COLOR
ENCYCLOPEDIA OF
GEMSTONES

COLOR ENCYCLOPEDIA OF GEMSTONES

Joel E. Arem. Ph.D. F.G.A.

VNR VAN NOSTRAND REINHOLD COMPANY
NEW YORK CINCINNATI TORONTO LONDON MELBOURNE

This book is dedicated to Abraham "Edge" Goldstein of Brooklyn, New York. His love of minerals and gems and his generosity and willingness to share his knowledge with others have been an inspiration to three generations of hobbyists. I consider myself fortunate to be numbered among those whom Edge considers his close friends.

Manufactured in the United States of America

Published by Van Nostrand Reinhold Company
135 West 50th Street, New York, N.Y. 10020

Van Nostrand Reinhold Limited
1410 Birchmount Road
Scarborough, Ontario MIP 2E7, Canada

Van Nostrand Reinhold
480 Latrobe Street
Melbourne, Victoria 3000, Australia

Van Nostrand Reinhold Company Limited
Molly Millars Lane
Wokingham, Berkshire, England

15 14 13 12 11 10 9 8

Library of Congress Cataloging in Publication Data

Arem, Joel E   1943-
Color Encyclopedia of gemstones.

   Bibliography: p.
   Includes index.
   1. Precious stones.   I. Title.
QE392.A69   553'.8'03   77-8834
ISBN 0-442-20333-0

Contents

Acknowledgment

Many people, directly and indirectly, have a role in the creation of a book of this type. Among these are people whose assistance is both significant and critically needed. I am delighted to gratefully acknowledge the following for such contributions:

Floyd Beattie, Casper Beesley, Bernard Cirlin, Carlton Davis, Denver Museum of Natural History, William Dippel, Pete J. Dunn, Mike Evick, Gemological Institute of America, A. Edge Goldstein, Alberta Gordon, Elvis Gray, Mike Gray, A.V. Gumuchian, George Harlow, John Holcombe, William T Huff, Kuhn's Baltic Amber Specialties, William Larson, Jim Leone, Richard T. Liddicoat, Betty Llewellyn, Joseph Longstreth, Barry Nathan, C.D. ("Dee") Parsons, William Pinch, John Saul, Sonja Schwartzman, John Sinkankas, Kenneth Sumner, Lillian Turner, Martin Zinn.

Very special thanks are extended to Karen Lou Johnson.

The author welcomes comments, criticisms, additions and corrections, in the hope of making future editions of this book more accurate, comprehensive and useful. Please address all correspondence to: Dr. Joel E. Arem, P.O. Box 996, Laytonsville, Md. 20760.

Introduction

Gemstones are among man's most treasured objects. They have been held in high esteem throughout history, by all societies, in all parts of the world. The histories of certain individual gemstones can be traced over a span of centuries, and gems have the same associations of wealth, prestige, status and power as gold and silver.

In the earliest periods of civilization, man became curious about natural objects, including minerals. Minerals are naturally occurring inorganic chemical elements and compounds. Scientists today have amended this definition, in light of discoveries about the arrangements of atoms in crystals. A mineral species is therefore also defined in terms of a definite crystalline structure. The chemical composition of a mineral may vary, but only within defined limits. If the composition varies outside these defined limits, the mineral may be given a new name and considered a distinct species.

Early man discovered pebbles and fragments of various brightly colored minerals, in fields and stream beds, on mountain slopes and in barren deserts. Some of these he made into ornaments. Others were ascribed mystical powers or symbolic religious significance. For centuries gem materials held a position of tremendous influence over the lives and destinies of mankind. But there was no science of gemology. The primary attribute of any gemstone was color, yet no reliable ways existed for differentiating minerals of the same or similar colors. It's not surprising that confusion reigned in both the literature and the marketplace. There are literally hundreds of references to gemstones in the Bible. Yet in many cases it is not known today exactly what stones were being described. Some incorrect names that were in use nearly 2,000 years ago are still employed today!

The modern science of gemology is a relatively recent development. Fairly accurate methods of chemical analysis existed more than 100 years ago. Yet even as recently as 1910 the nature of the internal structure of crystals was not firmly established. When X-rays first revealed the magnificent atomic geometry of crystals in the years following 1914, mineralogy, chemistry, and gemology all entered a new age of sophistication.

Progress, however, often adds complications and problems. At the same time that scientists worked to improve identification methods, other men developed ways of duplicating nature's gem masterpieces in the laboratory. Accurate detection technology was, in a sense, developed just in time to prevent collapse of the market for various gemstones.

A large part of the value of a fine gem lies in its scarcity as a rare natural object. People are therefore less likely to spend a large sum of money for a stone that might turn out to be man-made. The overall question of the reasons for the value of gems is complex, and will be discussed in following pages.

Gemology, in the last decades of the 20th century, is at a major turning point in its growth. Worldwide affluence has created an unprecedented demand for gems of fine quality, vastly raising their cost. Political problems in gem-producing areas have created restrictions in the supply of gem materials, further raising gem prices. Synthesis technology is developing new materials never found in nature, with very desirable properties, as well as laboratory equivalents of the more valuable natural gemstones. It has become essential to devise ways of distinguishing natural and synthetic materials, as well as revealing simulations and methods of color enhancement by chemical and physical treatment.

This book is an encyclopedia of gemstones. It is an attempt to provide basic information about all the mineral species that have been cut as gems, including their color varieties. But this introduction must first speak to the most basic question at hand: what is a gem?

WHAT IS A GEM?

World literature abounds with references to *precious* and *semiprecious* gems. The terms are used even today, quite without rigor, by the public and jewelry trade alike. But just what do these terms mean?

In antiquity, the so-called precious stones were diamond, ruby, emerald, sapphire, pearl, and occasionally opal. The dictionary (*Webster's New Collegiate Dictionary*, 7th ed., 1967) defines *precious* as "of great value or high price"; *semiprecious* is defined as meaning "of less commercial value than precious".

This indicates clearly that *precious* is a marketing term, applying to any expensive item. It is worth noting that a diamond can be purchased for as little as $200 per carat, yet certain colors of garnet are currently selling at prices over $1,000 per carat. Garnet has always been regarded as semiprecious, so it is obvious that these terms, as applied to gems, have little relevance or meaning. Therefore, aside from considerations of historical usage, the terms *precious* and *semiprecious* should be completely abandoned.

We are still left with the fundamental issue: what is a gem?

Nobody will argue with the statement that diamond, ruby, sapphire, and emerald are gems. Opal is a gem. So are jade, lapis, garnets and turquoise. But what do we do with andalusite, diopside, and sphene?

A material, to be considered a gem, must have beauty, durability, and scarcity, according to most accepted authorities. But all of these terms are subjective and open to wide interpretation. Opal, a gem, has a hardness of only 5.5 on the Mohs scale (see page xx), which is really too soft to wear in a ring. Opal is also quite fragile and brittle, and may crack spontaneously because of internal dehydration. If durability is a major criterion, opal is not a very good gem. Yet it *is* a gem and has always been considered as such, because of its other properties and beauty.

Proustite, a silver arsenic sulfide, is a rare mineral that is seldom faceted, and then only for collectors. Its red color is one of the richest in the mineral kingdom, far surpassing in intensity the hue of most rubies. Anyone who sees a cut proustite is likely to comment on its great beauty. There may be fewer than 50 cut proustites in the entire world, so the scarcity factor is indisputable. Is a cut proustite a gem or not?

Zoisite has been known as a mineral for decades. It is usually gray or pinkish and opaque, and seldom cut, even by collectors of the unusual. Then in the late 1960s fine, blue-violet, transparent zoisite crystals were discovered in Tanzania, and a few stones were cut from them. The cut stones were sold to a few collectors and connoisseurs of unusual faceted minerals. Eventually one of the world's major jewelry establishments, Tiffany & Co., noted that cut blue zoisite resembles fine sapphire,

dubbed the new material *tanzanite* and launched a major promotion of the "new gemstone." Today, tanzanite is accepted as a gem and large stones bring rather high prices. Here is an example of a mineral that was not a gem by accepted criteria before 1967, but "became" a gem by promotion. This is a double standard that leads one to ask for an objective criterion in the definition of a gem.

The dictionary is again consulted, and we find that a gem is "a precious or sometimes semiprecious stone cut and polished for ornament." If we omit the terms relating to price, as discussed earlier, we have the basis of a simple and unambiguous definition.

A gem is any mineral cut and polished for ornamental purposes.

There are nearly 3000 known minerals. Any of them could be used as a gem if it were found in a form solid, massive or attractive enough to warrant the effort. The definition of a mineral is unambiguous. The definition allows for all the rare and unusual materials that have been cut and which heretofore have been difficult to classify or discuss. Our definition of a gem is thus very tight, but we must allow for several exceptions, which are considered gems through the necessity of thousands of years of acceptance as such. These exceptions are pearl, coral, and amber. Pearl and coral actually are made up of mineral material (calcite and aragonite) but created through the agency of organic processes. Amber is the petrified, hardened sap of ancient pine trees, and is an organic material.

The term *ornamental material* could be more aptly applied to amber and coral, as well as ivory, jet, shell, and wood. All of these are natural materials of organic origin that are polished and used in jewelry. But they would not be called "gems" under the proposed terminology.

A problem in nomenclature now arises regarding man-made compounds and crystals that are sometimes cut for jewelry purposes. The term *synthetic* is derived from words that mean, literally, "put together" (from components), which, by itself, is noncommittal as to origin. The terms *created* and *cultured* have also been used in regard to laboratory products. The public has come to accept the term *synthetic* in connection with jewelry stones created in the laboratory. It should always be remembered, however, that a synthetic gemstone is a contradiction in terms, since a gem is by definition a mineral, which is a *naturally* occurring material.

The following classification avoids the confusions of current usage: a *gem* is a mineral cut and polished for ornamental use; a *gemstone* is a crystal, fragment, or pebble of gem material (this term is also used to describe the cut stone); a *jewel* is a combination of gemstone and metal setting allowing the gem to be worn easily; a *synthetic* is a man-made material which may either be physically and chemically equivalent to a mineral, or a compound unknown in nature but which can be grown in transparent crystals suitable for cutting; a *simulant* is a material that resembles another (usually more costly) material (for example, glass used as a substitute for ruby or emerald).

SCOPE OF THIS BOOK

Unlike other books about gems, this work does not provide history and lore of stones, descriptions of occurrences, mining and cutting techniques, or market and price data which are rapidly outdated. It is, rather, a comprehensive compendium of data organized in a format that provides rapid access to the basic properties of gemstones, especially those data that would be useful in identification.

The book's major asset is the large array of color plates. The photographs are a result of nearly three years of concentrated effort to develop specific techniques for gem photography. The ultimate goal is to capture on film the exact color of a faceted gemstone, while displaying to best advantage the cut and brilliance derived from the cutting. At the same time, hot spots or specular reflections from individual facets must be avoided, and the gem as pictured should have solidity and dimension, rather than appear flat or look like a painting. It is a major photographic challenge to achieve all these features simultaneously. The color plates in this book represent the author's current stage of technical competence, as modified by the limitations of converting color transparencies to images on paper, and there is considerable room for improvement. In many cases, however, the photos clearly show the degree of birefringence in a gem and also inclusions that are present, making the photos especially useful to the gemologist who is concerned with such matters.

There are nearly 210 species included in this volume. It must be remembered, of course, that any mineral species can be considered a gemstone if suitable cutting material can be found. Some minerals have been known for decades or centuries, but have not been considered gem materials because pieces of sufficient size, cohesion or transparency have never been available. This situation may change at any time with respect to a given mineral, so the list of gem species will undoubtedly increase with time.

The data presented herein have been compiled from many sources. The primary sources are standard reference works in the mineralogical and gemological literature. These provided a framework of basic information about all the species covered. Gaps were then filled by research into the periodical literature of mineralogy and gemology. This yielded current information about localities, new gemstones, additional basic data and some information on gemstone sizes. In some cases, as in the case of dispersion, mineralogical data have been reworked into a form more familiar to the gemologist. Specifically, a Hartman dispersion net was used to plot refractive index vs. wavelength information, and the interval B–G was extracted and reported as the dispersion of the material in question.

Spectral data have been provided only where a spectrum is distinctive enough to be useful in identification. Some spectra are complex and variable for a given mineral species, and in such cases the text lists only the pervasive or especially diagnostic lines.

Information on stone sizes comes from diverse sources. These sources include the standard literature, specialized books on specific gems (such as amber, pearl, opal, and diamond) and personal communications from cutters, dealers, collectors and museum curators. There are sure to be omissions in noting the existence of large and important gems, for which the author assumes full responsibility. Such omissions can be eliminated in future editions through the assistance of readers of this book in sending the author relevant information (see page vi).

Information on wearing characteristics of gems is inferred from analysis of mineral properties, comparison with other gems typically worn in jewelry, or from direct observation. No attempt has been made to disparage any particular gemstone, but rather an effort has been made to offer realistic advice on the liabilities and care of gems. The aim is the prevention of loss due to mishandling of more fragile or softer gems. Some gemstones are a poor choice for a ringstone, but make lovely earring or pendant stones.

The information presented in the text portion of this book is highly condensed. A basic familiarity with the principles and terminology is assumed, although a brief summary of important concepts is presented in the following pages. Further information is easily obtained from the many excellent specialized books available to interested readers, as listed in the Bibliography (see page 139).

Sins of omission, in preparing a book of this type, are easily made and easily criticized. It is likely that many of the finest stones in existence are not on display, but rather are held in private safe deposit boxes. There are probably a number of mineral species that have been faceted by hobbyists and either never reported in the literature or inadequately referenced. In all such cases, a plea is again made for assistance from readers in making future editions of this work more complete, comprehensive and accurate.

THE NATURE OF GEMS

As we have seen, gems are, with few exceptions, minerals. Minerals are naturally occurring chemical elements and compounds. Every mineral is characterized by a definite crystalline structure and a chemical composition that varies within defined limits.

The universe is made of atoms, which are the basic chemical units of matter. Every chemical element consists of atoms of a type characteristic of that element. Within the atom are yet smaller particles, some of which have electrical (+ or −) charges. The positively charged particles are called *protons*, and are concentrated in the center, or *nucleus* of the atom. Negatively charged particles, called *electrons*, spin about the nucleus at tremendous speed.

An isolated atom is electrically neutral, because the number of positive charges within it is balanced by an equal number of negative charges. However, atoms may borrow electrons from each other, some atoms thus acquiring a net + charge and some a net − charge. Charged atoms are called *ions*. Positive ions are known as *cations*, and negative ions are called *anions*.

An atom that loses an electron seldom gives it up entirely. Usually the loan is half-hearted, and the donor atom shares the electron(s) with the recipient atom. Neither atom will give up the electron(s) completely, and the result is an endless tug-of-war that keeps the atoms involved joined together.

In some cases, however, atoms do gain or lose electrons entirely and become ions. But the atom losing an electron thus acquires a positive charge, and a neutral atom gaining an electron becomes negatively charged. Since it is a basic law of nature that unlike charges attract each other, the ions are held close to each other in a way similar to the atoms merely sharing electrons.

The forces holding atoms together are called *bonds*. Electron sharing produces *covalent* bonds, which are usually very strong. The second example mentioned above, involving the attraction of ions, is called an *ionic* bond. Other types of bonds are generally weaker than these bond types.

A group of atoms held together by bonds in such a way as to form a cohesive unit is called a *molecule*. The molecule is the smallest amount of a chemical compound that displays all the characteristics of the compound.

At a temperature of absolute zero ($-273°C$), atoms are completely at rest and do not vibrate. But at all temperatures above this, atoms are in motion. At high temperatures, atomic vibration is so violent that bonds may form but are immediately broken. This is the situation in a gas or vapor, where atoms and molecules fly about at random and occupy all the space available to them.

At lower temperatures atoms stay in contact for a longer period of time, and may become bonded together but still retain a large degree of freedom of motion. This is the characteristic of liquids, in which atoms slide over each other but remain essentially in contact. Lowered temperatures further slow down atomic vibrations and prevent the atoms from breaking the bonds that form as a result of electrical attraction.

If the vibration is slowed down enough, the atoms become locked in fixed positions relative to one another.

Every atom in a given mixture of atom types tries to surround itself with specific kinds of other atoms, all at fixed distances and relative positions. This becomes a kind of unit of pattern in three dimensions. The pattern is analogous to wallpaper, in which a (perhaps geometric) unit of pattern is repeated at regular intervals. The repetition of molecular pattern units in three dimensions results in a *crystal structure*.

Crystal structures are both repetitive and symmetrical. One can discern, within a structure, planes of atoms of a specific type. These may be bonded to adjacent planes of atoms of a different type. The bonds between all these atom pairs are the same strength. If these bonds happen to be weak, the plane of bonds may be a zone of structural weakness in the material. On a macroscopic scale, the crystal might tend to split along such planes.

Furthermore, light traveling through the material interacts with the atoms in the crystal structure. The interaction involves the light energy itself and the electrons surrounding the atoms in the structure. Bonds between atoms are, in a sense, regions in which electrons are more highly concentrated, and therefore bond energies in a structure are localized in regions between specific sets of atoms. Bond strengths within a crystal vary greatly in direction. Consequently light is affected in different ways, depending on the path it takes through the crystal.

Crystal properties are directional, because the bonding within a crystal structure varies with direction, as well as the types of atoms involved. This concept is critical in understanding the properties of gems and minerals.

CRYSTAL STRUCTURES AND PROPERTIES

All solids are crystals, and every mineral is characterized by a crystal structure. Different minerals may have structures that are built of similar or even identical pattern units. However, no two minerals have exactly the same structural pattern *and* chemical composition.

A glass is rigid, but is not considered a true solid because the atoms within it are not organized in a long-range periodic array. A glass may form when, upon cooling from a molten state, a material solidifies before the atoms can arrange themselves into a pattern. The strong bonds linking the atoms together overcome random motion of the atoms, and the material may become both rigid and hard. There is no single temperature at which all the bonds loosen and allow the atoms to move again. Consequently glasses have no specific melting point, but rather soften gradually and eventually begin to flow. Obsidian and tektites are examples of naturally occurring glasses.

Chemical composition and structure both play a role in determining the properties of a mineral or gemstone. For example, consider the minerals halite (NaCl) and cerargyrite (AgCl). Both substances crystallize in the isometric system, form cube-shaped crystals, are colorless and transparent. The crystal structures are identical: each chlorine atom is surrounded by six metal atoms at equal distances. A plane of atoms in the structure parallel to a cube face would contain rows of alternating chlorine and metal atoms, in both minerals.

The properties of these minerals, however, are very different. The specific gravity of halite is 2.17, that of cerargyrite is 5.55! The refractive index of halite is 1.54, while that of cerargyrite is 2.07. These large differences may be attributed to the presence of silver in cerargyrite, as opposed to sodium in halite.

In the above instance the structures and compositions of the minerals discussed are very simple, and the metal atoms are major essential components of the formulas. A study of mineral properties reveals, however, that even small variations in chemistry can have a major effect on physical properties. This applies both to different minerals with slightly different formulas, and also to variations in chemistry within a single mineral species.

A good example of this is the mineral beryl, which is beryllium aluminum silicate. Pure beryl is colorless. However, a relatively small amount (less than 1%) of chromium, substituting for aluminum in the structure, is sufficient to produce a brilliant, intense green color. The substitution occurs because the ions of aluminum and chromium are both trivalent (have a net charge of $+3$) and are about the same size. If there is chromium present in the solution from which the beryl crystal grows, an occasional chromium atom is incorporated in the structure in the site normally occupied by an aluminum atom. As few as 2 chromium atoms in 5,000 aluminum sites will produce a green color. Iron in the beryl structure results in yellow or blue coloration, while manganese produces a pink color.

Many minerals may have their color so altered by impurities. In most cases the impurity atoms are present in sufficiently large quantities to also affect physical properties, such as specific gravity and refractive index. In general, impurities do not affect cleavage or hardness. Moreover, an impurity atom in a crystal structure is usually somewhat different in size and charge from the element it replaces. The result is that the structure can tolerate the presence of only a limited amount of the impurity, before the strain on the structure becomes so great that the crystal cannot grow at all. Most cases of chemical substitution involve amounts of impurities ranging from less than 1% to as much as 10%.

There are, however, numerous examples of minerals in which complete substitution is possible. An example is the mineral siderite ($FeCO_3$), a very common carbonate in ore deposits. The element manganese may substitute for iron in the siderite structure, in any amount. If 49% of the iron is replaced by manganese, the mineral is termed a "highly manganiferous siderite." But if the manganese content exceeds the iron content, the mineral is consid-

ered a new species: rhodochrosite. Pure rhodochrosite has the formula $MnCO_3$, and we might say that iron can substitute for manganese in any amount in the rhodochrosite structure. Obviously, the structures of siderite and rhodochrosite are identical. These two minerals comprise what is known as a *solid solution series*. The physical and chemical properties vary *continuously* from one end member of the series (in this case, pure rhodochrosite or pure siderite) to the other.

In many cases the variation in properties is said to be *linear*. That is, you can make a graph showing the variation in a parameter such as refractive index as the composition changes along the series, and the graph will turn out to be a straight line. This type of relationship is very useful, because within such a solution series you can determine the chemical composition just by measuring the refractive index! A graph of specific gravity vs. composition might show a similar relationship. A major problem in using such graphs is the oversimplification of the relationship between properties and chemistry. Usually more than one element may substitute for another in a crystal structure, and one must first sort out the separate effects of each substitution before a simple graph can be used with confidence.

Gemologists sometimes have a tendency to overlook mineralogical literature in evaluating gemstones, especially in cases where solid solutions are involved. The following is an example of this oversight.

Mineralogical convention states that, in the case of a simple two-component solid solution series, the 50% composition marks the dividing line between the two end-member species. One of these two species may be much more familiar than the other. A good example is the case of amblygonite: $(Li, Na)Al(PO_4)(F, OH)$. Analyses have shown that there is complete substitution possible between fluorine (F) and hydroxyl (OH) in the structure. Chemical analysis for these anions is tedious and beyond the range of the gemologist. However, measurable physical properties are markedly affected by the $F-OH$ substitution. When hydroxyl is present in greater amounts than fluorine, we have a new species, called montebrasite.

Most gems cut from members of this series are amblygonite. But many stones have been discussed in the literature as amblygonite, when a glance at the optical data reported for the gem reveals properties belonging to montebrasite! Montebrasite is not discussed at all in standard gemological literature, whereas this may be the correct species designation for many gems now labeled amblygonite in collections. A much greater awareness of the variation of physical properties with chemistry is required in gemological work; much of the needed information is readily available in standard mineralogy texts, and is reported in this book.

It is important to remember that chemical variations in minerals are seldom simple. The geological environments in which minerals form are extremely complex, and a growing crystal often has a wide variety of elements competing for space in its structure. A parameter such as refractive index is very sensitive to small variations in chemical composition. In addition, most minerals have several structural sites (positions), each of which can accommodate a variety of different atoms. For example, in the mineral diopside ($CaMgSi_2O_6$), sodium may substitute for calcium, titanium for magnesium, and aluminum for silicon, all at the same time, and in different amounts! In such cases it is not a simple matter to correlate changes in physical properties with compositional variations.

The above discussion makes it clear that the gemologist should become accustomed to thinking about gems in terms of families, or groups of minerals. Diopside, for example, is a member of a group of about 8 minerals with essentially the same structure, and differing in composition. The appearance of many of these species is similar, and they have many similar properties. A gemstone can be initially identified as a member of the diopside—hedenbergite series, for example, and then further testing may indicate exactly where the gem in question lies within the series. Other well-known mineral groups, in which this approach is useful, are the garnets, feldspars, spinels, humites, sodalite, and tourmaline.

A listing of the members of important groups of gem minerals is found on page 141. The group concept of relating similar gem species has been used throughout this book.

ORIGIN OF GEMSTONES

Rocks make up the crust of the earth. They are the most familiar of geological materials and their study provides clues about the long and turbulent history of our planet.

Rocks are made up of minerals, which are the chemical building blocks of the earth. A rock can consist of one mineral, as in the case of a pure limestone, which is composed entirely of the mineral calcite. Most rocks, however, are made up of several minerals. These are usually present in the form of crystals or grains. The history and origin of a rock can be deciphered from its mineral content and the way the mineral grains contact each other. This latter feature, known as *texture*, is especially important in classifying rocks.

ROCK CLASSIFICATION

Rocks are classified according to their overall chemical composition, the minerals they contain, the rock texture, the size of the mineral grains or crystals present, and obvious physical features such as lamination or banding. There are three basic types of rocks.

Igneous rocks form as a result of the cooling of molten material called *magma*, that usually originates deep in the earth, below the upper layer called the *crust*. Magma may have varying composition, and different types of magmas produce different types of igneous rocks. A magma rich in water and silica (SiO_2) may cool to yield a light colored rock known as granite; a silica-deficient magma may produce a black, dense rock called gabbro. A given magma may produce various types of rocks, depending on the cooling history, including rate of cooling and pressure changes within the molten material.

If magma solidifies deep within the earth and cools very slowly, crystals have a chance to grow to large size, resulting in a rock with *coarse texture*. Igneous rocks that cool more quickly, as they would nearer the earth's surface, develop a *fine texture*. An extreme example of a fine-textured rock is volcanic glass, which cools so quickly that crystals do not have a chance to develop at all. Two different rocks may contain the same minerals, and in the same proportions. They are differentiated according to grain size, which is a reflection of their cooling history.

Igneous rocks formed within the earth are called *intrusive* or *plutonic*, and usually have coarse textures. *Extrusive rocks* are formed when magma is ejected at the earth's surface, as in a volcanic eruption, and are fine grained as a result of rapid cooling.

Light-colored igneous rocks are sometimes called acidic, a misnomer relating to the time when it was believed that mineral acids such as "silicic acid" were responsible for rock formation. The chemical opposite of an acid is a base, and basic rocks are dark-colored rocks that were once presumed deficient in "silicic acid." The terms are no longer valid, but are mentioned here because they are occasionally used in the literature.

Sedimentary rocks are so named because they are composed of sediments, which are either rock and mineral fragments or the mineral and chemical weathering products of these materials. About 75% of the rocks exposed at the earth's surface are sedimentary, and they form by the deposition, in water or air, of rock and mineral particles or by the precipitation of mineral material in water. The most obvious and distinctive feature of sedimentary rocks is banding, or layering, known as *stratification*. *Mechanical* or *detrital* sediments include sand, gravel, clay, silt and mud. These particles may become rock through the processes of cementation or compaction. The first step in the hardening process is *consolidation*, accompanied by the expulsion of water and volatile materials, and the entire process may be referred to as *lithification*. An *evaporite* is a sedimentary rock formed by the evaporation of saline water (either an ocean or lake) with the consequent precipitation of salts, such as halite, gypsum, and borates. *Coal* is a sedimentary rock composed of the remains of plants that lived millions of years ago. Chemical sedimentary rocks are formed by accumulation of marine precipitates, usually calcium carbonate. The most familiar rock formed in this way is *limestone*. Solutions containing magnesium may later alter a limestone bed, producing a massive bed of the mineral *dolomite*. Some sedimentary rocks are created by consolidation of particles laid down by winds or even glaciers.

Metamorphic rocks are created when earth pressures and heat alter previously existing rocks. Metamorphism is a word derived from the Greek, meaning "change of form." Any kind of rock may be metamorphosed, and the major result is a reorganization of the mineral and chemical components of the previous rock. Some minerals, that form in a given set of geologic conditions, are unstable in drastically different conditions. In the latter eventuality they actually break down, decompose, and *recrystallize* into other minerals that are more stable in the new conditions. Rocks can be metamorphosed on a wide scale, as a result of the kinds of forces that produce mountain ranges. These are known as *regionally metamorphosed* rocks. Alternatively, a rock bed, such as a limestone, may be invaded by magma forced up from deep within the earth. The heat and chemical components of the magma chemically and physically alter the limestone, resulting in the formation of a wide range of new minerals. This process is called *contact metamorphism*. Certain minerals are very characteristic of either regional or contact metamorphism, and one can determine the extent of metamorphism in an area by examining the mineralogy of the rocks over a wide area. Metamorphic rocks are classified according to bulk chemistry, reflecting the composition of the original, unaltered rock, and the metamorphic minerals present, which indicate the temperature and pressure reached during metamorphism.

The earth is in a constant state of change. Rocks in some places are being melted or pulled into the interior; others are being created in spectacular volcanic episodes. Sediments are being deposited and compacted in oceans throughout the world. The earth is a closed system, with nothing added or removed (noting the negligible addition of meteoritic material). The chemical elements of the earth are thus repeatedly mixed and separated by geologic processes. The entire process of rock genesis, destruction, and alteration comprises a cycle. Sedimentary rocks are formed as a result of the breakdown of other rocks. Igneous rocks are created by volcanism, or are exposed at the earth's surface by weathering. Metamorphic rocks result from the transformation of igneous and sedimentary rocks by heat and pressure. All of these rocks, in their turn, are worn down and become new sediments. The so-called *geologic cycle* is thus revealed as a complex mechanism of creation and destruction of rocks.

Geologic structures may be characteristic of certain rock types. For example, a volcano is clearly composed of igneous material. Large folds visible in rocks exposed on a mountain slope are evidence of the action of metamorphic forces. Terraced cliffs, such as those exposed in the Grand Canyon of Arizona, are clearly derived from the weathering of bedded sedimentary rock layers.

It is important to remember that gems are simply minerals, albeit of a very special quality. Minerals are components of rocks. Every mineral species is characterized by a definite structure and chemical composition. The same chemical ingredients may crystallize in different structural arrangements, depending on external parameters, such as temperature and pressure. Although they may have the same composition, these different structural arrangements qualify as distinct mineral species, such as, for example, rutile, anatase and brookite, which are all composed of titanium oxide. The conditions at the time of mineral formation determine which of the three mineral species with this composition will form from titanium and oxygen present.

The controlling influence of physical conditions is most clearly seen in metamorphic rocks. During metamorphism the temperature and pressure conditions in a region may rise greatly over a period of time. A given assemblage of chemical ingredients may be stable in the form of a certain mineral at low pressure and temperature. But when these conditions change beyond a certain point, that mineral may no longer be stable. The mineral then decomposes, and the chemical constituents arrange themselves in a way that is more stable in the new conditions.

A good example of this is the mineral quartz, the most common mineral on earth. Quartz, in the form we see as pretty crystals or as a component of beach sand, is stable up to a temperature of 870°C. Above this temperature the framework of Si and O atoms characteristic of quartz vibrates too rapidly to hold together in the pattern of the quartz structure. An *inversion*, or change in structural arrangement, occurs and we have a new mineral called tridymite. Tridymite has the same composition as quartz (SiO_2) but a different structure that is stable at higher temperatures than the quartz structure. The tridymite structure, in fact, is more "open," allowing it to accommodate the increased vibrational movement of the atoms at higher temperatures. But even this structure is torn apart by atomic vibration at 1470°C, and a totally new mineral forms, known as cristobalite. The cristobalite structure is capable of handling very large atomic vibrations, but only up to a temperature of 1710°C. At this temperature no structure of Si and O atoms is stable, and cristobalite melts to a very viscous liquid. The atoms in the melt are then free of the relatively rigid atomic bonds that hold a crystal structure together, and can vibrate as much as is necessitated by higher temperatures within the melt.

A given rock, with a particular history of formation, therefore characterizes a very specific range of conditions in which minerals can form. The environment of formation of a mineral is thus a combination of specific conditions, such as temperature and pressure, available chemical components, and such miscellaneous factors as solution flow, metamorphic directional stresses, and rates of cooling or heating. The chemical environment is determined by local rock types and their mineral content, plus the introduction of materials by migrating waters or vapors.

Obviously, the formation of a mineral is often a complex affair. But, conceptually, the whole subject of mineral environment and formation, collectively known as *paragenesis*, can be reduced to a simple rule. *Minerals are found where they ought to be.* This seemingly simple statement is really the first rule of mineral exploration.

For example, if you want to locate a source of peridot, you must first know that peridot is the gem form of the mineral olivine. Olivine is characteristic of basaltic rocks. A basaltic magma has the right chemical ingredients for the crystallization of olivine, and also exists at the right temperature. Olivine is, in fact, the mineral with the highest melting point in a basaltic magma, and therefore is the first to crystallize when the magma cools. The olivine crystals that appear within the melt are heavier than the surrounding liquid, and consequently sink. Thus, in a large body of basalt that formed as a thick lava flow, or in an intrusive dark-colored igneous rock mass, olivine crystals of large size would most likely be found at the bottom. In fact, we do find zones of coarse grained olivine at the lower part of lava flows or large intrusive bodies.

Gemstone occurrences are usually somewhat more complex. Gems are very special mineral oddities, in that they are very pure, or have formed under special conditions that allowed crystals to grow free of imperfections, inclusions, cavities and fractures.

GEM SCARCITY

The environment of formation of a gem crystal may be the same as for any other crystal of the same species. But chance has acted in a way that produces especially fine crystals, or larger crystals, or crystals of a better color than is usually encountered in the species. In this sense, gems are actually mineralogical freaks. They are not abundant, and are restricted in occurrence *only* to those localities where conditions were suitable for their formation. If the mineral in question is rare, gem quality crystals of that species are much rarer. A particular mineral species, such as topaz, for example, may be widespread and abundant throughout the world. However, large transparent crystals of a deep pink or orange color are exceedingly uncommon. Pink and orange gem topaz, when viewed in a geological context, are thus seen to be so rare as to present us with the amazing mystery of how they have been found at all!

Rarity in gems is thus a function of several factors. In some cases the requirements of composition and conditions of formation of a species are seldom fulfilled simultaneously, as in the case of proustite and manganotantalite. Such *species* are therefore rare in their own right, regardless of whether they form crystals transparent enough to cut.

Sometimes a mineral species is not rare, but transparent, cuttable crystals are very seldom encountered. This is the situation for most of the so-called collector gems.

Another case is rarity of color. A good example is emerald, the deep green variety of the mineral beryl. Beryl occurs throughout the world, usually found in pegmatites (see page xv). Emerald owes its green color to the element chromium. Chromium, however, is *not* usually present in pegmatites. Its geochemical environment is rather in dark-colored (basic) igneous rocks. Beryl is rarely found in these latter geologic environments, largely because its primary constituent, beryllium, is rare in basic rocks. The conditions necessary for the occurrence of emerald, i.e., the formation of beryl plus the availability of chromium, are thus seen to be mutually incompatible! This accounts for the worldwide paucity of emerald. The reasons become obvious when one understands the geologic factors.

Finally, there is scarcity in size. Topaz, for example, occurs in crystals that weigh hundreds of pounds. These are usually colorless or very pale yellow or blue. But topaz crystals of a fine pink color are never seen in sizes larger than a few inches. A huge faceted gem of white topaz is not rare, but a 10 carat pink topaz would be.

Likewise, rubies of very fine quality (color and transparency) are extremely rare over about 10 carats. But sapphires, which are mineralogically equivalent to ruby (both are the mineral corundum), are encountered in crystals weighing hundreds of carats.

Large amethyst crystals are found in many localities. However, pieces free of inclusions weighing more than 50 carats are quite rare. In general, it is clear that rarity is a combination of a number of factors, all of which depend on the basic geology of a gem species plus the status of the marketplace. Scarcity is a function of the following factors: geologic abundance of the species in question; desirable color, size, and freedom from imperfections; market availability (number of producing localities and the sizes of the deposits); demands of the market.

A gemstone occurrence is a very rare and transient geologic feature. Once exhausted, it cannot be replenished within the span of human lifetimes. Synthetics can be manufactured in the laboratory, but the value of natural gems will not be affected as long as they can be distinguished as rare *natural* objects of great beauty.

The gem market is continually faced with the threat of depletion of known gem deposits, or loss of production due to political factors. This puts great pressure on other known sources to meet world demand. Depletion of supply coupled with high demand creates rising prices. This is a major reason why gems have had great appeal throughout history as an investment medium and a way of storing wealth. Gems are what might be called "real value" commodities, with desirability in all cultures, throughout all the periods of human history.

Geological scarcity accounts for such rare gems as painite and taaffeite. Only one painite crystal has been found, and less than half a dozen cut taaffeites are known. To be sure, more specimens of both materials may exist; painite may resemble ruby and taaffeite looks like mauve spinel, and misidentified cut stones may exist in various collections and inventories. Nonetheless, such rare collector gems offer a situation comparable to art. Rembrandt is dead, and no additional *original* Rembrandts can be produced. By analogy, an exhausted gem deposit can produce no more gemstones.

With this in mind, consider the future of gem prices. We may some day see rare stones command prices comparable to the levels of great art. There may be only one da Vinci "Last Supper", but there is (at least, at the time of this writing) also only one painite.

ROCK TYPES

Igneous Rocks

INTRUSIVE

Granite—core of many mountain ranges. Coarse texture, composed of potassium feldspar, quartz, plus some mica or hornblende and accessory minerals.
Syenite—similar to granite; contains little or no quartz; fine grained.
Pegmatite—very coarse grained rock, composition like granite. Frequently contains immense crystals and rare, exotic elements. Home of many gem minerals.
Diorite—dark-colored, contains plagioclase feldspar, little quartz, some biotite.
Granodiorite—like diorite, but richer in potassium feldspar.
Tonalite—like diorite, but contains some quartz.
Monzonite—intermediate between syenite and diorite.
Gabbro—diorite rich in calcic plagioclase feldspar; contains pyroxenes as opposed to amphiboles.
Anorthosite—rock composed almost entirely of plagioclase feldspar.
Diabase—fine grained gabbro typical of small intrusive bodies.
Peridotite—dark rock composed of pyroxene and olivine.
Dunite—peridotite-like rock containing chiefly olivine.
Kimberlite—an altered peridotite characterized by high-pressure minerals.

EXTRUSIVE

Rhyolite—light-colored, fine grained rock, with composition like granite.
Obsidian—volcanic glass, with overall composition like rhyolite.
Pumice—"frothy" volcanic rock, full of gas bubbles, and will float on water!
Porphyry—igneous rock with different grain sizes, reflecting cooling history; larger crystals called *phenocrysts* lie in fine grained *groundmass*. The phenocrysts formed by slow cooling, and then the rock was suddenly chilled.
Basalt—dark-colored, fine grained rock, typical of lava flows. Very widespread. Also known as *traprock*.
Scoria—porous, cinderlike rock seen at tops of lava flows.
Andesite—volcanic equivalent of diorite, dark-colored.
Trachyte—volcanic equivalent of syenite.

Sedimentary Rocks

Conglomerate—made of large, rounded pebbles and smaller grains, cemented together.
Sandstone—composed of sand-size (between 1/16 and 2 mm) particles. Sandstone refers to particle size, not composition; therefore, quartz sandstone is made of quartz grains.
Arkose—sandstone composed chiefly of feldspar and quartz grains.
Graywacke—dense, dark-colored sandstone with rock fragments and clay particles.
Shale—fine grained rock composed of clay or silt-sized particles (microscopic).
Limestone—chemical precipitate of calcium carbonate in sea water. Sometimes the fossil remains of large reefs, built by corals and other animals long ago.
Chalk—calcareous chemical precipitate, composed of tiny marine plants and animal skeletons, plus biochemically deposited calcite.
Dolomite—massive sedimentary rock composed chiefly of the mineral dolomite.
Travertine—limestone formed in caves by slow evaporation of solutions.

SEDIMENTARY FEATURES

Concretions are masses of cementing material, the same cement (such as silica or iron oxide) that caused lithification of nearby sediments. Usually spherical, they sometimes assume fantastic and grotesque shapes.

Nodules are masses of mineral material differing in composition from the rocks in which they are found.

Geodes are hollow, more or less round objects, often containing an interior lining of terminated crystals. Geodes are usually made of quartz, but may contain a wide variety of other minerals. Geodes commonly occur in shales, but also form in gas pockets in igneous rocks and accumulate in the soils resulting from the weathering of such rocks.

Metamorphic Rocks

Slate—formed by the low-grade metamorphism of shale. Pressure causes aligning of the clay particles in the shale, resulting in easy breakage of the rock into layers.

Phyllite—next step upward in metamorphism from slate. May have a shiny appearance on broken surfaces, due to parallel alignment of recrystallized mineral grains.

Schist—can be derived from various rock types by intense recrystallization; tends to break between layers to produce characteristic uneven, wavy surface. Schists are named according to the minerals they contain. Often characterized by folded, crumpled look.

Gneiss—coarse grained, banded rock due to intense metamorphism. Does not show tendency to split along planes, but minerals are arranged in parallel layers.

Marble—coarse grained calcareous rock produced by metamorphic recrystallization of limestone.

Quartzite—dense, compact rock, produced by recrystallization of quartz grains in a sedimentary quartzite or sandstone.

Skarn—complex mineral assemblage produced by contact metamorphism of an impure limestone or dolomite. Minerals of economic value in such assemblages are often called *contact deposits*.

IDENTIFICATION OF GEMSTONES

There are approximately 3000 known mineral species. A few new minerals are added every year, and occasionally an existing species is discredited when careful analysis reveals it to be a mixture of other minerals. The number of mineral species is very small in comparison to the huge list of compounds known to chemistry. This is because minerals are naturally occurring chemical elements and compounds. There are geochemical restrictions that limit the number of possible mineral species, namely the tendency for certain elements to be restricted to specific geochemical environments. Random chance also plays a major role in the formation of minerals, in the temperature and pressure that happen to be prevalent in the environment where chemical reactions occur and minerals are forming.

Very rarely is a new mineral species found in large, well-formed crystals. An example of such an occurrence is the mineral brazilianite, which was described on the basis of spectacular, large, and even gemmy crystals

discovered in Brazil. Usually, however, a new mineral is recognized only with great difficulty. An astute observer may be studying a complex mineral assemblage and recognize a few grains of a mineral which is unfamiliar to him. Detailed analysis may show that the material has a chemical composition slightly different from another, well-known species; the difference may be large enough to warrant calling the unknown material a new species. In some cases there is barely enough of the new mineral even to perform a complete chemical analysis! Most of the new minerals added to the known list are in this category of obscure grains very limited in quantity. Very sophisticated analytical devices are required for this type of descriptive work.

The situation with gems is not so demanding. Usually the gemologist's major problem is to pin down the composition of a gemstone in order to locate the material within a solid solution series, as for example in the case of garnets and feldspars. In some such cases a measurable property, such as refractive index, may vary linearly with chemical composition. The composition may therefore be determined by carefully measuring refractive index and using a graph to pick off the corresponding chemistry. This type of analysis works only in simple cases, such as in the olivine series, where the only major chemical variable is the ratio of iron and magnesium. In most solid solution series, however, the chemistry is far too complex for simple correlations, and a combination of tests is needed for identification.

The most useful instrument for gemstone identification is the microscope, especially a stereoscopic type fitted with special darkfield illumination in which light enters the gemstone from the sides only. This instrument is ideal for the examination of inclusions, which are frequently diagnostic in identification. Magnification also reveals cleavage developed on a small scale, as well as the degree of surface finish on a stone, which allows an estimate of hardness. Fracture may also be determined by observing small chips on the girdle of a faceted gem.

The refractometer allows measurement of refractive index of most gems, as well as birefringence. Some gems have indices too high for measurement with a standard refractometer; the microscope can sometimes be used for direct measurement of refractive index, using a technique discussed in standard gemological texts (see Bibliography on page 139). Specific gravity may be determined with heavy liquids or with torsion balances. Gravity measurement plus refractive index usually allows for unambiguous identification of a gemstone. In some cases the spectroscope provides very rapid and unambiguous analysis, as for example in distinguishing between almandine garnet and ruby. The polariscope is also useful in determining the optical character of a gemstone.

There are only about 200 mineral species that have been cut as gems, a fact that makes the gemologist's life easier than that of the mineralogist, who is concerned with more than 3000 species. It is important to remember, however, that at any time a mineral species may be encountered in a form with gem potential. If such a material is brought to a gemologist for identification, he may be mystified when the properties of the substance do not match anything in his standard gemological reference tables. In such cases it is necessary to resort to more powerful techniques for identification.

An extremely powerful diagnostic tool, routinely used by the mineralogist, is virtually unknown to the gemological fraternity. This is the X-ray powder diffraction camera, a device that can, in most instances, provide unambiguous identification of a mineral in a period of a few hours.

The detailed principles of X-ray methods are too complex for elaboration here. A brief summary of the approach is, however, warranted. X-rays are a form of energy, like light and heat, but with very short wavelengths. The level of energy in an X-ray beam is on the same order of magnitude as the energy associated with the electrons that spin about the nucleus of all types of atoms. Consequently, if an X-ray beam enters a crystal it can interact with the electrons of the atoms in the crystal structure. The more electrons an atom has (i.e., the heavier the atom) the greater the degree of interaction.

The incoming X-ray beam enters the crystal in one specific direction. However, the electrons in the crystal's atoms absorb the X-ray energy, and re-emit this energy almost instantaneously in *all* directions (radially). The situation is as if each electron were itself acting as a source of X-rays. All the electrons that are affected within a particular atom combine their radiations and the atom itself acts as an X-ray source.

Intuitively, one would expect that the X-rays emerging from the crystal would be in the form of a glow or diffuse spherical emanation of uniform intensity. However, the atoms in the crystal are arranged in rows and layers, with definite spacings between them. The spacings in a crystal structure are about the same size as the wavelength of the X-rays. This situation is analogous to an optical device known as a *diffraction grating*, the principles of which may be found in any standard physics textbook. When diffraction occurs off a grating, radiation emitted from a row of regularly spaced point sources is reinforced along certain directions, and completely cancelled out along other directions! These directions can be predicted and described mathematically, based on the wavelength of the radiation and the spacing between the point sources. The case of crystals is much more complex, because the diffraction takes place in *three* directions (dimensions) simultaneously, and the exact interaction of the various beams is enormously difficult to calculate. The result of all this is that whereas a single X-ray beam enters the crystal, a divergent array of diffracted beams comes out.

These diffracted beams come out in specific directions. In addition, each beam is the result of interactions with various rows of atoms and a variety of types of atoms, each type contributing radiation based on its particular electronic makeup. The intensities of all the diffracted beams therefore vary widely.

A special camera has been devised in which a crystal being irradiated with X-rays is surrounded by special photographic film. The film records the positions and (through degree of darkening) the intensities of the diffracted X-ray beams. These parameters are measured on the film and listed as a set of line spacings and intensities. Such parameters have been measured and tabulated for nearly all the known mineral species. A rapid search of the tabulation usually allows the crystal to be quickly and unambiguously identified, in a matter of a few minutes.

A major advantage of the X-ray approach is that powder analysis requires a very small amount of sample. In the case of a faceted gem, a tiny bit of material can be scraped from the girdle with a diamond stylus, without materially damaging the stone. This amount of powder is sufficient for the X-ray analysis.

X-ray methods can be used advantageously in cases where optical and other data acquired by normal means are ambiguous. In some cases a gem is encountered that is a very rare cut example of a mineral not usually found in gem quality. In this instance the standard gemological measurements are not present in tabulations in textbooks, and the mineralogical literature must be consulted. In another case, a gemologist may encounter a synthetic gem material, such as a rare-earth garnet, the properties of which are also not tabulated in the gem literature. X-ray analysis would be definitive here, because the tabulation of X-ray measurements extends to the entire range of organic and inorganic compounds, as well as minerals.

X-ray equipment is expensive and requires great care in use. The X-ray beams produced for mineral analysis are extremely potent and capable of great damage to human tissues. Many large cities do have complete analytical laboratories that may offer diffraction as a service. The active gemologist should make an effort to locate such a laboratory for those times when diffraction offers special advantages in identification.

The gemologist should always remember that the chemical composition of minerals varies widely, with corresponding variation in physical properties. There is almost always a range of values in parameters such as refractive index, specific gravity and optical spectrum (presence or absence of diagnostic lines). By maintaining a continual awareness of the principles of crystal chemistry, the gemologist can avoid confusion and increase by many times the power of his analytical abilities.

Sources of Data Used in Text

FORMULA

The chemical composition of a mineral is a primary aspect of its definition as a species. The reader is referred to a periodic table of the chemical elements (page 143) for the meaning of standard abbreviations of the names of elements.

Many formulas contain parentheses within which are listed several elements, for example (Fe, Mg). This indicates that there is a specific position in the crystal structure that may be occupied by either iron, or magnesium, or both. The element listed first within the parentheses is the one present in greater amount on the structural site. In some cases this determines the species! For example, amblygonite is $(Li, Na)Al(PO_4)(F, OH)$. But if the formula reads $(Li, Na)Al(PO_4)(OH, F)$ we have a new species in which hydroxyl exceeds fluorine, and the species is now called montebrasite. Furthermore, if the formula is $(Na, Li)Al(PO_4)(OH, F)$, sodium exceeds lithium and the mineral is classed as yet another species, natromontebrasite. Obviously, the degree of complexity associated with solid solution can be very great. Any substitution of elements on a crystallographic structural site may (or may not) have an effect on physical properties.

Impurities also affect properties. A good example is beryl, $Be_3Al_2Si_6O_{18}$, but often containing such elements as Fe, Mn, Cr, V, and Cs. These elements are usually present in such small quantities that they are not written into the formula. However the mineralogist understands that Cr, for example, which makes beryl the rich green color we know as emerald, substitutes for Al in the formula. A detailed knowledge of chemical substitutions and color changes in crystals requires a much greater sophistication in crystal chemical principles than can be expounded here.

Formulas given in this book are based on the most re-cent mineralogical studies. Chemical elements listed after a "plus" sign (+) following the formula are those most often noted as substituting for elements in the formula.

CRYSTALLOGRAPHY

The reader is referred to standard books on mineralogy or crystallography for a detailed background in crystallography and terminology. It will suffice here to say that crystals grow in such a way that their component atoms and molecules are locked together in periodic arrays, like three-dimensional wallpaper patterns. These arrays have symmetry of various types that can be described and categorized. When this is done it is discovered that all known crystals can be organized according to six major crystal systems: *isometric, tetragonal, hexagonal, ortho-rhombic, monoclinic* and *triclinic*. A subclass of the hexagonal system that is sometimes (though erroneously) regarded as a seventh crystal system is known as *trigonal*. Each crystal system is defined in terms of crystal *axes*, which are imaginary lines in space that intersect at a common point, and whose lengths may be described as equal or unequal to each other. The systems are further described in terms of the angles that these axes make with each other.

Various descriptive terms may be used in describing the crystals exhibited by various mineral species. These terms include prismatic (elongated), bladed, acicular (needle-like), filiform (hair-like), equant (roughly equal-length sides), pyramidal (looking like single or double pyramids), and tabular. Sometimes terms are used that refer to specific forms characteristic of specific crystal systems (octahedron, pyritohedron, etc.). Other terms used to describe a mineral's appearance refer to state of aggregation: massive (solid and chunky), compact (solid and dense), cleavable (crystalline masses that can be cleaved), granular (masses of compact grains), stalactitic (resembling the form of stalactites), oolitic (masses of spherical grains), earthy (masses of densely packed powder).

The appearance of a mineral is largely a function of the growth process and the environment of formation. Minerals deposited in sedimentary environments tend to be earthy, stalactitic, oolitic, and sometimes massive. Igneous minerals tend to be crystalline or massive, sometimes cleavable. All these terms are somewhat subjective but are useful in getting a mental image of the appearance of a mineral as it occurs in the earth.

COLOR

Color is perhaps the least diagnostic aspect of a mineral or gemstone, except in rare cases, where the color can be truly diagnostic and useful in identification. The colors reported include all those mentioned in the mineralogical or gemological literature. The mineral literature is relied on heavily here, because it indicates the potential range of color for a given species. At any time a mineral may occur in gem quality in an unfamiliar color (for example, blue zoisite = tanzanite) and the tabulation will therefore indicate what might be expected in the future.

The streak (color of a powdered mineral) is listed where it is a useful diagnostic parameter in identification. Streak is useful almost exclusively in the case of opaque metallic minerals. The powder of most transparent minerals is white or colorless.

LUSTER

This property is considered a basic descriptive parameter for minerals, but varies somewhat even within a single crystal, and its usefulness is therefore limited. Lusters include: vitreous (the luster of glass—characteristic of most gem minerals); pearly (iridescent, pearl-like); resinous (luster of resin); greasy (appears covered by oil layer); adamantine (hard, steely brilliance like the reflection from a diamond); silky (fibrous reflection of silk); dull.

Luster is a phenomenon of reflected light and is mostly due to the state of aggregation of the mineral. For example, gypsum may have a vitreous luster on some crystal faces; the luster is pearly on surfaces parallel to the excellent cleavage of this mineral; and if the mineral occurs in aggregates of long fibers (satin spar) it has a silky luster. Luster can hardly be a useful diagnostic property in identifying gypsum under these circumstances!

Luster is primarily divided into two types: *metallic* and *nonmetallic*. There are also intermediate types, called *submetallic*. Any mineral that does not have a metallic appearance is described as nonmetallic, and the above descriptive terms are applied.

HARDNESS

Hardness is the resistance to scratching of a smooth surface. Hardness has little use to the gemologist, since gems are not normally scratched as a part of gem testing. A hardness is sometimes taken on the back of a statue, as for example to differentiate between jade and serpentine. But even using the girdle of a gem to perform a hardness test results in chipping on occasion.

Hardness depends on the bonding that holds the atoms together within a crystal structure. This bonding is reflected in the ease with which the layers of atoms at a surface can be separated, by applying pressure with a sample of another material. If the second material is harder than the first, it will leave a furrow, or scratch, which represents the breaking of millions of atomic bonds on a microscopic scale. The hardness of a mineral is, specifically, its "scratchability," and all minerals can be ranked in order of which one will scratch which other ones.

A mineralogist named Friedrich Mohs established a reference scale of 10 common minerals, ranked in order of increasing hardness, as follows:

1. Talc	5. Apatite	9. Corundum
2. Gypsum	6. Feldspar	10. Diamond
3. Calcite	7. Quartz	
4. Fluorite	8. Topaz	

In reality, diamond is very much harder than corundum, even though the scale says that they are only one division apart. The Mohs scale is approximately linear from 1 through 9; the curve climbs sharply upwards at corundum, however.

A mineral may be both hard and brittle, as in the case of diamond. Diamond will scratch any other material known to man, but a strong hammer blow can shatter a diamond into thousands of pieces. The perfect cleavage of diamond, in fact, allows it to be more expeditiously cut. Cleavage may be an initial diamond cutting operation, as opposed to the long and tedious process of sawing.

Hardness in a gemstone will determine the degree to which it will show wear. An opal, for example, which is quite soft for a ringstone, rapidly becomes covered with fine scratches in daily use, and the polish is quickly lost. A ruby, on the other hand, will remain bright and lustrous for years, because the material is harder than most of the abrasive particles in the atmosphere which contribute to gem wear.

The hardness of a material may vary slightly with composition and also with state of aggregation. The measurement of hardness is very tricky and often a mark that looks like a scratch is actually a trail of powder left by the supposedly harder material! It is really not critical whether the hardness of a mineral is 5 or $5\frac{1}{2}$. Fractional hardnesses are reported where the literature has indicated an intermediate value. A range in hardness is much more meaningful, and the values reported in this book represent all values encountered in the literature. In only one case (kyanite) does the hardness of a mineral vary very widely even within a single crystal. In most cases the hardness range reported is very small (one unit).

DENSITY

Density, or specific gravity, is a bulk property of a material. That is, it is independent of direction and is uniform within a mass of material under ideal circumstances.

In actuality, the density of a mineral varies widely, even within a single crystal, due to the presence of impurities, cracks, and bubbles. The density is a useful parameter in gem identification, and so the problems in its determination should be well understood.

Specific gravity is the ratio expressing the weight of a given material compared to that of an equal volume of water at 4°C. Thus, a specific gravity of 3 means that, at 4°C, one cubic inch of the material in question weighs 3 times as much as one cubic inch of water.

The density of a compound is a function of several factors, including chemical composition and crystal structure. For example, consider diamond and graphite, both of which are crystalline forms of the element carbon. Diamond has a density of 3.5 because the carbon atoms are tightly packed together in the structure; graphite, with a much more loose, open structure, has a density of only 2.2.

The density of minerals within a solid solution series may vary linearly with change in composition. The effect of chemical substitution is seen dramatically in the case of the orthorhombic carbonate minerals, aragonite and cerussite. Aragonite is $CaCO_3$ and has a specific gravity of 2.95; cerussite, with the same structure, is composed of $PbCO_3$ and has a specific gravity of 6.55! This clearly shows the role of lead versus calcium in the structure in influencing specific gravity.

Specific gravities are usually measured with heavy liquids. A liquid is prepared, such as a mixture of bromoform and toluene, to have a specific density value. An unknown material dropped into the liquid may sink, float, or remain suspended in one place within the liquid. If the material sinks, it is denser than the liquid, and if it floats it is lighter. If it remains at one level it has the same density as the liquid. Very accurate measurements of specific gravity can be made by changing the density of a column of liquid through temperature variations, and suspending density standards in the column.

An alternative method of measurement is the use of so-called torsion balances, such as the Berman balance used by mineralogists. These devices are designed to weigh a sample first in air, and then suspended in a liquid, such as water or toluene. The weights in both media can be measured quite accurately and specific gravities can sometimes be reported to two decimal places.

In all density measurements a major problem is the presence of impurities within the crystal being studied. These impurities hardly ever have the same specific gravity as the host material, and their presence leads to incorrect results. Surface tension may also "float" a mineral grain in both heavy liquids and the torsion balance, resulting in an erroneously low specific gravity measurement. Accurate density measurement involves absolute cleanliness, great care in specimen preparation, accurate temperature control, and replicate measurements.

The specific gravity measurements reported in this book represent values taken from both the mineralogical and gemological literature. In most cases a range is reported, as well as a typical value or (where reported) the value of the pure material.

CLEAVAGE

Hardness, as discussed earlier, is the scratchability of a material. Cleavage and the related property, *fracture*, are both manifestations of the tendency of certain crystals to break along definite plane surfaces. As in the case of hardness, the underlying principle is that of relative bond strengths. If there are planes in a crystal structure along which the atomic bonds are relatively weak, the crystal may tend to break along such planes. Under ideal circumstances, a cleavage plane might be smooth and flat, virtually on an atomic scale.

The atomic arrangement within a crystal is symmetrical; consequently the planes of specific bonds are symmetrically disposed within the crystal. Cleavage planes are therefore as symmetrical as crystal faces. By the same reasoning, glass can have no cleavage whatever. Glass is not crystalline, but is rather a supercooled liquid, in which the atoms are not arranged in a long range periodic array. There can therefore be no uniform bond layers, and hence no cleavage.

Cleavage is usually described with reference to crystallographic axes and directions. However, this nomenclature is beyond the scope of this book, so in all cases only the number of cleavage directions in a gem species has been indicated, and whether the cleavage is perfect (eminent), good, fair, or poor. Sometimes there are different degrees of cleavage perfection in different directions within the same crystal, and these have been so indicated in the text.

The term *parting* refers to breakage of minerals along directions of structural weakness. Unlike the situation in cleavage, parting is not present in all specimens of a given species.

Fracture is the way a mineral breaks other than along cleavage directions. The descriptive terms for this property are: conchoidal (shell-like, distinguished by concentric curved lines; this is the way glass breaks); fibrous; splintery; hackly (consisting of sharp-edged and jagged fracture surfaces); uneven.

Gems with perfect cleavage must be set carefully and worn carefully, as a sharp blow to the stone along a cleavage direction may easily split the gem. Spodumene is well known for its difficulty in cutting, and even topaz offers occasional problems to the cutter who is not aware of the cleavage direction.

OPTICS

Accurate measurements of the optical properties of gems are very useful because optical properties are extremely sensitive to minute changes in composition and strain in the crystal structure.

The basis of crystal optics is the premise that light travels in the form of waves, like ripples on a pond. The distance between successive crests or troughs of such a wave is known as the *wavelength*, and the *amplitude* of the wave is the height of the wave above the median (middle position between crest and trough). In familiar terms, different colors are different wave lengths, and the amplitude is the intensity of the light. Light vibrates at right angles to its direction of motion, and the vibration takes place in all directions perpendicular to the light path.

When light passes from one medium (such as air) into another (such as water) the light is actually slowed down. In addition, the light path is bent. The deviation is always referred to a line perpendicular to the interface between the two media, which is known as the *normal* to the interface. The light is always bent towards the normal in the medium in which the light travels slower.

The ratio between the velocity of light in the two media is called the index of refraction or *refractive index;* the first medium is usually taken to be air, in which the light velocity is considered unity (1). The refractive index then becomes $1/v$, where v is the velocity of light in the denser medium. Refractive index (usually abbreviated n) is also frequently described in terms of the angle to the normal made by the incoming light beam (incident ray) and that made by the refracted beam (traveling within the denser medium). Index of refraction in these terms equals the sine of the angle of incidence divided by the sine of the angle of refraction.

It is possible for light traveling from a given medium into a less dense medium, as, for example, from a crystal into air, to strike the interface at such an angle that the light is totally reflected at the interface, back into the denser medium. The incidence angle at which this takes place is known as the *critical angle*. This angle has great significance in terms of gem cutting. If the angles at which the gemstone are cut are incorrectly matched to the refractive index of the material, light refracted within the stone at the top may "leak out" the bottom of the gem, causing a loss of brilliance. If the angles are correct at the bottom of the stone, light is totally reflected internally and returns to the eye of the viewer, creating brilliance that is most pleasing, and, in fact, the whole reason for cutting facets on gemstones.

The optical properties of gemstones and minerals are determined by the crystallographic symmetry of these materials. For example, isometric crystals have crystal structures that are highly symmetrical in all directions; the result is that light traveling in an isometric crystal, or a glass (which is amorphous and has no crystal structure) travels at the same speed in any direction, and is not slowed down measurably in any one direction within the material. Such a material is termed *isotropic* and is characterized by a single refractive index, abbreviated in this book as N.

However, in all other crystals light is separated into two components. These two rays are *polarized*, that is, they each vibrate in a single plane rather than in all directions perpendicular to the direction of travel of the light. The two rays arising in such crystals are known as the *ordinary ray* and the *extraordinary ray*. All crystals other than isometric ones cause this splitting of incident light, and are termed *anisotropic*.

The existence of polarized light can be demonstrated by means of a special prism known after its inventor as the *Nicol prism*. This contains specially cut pieces of the mineral calcite that are oriented in such a way as to allow only light polarized in a single plane to pass through. If two Nicol prisms are lined up and turned with their polarization directions at right angles to each other, no light may pass at all. Similarly, a Nicol prism (or similar device) can be used to test for the polarization directions of light that has traveled through a crystal specimen or gemstone. This is the basic function of such devices as the *polariscope* and *polarizing microscope*.

In tetragonal and hexagonal crystals there is a "unique" crystal axis, which is either longer or shorter than the other two axes in the crystal. Light traveling in a direction parallel to this axis vibrates in the plane of the other two axes. But since the other two axes are equivalent, this vibration is uniform and resembles the light vibration in an isotropic crystal. If a pair of Nicol prisms is placed in line with light traveling in this direction in such a crystal, and the prisms are rotated so that the polarization directions are "crossed" (perpendicular), no light will be seen emerging from the crystal. As a result of the presence of this unique optical direction in tetragonal and hexagonal crystals, substances crystallizing in these crystal systems are termed *uniaxial*.

All other crystals contain *two* directions in which light vibrates uniformly perpendicular to the direction of travel. Consequently, crystals in the orthorhombic, monoclinic and triclinic systems are termed *biaxial*. The complete description of the behavior of light in such crystals is very complex, and beyond the scope of this book. The interested reader is referred to standard works on optical crystallography indicated in the Bibliography on page 139.

The ray in uniaxial crystals that travels along the optic axis, and which vibrates equally in a plane at right angles to this direction, is the ordinary ray. The other ray, which vibrates in a plane that includes the unique crystal axis direction, is the extraordinary ray. The refractive indices for these rays (directions) are the basic optical parameters for a uniaxial mineral, and are listed in this book as o and e. If the o-ray has a velocity in the crystal greater than the e-ray, such a crystal is termed *positive* ($+$); the crystal is considered *negative* ($-$) if the e-ray has a greater velocity. The *birefringence* in a uniaxial crystal is the difference between the refractive indices for o and e.

In biaxial crystals there are three different crystallographic axes, and in addition there are the two unique directions within the crystal that resemble the unique optic axis in a uniaxial crystal. The refractive indices of a biaxial crystal are designated by the Greek letters α (alpha), β (beta), and γ (gamma). Alpha is the lowest index, is referred to a direction in the crystal known as X, and is associated with the fastest light speed within the crystal. Beta is an intermediate index, corresponds to the Y crystallographic direction, and represents an intermediate ray velocity. Gamma is the highest refractive index, corresponds to the Z crystallographic direction, and is associated with the lowest ray velocity.

The birefringence in a biaxial crystal is the difference between the alpha and gamma index. The acute angle between the two optic axes within the crystal is designated $2V$ and is a useful parameter to the mineralogist. It turns out that if the beta index is exactly halfway between alpha and gamma, the $2V$ angle is exactly $90°$. Finally, if beta is closer in value to gamma than to alpha, the crystal is considered negative. If the value of beta is closer to that of alpha, the crystal is termed positive.

Both refractive indices and birefringence are useful parameters in characterizing and identifying crystals, and both change with composition, the presence of impurities and may vary even within a single crystal.

It should always be remembered that the refractive index is basically a measure of relative light velocity. Every wavelength of light travels through a given medium (other than air) at a *different* velocity, and consequently every wavelength has its own refractive index. The difference in refractive index with variation in wavelength is known as *dispersion*.

Dispersion is what makes a diamond sparkle with colors. The difference in refractive index for red vs. blue light in a diamond is quite large. As light travels through a cut gemstone, the various wavelengths (colors) therefore diverge, and when the light finally emerges from the stone the various color portions of the spectrum have been completely separated.

Dispersion is reported as a dimensionless number (i.e., no units), but there is some degree of choice in selecting the wavelengths to use as reference points. By convention, the dispersion of a gemstone is taken as the difference in refractive index as measured using the Fraunhofer B and G lines. These are spectral lines observed in the spectrum of the sun, respectively at 6870 and 4308 Å (Ångstrom units: one Ångstrom is equal to one ten-billionth of a meter. This is a unit of length used to describe light wavelengths).

In some cases, no dispersion information exists for a mineral or gemstone in the gemological literature; however, the mineralogical literature may have data for the refractive index measured at certain different wavelengths (not including the B and G wavelengths). In such cases it is possible to calculate the dispersion, by means of a special type of graph paper known as a *Hartman Dispersion Net*. This is a logarithmic-type paper on which one can plot refractive indices at specific wavelengths covering the entire useful range. Such plots are linear, and can be extrapolated to the positions of the B and G lines. The B–G dispersion is then simply picked off the graph. Approximately 20 gemstone dispersions, never before reported, are included in this book based on such calculations.

In some cases, as with opaque or translucent materials, the gemologist using only a refractometer cannot measure accurate refractive indices; rather, his instrument gives only a vague line representing a mean index for the material. Since this number is useful, in that it indicates what can be expected in routine work, it has sometimes been included in the text of this book.

Light may be absorbed differently as it passes through a crystal in different directions. Sometimes the differences are only in degree of absorption, or intensity. In other cases, however, different wavelength portions of the transmitted light are absorbed in different directions, resulting in colors. This phenomenon is termed *pleochroism*. In the case of uniaxial materials, there are only two distinct optical directions and the phenomenon is termed *dichroism*. Other materials may be *trichroic*, and the pleochroic colors are sometimes very distinct and and strong, and are useful in identification. The pleochroic colors reported for various gems are presented in this book in the order $X/Y/Z$, separated by slashes.

Since isotropic materials (including glasses) do not affect the velocity or properties of light passing through them in different directions, isotropic materials never display pleochroism. Occasionally, however, an isotropic material may display anomalous colors in polarized light. These effects are generally attributed to strain.

SPECTRAL

The optical spectrum of a gemstone may be extremely useful in identification, or in rapidly distinguishing between two similar gemstones with similar optical properties.

The principle of the spectroscope is fairly straightforward. Light we call white actually consists of a mixture of all the wavelengths in the visible range. When such light passes through a colorless material, none of the light is absorbed, and the white light emerges unchanged. However, some materials absorb various portions of the white light, allowing other portions to emerge and reach our eyes. The remaining portions consist of white light from which certain wavelengths have been subtracted. Consequently, if a material absorbs red, orange, and most of the yellow from the original white light, all that remains is blue and green and the material appears to us as a blue-green color. A ruby appears red to us because it absorbs much of the blue and green and nearly all of the violet light passing through it.

The optical spectroscope is a device that separates white light into a spectrum of component colors, using either a prism or a diffraction grating. The spectroscope allows light to enter through a narrow slit, the opening of which is usually controllable. The spectrum seen in the device consists of a closely packed array of thousands of images of the slit, each produced by a different wavelength. A gemstone placed between the light source and the slit absorbs some wavelengths, causing the corresponding slit images to be missing. Visually this appears as a continuous spectrum broken by sharp lines or broad bands, corresponding to the wavelengths being absorbed by the gemstone.

Certain gemstones have very distinctive spectra. In general, an optical spectrum is created through the agency of certain atoms in the crystal structure, which are, in the final analysis, responsible for the light absorption. Emerald, for example, contains chromium by definition; in fact, the spectrum of emerald contains very distinctive absorption lines representing chromium, located in the far red portion of the spectrum. Such minerals as apatite, zircon, olivine, sinhalite, and idocrase have characteristic lines that are frequently used in identification. A glance through a spectroscope is instantly sufficent to distinguish between a garnet and a ruby, for example.

The absorption spectra of many gemstones have not yet been reported in the gem literature. In other instances the spectrum has no distinctive or useful features. In both cases the abbreviation N.D. (No Data) has been used. Hopefully, the next edition of this book will contain complete spectral information on all the rare gems for which data are currently not available.

INCLUSIONS

Inclusions are crystals of minerals, cracks, healing fissures, bubbles, hoses, and other internal features of minerals that are useful in identification. Inclusions represent minerals that were floating in solutions from which other minerals formed; they are bits of liquid and gas bubbles trapped in a mineral as it grew; they are fractures surrounding radioactive minerals contained within a host mineral. The world of gemstone inclusions is beautiful, vast, and exciting, and one to which knowledge is continually being added.

The instrument for study of inclusions in gems is the microscope, preferably one with darkfield illumination. Sometimes inclusions are too small to be resolved with the 30–60X usually reached by stereoscopic microscopes, and magnifications of 200X or more are required.

An expert in the field of mineral and gemstone inclusions may be able, not only to identify a gemstone and pronounce unambiguously whether it is natural or synthetic, but also to indicate the very mine from which it came! Inclusions are the most powerful means of distinguishing the bewildering variety of man-made stones from the much more valuable natural gems they attempt to imitate. Inclusion information in this book represents a summary of what is in the available literature; information is lacking for many of the rarer gemstones, which will hopefully be provided for future editions of this book.

LUMINESCENCE

Certain electrons in atoms within the crystal structure of a mineral may be able to absorb energy and release the energy at a later time. This creates a phenomenon known as *luminescence*. If the absorbed energy is released almost immediately, the effect is called *fluorescence;* if there is a delay (ranging from seconds to hours) in the release of the energy the effect is called *phosphorescence*. The excitation energy may be X-rays, visible light, or even heat, but the most widely used energy source is ultraviolet light. Ultraviolet (UV) light is generated by several different kinds of lamps, basically of two types: long-wave (LW) UV at 3660 Å, which is generated by fluorescent-type lamps, and short-wave (SW) UV, at 2587 Å, generated by special quartz tubes.

Some minerals react in LW, some in SW, some in both, and some in neither. In many cases a mineral is not excited by UV light, unless it contains an impurity element which acts as an activator. The element manganese plays such a role in many minerals. Conversely, the element iron quenches fluorescence in most minerals. The detailed reasons for this behavior are beyond the scope of this book.

Luminescence effects are useful in gemstone identification, especially in certain cases in distinguishing synthetics. However, luminescence is best used in conjunction with other gemological tests.

OCCURRENCE

The occurrences reported in this book are condensed from both the mineralogical and gemological literature. Where possible an attempt has been made to indicate the general rock types and geological environments in which a mineral occurs. Following this is a listing of specific localities that have been reported, noting, where possible, whether the material found is of major gemological significance.

It should be remembered that a mineral may be reported from a locality, and none of it is of gem quality (i.e., attractive in color, transparent, etc.). However, an occasional piece may be encountered that is suitable for cutting, and this is sufficient to establish the material in the literature as occurring in gem quality in that locality. Such possibilities are always open. The main emphasis of this section in the book is to indicate how widespread the material is, and from what parts of the world it is best known.

STONE SIZES

This section of the book will, perhaps, never actually be completed, but rather will continually focus on adding information as obtained.

The objective is to indicte what constitutes a "large one" for a given species in question, with respect to cut gems. In some cases catalog information for major museums exists. Much information has been compiled from verbal sources, information in the minds of expert cutters, museum curators, and collectors. In some cases the author has seen no cut examples of a gem in question, but he has seen references to such gems in the literature or in private communications. Here only an indication can be provided of expectable gem sizes. The author freely acknowledges major omissions in the information presented in this portion of the text, and hopes that interested readers will make the next edition more useful by providing corrections and additions.

Gemstones of major importance exist in museum collections throughout the world. Some museums have especially complete collections of rare gems, and these institutions have been mentioned frequently in the text. Abbreviation used for some of these museums are as follows:

BM: British Museum (Natural History) (London, England);

SI: Smithsonian Institution (Washington, D.C.);

DG: Devonian Group (Calgary, Alberta, Canada);

AMNH: American Museum of Natural History (New York);

ROM: Royal Ontario Museum (Toronto, Ontario, Canada);

PC: Private Collection.

The metric carat is a unit of weight equal to one-fifth of a gram. It is the standard measure of gemstones. Where sizes are given in this book without a unit of measurement, the weight in carats is intended. Lower-cost cabochons are measured in millimeter size.

COMMENTS

This section contains general comments on wearing characteristics of gemstones, miscellaneous notes on occurrence, what constitutes high or low quality in the stone, general availability, and scarcity.

A

ACHROITE   See: Tourmaline.

ACTINOLITE   See also: Tremolite; Nephrite.
Formula: $Ca_2(Mg, Fe)_5Si_8O_{22}(OH)_2$.
Crystallography: Monoclinic; bladed crystals, usually elongated; fibrous, columnar aggregates. Also massive, granular. Often twinned.
Colors: Pale to dark green, blackish green, black.
Luster: Vitreous, sometimes dull.
Hardness: $5\frac{1}{2}$.
Density: Usually 3.05; Tanzania: 3.03–3.07; Max.: 3.44.
Cleavage: 2 directions good, often fibrous nature. Brittle. Compact variety tough.
Optics: $\alpha = 1.619$–1.622; $\beta = 1.632$–1.634; $\gamma = 1.642$–1.644 (Tanzanian material). See diagram on p. 124. Biaxial (−); $2V = 78°$.
Birefringence: 0.022–0.026.
Pleochroism: Yellow to dark green. Material transparent to nearly opaque.
α: pale yellow/yellowish-green.
β: pale yellow green/green.
γ: pale green/deep greenish blue.
Spectral: Faint line at 5030.
Luminescence: None (due to presence of Fe).
Occurrence: Contact metamorphic limestones and dolomites; magnesium-rich limestones and ultrabasic rocks; regionally metamorphosed rocks.
Chester, Vermont.
Madagascar: small, dark green crystals. Many of these are clean and suitable for faceting.
Tanzania: transparent crystals.
(See also localities for nephrite.)
Stone Sizes: Actinolite is rarely facetable and usually in small fragments. Material from Chester, Vt. could provide stones to about 10 carats.
DG: 2.06 (greenish, step cut, Africa).
Comments: Actinolite is a member of a series that contains varying amounts of iron and magnesium. Tremolite is the Mg end, and ferroactinolite the Fe end, with actinolite in the middle. Actinolites with more than 50% Fe are very rare. *Catseye* actinolite exists (S.G. 3.0, R.I. 1.63); when chatoyant material is cut it exhibits a fine eye. Actinolite is easy to cleave and hard to cut, and would make a poor jewelry stone. Actinolite is the chief constituent of nephrite (jade).
Name: Greek *aktis,* meaning *ray,* due to the fibrous nature.

ADAMITE
Formula: $Zn_2(AsO_4)OH + Co, Cu$.
Crystallography: Orthorhombic; crystals elongated or equant; druses, radial aggregates, and spheroids on matrix.
Colors: Colorless, pale green, yellowish green, yellow (various shades), bluish green, green (contains Cu); rose and violet shades (color zoned, contains Co).
Luster: Vitreous.
Hardness: $3\frac{1}{2}$.
Density: 4.32−4.48.
Cleavage: good 1 direction. Fracture subconchoidal to uneven.
Optics:

Locality	α	β	γ	Birefringence
Mapimi, Mexico	1.722	1.742	1.763	0.041
Tsumeb, S.W.A. (Cu)	1.742	1.768	1.773	0.031
Tsumeb, S.W.A. (Co)	1.722	1.738	1.761	0.039
Laurium, Greece	1.708	1.734	1.758	0.050

Biaxial (+); $2V = 15°$ (Cu var.) to 88°.
Large variations in composition lead to wide variations in optical properties.
Dispersion: Strong.
Pleochroism:
Colorless/blue-green/yellow-green.
Pale rose/pale rose/pale purple.
Pink/pale rose/colorless.
Spectral: Not diagnostic.
Luminescence: Intense green in SW, LW; also lemon yellow in SW.
Occurrence: Secondary mineral in the oxidized zone of ore deposits.
Utah (various localities); California; Nevada.
Laurium, Greece: often containing copper, in lovely blue and green shades.
Mapimi, Mexico: fine sprays of crystals in limonite matrix.
Tsumeb, S.W. Africa—fine crystals, sometimes colored purple by cobalt.
Cap Garonne, France.
Also *Chile, Italy, Germany, Turkey, Algeria.*
Stone Sizes: Violet crystals noted up to 1 cm long and transparent, would yield stones up to about 1−2 carats. Green material usually not clean, would provide only small faceted gems (1−3 carats).

Comments: Exceedingly rare as a cut gem, although the mineral occurs in many localities. Much too soft and fragile for jewelry; strictly collector item.

Name: After Mr. Gilbert Adam, mineralogist, of Paris, who supplied the first specimens for study.

ADULARIA See: Feldspar.

AGALMATOLITE See: Pyrophyllite.

AGATE See: Quartz.

ALABASTER See: Calcite, Gypsum.

ALBITE See: Feldspar.

ALGODONITE Also: Domeykite, Mohawkite.

Formula: Cu_6As (Domeykite = Cu_3As).

Crystallography: Hexagonal crystals rare; usually massive, granular, reniforn. Domeykite is Isometric.

Colors: Silver white to steel gray; tarnishes rapidly to a dull brown.

Luster: Metallic; opaque.

Hardness: 3–4 (Domeykite: 3–3.5).

Density: 8.38 (Domeykite: 7.92–8.10).

Cleavage: None. Fracture uneven in domeykite, subconchoidal in algodonite.

Occurrence: Localities that produce copper arsenide minerals.
Algodonite from *Painsdale, Michigan* in fine crystals. In masses from the *Algodones Mines, Coquimbo, Chile,* and *Cerro de Los Aeguas, Rancagua, Chile.*
Mohawkite is a mixture of algodonite and other copper arsenides, from the *Mohawk Mine, Keweenaw Peninsula, Michigan.*
Domeykite is from the *Mohawk Mine, Michigan; Lake Superior district, Ontario, Canda; Guererro, Mexico;* also from *Chile, Germany, Sweden,* and from *Cornwall, England.* Related minerals are found at *Beloves, Czechoslovakia* and *Mesanki, Iran.*

Stone Sizes: Cabochons could be cut to almost any size, depending on the availability of large masses of metallic rough.

Comments: Cabochons of these arsenides are bright, silvery and metallic and are both attractive and unusual. However, they tarnish rather quickly and the surfaces turn a drab brown and lose their luster. Cut stones are rarely seen even in collections, although they are strikingly beautiful when cut and polished to a high luster. They must be sprayed with lacquer to prevent tarnishing. Algodonite and domeykite are heat sensitive, and care must be exercised in cutting.

Name: After the Algodones Mine, Coquimbo, Chile.

ALLANITE See: Epidote.

ALMANDINE See: Garnet.

AMAZONITE See: Feldspar.

AMBER Also: Succinite.

Formula: Approximately $C_{10}H_{16}O + H_2S$.
A mixture of hydrocarbons, plus resins, succinic acid, and oils.
Amber is the hardened resin of pine trees, sp. *Pinus succinifera,* age ca 30 million years.

Crystallography: Amorphous.

Colors: Yellow, brown, whitish yellow, reddish, cream color, orange shades. Rarely blue, greenish, violetish.

Luster: Greasy.

Hardness: 2–2.5.

Density: 1.05–1.096 Usually ca 1.08.

Cleavage: None. Fracture conchoidal.

Optics: R.I. ca 1.54.

Spectral: Not diagnostic.

Luminescence: Yellow in SW (Texas); bluish white or greenish in LW. Baltic amber may fluoresce grayish blue in SW. Inert in X-rays.
Sicilian amber is noted for its fluorescence.

Occurrence: In sedimentary deposits and on shorelines, due to the action of waves and currents in bringing material up from offshore beds.
E. Prussia: Succinite (now U.S.S.R.).
Entire Baltic Sea region, including *Poland, E. Germany, Norway, Denmark;* also *Rumania, Sicily.* Sicilian material may be opalescent blue or green.
Rarely found in *England.* Southern *Mexico* produces golden yellow material.
Burma: brownish yellow and brown amber; also colorless, pale yellow and orange.
Lebanon: scarce, from very old deposits.
Dominican Republic: mined from sedimentary rocks, yellow, orange, and red colors; this amber often contains well preserved insects, and sometimes displays a strong bluish tone in reflected light.

Stone Sizes: The normal size of amber fragments is less than half a pound, but pieces weighing several pounds have been found. Amber is used often in making pipestems, as beads (tumble polished or faceted), pendants, earrings and rings. It is also carved, sometimes ornately; used as inlay material, umbrella handles, etc.

Inclusions: Amber is noted for its inclusions, which are chiefly insects and pollen, as well as leaves and other organic debris. These were trapped in the sticky fluid that oozed from the pine trees millions of years ago, and provide an intimate look at plant and insect life of that time period.

Comments: Amber is classed in various types: sea amber (found in the sea), pit amber (dug up, especially from the Baltic area), clear, massive, fancy, cloudy, frothy, fatty and bone amber.

Frequently seen in amber are flattened starburst shapes, known as *sun spangles*. These are internal feathers and are caused by stress. Amber softens at about 150°C. and melts at 250–300°C. *Pressed amber*, or *ambroid*, is made by melting small pieces of amber together under great pressure. This is usually detectable by careful microscopic investigation. Amber often darkens with age to a fine red-brown color. Pressed amber, however, may turn white with age.

Amber is in great demand today, as it has been for centuries, and very large material is extremely rare, as are the more unusual colored varieties (blue, green). Good quality material is seldom used for anything but jewelry.

Name: Arabic *anbar*, which the Spanish converted to *ambar*, then later to amber. Succinite is from *succinum*, the Latin word for amber, meaning *juice*.

AMBLYGONITE Also: Montebrasite (OH exceeds F); Natromontebrasite (Na exceeds Li).

Formula: $(Li, Na)Al(PO_4)(F, OH)$.
Usually Li greatly exceeds Na.

Crystallography: Triclinic; crystals equant to short prismatic, rough faces. Twinning common. Usually in cleavable masses.

Colors: Colorless, white, grayish white, yellow, pinkish, tan, greenish, bluish.

Luster: Vitreous to greasy; pearly on cleavages.

Hardness: 5.5–6.

Density: Approximately 2.98–3.11.
Amblygonite = 3.11;
montebrasite = 2.98;
natromontebrasite = 3.04–3.1.

Cleavage: Perfect 1 direction, good 1 direction.

Optics:

Luminescence: Pale blue in SW (Keystone, S.D.). Weak orange or bright green in LW, or pale brown in LW (Pala, Calif.).

Inclusions: Commonly veil-type inclusions, usually clouds in parallel bands.

Occurrence: Granite pegmatites.
Brazil: origin of most gem material, in crystals and masses, fine yellow color.
Custer Co., S.D.: masses up to 200 tons (non-gem) and at Tinton, S.D. in masses.
Also from *Arizona; New Mexico; California; New Hampshire; Pala, California;* and *Newry, Maine* in crystals up to more than 3 × 4 inches. These were found in 1940–41; they were heavily included and provided only small gems.
France; Germany; Varutrask, Sweden.
Montebras, France: Montebrasite.
Karibib, S.W. Africa: Montebrasite.
Sakangyi, Burma.

Stone Sizes: The largest cut amblygonite is ca 70 carats, cut from Brazilian material. The normal size is 1–15 carats. Facetable material is known from Maine, Brazil, and Burma, but cut gems over 10 carats are scarce.
SI: 62.5 (yellow, Brazil), 19.7 (yellow, Burma).
ROM: 15.6.
AMNH: 3 (colorless, Maine).
DG: 47 (yellow, Brazil).

Comments: Gems are usually pale straw yellow, and highly prized if the color is darker. Large stones have been cut but are extremely rare. Amblygonite is too soft and cleavable to make a good ringstone. The material from Karibib, S.W.A. is lilac in color and quite beautiful when faceted, as well as being extremely rare. It should be noted that many of the "amblygonites" reported in the literature are optically (+) and are therefore really montebrasites. Many gems in collections should probably be reexamined and relabeled if necessary. Most yellow gems in collections and on the market are

Species	Locality	α	β	γ	Birefringence	Density
Amblygonite	*Chursdorf, Germany*	1.578	—	1.598	.020	3.101
Amblygonite	*Uto, Sweden*	1.591	1.605	1.612	.021	3.065
Montebrasite	*Karibib, S.W. Africa*	1.594	1.608	1.616	.022	3.085
Montebrasite	*Kimito, Finland*	1.611	1.619	1.633	.022	3.00
Natromontebrasite	*Fremont Co., Colo.*	1.594	1.603	1.615	.021	3.04

Note that refractive indices and optic angle decrease as Na and F content increase. Montebrasite is optically (+) and amblygonite is (−). The change in optic sign (where $2V = 90°$) occurs ca 60% (OH). There appears to be a complete series of (OH, F) substitutions.

Pleochroism: None.

Spectral: Not diagnostic.

amblygonites from Brazil; however, stones from Mogi dãs Cruzes, Sao Paulo, Brazil are montebrasite.

Names: *Amblygonite* is from the Greek words for *blunt* and *angle* in allusion to the shapes of crystals.
Montebrasite is from the French locality where found.

AMETHYST See: Quartz.

ANALCIME Zeolite Group. See also: Pollucite.

Formula: $NaAlSi_2O_6 \cdot H_2O$.

Crystallography: Isometric; good crystals are common, usually trapezohedra. Massive, granular.

Colors: Colorless, white, gray, yellowish, pink, greenish.

Luster: Vitreous.

Hardness: 5–5.5.

Density: 2.22–2.29.

Cleavage: Indistinct. Fracture subconchoidal. Brittle.

Birefringence: Anomalous in polarized light.

Optics: Isotropic; $N = 1.479 – 1.493$.

Pleochroism: None.

Spectral: Not Diagnostic.

Luminescence: Cream white in LW (Golden, Colo.).

Occurrence: Secondary mineral in basic igneous rocks; also in sedimentary rocks such as siltstones and sandstones.
Washington, Oregon, and *California* (Columbia Plateau area).
Houghton Co.,Mich.
New Jersey: Watchung basalt flows.
India: Deccan Plateau.
Nova Scotia: Bay of Fundy area.
Mt. Ste. Hilaire, Quebec.
Also: *Scotland, Ireland, Iceland, Norway, Italy, Czechoslovakia, Germany.*

Stone Sizes: Gems are nearly always colorless, and less than 1–2 carats when faceted. Large crystals from Mt. Ste. Hilaire are white but may have small facetable areas. Crystals in general do not exceed $\frac{1}{4}$ inch in size in basaltic cavities and remain transparent.

Comments: Large colorless crystals are a great rarity in analcime, although small transparent crystals are abundant. Faceted gems are extremely rare, and seldom seen even in large collections. The hardness is marginal for wear, but the mineral has no cleavage and should present no difficulties in cutting.

Name: From the Greek *analkis*, meaning *weak*, because of the weak electric charge analcime develops when it is rubbed.

ANATASE Also called: Octahedrite. See: Brookite, Rutile.

Formula: TiO_2.

Crystallography: Tetragonal; crystals pyramidal, striated; also tabular and prismatic.

Colors: Black, red-brown, brown, deep indigo-blue; colorless to grayish, greenish, blue-green, lavender. Banding due to zonal growth often visible.

Luster: Adamantine, sometimes slightly metallic.

Hardness: 5.5–6.

Density: 3.82–3.97.

Cleavage: Perfect 2 directions. Fracture subconchoidal. Brittle.

Birefringence: 0.046–0.067.

Optics: $o = 2.534 – 2.564$; $e = 2.488 – 2.497$.
Refractive indices are extremely variable, depending on temperature and wavelength.
Anatase is sometimes biaxial with small $2V$ (dark-colored crystals).

Dispersion: 0.213 (o); 0.259 (e).

Pleochroism: Strong in deeply colored crystals: brown/yellow-brown/greenish-blue.

Spectral: Not diagnostic.

Luminescence: None.

Occurrence: Gneisses, schists, and other metamorphic rocks; as detrital grains, as an accessory mineral in granites, and in various other igneous rocks.
California; Gunnison Co., Colorado; Arkansas; Massachusetts; Virginia; North Carolina.
Canada; Brazil; Cornwall, England; Wales; Norway; France; Italy; U.S.S.R.
Switzerland: gem material from the Alpine regions.
Brazil: found in diamondiferous gravels.

Stone Sizes: Faceted gems are exceedingly rare and always very small (less than 1–2 carats). Usually the material is very dark and unappealing. Cut gems are known as large as ca 6 carats.

Comments: Anatase is usually found in very small crystals, seldom transparent, and even then very dark-colored. Gems have been cut as curiosities, but are almost never seen on the market for sale because of scarcity.

Name: Greek *anatasis*, meaning *erection* because the "octahedron" of anatase is really a tetragonal bipyramid and elongated with respect to the octahedron of the isometric system.

ANDALUSITE Varieties: Chiastolite, viridine. See: Kyanite, Sillimanite.

Formula: Al_2SiO_5.

Crystallography: Orthorhombic. Crystals prismatic, striated, square in cross section. Massive, compact.

Colors: Pinkish, reddish brown, rose red, whitish, grayish, yellowish, violet, greenish.
Chiastolite: gray crystals with black, carbonaceous cruciform pattern in interior.

Luster: Vitreous to subvitreous.

Hardness: 6.5–7.5.

Density: 3.13–3.17.

Cleavage: Distinct 1 direction. Fracture even to subconchoidal. Brittle.

Optics: $\alpha = 1.629 – 1.640$; $\beta = 1.633 – 1.644$; $\gamma = 1.638 – 1.650$.

Viridine: 1.66–1.69.
Biaxial (−), $2V = 73–86°$.

Birefringence: 0.007–0.011.

Dispersion: 0.016.

Pleochroism: Strongly pleochroic: olive green to flesh-red (Brazil).
Usually: yellow/green/red.

Spectral: Deep green varieties from Brazil display Mn spectrum: knife-edge shadow at 5535, fine lines at 5505, 5475; faint lines at 5180, 4950 and 4550.

Inclusions: Veil inclusions are common. Carbon inclusions in chiastolite.

Luminescence: None in LW. Brown fluorescence in SW (Lancaster, Mass.). Dark green or yellow-green fluorescence in SW (brown-green gems from Brazil).

Occurrence: Metamorphic rocks, usually slates and schists as a contact mineral, or developed within mica schist or gneiss. Also as a detrital mineral, and very rarely in pegmatites and granites.
California; South Dakota (Black Hills); *Colorado; New Mexico; Pennsylvania; Maine; Massachusetts.*
East Africa.
Brazil: main gem source today; found as pebbles in stream beds or on hillsides under layers of clay.
Ceylon: gem material found as waterworn pebbles, sometimes large size.
Burma: dull green material in gem gravels.

Stone Sizes: Gems from Brazil reach 75–100 carats. Usually gems are 1–5 carats; stones in the 5–10 carat range are available at several times the cost of the smaller ones. Stones over 10 carats are quite rare, and over 20 carats extremely rare.
SI: 28.3 (brown, Brazil), 13.5 (green/brown, Brazil).
ROM: 12.44 (Brazil).

Comments: Andalusite is a slightly brittle material and care is required if it is set as a ringstone. The pleochroism of andalusite is distinctive and extremely attractive. Sometimes gems are cut to show the pink and almost colorless shades; others display green in the center with brown tips, or various other combinations depending on how the rough was oriented before cutting. Catseye andalusites are known when fibrous inclusions are present, but are extremely rare.
Viridine is a deep green variety containing manganese.
Chiastolite is cut more or less as a curiosity, since it is always opaque; cross sections showing a well-formed black cross on a gray background are quite attractive. Chiastolite, because of its contained impurities, has a lower hardness and density than other varieties of andalusite.

Name: After the first noted locality, Andalusia (Spain). Chiastolite is from the Greek *chiastos, arranged diagonally,* because the pattern of carbon inclusions resembles the Greek letter *Chi,* which is written χ.

ANDESINE   See: Feldspar.

ANDRADITE   See: Garnet.

ANGLESITE

Formula: $PbSO_4$.

Crystallography: Orthorhombic. Crystals usually tabular, prismatic; granular; massive; stalactitic.

Colors: Colorless, white, yellowish gray, pale green and bluish shades.

Luster: Adamantine to vitreous.

Hardness: 2.5–3.

Density: 6.30–6.39; usually 6.38.

Cleavage: Good 1 direction. Fracture conchoidal. Brittle.

Optics: $\alpha = 1.877$; $\beta = 1.883$; $\gamma = 1.894$.
Biaxial (+), $2V$ ca 75°.

Birefringence: 0.017.

Dispersion: 0.044.

Pleochroism: None.

Spectral: Not diagnostic.

Luminescence: Weak yellowish fluorescence in SW and LW.

Occurrence: Secondary mineral in lead deposits, due to oxidation of galena (PbS). There are many localities, and many have the potential of yielding gemmy crystals.
Chester Co., Pennsylvania; Tintic, Utah; Arizona; New Mexico; Coeur d'Alene district, Idaho.
Chihuahua, Mexico; England; Scotland; Wales; U.S.S.R.; Germany; Sardinia; Broken Hill, N.S.W., Australia; Dundas, Tasmania.
Morocco: gem crystals.
Tsumeb, S.W. Africa: large transparent yellowish crystals, sometimes colorless, gemmy.
Tunisia: gemmy crystals.

Stone Sizes: Usual range is 1–6 carats for faceted gems. Anglesites very rarely are large enough to cut bigger stones than this, but some rough has yielded 100 carat gems, notably the material from Tsumeb.
DG: 88.75 (yellow, coffin-shaped triangle, Tsumeb, S.W.A.), perhaps world's largest.

Comments: Anglesite gems are colorless to pale brown and are available from only a few localities. But the dispersion is equal to that of diamond, and properly faceted gems are truly magnificent and bright. Low hardness and cleavage indicate great care is required in cutting, and wear is not recommended. Cut anglesites are true rarities and seldom seen except in very complete collections.

Name: Anglesey, the English locality where first found.

ANHYDRITE

Formula: $CaSO_4$.

Crystallography: Orthorhombic. Crystals equant, thick, tabular or (rarely) prismatic; massive, cleavable.

Colors: Colorless, white-gray, bluish, violet, pinkish, reddish, brownish.

Luster: Greasy; pearly on cleavage; vitreous in massive varieties.

Hardness: 3–3.5.

Density: 2.9–2.98.

Cleavage: Perfect 1 direction, nearly perfect 1 direction.

Optics: $\alpha = 1.570$; $\beta = 1.575$; $\gamma = 1.614$. Biaxial (+), $2V$ ca 43°.

Birefringence: 0.044.

Dispersion: 0.013.

Pleochroism: In violet crystals: colorless–pale yellow/pale violet –rose/violet.

Spectral: Not diagnostic.

Luminescence: Red color in LW (Germany).

Occurrence: A rock-forming mineral, associated with gypsum beds, halite and limestones. Also occurs in hydrothermal veins, cavities in basalts and other traprocks.

South Dakota, New Mexico, New Jersey, Texas.
Nova Scotia.
France, India, Germany, Austria, Poland.
Faraday Mine, Bancroft, Ontario, Canada: large purplish masses, some facetable.
Simplon Tunnel, Switzerland: pale purple cleavages, facetable.
Mexico: large blue masses, very lovely color.
Volpino, Italy: a white-gray, marble-like textured material known as *vulpinite* and used as a decorative stone locally, and made into cabochons.

Stone Sizes: Faceted gems are quite unusual, usually small (1–5 carats), but potentially much larger. Gems up to 9 carats have been cut, but cleavage masses could provide larger rough. Faceted gems are usually purplish or pale pink, from the Swiss and Canadian localities.

Comments: The blue or violet color disappears on heating and can be restored by gamma ray bombardment. The natural color may therefore be caused by natural radiation. Gemstones are very fragile due to excellent cleavages and must be cut and handled with great care.

Name: Greek *without water* in allusion to composition.

ANKERITE See: Dolomite.

ANORTHITE See: Feldspar.

ANORTHOCLASE See: Feldspar.

ANTIGORITE See: Serpentine.

APACHE TEARS See: Obsidian.

APATITE Group name. Also called: Asparagus Stone.

Formula: $Ca_5(PO_4)_3(F, OH, Cl)_3$.
Ca often replaced by Sr, Mn.
Also contains: Ce, rare earths, U, Th.
PO_4 replaced by $SO_4 + SiO_2$.
Carbonate apatites contain CO_2.

Crystallography: Hexagonal. Crystals usually prismatic or stubby; massive, granular, compact; oolitic, earthy.

Colors: Colorless, green, white, blue, brown, yellow, purple, violet, gray, pink, and various shades of most of these colors.

Luster: Vitreous in crystals.

Hardness: 5 (some massive varieties 3–4).

Density: 3.10–3.35 (massive varieties 2.5–2.9).

Cleavage: Poor. Fracture conchoidal to uneven. Brittle.

Optics: $e = 1.598-1.666$; $o = 1.603-1.667$. Very variable with composition.
Gem varieties: $o = 1.632-1.649$, $e = 1.628-1.642$.
Uniaxial (−); francolite may be biaxial, $2V = 25-40°$.

Birefringence: 0.001–0.013.
Chlorapatites have the lowest birefringence (ca 0.001); fluorapatites medium (0.004); hydroxylapatites higher (0.007); carbonate apatites as high as 0.008; and francolite as high as 0.013.

Dispersion: 0.013.

Pleochroism: Distinct in blue-green varieties; otherwise weak.
Gem blue apatite shows strong dichroism: blue/yellow.

Spectral: Blue and yellow apatites display a rare earth spectrum. Yellow gems have 7-line group at 5800 and 5 lines at 5200. Blue gems give broad bands at 5120, 4910 and 4640.

Luminescence: Yellow gems fluoresce lilac-pink in SW and LW (stronger in LW). Blue apatite fluoresces violet-blue to sky blue, and violet material fluoresces greenish-yellow (LW) or pale mauve (SW). Green apatite fluoresces a greenish mustard color, LW stronger than SW. Manganapatite fluoresces pink in SW.

Occurrence: Apatite is found in a wide variety of rock types. Igneous rocks are usually characterized by F and OH varieties, some containing Mn. Apatite occurs in pegmatites, hydrothermal veins and cavities, metamorphic rocks, and as detrital grains in sedimentary rocks and phosphate beds.

Blue: Burma; Ceylon; Brazil.

Refractive Indices

Type	Locality	Color	o	e	Birefrin-gence	S.G.
Chlorapatite	Japan	yellow	1.658	1.653	.005	—
Hydroxylapatite	Holly Springs, Ga.	—	1.651	1.644	.007	3.21
Fluorapatite	Finland	blue-green	1.629	1.633	.004	3.2
Hydroxylapatite	Sweden (with Mn)	blue-green	1.646	1.641	.005	3.22
Fluorapatite	Sweden	colorless	1.634	1.631	.003	3.27
Carbonate apatite with fluorine	Devonshire, Engl. (francolite)	—	1.629	1.624	.005	3.14
Hydroxylapatite	Mexico	yellow	1.634	1.630	.004	—
Fluorapatite	Canada	green	1.632	1.629	.003	—
Fluorapatite	Maine	purple	1.633	1.630	.003	—
Carbonate apatite	St. Paul's Rocks, Atlantic Ocean	—	1.603	1.598	.005	—
Cut gemstone	Kenya	dark green	1.641	1.637	.004	—
Cut gemstone	Rhodesia	yellow-green	1.643	1.638	.005	—
Cut gemstone	Mexico	yellow	1.637	1.633	.004	—
Cut gemstone	Madagascar	dark green	1.637	1.632	.005	—
Cut gemstone	Burma	green	1.636	1.632	.004	—
Cut gemstone	Brazil	deep blue	1.638	1.632	.006	—
Cut gemstone	Canada	green	1.632	1.628	.004	—
Cut gemstone	Ceylon (catseye)	brown	1.647–1.649	1.640–1.642	.007	—

Blue-green: Arendal, Norway (variety called moroxite).
Violet: Germany; Maine; California.
Yellow: Durango, Mexico; Murcia, Spain; Canada; Brazil.
Green: India; Canada (trade-named Trilliumite); *Mozambique; Madagascar; Spain; Burma.*
Brown: Canada.
Colorless: Burma; Italy; Germany.
Catseye: Blue green and green from *Ceylon* and *Burma; Ceylon* also produces yellowish catseye apatite. Green catseyes also occur in *Brazil.*

Stone Sizes: The Roebling purple apatite in *SI* is ca 100 grams, superb crystal. Cut apatites are not common in museum collections. Blue gems (Brazil) are almost always small (1–2 carats). Burma produces 10 carat blue gems, but this color is very scarce in larger sizes. Yellow gems up to 15–20 carats are known from Mexico, but larger ones are quite rare. Violet stones are the rarest and smallest in general, usually under 2 carats. Blue-green clean stones are usually less than 5 carats, rare if larger. Green apatite occurs in large crystals; Canadian material has yielded 100 carat stones, flawless. The world's largest golden green gem may be a 147 carat stone from Kenya. Yellowish catseyes range up to about 15 carats, and green catseyes a bit larger (20 carats).

Comments: Fluorapatite is the commonest apatite variety. Apatite is abundant throughout the world, and is, in fact, the main constituent of bones and teeth. It is also the most abundant phosphorus-bearing mineral, especially collophane, the massive type that makes up large beds in some localities. Apatite is brittle and heat sensitive, and must be cut and worn with care. Properly cut stones are truly magnificent, however, since they are both bright and richly colored. It is possible to assemble suites of as many as 20 gems, all different colors.

Mexican yellow apatite is perhaps the most abundant material available, and thousands of crystals exist that would cut stones up to 5 carats. Larger pieces are rare, however, even from this locality. The Mexican material may be turned colorless by careful heating.

Lazurapatite is a mixture of lapis and apatite that is found in Siberia.

Name: From the Greek, meaning *to deceive* because mineralogists had confused apatite with other species.

APOPHYLLITE

Formula: $KCa_4Si_8O_{20}(F, OH)\cdot 8H_2O$.

Crystallography: Tetragonal. Crystals pseudocubic; tabular, prismatic, sometimes pyramidal.

Colors: Colorless, white, grayish, pale yellow, pale green, dark green, reddish.

Luster: Vitreous, pearly on cleavage.

Hardness: 4.5–5.

Density: 2.3–2.5.

Cleavage: Perfect 1 direction. Fracture uneven. Brittle.

Optics: $o = 1.53–1.54$; $e = 1.53–1.54$ (variable). Optically (+) or (−); uniaxial.

Birefringence: 0.001 or less. May appear isotropic.

Pleochroism: None.

Spectral: Not diagnostic.

Luminescence: None.

Occurrence: Secondary mineral in basic igneous rocks, such as basalts and traprocks.
New Jersey; Oregon; Washington; Colorado; Michigan; Virginia; Pennsylvania.
Guanajuato, Mexico; Brazil; Canada; Sweden; Scotland; Germany; Ireland; Faroe Islands, Iceland; Bay of Fundy, Nova Scotia.
Bombay, India: colorless crystals and also intense apple green color, due to Fe (*Poona, India:* o = 1.530, e = 1.533, birefringence 0.003, S.G. = 2.37).

Stone Sizes: Apophyllites are seldom faceted, and rough to cut greater than 10 carats is very rare. Stones are usually colorless, though green Indian material is also cut.
SI: 15.4 (colorless, step-cut).
D.G.: 7.05 (colorless, Poona, India).

Comments: Apophyllite is very brittle and fragile, with an extremely perfect and easy cleavage. It is unsuited for jewelry, but colorless apophyllite is perhaps the whitest of all gems. The cut stones are so devoid of any trace of color that they almost appear silvery. The cleavage indicates an orientation with the table of a faceted stone not perpendicular to the long axis of the crystals. The green, iron-rich apophyllite from India occurs in magnificent crystal groups, but facetable material is quite scarce and usually smaller than the colorless.

Name: From Greek words describing the tendency of apophyllite to exfoliate when strongly heated.

AQUAMARINE See: Beryl.

ARAGONITE *Dimorphous with* Calcite.

Formula: $CaCO_3$ + Pb, Sr, rarely Zn.

Crystallography: Orthorhombic. Pseudohexagonal, crystals often acicular, chisel-shaped, prismatic; also massive, columnar, fibrous, stalactitic, coralloidal. Frequently twinned.

Colors: Colorless, white, yellow, gray, green, blue-green, lavender, reddish, brown.

Luster: Vitreous to resinous.

Hardness: 3.5–4.

Density: 2.947 (pure). Usually 2.93–2.95; up to 3.0 if Pb present.

Cleavage: Distinct 1 direction. Fracture subconchoidal. Brittle.

Optics: $\alpha = 1.530$; $\beta = 1.681$; $\gamma = 1.685$.
Biaxial (−), $2V = 18°$. Sector twinning observed.

Birefringence: 0.155.

Pleochroism: None.

Spectral: Not diagnostic.

Inclusion: Usually veil-type inclusions observed.

Luminescence: Pale rose, yellow, tan, green, rarely bluish in LW; may phosphoresce green in LW (Sicily). Yellowish, pinkish-red, tan, white in SW, also pink (Sicily).

Occurrence: Worldwide occurrences, especially in limestone caverns, hot springs, and in the oxidized zone of ore deposits.
Molina de Aragon, Spain: type locality, in stubby twinned crystals.
Austria; England; Peru; S.W. Africa; Czechoslovakia.
Agrigento, Sicily: with sulfur crystals.
Chile: blue material.
Guanajuato, Mexico. Laurium, Greece: blue aragonite.
Many localities in U.S., including *New Mexico, South Dakota, Virginia, Colorado.*
Fibrous aragonite from *Wyoming, California, Iowa.*

Stone Sizes: Faceted gems usually only a few carats. Potential exists for much larger stones. Most faceted gems are colorless, since colored material is usually massive. Straw yellow crystals from Horschenz, Germany have yielded stones to 10 carats. The largest known cut specimens are in the 40–50 carat range.
D.G.: 7.85 (Germany).

Comments: The hardness of aragonite is too low to allow for safe wear. Aragonite is not as abundant or widespread as calcite, except (in gem use) insofar as it is the major constituent of pearls. Faceted gems are almost always very small, as opposed to calcite, which occurs in huge transparent masses or crystals. Faceted gems are thus truly rare collector items.

Name: Locality, Molina de Aragon, Spain.

AUGELITE

Formula: $Al_2PO_4(OH)_3$.

Crystallography: Monoclinic. Crystals tabular and thick; prismatic; acicular. Also massive.

Colors: White, yellowish, pale blue, pale rose.

Luster: Vitreous. Pearly on cleavage surfaces.

Hardness: 4.5–5.

Density: 2.696–2.75.

Cleavage: Perfect 1 direction, good 1 direction.

Optics: $\alpha = 1.574$; $\beta = 1.576$; $\gamma = 1.588$.
White Mountain, California material: $\alpha = 1.570$; $\beta = 1.574$; $\gamma = 1.590$.
Biaxial (+), $2V$ ca 50°.

Birefringence: 0.014–0.020.

Pleochroism: None.

Spectral: Not diagnostic.

Luminescence: None.

Occurrence: Crystals from the *Champion Mine, Mono Co., California* reach a size of about one inch; this

locality is now depleted. It furnished cuttable gem material.
Masses occur at *Keystone, South Dakota* (non-gem).
Palermo Mine, New Hampshire.
Potosi, Bolivia: in crystals.
Sweden: massive.
Uganda.

Stone Sizes: Most gems in existence, from the California material, are less than 1 carat up to about 3 carats. Larger stones are exceedingly rare, in the case of what is already a rare mineral.

Comments: Augelite is soft and brittle, unsuited for wear. However, the gems cut from rare transparent crystals are true collector items, and seen only in very complete collections.

Name: From a Greek word meaning *luster*, because of the glassy appearance of the mineral.

AVENTURINE   See: Quartz.

AXINITE   *Group name.*
Formula: $(Ca, Mn, Fe, Mg)_3Al_2BSi_4O_{15}(OH)$.
$$+Mg = magnesioaxinite$$
$$If\ Fe > Mn = ferroaxinite$$
$$If\ Mn > Fe = manganaxinite$$
If Mn > Fe and Ca < 1.5 = *tinzenite*

Crystallography: Triclinic. Distinctive wedge-shaped crystals, also tabular.

Colors: Violet-brown, colorless, yellowish (Mn), pale violet to reddish (Mn), blue (Mg).

Luster: Vitreous.

Hardness: 6.5–7; variable with direction.

Density: 3.26–3.36; magnesioaxinite = 3.18.

Cleavage: Good 1 direction. Fracture uneven to conchoidal. Brittle.

Optics: $\alpha = 1.674-1.693$; $\beta = 1.681-1.701$; $\gamma = 1.684-1.704$.
Magnesioaxinite: $\alpha = 1.656$; $\beta = 1.660$; $\gamma = 1.668$.
Biaxial (–), $2V = 63-80°$ or more.

Birefringence: 0.010–0.012.

Dispersion: Large.

Pleochroism: Intense in all colored varieties:
Cinnamon brown/violet-blue/olive green, yellow, or colorless.
Luning, Nevada: pale brown to colorless/deep brown/brownish red.
Pale blue/pale violet/pale gray (magnesioaxinite).

Spectral: Narrow line at 5120, broad lines at 4920 and 4660, also 4150. Sometimes lines visible at 5320, 4440 and 4150 (latter may be strong).

Luminescence: Red in SW (Franklin, N.J.). Dull red in SW, orange-red in LW (Tanzania: magnesioaxinite).

Occurrence: Axinite is found in areas of contact metamorphism and metasomatism.
Yuba Co., Calif.: gemmy crystals. Also gem material from *Coarse Gold, Madera Co., Calif.*
Luning, Nevada: masses.
Pennsylvania; New Jersey.
Cornwall, England; Germany; Norway; Finland; U.S.S.R.; Japan; Tasmania.
Bourg d'Oisans, France: S.G. 3.28, R.I. = 1.68–1.69, in pockets in schist.
Switzerland: tinzenite.
Tanzania: magnesioaxinite.

Stone Sizes: Axinite is rare in faceted gems over 10 carats. Material from Baja California will yield gems to about 25 carats, but most stones, if clean, are less than 5 carats.
SI: 23.6 (brown, Mexico).
PC: 16.5 (Baja).
Geol. Mus., London: 0.78 (magnesioaxinite, Tanzania).

Comments: Cut axinites are usually intensely trichroic, with the brown and purple colors dominating. The material is exquisite, but is almost never completely free of flaws and feathers. Axinite is actually an extremely rare cut gem, and could be one of the most magnificent because of its rich colors and brilliance. Clean stones over 5 carats are difficult to find and worthy of museum display. Axinite is hard enough to be worn in jewelry, though it is a bit brittle.

Name: From a Greek word meaning *axe*, in allusion to characteristic crystal shape.

AZURITE
Formula: $Cu_3(CO_3)_2(OH)_2$.
Crystallography: Monoclinic. Crystals may be large and perfect, tabular, prismatic; also massive, earthy, banded, stalactitic.
Colors: Light and dark azure blue.
Luster: Vitreous (crystals) to earthy or dull.
Hardness: 3.5–4.
Density: 3.77.
Cleavage: Perfect 1 direction. Fracture conchoidal. Brittle.
Optics: $\alpha = 1.730$; $\beta = 1.758$; $\gamma = 1.836$.
Biaxial (+), $2V$ ca 67°
Birefringence: 0.110.
Pleochroism: Strong, in shades of blue.
Spectral: Not Diagnostic.
Luminescence: None.
Occurrence: Secondary mineral in copper deposits.
Chessy, France: chessylite, fine crystals in large groups.
Morenci and Bisbee, Arizona: banded and massive material, also crystals.

Kelly, New Mexico and other localities in that state.
Italy; Greece; U.S.S.R.; Australia.
Tsumeb, S.W. Africa: fine, tabular crystals, some facetable in small bits.
Zacatecas, Mexico: fine crystals (small).

Stone Sizes: Facetable crystals are always tiny, and cut gems are all less than 1 carat. It is pointless to cut larger stones, as they would be so dark as to be opaque. Dark blue crystalline material is sometimes cabbed, and cabochons may be several inches across.

Comments: Faceted azurite is a great rarity, but even small stones are extremely dark, virtually black. *Azurmalachite* is a mixture of azurite and another copper carbonate, malachite. *Burnite* is a mixture of azurite and cuprite (copper oxide). Azurite occurs in fine crystals in many localities, but in massive form is almost always mixed with malachite. In this form it is cut as very attractive cabochons and large decorative items, such as boxes. The intense blue color is distinctive and makes azurite very desirable among mineral collectors and gem hobbyists.

Name: In allusion to the color, derived from the Persian word *lazhward*, meaning *blue*.

AZURMALACHITE   See: Azurite.

B

BALAS RUBY   See: Spinel.

BARBERTONITE   See: Stichtite.

BARITE

Formula: $BaSO_4$ + Ca, Sr.

Crystallography: Orthorhombic. Tabular crystals, aggregates and rosettes; massive, granular, fibrous, earthy, stalactitic.

Colors: White, grayish, yellowish to brown, blue, green, reddish. May be color zoned.

Luster: Vitreous to resinous; pearly on cleavage.

Hardness: 3−3.5.

Density: 4.50 (pure); usually 4.3−4.6.

Cleavage: Perfect 1 direction. Fracture even. Brittle.

Optics: $\alpha = 1.636$; $\beta = 1.637$; $\gamma = 1.648$.
Biaxial (+), $2V = 37°$.

Birefringence: 0.012.

Dispersion: 0.016.

Pleochroism: Weak if crystal is colored:
Brown crystal: straw yellow/wine yellow/violet.
Yellow crystal: pale yellow/yellow-brown/brown.
Green crystal: colorless/pale green/violet.

Luminescence: In SW: white (Germany, Ohio), blue-green (Germany, England), gray (Germany). In LW: greenish white (Germany), pinkish white (Ohio), cream-white (South Dakota), yellow-green (Germany).

Occurrence: Barite is common in low-temperature hydrothermal vein deposits; also as a component of sedimentary rocks, sometimes in large beds; as concretions, in clay deposits, and rarely in cavities in igneous rocks. Good crystals abundant worldwide.
Meade Co., South Dakota: fine brown crystals, facetable.
Colorado: exquisite blue crystals, some facetable (Sterling area).
Illinois.
Thunder Bay Dist., Ontario: colorless crystals suitable for cutting.
Rock Candy Mine, Brit. Columbia: facetable yellow crystals, up to 4 inches long.
Cumberland, England: fine crystals, sometimes very large, facetable areas.
Many other localities worldwide, many with potential for clean material.

Stone Sizes: Large crystals are known, usually flawed, but many have facetable areas. English material will yield stones up to about 50 carats; one is known over 300 carats. Yellow-brown crystals from France have been cut into gems as large as 65 carats. Colorado gems are usually 1−5 carats.

Comments: Massive white barite looks like marble and coule be used for decorative purposes. Faceted gems are hard to cut, and facet junctions tend to be rounded. The perfect cleavage makes wear very risky, and the low hardness would also prevent use in jewelry. In spite of the abundance of good crystals, cut barites are not commonly seen, especially in rich colors. With very few exceptions, large stones could be obtained in almost any desired color.

Name: Greek *baros*, heavy, because of the high specific gravity.

BASTITE   See: Enstatite.

BAYLDONITE

Formula: $(Pb, Cu)_3(AsO_4)_2(OH)_2$.

Crystallography: Monoclinic. Fibrous concretions; massive, granular.

Colors: Various shades of yellowish green.

Luster: Resinous.

Hardness: 4.5.

Density: 5.5.

Cleavage: Not observed.

Optics: $\alpha = 1.95$; $\beta = 1.97$; $\gamma = 1.99$.
Biaxial (+), $2V$ large.

Birefringence: 0.04.

Dispersion: No data.

Pleochroism: No data.

Spectral: Not diagnostic.

Luminescence: None.

Occurrence: Secondary mineral in Pb−Cu deposits.
England; France.
Tsumeb, S.W.Africa: only major occurrence.

Stone Sizes: Cabochons only from massive, fibrous material from Tsumeb.

Comments: Bayldonite is a nondescript greenish material that has been cut into cabochons by enterprising collectors of the unusual. Cut bayldonites are a rarity, nonetheless, and seldom seen in collections. The luster of cabochons is sometimes almost metallic and provides a curious appearance to the cut stones. Bayldonite is compact but too soft for rings; it could be worn in bola ties and pendants.

Name: After Mr. John Bayldon.

BENITOITE

Formula: $BaTiSi_3O_9$.

Crystallography: Hexagonal. Crystals triangular in shape, flattened, very distinctive.

Colors: Blue (various shades), purple, pink, white, colorless. Sometimes zoned.

Luster: Vitreous.

Hardness: 6–6.5.

Density: 3.64–3.68.

Cleavage: Indistinct. Fracture conchoidal to uneven. Brittle.

Optics: $o = 1.757$; $e = 1.804$.
Uniaxial (+).

Birefringence: 0.047.

Dispersion: 0.046.

Pleochroism: Strong: o = colorless, e = blue.

Luminescence: Intense blue in SW only, no reaction to LW.

Occurrence: *Rush Creek, Fresno Co., Calif.; Texas. Belgium.*
Only gem locality is in *San Benito Co., California*, as superb crystals in a massive, fine-grained, white natrolite. The crystals reach a size of ca 2 inches across, colored white and various shades of blue, rarely pinkish or colorless, zoned. Though crystals are large, facetable areas are always very small.

Stone Sizes: Always small, because crystals are badly flawed. Also, best color (along *e*) is seen in an unadvantageous direction in terms of the flattening of the crystals, giving smaller gems with good color. The largest stone on record is in *SI*, 7.8 carats. A large gem of 6.52 carats was cut for a private collector but stolen in transit. Most gems are under 1 carat, up to about 2–3 carats. Larger stones are exceedingly rare. The deposit has been largely worked out and available gems sold, so benitoite is becoming very difficult to obtain in cut form.

AMNH: 3.57.

Comments: Benitoite is one of the most beautiful of all the rare gems, with the color of fine sapphire and the dispersion of diamond! It was discovered in 1906 and first thought to be sapphire. The dispersion is usually masked by the intense blue color. Benitoite is one of the most desirable, beautiful, and scarce of all gemstones.

Name: After the occurrence in San Benito County, California.

BERYL

Formula: $Be_3Al_2Si_6O_{18}$ + Fe, Mn, Cr, V, Cs.

Crystallography: Hexagonal. Crystals prismatic, elongated or flattened, equant; often striated or etched; rolled pebbles; massive.

Colors: Colorless, white, light green, olive green, blue-green to blue (aquamarine), deep green (emerald), pink or peachy pink (morganite), greenish yellow, yellow (heliodor), pinkish orange, red (bixbite).

Beryl is one of the most familiar minerals because of the many famous gem varieties it offers. These specific gem types are named according to color and chemistry. The colorless variety, pure beryl, is termed *goshenite*. A trace of manganese adds a pink or salmon-peachy-pink color, and we have the variety known as *morganite*. *Heliodor* or *golden beryl* derives its color from ferric iron, and the color ranges from pale yellow to deep yellowish-orange. *Aquamarine* also gets its color from iron, but in the ferrous (reduced) state, and the range is from blue-green to deep blue. *Emerald* is the best known color variety, the color of which, a fine, intense green, is due to a trace of chromium replacing aluminum in the beryl structure. Emerald is, by definition, the green beryl colored by chromium. Other green beryls of various shades exist, which are simply termed *green beryl*, where Cr is not present and does not reveal a chromium spectrum; this also includes a deep green beryl colored by vanadium, which is technically speaking *not* emerald. A deep rose-red colored beryl, in small crystals from the mountains of Utah, has been named *bixbite;* this color is also due to manganese.

Luster: Vitreous.

Hardness: 7.5–8.

Cleavage: Indistinct. Fracture conchoidal to uneven. Brittle.

Density:
Goshenite: 2.6–2.9;
morganite: 2.71–2.90;
aquamarine: 2.68–2.80;
emerald: 2.68–2.78.

Inclusions: Beryl is characterized by long, hollow tubes, sometimes filled with liquid; the tubes are parallel and run the length of prismatic crystals, sometimes have a brownish color and may contain gas bubbles. *Negative* crystals are also seen, as well as flat inclusions that resemble snowflakes and have a metallic look, known as *chrysanthemum* inclusions. Aquamarines contain, in addition to the above, crystals of biotite, phlogopite, rutile, pyrite, hematite, and ilmenite in skeletal crystals that sometimes allow the cutting of *star beryls*. Some aquamarines contain *snow-stars:* irregular liquid droplets in starlike patterns. These were especially noted in the Martha Rocha, a famous and large aquamarine.

Inclusions in Emeralds

Habachthal, Austria: Straight, broad-stemmed tremolite rods; biotite, rounded mica plates; tourmaline; epidote; sphene; apatite; rutile.

Colombia:
  Chivor Mine, 3-phase inclusions; pyrite; albite.
  Muzo Mine, 3-phase inclusions; parisite crystals (*only* known from Muzo mine), in yellow-brown prisms; calcite rhombs.
  Borur Mine, 3-phase inclusions.
  Gachala Mine, parallel growth bands, needle-like growth tubes; 3-phase inclusions: albite, pyrite; 6-sided cleavage cracks.
Bahia, Brazil: 2-phase inclusions; biotite; talc; dolomite crystals; liquid films.
U.S.S.R.: Actinolite crystals, singly or in groups, resembling bamboo-cane; mica plates.
Australia: Biotite (abundantly); actinolite; calcite; some 3-phase inclusions seen.
Transvaal, S.W. Africa: Brown mica (makes gems dark in color); curved molybdenite crystals.
Rhodesia: Fine, long curving tremolite needles; also short rods or fine curved fibers; color zoning; garnets; hematite; feldspar.
India: Oblong cavities parallel to long crystal axis, with gas bubbles; parallel to basal plane are biotite crystals, fuchsite, 2-phase inclusions; apatite crystals; groups of negative twin crystals with comma shape.

W. Pakistan: 2-phase inclusions; thin films; some liquid inclusions, few mineral crystals.
Tanzania: 2-phase and 3-phase inclusions; square-shaped cavities and tubes; actinolite, mica.
Zambia: Biotite (black crystals) as small specks or dots; pinpoints, breadcrumb inclusions.
Norway: Mossy inclusions; also interconnected tubes (make crystals turbid).
North Carolina: Quartz crystals sometimes seen.

Optics: Beryl is uniaxial $(-)$, and refractive indices vary with composition:
Goshenite: $o = 1.566 - 1.602$; $e = 1.562 - 1.594$; Birefringence $= 0.004 - 0.008$.
Morganite: $o = 1.572 - 1.592$; $e = 1.578 - 1.600$; Birefringence $= 0.008 - 0.009$.
Aquamarine: $o = 1.567 - 1.583$; $e = 1.572 - 1.590$; Birefringence $= 0.005 - 0.007$.
Maxixe beryl, rich in cesium: $o = 1.584$, $e = 1.592$, Birefringence 0.008.
Emerald: see table.

Dispersion: 0.014 (low).

Pleochroism: Distinct in strongly colored varieties: Aquamarine: blue/colorless (sometimes greenish).

Characteristics of Emeralds—Worldwide Localities.

Locality	Occurrence	o	e	Density	Birefringence	Comments
Austria (Habachthal)	biotite schist	1.591	1.584	2.74	0.007	
Colombia						
Chivor Mine	cracks in dark schist	1.577	1.571	2.69	0.006	blue-green
Muzo Mine	calcite veins in dark shale	1.584	1.578	2.71	0.006	
Borur Mine		1.576	1.569	2.70	0.007	fluorescent
Gachala Mine		1.576	1.570	2.70	0.006	
new deposit (1976)		1.588	1.581	2.77	0.007	
Brazil						
Carnaiba, Bahia	in mica schist	1.588	1.582	—	0.006	
Bahia	pale yellow-green	1.572	1.566	2.72	0.006	
U.S.S.R. (Urals)	biotite-chlorite schist	1.588	1.581	2.74	0.007	
Australia (Poona)	in schists	1.579	1.572	2.70	0.007	
S. Africa						
Cobra Mine, Transvaal	acid pegmatites and schists in contact with them	1.593	1.586	2.76	0.007	
Rhodesia (Sandawana)	granite pegmatites cutting schist	1.593	1.586	2.76	0.007	nonfluorescent
		1.589	1.583	2.74	0.007	
India	biotite schist	1.593	1.585	2.73	0.007	
W. Pakistan (Swat area)		1.595–1.600	1.588–1.593	2.75–2.78	0.007	
Tanzania (Lake Manyara, Arusha)	mica schists	1.585	1.580	2.73	0.005	
Zambia						
Miku	in schists	1.590	1.581	2.74	0.009	nonfluorescent
Mufulira		1.588	1.581	2.68	0.007	
Norway (Eidsvoll)	in granite	1.591	1.584	2.68	0.007	
North Carolina (Hiddenite)	in albite matrix	1.588	1.580	2.73	0.008	fluoresces in LW
Ghana	poor quality material	1.589	1.582	2.70	0.007	
Colombia	trapiche emerald in albite	1.583	1.577	2.70	0.006	

Maxixe-type aquamarine = blue/blue.
Morganite: deep bluish-pink/pale pink.
Heliodor: brownish-yellow/lemon yellow.
Emerald: blue-green/yellowish-green.

Spectral: *Aquamarine* spectrum due to ferrous iron; broad band at 4270, weak and diffuse band at 4560. Also weak line may be seen at 5370 (absent if stone has been heated).
Maxixe beryl has narrow line at 6950, strong line at 6540, and weak lines at 6280, 6150, 5500, 5810.
Emerald spectrum very diagnostic: there are fine lines in the red, weak ones in the blue and a broad absorption in the violet; *e* and *o* have *different characteristics:*
> *o:* 6830/6800 doublet plus 6370 line; broad band 6250−5800; narrow lines 4775 and 4725.
> *e:* 6830/6800 doublet, very strong; no 6370 line, but see diffuse 6620 and 6460 lines; broad absorption band is weaker, no lines visible in the blue at all.

Luminescence: Emerald sometimes green in SW; very seldom weak red, orange in LW. If red fluorescence is seen the color is visible in the Chelsea filter. Fluorescence is quenched by Fe, as in the S. African and Indian emeralds. Morganite may fluoresce weak lilac.

Occurrence: Beryl occurs in granitic rocks, especially granite pegmatites; also in schists (emerald), metamorphic limestones (emerald) and hydrothermal veins. Occurrences are worldwide.
Goshenite:
> *California; Maine; South Dakota; Utah; Colorado; North Carolina; Connecticut; Idaho; New Hampshire. Canada; Mexico; Brazil; U.S.S.R.*

Morganite:
> *California:* San Diego Co., in several localities—fine crystals and gem material.
> *Thomas Range, Utah:* deep rose-red bixbite variety.
> *Madagascar:* in pegmatites and as alluvial material.
> *Minas Gerais, Brazil:* fine crystals and gem material.

Heliodor:
> *Madagascar:* gemmy crystals.
> *Brazil:* greenish yellow to fine deep orange colored material, much of it gemmy.
> *S.W. Africa:* in pegmatites.
> *Connecticut:* small but fine colored crystals, some gemmy.

Aquamarine:
> *Maine; North Carolina; Mt. Antero, Colorado; Connecticut:* some gem.
> *San Diego Co., California:* not much gem material.
> *Rhodesia.*
> *Minas Gerais, Brazil,* also *Rio Grande do Norte, Ceara,* other localities: Brazil is the world's major source of fine aquamarine gems.
> *Mursinsk, U.S.S.R.:* also other localities.
> *Madagascar:* fine blue gem material, more than 50 specific localities.

Burma and *Ceylon:* aquamarine has been found, not common there.
Rossing, S.W. Africa: in pegmatites.
India: at *Madras* and *Kashmir,* medium blue color.

Emerald:
> *Hiddenite, North Carolina.*
> *Habachthal, Austria; Brazil; U.S.S.R.; Sandawana, Rhodesia; Poona, Australia; Cobra Mine, Transvaal, S. Africa; Arusha, Tanzania; Lake Manyara, Tanzania; Ghana.*
> *Colombia:* at Chivor, Muzo, Gachala, and Borur Mines.
> *Swat* area, *W. Pakistan.*
> *Zambia:* at Miku and Mifulira.
> *Eidsvoll, Norway:* in granite.

Stone Sizes: Beryl crystals weighing many tons have been found in pegmatites, but these are never of gem quality. Aquamarine and green beryls, however, may be completely transparent and still be very large. A crystal weighing 243 pounds was found in Brazil in 1910 that was completely transparent; another in 1956 weighed about 135 pounds. Some very large gems have been cut from this type of material. Morganites are usually smaller, up to about 6 inches in diameter, and the largest emeralds known are less than 10 pounds. Bixbite occurs in crystals up to about 2 inches in length, and these are seldom transparent, even in small areas. The very few stones known are less than 3 carats.

Goshenite:
SI: 61.9 (colorless, Brazil).

Morganite:
SI: 287 (pink, Brazil) and 235 (pink, Brazil); 178 (pink, California); 113 (peach, California); 56 (pale pink, Madagascar).
Leningrad Museum: 598.7 (Rose-pink, step cut, Madagascar).
Natural Hist. Museum, Paris: 250 (pink, Madagascar).
ROM: 118.6 (pink, catseye).
BM: rose-red crystal from California weighing 9 pounds.
AMNH: 58.8 (heart-shape, Madagascar).
PC: three very large cut gems with carved tables, total weight ca 1500 carats, tables carved in religious motifs.

Heliodor:
BM: 82.25 (yellow).
ROM: 78.8 (yellow, step cut, Brazil).
SI: 133.5 (yellow, Madagascar); 43.5 (golden catseye, Madagascar); 17.5 (yellow, U.S.S.R.).

Aquamarine:
BM: 67.35 (blue) and 60.90 (greenish); 879 (sea-green, oval). A crystal was found in Marambaia, Teofilo Otoni, Brazil, blue-green, an irregular prism 19 inches long and 16 inches across and weighed 110.2 kg. It was transparent end to end.
AMNH: 272, 215, and 160; also 355 (Ceylon), 144.5 (Brazil).

Hyde Park Museum, New York: 1847 carats.

SI: 1000 (blue-green, fine color, Brazil); 911 (blue, Brazil); 263.5 (blue, U.S.S.R.); 71.2 (pale blue, Ceylon); 66.3 (pale blue-green, Maine); 20.7 (pale blue, Madagascar); 15.3 (blue-green, Idaho); 14.3 (blue, Connecticut).

Other Colors:

SI: 2054 (green-gold, Brazil); 1363 (green, Brazil); 133.5 (golden yellow Madagascar); 98.4 (pale green, Brazil); 40.4 (pale green, Connecticut); 23 (green, Maine); 19.8 (brown, star, Brazil).

Emerald:

The largest emerald crystal extant weighs 16,020 carats, and is from the Muzo Mine in Colombia. Many museums around the world display fine and large emeralds, both crystals and faceted gems, as well as some carvings and tumble-polished stones.

SI: 117 (green, Colombia); 10.6 (North Carolina); 4.6 (green catseye, Colombia).

Moscow: 136 (nearly flawless, deep blue-green, step cut) (in the Diamond Fund).

Kunsthistorisches Museum, Vienna: 2681 carat vase, carved.

Topkapi Museum, Istanbul: 6 cm hexagonal crystal; fine 8 cm crystal; 3 other large crystals.

Banque Markazi, Teheran: Many cabochons between 100 and 300 carats; one is 175 carats, another 225. There are also faceted gems of 100 and 110 carats; unmounted cabochons of 320, 303, 144.4, and two others over 250 carats.

BM: "Devonshire emerald", a crystal 51 mm. long, weighs 1384 carats, fine color.

AMNH: Crystal 1200 carats, fine color, the *Patricia emerald.*

PC: Atahuallpa emerald, 45 carats, set in *Crown of the Andes,* a magnificent gold headpiece with 453 emeralds totaling 1521 carats.

Comments: The beryls are among the most popular, and also the most expensive, of all gems. A wide range of color is represented, from colorless to black. Beryls can be large and flawless, but these are best displayed in museums rather than worn. Emerald is acknowledged as one of the most desirable gemstones, and aquamarine has recently sustained an unprecedented rise in price. Goshenite has never achieved great popularity and colorless beryls are easy to obtain at modest cost. The same general comment applies to yellow beryls, although darker-colored gems over 10–15 carats are in greater demand. Green beryls and olive-colored stones are not well known to the gem-buying public and therefore are in slight demand. Aquamarine of large size (15–25 carats) and very deep blue color has become extremely scarce and very expensive. Large gems continue to be available but at ever higher prices. A major problem in aquamarine is the so-called Maxixe-type beryl, which can be irradiated to improve the color. The deeper blue is not stable, however, and such gems may rapidly fade in sunlight. The dichroscope reveals the Maxixe beryl, both windows remaining blue whereas in normal aquamarine one window would be colorless or pale yellowish.

Some controversy exists as to the definition of emerald. The type of definition involving a shade of green or depth of color is totally inadequate, because it is completely subjective. A rigorous, adequate and objective definition involves simply the presence or absence of chromium and the corresponding presence of the chromium absorption spectrum, plus (usually) a red color in the Chelsea filter. The deep green beryls colored by vanadium are therefore not emeralds, despite potentially high prices.

Bixbite is a very rare, raspberry-red beryl from Utah, seldom seen as a cut gem and then only in very small size (1–2 carats). Indices are $o = 1.576$, $e = 1.570$.

Catseye and star beryls are strange curiosities. Catseye aquamarine and emerald are known, sometimes rather large. Oriented ilmenite inclusions in pale green aquamarine from Gouvernador Valadares, Brazil create a brown body color and cause a sheen or Schiller effect that, when included in a cabochon, creates a star. Black star beryls have no fluorescence or distinctive absorption spectrum, and are also known from Alta Ligonha, Mozambique. They strongly resemble black star sapphire, and are often confused with the latter.

Most aquamarine is heated at 400–450°C to reduce any ferric iron present and eliminate the accompanying yellowish color. This has the effect of making blue-green material pure blue, which is considered a more desirable color on the marketplace. This heating is done just after cutting, in Brazil, and does not affect the value of the cut stone, since virtually all aquamarine is heated in this manner.

Emeralds from Muzo and Chivor can be distinguished in a general way, because Muzo material is yellowish green, whereas that from Chivor is blue-green. It sometimes takes a trained eye to see the distinction in color, however. The inclusions in emerald may weaken the material, and hence cut gems are fragile and brittle and may be easily chipped. Care should always be taken in wearing an emerald, especially a ringstone.

Names: *Beryl* is of Greek origin but uncertain derivation. *Aquamarine* comes from Latin for *sea water* in allusion to the color. *Morganite* is named after J.P. Morgan, the investment banker and financier. *Goshenite* is named after Goshen, Massachusetts. *Heliodor* is from the Greek *helios* (*sun*), in allusion to the color. *Emerald* is from the Greek *smaragdos* (green), through the Latin "smaragdus" to Middle English "esmeralde." *Bixbite* is named after a Mr. Bixby.

BERYLLONITE

Formula: $NaBePO_4$.

Crystallography: Monoclinic. Crystals tabular or

prismatic, usually etched. Twinning common. May be pseudo-orthorhombic.

Colors: Colorless, white, pale yellow.

Luster: Vitreous; pearly on cleavage.

Hardness: 5.5–6.

Density: 2.84 (pure); usually 2.80–2.85.

Cleavage: Perfect 1 direction, good 1 direction. Fracture conchoidal. Brittle.

Optics: $\alpha = 1.552$; $\beta = 1.558$; $\gamma = 1.561$. Biaxial (−), $2V = 68°$

Birefringence: 0.009.

Dispersion: 0.010.

Pleochroism: None.

Spectral: Not diagnostic.

Luminescence: None.

Inclusions: Hollow canals and fluid cavities arranged parallel to crystal axis. Material from Stoneham, Maine has tubes, gas bubbles, and acicular crystals.

Occurrence: Granite pegmatites.
Newry, Maine: opaque white crystals, not really possible to cut.
Stoneham, Maine: only cuttable crystals ever found; also crystalline masses up to 1–2 inches, but only small clean areas within such masses could be cut.

Stone Sizes: All gems less than 5 carats. The mineral itself is very rare, and gems are only known from Maine localities. Stones up to 10 carats have been cut, but they are not clean.
SI: 2.5, 3.3, 3.9, 5.10 (all Maine).
DG: 5.70 (colorless, Maine).

Comments: Beryllonite is really not suited for wear, and since it is available only as small colorless stones there is not much incentive to make jewelry out of it. However, beryllonite is one of the truly rare collector gems and should be greatly prized as a cut stone. The cleavage makes gems hard to cut.

Name: In allusion to the composition.

BISMUTOTANTALITE   See also: Tantalite, Stibio-tantalite.

Formula: $(Bi, Sb) (Ta, Nb)O_4$.

Crystallography: Orthorhombic. Crystals sometimes large; massive; stream pebbles.

Colors: Light brown to black.

Luster: Adamantine to submetallic.

Streak: Yellow-brown to black.

Hardness: 5.

Density: 8.84 (Brazil).

Cleavage: Perfect 1 direction. Fracture subconchoidal. Brittle.

Optics: $\alpha = 2.388$; $\beta = 2.403$; $\gamma = 2.428$. Biaxial (+), $2V = 80°$

Birefringence: 0.040.

Dispersion: No data.

Pleochroism: No data.

Spectral: Not diagnostic.

Luminescence: None.

Occurrence: Pegmatites.
Gamba Hill, Uganda; Acari, Brazil.

Stone Sizes: Cut gems always small, less than 5 carats.

Comments: Extremely rare as a cut gem, even in very complete collections. Many of the minerals in the tantalite group have been faceted; bismutotantalite is perhaps the rarest of them all. The color is attractive, but low hardness and good cleavage make use in jewelry unadvisable.

Name: On account of the composition.

BIXBITE   See: Beryl.

BLENDE   See: Sphalerite.

BLOODSTONE   See: Quartz.

BOEHMITE   See: Diaspore.

BOLEITE

Formula: $Pb_9Ag_3Cu_8Cl_{21}(OH)_{16} \cdot H_2O$.

Crystallography: Tetragonal. Pseudocubic. Crystals usually cube shaped, sometimes modified by other faces, and in parallel growths.

Colors: Indigo blue to Prussian blue, blackish blue.

Streak: Blue with a greenish tinge.

Luster: Vitreous, pearly on cleavage.

Hardness: 3–3.5.

Density: 5.05.

Cleavage: Perfect 1 direction, good 1 direction.

Optics: $o = 2.05$; $e = 2.03$. Uniaxial (−).

Birefringence: 0.020.

Pleochroism: None.

Spectral: Not diagnostic.

Luminescence: None.

Occurrence: Secondary mineral in Cu and Pb deposits.
Chile; Broken Hill, N.S. W., Australia.
Boleo, Baja California: magnificent single crystals and groups on matrix, with single crystals up to nearly $\frac{1}{2}$ inch.

Stone Sizes: Crystals up to 2 cm on an edge have been found. Crystals, however, are usually nearly opaque, and facetable material is exceedingly rare. Stones up to about

1 carat have been cut, and even these are not entirely clean.

Comments: Cut boleite is strictly for collectors, since it is soft and very rare. Faceted gems of any transparency should be considered among the rarest of all gemstones. The color is so attractive that any available stones would be quickly snapped up.

Name: Boleo, Santa Rosalia, Baja California.

BORACITE

Formula: $Mg_3B_7O_{13}Cl$.

Crystallography: Orthorhombic. Pseudotetragonal. Crystals small and equant.

Colors: Colorless, white, gray, yellow, pale to dark green, bluish-green.

Luster: Vitreous.

Hardness: 7−7.5.

Density: 2.95.

Cleavage: None. Fracture conchoidal to uneven.

Optics: $\alpha = 1.658-1.662$; $\beta = 1.662-1.667$; $\gamma = 1.668-1.673$.
Biaxial (+), $2V = 82°$.

Birefringence: 0.011.

Dispersion: 0.024.

Pleochroism: None.

Spectral: Not diagnostic.

Luminescence: Weak greenish (SW).

Occurrence: Sedimentary deposits formed in evaporite sequences (seawater).
Choctaw Salt Dome, Louisiana; Otis, California.
Aislaby, England; Luneville, France;
Stassfurt and Hanover districts, Germany: source of the only cuttable crystals. Crystals usually small, pale colored.

Stone Sizes: Boracite crystals are very small and yield stones up to 1−2 carats. Gems over 2 carats would be considered an extreme rarity.

Comments: Boracite is not a common mineral; its occurrence is restricted to salt deposits and similar environments, resulting from the evaporation of sea water in enclosed basins. However, the mineral has no cleavage and a high hardness, so it is a shame it is not larger or more abundant. The colors of cut gems are usually delicate shades of light blue and green, and the dispersion is moderate. Cut boracite is one of the rarer of collector gems.

Name: In allusion to the borax in the composition.

BORNITE

Formula: Cu_5FeS_4.

Crystallography: Tetragonal. Crystals rare, twinned; usually massive, compact.

Colors: Copper red to bronze. Tarnishes to an iridescent purple color.

Streak: Light grayish black.

Luster: Metallic; opaque.

Hardness: 3.

Density: 5.08.

Cleavage: Traces. Fracture uneven to conchoidal. Brittle.

Spectral: No data.

Occurrence: Low temperature copper deposits.
Bristol, Connecticut; Virginia; North Carolina; Montana; Arizona; Colorado; California.
Canada; Chile; Peru; England; Italy; Germany; S. Africa; Madagascar.

Stone Sizes: Cabochons could be very large, several inches long, because the massive material from ore veins is available in large pieces.

Comments: Bornite is suitable only for cabochons. The bronzy color rapidly tarnishes in air to a magnificent iridescent color display, mostly purple, but also with blue and green tones. Bornite is too soft and brittle for anything but a collector curiosity, although cabochons are quire attractive when they tarnish. The material is not rare, so cabochons have no great value beyond the effort of cutting.

Name: After Ignatius von Born, 18th Century mineralogist.

BOWENITE See: Serpentine.

BRAZILIANITE

Formula: $NaAl_3(PO_4)_2(OH)_4$.

Crystallography: Monoclinic. Crystals equant, prismatic, spear-shaped; also striated.

Colors: Colorless, pale yellow, yellowish-green, greenish.

Luster: Vitreous.

Hardness: 5.5.

Density: 2.980−2.995.

Cleavage: Good 1 direction. Fracture conchoidal. Brittle.

Optics: $\alpha = 1.602$; $\beta = 1.609$; $\gamma = 1.621-1.623$.
Biaxial (+), $2V = 71°$.

Birefringence: 0.019−0.021.

Dispersion: 0.014.

Pleochroism: Weak—merely a change in shade of color.

Spectral: Not diagnostic.

Luminescence: None.

Occurrence: Hydrothermal mineral in pegmatitic cavities.

Palermo Mine, Grafton, New Hampshire.

Conselheira Pena, Minas Gerais, Brazil: only source of gem material, in crystals up to large size.

Stone Sizes: Crystals from Brazil are up to 12 x 8 cm. Some large gems have been cut.

AMNH: 23 (emerald cut, Brazil), 19 (round, yellow).

SI: 41.9 and 17.0 (yellow, Brazil).

PC: 24 (yellow, Brazil).

Most gems are 1–10 carats, or even smaller. Cut stones over 5 carats are scarce today.

Comments: Brazilianite was discovered in 1944. Gems are suitable only for collections, but the color is lovely. Faceted stones are often flawed in large sizes, so a clean gem over 15 carats is a great rarity. Many crystals that are in museums would yield very large gems but these are retained as crystal specimens and it is unlikely that they will ever be cut.

Name: After occurrence in Brazil.

BREITHAUPTITE

Formula: NiSb.

Crystallography: Hexagonal. Crystals are rare, usually massive, compact.

Colors: Light copper-red, violetish.

Streak: Reddish brown.

Luster: Metallic; opaque.

Hardness: 5.5.

Density: 7.59–8.23.

Cleavage: None. Fracture subconchoidal to uneven. Brittle.

Pleochroism: Strong in reflected light.

Luminescence: None.

Occurrence: In massive Ni sulfide orebodies.

Cobalt district, Ontario, Canada; Sarrabus, Sardinia; Adreasburg, Harz, Germany.

Stone Sizes: Massive material could cut gems to hundreds of carats, but only as cabochons.

Comments: Breithauptite is a curiosity cut for collectors, although it could be worn in jewelry, with care. The color is extremely lovely, a delicate reddish or violet with metallic luster that is both unique and attractive. Sometimes the reddish sulfide is veined with streaks of native silver or colorless gangue minerals providing interesting patterning to the color. The material is not very rare, but seldom encountered in cut form.

Name: After G.W.A. Breithaupt, a German mineralogist.

BRONZITE See: Enstatite.

BROOKITE

Formula: TiO_2.

Crystallography: Orthorhombic. Occurs only in crystals; tabular, prismatic, pyramidal; often striated.

Colors: Brown, yellowish brown, reddish brown, dark brown to black; rarely blue.

Luster: Adamantine to submetallic.

Hardness: 5.5–6.

Density: 4.14 normal; range 3.87–4.14.

Optics: $\alpha = 2.583$; $\beta = 2.584$; $\gamma = 2.700–2.740$. Biaxial (+).

Birefringence: 0.122–0.157.

Dispersion: Strong, ca 0.131.

Pleochroism: Strong: yellow-brown/reddish-brown/orange to golden brown. An hourglass-shaped zonal coloration is sometimes seen in bluish crystals.

Spectral: Not diagnostic.

Luminescence: None.

Occurrence: In gneisses, schists and sometimes in igneous rocks; contact deposits.

North Carolina; Somerville, Massachusetts; Maine; California.

Magnet Cove, Arkansas: contact metamorphic rocks.

Ellenville, New York: hydrothermal deposits.

Tirol, Switzerland: typical Alpine deposits.

Minas Gerais, Brazil; Dartmoor, England; France; U.S.S.R.

Stone Sizes: Always less than 1–2 carats; larger stones are opaque.

Comments: Brookite is a very dark-colored mineral, transparent only in small fragments. Cuttable crystals are exceedingly rare, and attractive-looking cut stones are among the rarest of all gems. Most stones are in private collections.

Name: After the English mineralogist and crystallographer, J.H. Brooke.

BUERGERITE See: Tourmaline.

BURNITE See: Azurite.

BUSTAMITE

Formula: $(Mn, Ca)_3Si_3O_9$.

Crystallography: Triclinic. Crystals tabular, usually rounded and rough; massive.

Colors: Pale flesh pink to brownish red.

Luster: Vitreous.

Hardness: 5.5–6.5.

Density: 3.32–3.43.

Cleavage: Perfect 1 direction, good 1 direction.

Optics: $\alpha = 1.662-1.692$; $\beta = 1.674-1.705$; $\gamma = 1.676-1.707$.
Biaxial ($-$), $2V = 30-44°$.

Birefringence: 0.014−0.015.

Pleochroism: Weak: rose red/orange/orange.

Spectral: Not diagnostic.

Luminescence: None.

Occurrence: Manganese orebodies, usually of metasomatic origin.
Cornwall, England; Långban, Sweden.
Franklin and *Sterling Hill, New Jersey:* in fine crystals. *Iwate and Yamagata Prefectures, Japan:* gemmy crystals. *Broken Hill, N.S.W., Australia:* this material has high Mn content, in crystals up to 2 x 10 cm; S.G. = 3.41, $2V = 39°$, $\alpha = 1.688$, $\beta = 1.699$, $\gamma = 1.703$, Birefringence 0.015.

Stone Sizes: Faceted gems are usually small, less than 5 carats, and mostly in the 1−2 carat range. Catseyes are also known, up to about 5 carats.

Comments: Bustamite is very similar in appearance and properties to rhodonite. The Japanese crystals are very rich in Mn. The color, when fresh, is paler than rhodonite. Bustamite may also be fibrous, and then yields fine catseye gems, but these are extremely rare. Faceted bustamites are very attractive, especially in the pinkish shades, but stones over 1−2 carats are very rare collector items. The cleavage makes cutting difficult and wear ill advised.

Name: After the discoverer of the mineral, M. Bustamente.

BYTOWNITE See: Feldspar.

C

CAIRNGORM See: Quartz.

CALAMINE See: Hemimorphite.

CALCITE *Dimorph of* ARAGONITE. Also: Cobaltocalcite = Sphaerocobaltite = $CoCO_3$; Onxy = Travertine = Flowstone (found in caves); Iceland spar; Alabaster; Marble.

Formula: $CaCO_3$.

Crystallography: Hexagonal (R). Crystals common in a huge array of forms; massive; stalactitic; chalky.

Colors: Colorless (Iceland spar), white, gray, yellow, shades of pink, green, blue, purplish red (Co).

Luster: Vitreous to pearly.

Hardness: 3.

Density: 2.71 (pure)−2.94.

Cleavage: Perfect rhombohedral (3 directions).

Optics: $e = 1.486-1.550$; $o = 1.658-1.740$. Uniaxial (−).

Birefringence: 0.172−0.190.

Dispersion: Strong.

Pleochroism: None.

Spectral: Any lines seen are due to specific elements as impurities.

Luminescence: Common and from many localities around the world.
SW: red, orange, lemon yellow, shades of green, shades of blue, pink, white.
LW: orange, dull pink, tan, yellow, blue, gray.

Occurrence: Occurs in all types of rocks as the most abundant carbonate mineral on earth. Found in veins, ore deposits and as a constituent of rock limestone and marble. Crystals often large (many inches) and transparent. *Onyx* is the material of most limestone caves, usually banded in shades of tan and brown. *Iceland spar* is colorless calcite, transparent, sometimes in large masses. The name *alabaster* refers to gypsum and is incorrect when applied to calcite. Gem material is commonly seen from the following localities: *Missouri* (colorless), *Baja California* (brown), *Montana, England, Mexico, Iceland* (colorless), and the *U.S.S.R.* (pale yellow).

Stone Sizes: Rough material can be very large (hundreds of carats). Colorless material is usually step-cut or emerald-cut, up to about 100 carats. Brown material from Baja is usually seen up to 50 carats, normal range 5−25 carats. One yellowish stone of Russian material weighs 474 carats and may be the world's largest cut calcite. Purplish-red material from Paramca, Spain (cobaltian) is not transparent, usually cut 1−5 carat size. Onxy is opaque and yields cabochons and carvings of any desired size.
SI: 75.8 and 45.8 (golden-brown, Baja).
DG: 7.5 (cobaltocalcite, Spain).

Comments: Calcite is common and abundant throughout the world. The material has little intrinsic value because of lack of scarcity. However, calcite is one of the most difficult of all minerals to cut, because of the perfect cleavage in 3 directions. The cost of a faceted stone is therefore mostly in the labor of cutting. Cleavage also makes large sizes of cut gems rare. Normally a faceted stone breaks during cutting, and the finished gem is much smaller than the originally intended size. A cut calcite over 50 carats is therefore a great rarity. Faceted stones might turn up cut from material from many localities. But the lack of scarcity value is not encouraging to potential calcite cutters.

Onyx is usually cut into slabs, made into vases, lamps, ashtrays, bookends and many other decorative objects. It is usually banded in shades of brown, green, and buff. Marble is a metamorphic rock often used in construction and in making decorative carved objects. Coloration in the form of banding and streaks is due to impurities.

Name: *Calcite* is derived from the Latin *calx*, meaning *lime*.

CALIFORNITE See: Garnet.

CANASITE

Formula: $(Na, K)_5(Ca, Mn, Mg)_4(Si_2O_5)_5(OH, F)_3$.

Crystallography: Monoclinic. Occurs in tiny grains, usually twinned.

Colors: Greenish yellow.

Luster: Vitreous.

Hardness: No data.

Density: 2.707.

Cleavage: Very perfect 1 direction, perfect 1 direction. Brittle; grinds to feltlike powder.

Optics: $\alpha = 1.534$; $\beta = 1.538$; $\gamma = 1.543$. Biaxial (−), $2V$, ca 53°.

Birefringence: 0.009.

Spectral: Not diagnostic.

Occurrence: Occurs in pegmatite in the *Khibina Tundra, U.S.S.R.*

Stone Sizes: Massive blocks up to several inches have been found. Material is cut as cabochons and decorative objects.

Comments: The material usually seen on the market as "canasite" is purplish in color. It is frequently confused with another purplish material, a member of the serpentine family known as *stichtite*. However, stichtite occurs in elongated fibers that have a kind of lustrous sheen, almost asbestiform, whereas the canasite material is granular. Recent research seems to indicate that, in fact, the material being called canasite has no canasite in it, but is a new, distinct species.

CANCRINITE

Formula: $(Na, K, Ca)_{6-8}(Al, Si)_{12}O_{24}(CO_3, SO_4, Cl)_{1-2} \cdot nH_2O$.
Note: If $SO_4 > CO_3$ the species is termed *Vishnevite*.

Crystallography: Hexagonal. Crystals prismatic, but rare; usually massive.

Colors: Colorless, white, yellow, orange, pink to reddish, pale blue, bluish gray.

Luster: Vitreous; pearly on cleavage; greasy.

Hardness: 5-6.

Density: 2.42-2.51; Vishnevite: 2.3.

Cleavage: Perfect 1 direction. Fracture uneven. Brittle.

Optics:
  $o = 1.507-1.528$; $e = 1.495-1.503$. (cancrinite).
  $o = 1.490-1.507$; $e = 1.488-1.495$ (vishnevite).
Uniaxial(−); chlorine-rich variety (microsommite) is optically (+).

Birefringence: 0.022 (cancrinite); 0.002-0.012 (vishnevite).

Dispersion: Weak.

Spectral: Not diagnostic.

Luminescence: None in UV.

Occurrence: Primarily in alkali-rich rocks; also as an alteration product of nepheline.
Iron Hill, Colorado; Kennebec Co., Maine.
Norway; Romania; Finland; U.S.S.R.; Korea; China; Zaire; India; Uganda; Kenya.
Bancroft Dist., Ontario, Canada: fine gemmy material.

Stone Sizes: Masses occur up to several pounds, but cancrinite usually in veins a few inches across. Usually cut as cabochons and beads. The Canadian material is orangy yellow in color, with a greasy luster. Faceted stones are exceedingly rare, and always less than 1-2 carats.

Comments: Cancrinite is one of the most attractive of all opaque or translucent gem materials. It is a bit too soft for average wear, but its distinctive color is worthy of jewelry. Cancrinite may be tricky to cut, because it often contains numerous hard inclusions. Faceted gems even as large as 1 carat are considered great rarities.

Name: After Count Cancrin, Finance Minister of Russia.

CARNELIAN   See: Quartz.

CASSITERITE

Formula: $SnO_2 + Fe, Ta, Nb$.

Crystallography: Tetragonal. Crystals prismatic, pyramidal; also botryoidal, reniform with a radial fibrous structure. Twinning common.

Colors: Brown, brownish black, black, colorless, gray, yellowish, greenish, red.

Streak: White, grayish, brown.

Luster: Adamantine to vitreous; greasy on fracture surfaces.

Hardness: 6-7.

Density: 6.7-7.1; pure material 6.99.

Cleavage: Imperfect. Fracture subconchoidal to uneven. Brittle.

Optics: $o = 2.006$; $e = 2.097-2.101$.
Uniaxial (+); anomalously biaxial, $2V = 0-38°$, usually in zoned crystals.

Birefringence: 0.098.

Dispersion: 0.071 (nearly twice that of diamond).

Pleochroism: Weak to strong; greenish yellow or yellow brown/ red-brown. Most visible in strongly colored crystals.

Spectral: Not diagnostic.

Luminescence: None.

Occurrence: Principal ore of tin; occurs in medium to high temperature veins; metasomatic deposits; granite pegmatites; rhyolites; alluvial deposits.
Alaska; Washington; California; Nevada; South Dakota; South Carolina; Virginia.
Canada; Mexico; Cornwall, England; Portugal; Japan; China; Arandis, S.W. Africa; New South Wales, Australia.
Araca Mine, Bolivia: source of most of the gem material known: yellow, gray, colorless and light yellowish-brown to reddish-brown.
Spain: also provides gem material, in yellowish to red cuttable pieces.
Erongo tinfields, S.W.Africa: gem material occurs.

Stone Sizes: Cassiterite is quite rare in gems that are clean over 1 carat. Masses occur up to several pounds in weight, but these are opaque and are sometimes cut into cabochons. Pale brown to dark brown gems up to 15 carats have been cut; slightly flawed stones up to 25 carats are known, mostly Bolivian material.
PC: 9.6 (brownish, Tasmania); 11.83 (brown, England).

SI: 10 (yellow-brown, Bolivia).

DG: 14.85, 9.51 (brownish, Bolivia).

Comments: Cassiterite has tremendous dispersive fire, much more than diamond, and it is visible in pale colored gems that are properly cut. This lighter-colored material is, however, very rare except in small fragments. Cassiterite is a fine gemstone—it is rather hard, and there is no cleavage problem. It is unfortunate that cuttable rough is so scarce. Cassiterites under 5 carats are not among the rarest of rare stones, but large clean gems definitely are.

Name: The Greek word for tin is *kassiteros.*

CELESTITE

Formula: $SrSO_4$.

Crystallography: Orthorhombic. Crystals common, usually tabular; also nodules, earthy, massive.

Colors: Colorless, white, gray, blue, green, yellow, orange, and red shades.

Luster: Vitreous; pearly on cleavage.

Hardness: 3–3.5.

Density: 3.97–4.00.

Cleavage: Perfect 1 direction, good 1 direction. Fracture uneven. Brittle.

Optics: $\alpha = 1.622-1.625$; $\beta = 1.624$; $\gamma = 1.631-1.635$. Madagascar gems: $\alpha = 1.619$; $\gamma = 1.631$.
Biaxial (+), $2V = 50°$.

Birefringence: 0.009–0.012.

Dispersion: 0.014.

Pleochroism: Weak, in shades of indigo blue, bluish-green, and violet.

Spectral: Not diagnostic.

Luminescence: Blue in SW. Blue or dull yellow in LW. May phosphoresce blue-white.

Occurrence: Celestite occurs in sedimentary rocks, especially limestones; it is also found in hydrothermal vein deposits, sometimes in igneous rocks.
Clay Center, Ohio; Colorado; Chittenango Falls, New York; many localities in California.
San Luis Potosi, Mexico; Bristol, England; Girgenti, Sicily; Madagascar; Germany; France; Austria; Italy; Switzerland; U.S.S.R.; Egypt; Tunisia.
Lampasas, Texas: gemmy material (blue).
Put-in-Bay, Strontian Islands, Lake Erie: gemmy material.
Tsumeb, S.W. Africa: gem material.
Canada: orange crystals.

Stone Sizes: Celestite gems are usually under 3 carats and are generally colorless or pale blue, often step cut. However, some gems are known in the 30 carat range, and there is no reason why large transparent crystals

cannot be found and cut.

DG: 20.1 (blue, Madagascar).

Comments: Celestite is seldom seen in collections; perhaps it is because faceted gems have little fire, and are usually colorless or pale blue, rarely orange. Gems are soft and fragile, hard to cut, and cannot be worn with safety. Celestite is strictly for collectors, but large clean faceted gems are indeed rare, while transparent crystals per se are not.

Name: Latin *coelestis* means *celestial,* in allusion to the delicate and lovely pale blue color often displayed by this mineral.

CERULEITE

Formula: $Cu_2Al_7(AsO_4)_4(OH)_{13}$.

Crystallography: Usually massive, compact, earthy.

Colors: Turquoise-blue shades, cerulean blue.

Luster: Earthy, dull.

Hardness: 6.5 (conflicting data, may be softer).

Density: 2.7–2.8.

Optics: Mean index ca 1.60. Very fine grained.

Occurrence: Sedimentary material formed in the vicinity of copper deposits, like turquoise.
Cornwall, England.
Huanaco, Chile: original material.
Southern Bolivia: cabbing material of fine color.

Stone Sizes: Nodules are usually small, less than 1 inch, up to several inches in size. The material yields cabochons only.

Comments: Ceruleite is a little known gem material of truly exquisite color. It takes a very high polish, easily and quickly, and the color of polished gems is far deeper than that of the rough nodules. It is extremely rare in fine, solid cuttable pieces, and is consequently rather expensive. Few cut stones are to be seen in museum collections, and the total amount of fine Bolivian material may not exceed several hundred pounds.

Name: In allusion to its color; the Latin *caerulea* means *sky blue.*

CERUSSITE

Formula: $PbCO_3$.

Crystallography: Orthorhombic. Crystals common, elongated, tabular, often twinned and striated; acicular, massive.

Colors: Colorless, white, gray, "smoky," greenish (Cu inclusions), yellowish. Dark gray or black material is due to inclusions.

Luster: Adamantine to submetallic; vitreous; resinous; pearly.

Hardness: 3–3.5.

Density: 6.55

Cleavage: Distinct 1 direction. Fracture conchoidal. Extremely brittle.

Optics: $\alpha = 1.804$; $\beta = 2.076$; $\gamma = 2.079$. Biaxial (−), $2V = 9°$.

Birefringence: 0.274.

Dispersion: 0.055 (greater than diamond).

Pleochroism: None.

Spectral: Not diagnostic.

Luminescence: Pinkish orange (Utah) or yellow shades in LW. Pale blue or shades of green in SW.

Occurrence: Secondary mineral in the oxidized zones of lead deposits. Many localities known:
Tiger, Arizona; Colorado; Idaho; South Dakota; Utah; New Mexico; Montana; Nevada; California.
Broken Hill Mine, Zambia; Dundas, Tasmania; Broken Hill, N.S.W., Australia; Monte Poni, Sardinia; Leadhills, Scotland.
Tsumeb, S.W. Africa: source of the largest and finest gem material; colorless, gray and yellowish, in masses up to several pounds (completely transparent).

Stone Sizes: Large masses of transparent rough are known from Tsumeb, that could cut stones of several thousand carats. The real problem is cohesion of large stones. As a result, the largest known gem is ca 126 carats (*DG*).
Catseyes are known from 2−6 carats; the material is from Tiger, Arizona, also Tsumeb.
SI: 4.7 (pale yellow, Tsumeb).

Comments: Cut cerussite is as beautiful as diamond, since it has higher dispersion, is free of any color, and has an adamantine luster. However, cerussite is extremely soft and one of the most brittle and heat sensitive of all minerals. Cutting a gem is a major chore, and cutting a very large one without breaking it is almost impossible. Consequently, faceted cerussite is one of the rarest of all gems. Abundant rough material is available among the thousands of crystals and crystal fragments recovered from Tsumeb, S.W.A. Few cutters, however, have the skill and knowledge required to successfully fashion a gem from this rough. The cost of a cut stone will therefore largely reflect the cutting cost. Time, patience and TLC (tender loving care) are essential.

Name: From the Latin *cerussa*, the name of an artificial lead carbonate.

CEYLONITE See: Spinel.

CHABAZITE

Formula: $CaAl_2Si_4O_{12}\cdot6H_2O$.

Crystallography: Hexagonal. Crystals rhomb-shaped, tabular; frequently twinned.

Colors: Colorless, white, yellowish, pinkish, reddish white, salmon color, greenish.

Luster: Vitreous.

Hardness: 4−5.

Density: 2.05−2.16.

Cleavage: Distinct, 1 direction. Fracture uneven. Brittle.

Optics: Variable: 1.470−1.494. Uniaxial (+) or (−).

Spectral: Not diagnostic.

Luminescence: None.

Occurrence: Cavities in basalt and other basic igneous rocks; also hot spring deposits.
Nevada; California; Oregon; Colorado; New Jersey; Hawaii.
Bay of Fundy dist., Nova Scotia, Canada; Greenland; Scotland; Ireland; Italy; Germany; Hungary; U.S.S.R.; India; Australia; Czechoslovakia.

Stone Sizes: Cut chabazites are always very small, usually less than 1−2 carats. Crystals are never entirely transparent, and often only one corner of a pinkish or colorless crystal can be cut. Very few chabazites have been cut at all, and they are seldom seen in museum collections.

Comments: Chabazite is too soft for wear. The colors are pale, but attractive. Unfortunately, clean material is extremely scarce. Chabazite is not a terribly difficult material to facet, but finding suitable material is not easy. This is one of the rare gems seldom discussed or heard about. There may only be a handful of cut gems in existence.

Name: From the Greek *chabazios*, an ancient name applied to certain minerals.

CHALCEDONY See: Quartz.

CHALCOSIDERITE See: Turquoise.

CHAMBERSITE

Formula: $Mn_3B_7O_{13}Cl$.

Crystallography: Orthorhombic. Crystals shaped like tetrahedra, up to 1 cm on edge.

Colors: Colorless, brownish, lilac, purple.

Luster: Vitreous.

Hardness: 7.

Density: 3.49.

Cleavage: None.

Optics: $\alpha = 1.732$; $\beta = 1.737$; $\gamma = 1.744$. Biaxial (+), $2V$ ca 83°.

Birefringence: 0.012.

Spectral: Not diagnostic.

Luminescence: None.

Occurrence: Occurs in brines in storage well at *Barber's Hill salt dome, Chambers Co., Texas.*

Stone Sizes: Cut stones are not really transparent, and are usually under 2 carats. Gems are generally triangular in shape, and are cut by beveling and polishing off part of the tetrahedron of a crystal, to save weight. Cut stones are, in a sense, truncated crystals with their surfaces polished.

Comments: Chambersite is an exceedingly rare mineral, as might be gathered from the locality information. Crystals are generally tiny, and are recovered by skin diving to a depth of as much as 70 feet in brine. Cut stones are merely curiosities, and very few of them exist.

Name: From the Texas locality.

CHERT See: Quartz.

CHIASTOLITE See: Andalusite.

CHILDRENITE *Series to* EOSPHORITE *if Mn exceeds Fe.*

Formula: $(Fe, Mn)AlPO_4(OH)_2 \cdot H_2O$.

Crystallography: Orthorhombic. Crystals equant, pyramidal, platy, often doubly terminated.

Colors: Brown to yellowish brown, golden yellow.

Luster: Vitreous to resinous.

Hardness: 5.

Density: 3.2 (pure Fe end member).

Cleavage: Poor. Fracture uneven to subconchoidal.

Optics: $\alpha = 1.63 - 1.645$; $\beta = 1.65 - 1.68$; $\gamma = 1.66 - 1.685$.
Biaxial $(-)$, $2V = 40 - 45°$.

Birefringence: 0.030 - 0.040.

Pleochroism: Distinct: yellow/pink/colorless to pale pink.

Luminescence: None.

Spectral: May show lines of iron spectrum.

Occurrence: In granite pegmatites and hydrothermal vein deposits.
Cornwall, England; Greifenstein, Germany; Custer, S. Dakota.
Minas Gerais, Brazil: gemmy crystals. These are found to be Fe:Mn = 1:1, and could be termed "childro-eosphorite".

Stone Sizes: Childrenite occurs in brown, opaque crystals up to several inches long. Transparent material is much smaller, and facetable crystals yield stones up to about 3-4 carats. In general, cuttable material in this series is closer to the eosphorite end.
DG: 3.58 (Brazil).

Comments: Cut childrenite is a great rarity, and all

gems are small. Cut eosphorite is more abundantly available, though both materials are very scarce.

Name: J.G. Children, English mineralogist.

CHIOLITE

Formula: $Na_5Al_3F_{14}$.

Crystallography: Tetragonal; Minute dipyramidal crystals, commonly in masses.

Colors: Colorless, white.

Luster: Vitreous.

Hardness: 3.5 - 4.

Density: 2.998.

Cleavage: Perfect, 1 direction.

Optics: $o = 1.349$; $e = 1.342$. Uniaxial $(-)$.

Birefringence: 0.007.

Pleochroism: None.

Spectral: Not diagnostic.

Luminescence: None.

Occurrence: *Ivigtut, Greenland:* associated with cryolite.
Miask, Urals, U.S.S.R.: in a cryolite pegmatite.

Stone Sizes: Always tiny, 1-2 carat range, if clean. Large clean fragments do not exist for cutting. The mineral itself is quite rare.

Comments: Chiolite has nothing much to offer in the way of a gem. It is very soft, has perfect cleavage, has no appealing colors, and is usually small and nondescript. However, it has joined the ranks of minerals that have been cut by facetors who must try their hand at everything clean enough to cut. There may be less than one or two dozen cut stones in existence. It exists solely as a curiosity in the gem world.

Name: From the Greek words for *snow* and *stone* because in its white appearance it is similar to cryolite, whose name means *ice-stone.*

CHLORASTROLITE See: Pumpellyite.

CHLOROMELANITE See: Jadeite.

CHONDRODITE *Member of the* Humite group, *which includes:* Norbergite, Humite, Clinohumite.

Members of this group are easily confused with each other. The compositions are related in a very distinctive way:

Norbergite: $Mg(OH, F)_2 \cdot Mg_2(SiO_4)$
Humite: $Mg(OH, F)_2 \cdot 3Mg_2(SiO_4)$
Chondrodite: $Mg(OH, F)_2 \cdot 2Mg_2(SiO_4)$
Clinohumite: $Mg(OH, F)_2 \cdot 4Mg_2(SiO_4)$

All are biaxial $(+)$, all are yellowish brown in color.

	Norbergite	Chondrodite	Humite	Clinohumite
Crystallography	orthorhombic	monoclinic	orthorhombic	monoclinic
Colors	yellowish-tan	yellow, brown, red	yellow, deep orange	yellow, brown, white
Hardness	6.5	6.5	6	6
Density	3.15−3.18	3.16−3.26	3.20−3.32	3.21−3.35
Optics				
α	1.563−1.567	1.592−1.615	1.607−1.643	1.629−1.638
β	1.567−1.579	1.602−1.627	1.639−1.675	1.662−1.643
γ	1.590−1.593	1.621−1.646	1.639−1.675	1.662−1.674
$2V$	44−50	71−85	65−84	73−76
Birefringence	0.026−0.027	0.028−0.034	0.029−0.031	0.028−0.041
Pleochroism				
α	pale yellow	very pale yellow/ brownish yellow	yellow	golden yellow/ deep reddish yellow
β	very pale yellow	colorless/ yellowish green	colorless/ pale yellow	pale yellow/ orange yellow
γ	colorless	colorless/ pale green	colorless/ pale yellow	pale yellow/ orange yellow

TiO_2 present in humite and clinohumite strongly affects their optical properties. All members of this group have poor cleavage and a vitreous luster.

The following data relate to chondrodite, since this member of the humite group is the one represented by gem material.

Luminescence: Usually inert in SW, sometimes golden yellow; dull orange to brownish orange in LW.

Occurrence: In contact zones in limestone or dolomite. Rarely in alkaline rocks of igneous origin. This paragenesis is true for all members of humite group.
Wilberforce, Ontario, Canada.
Tilly Foster Mine, Brewster, New York: fine crystals of chondrodite, reddish brown, some rather gemmy, associated with humite and clinohumite. This locality is the source of most gem chondrodite.
Kafveltorp, Orebro, Sweden: yellowish material.
Pargas, Finland: yellowish material.
Loolekop, E. Transvaal: in a carbonatite.
Norbergite from: *Franklin, New Jersey; Orange Co., New York; Norberg, Sweden.*
Clinohumite from: *California; Ala, Italy; Malaga, Spain; L. Baikal, U.S.S.R.*

Stone Sizes: Cut humite minerals are always small, in the 1−3 carat range, because crystals are usually quite dark and filled with inclusions and fractures. Larger cut gems would be extremely rare.
AMNH: several round gems, ca 1−2 carats.

Comments: Faceted chondrodite is a great rarity, which is a shame because the color is very rich and the material has no strong cleavage and manageable hardness. Cutting presents no great difficulty, but rough is virtually unobtainable. Only tiny portions of crystals can be utilized. A transparent chondrodite may be considered one of the scarcest of all the attractive collector gems.

Name: Greek *chondros*, a grain, in allusion to the mineral's granular nature.

CHROMITE Chromite group, *extensive solid solution series. Note:* Magnesiochromite = $MgCr_2O_4$; Hercynite = $FeAl_2O_4$.

Formula: $FeCr_2O_4$.

Crystallography: Isometric. Octahedral crystals up to 1 cm on edge; massive.

Colors: Black, reddish brown.

Streak: Brown.

Luster: Submetallic; opaque, translucent in thin splinters.

Hardness: 5.5.

Density: 4.5−4.8.

Cleavage: None. Fracture uneven. Brittle. Sometimes weakly magnetic.

Optics: R.I. = 2.08−2.16. Isotropic.

Spectral: Not diagnostic.

Luminescence: None.

Occurrence: In igneous rocks rich in olivine; in serpentines; in stream and beach sands. Sometimes in massive deposits of large size.
California; Oregon; Washington; Wyoming; Maryland; North Carolina; Pennsylvania.
Canada; Cuba; Norway; U.S.S.R.; France; Rhodesia; India.

Stone Sizes: Any size could be cut from massive material. The possibility exists for some deep reddish crystals to contain very tiny facetable areas, but thus far none have been discovered.

Comments: Chromite is shiny and black, and makes a curious-looking cabochon with no special attraction.

Occasionally a cabochon has a reddish color. The stones have no value because the material is extremely abundant, but are cut as curiosities only.

Name: In allusion to the composition.

CHRYSOBERYL Also called: Catseye, Alexandrite.

Formula: $BeAl_2O_4$ + Fe, Ti.

Crystallography: Orthorhombic. Crystals tabular or prismatic, 6-ling twins common; also massive and as waterworn pebbles.

Colors: Yellowish green, yellow, gray, brown, blue-green, deep green, red, violet. Rarely colorless. *Alexandrite* varies in color with incident light: green, blue-green, or pale green in daylight; mauve, violet to red, purplish in incandescent light. *Catseye* usually dark yellowish brown to pale yellow, honey yellow, greenish.

Luster: Vitreous.

Hardness: 8.5.

Density: 3.68–3.73; colorless 3.70; gems usually higher.

Cleavage: Distinct 1 direction, varies to poor. Fracture conchoidal. Brittle.

Optics: α = 1.744–1.759; β = 1.747–1.764; γ = 1.753–1.770.
Biaxial (+), $2V$ = 70°. Indices vary with Fe content.

Birefringence: 0.008–0.010.

Alexandrite from Various Localities—Properties

	Urals	Ceylon	Burma	Brazil	Rhodesia
Density	—	—	3.71	3.68	3.64–3.77
Optics					
α	1.749	1.745	1.746	1.747	
β	1.753	1.749	1.748	1.748	1.748
γ	1.759	1.755	1.755	1.756	(Mean index)
Birefrin-gence	0.009	0.010	0.009	0.009	—

Dispersion: 0.015.

Pleochroism: Distinct, shades of yellow and brown. Alexandrite: deep red/orange-yellow/green. *NOTE:* Burma gem (anomalously): purple/grass-green/blue-green.

Spectral: Yellowish and brown gems have strong band at 4440 due to Fe, especially Ceylon gems. Also may be bands visible at 5040 and 4860. Alexandrite has narrow doublet at *6805/6875*, with weak, narrow lines at 6650, 6550, 6490, and broad band at 6400–5550. Total absorption below 4700.

Luminescence: Alexandrite fluoresces weak red in SW and LW; pale green (Connecticut) to yellow-green in SW also noted.

Inclusions: In catseye, there are short needles and tubes parallel to the long axis of the crystal. Liquid-filled cavities with two-phase inclusions; stepped twin planes.

Occurrence: Occurs in pegmatites, gneiss, mica schist, dolomitic marbles; also is found as stream pebbles and detrital grains.
South Dakota; Colorado; Maine; New Hampshire; Connecticut; New York.
Finland; Zaire; Madagascar; Japan; Australia.
U.S.S.R.: alexandrite of fine quality near Sverdlovsk, in mica schist.
Brazil, especially *Bahia (Jacuda):* facetable material, also catseye and alexandrite.
Ceylon: all types, most especially catseye (world's finest) and alexandrite.
Burma: rarely colorless facetable chrysoberyl; some alexandrite.
Rhodesia: fine alexandrite, intense color change.

Stone Sizes: The largest of the fine Russian alexandrites is in the 30 carat range. Facetable chrysoberyl up to hundreds of carats is known, and catseyes of hundreds of carats have been found. Star chrysoberyls are known but very rare.

BM: 29.4 (Ceylon, yellow-green); catseye: *Hope Chrysoberyl*, 45 carats, oval, flawless.
PC: 185 (Brazil, not clean); catseye over 300 carats in U.S. collection.
ROM: 42.72 (Ceylon, chartreuse green).
AMNH: 74.4 (emerald cut, yellowish-green)—may be world's finest of this color.
SI: catseyes: 171 (Ceylon, gray-green); also 47.8 (Ceylon); 58.2 (Ceylon: *the Maharani*).
    faceted: 114.3 (Ceylon, yellow-green); 120.5 (Ceylon, green); 46.3 (green-yellow, Brazil); 31.7 (Ceylon, Brown); 6.7 (star, Brazil).
Crown Jewels of Iran: Catseye, 147.7 (chartreuse color, Ceylon); 25 (catseye, gray-green). *Note:* Catseye of 475 carats has been reported in the literature (Ceylon).
Alexandrites:
  SI: 65.7 (Ceylon); also 16.7 and 11 (Ceylon).
  BM: 43, 27.5 (Ceylon).
  Inst. of Mines, Leningrad (St.Petersburg): crystal cluster 6 x 3 cm (3 crystals)—Urals.
  Fersman Museum, Leningrad: Crystal group 25 x 15 cm, crystals up to 6 x 3 cm (Urals).
  PC: U.S. dealers have reported stones up to about 50 carats.

Comments: Transparent chrysoberyl makes a handsome faceted gem, and also one of the hardest and toughest for jewelry purposes. Cleavage is not distinct, and the hardness is just below that of sapphire and ruby. In general the bright yellow and yellow-green shades are the most desirable, but some browns are also handsome.

Properly cut gems are very brilliant, although they lack fire due to low dispersion.

Catseye gems of such minerals as apatite, tourmaline and diopside are well known, but when the term *catseye* is used alone it always refers to chrysoberyl. The eye in a chrysoberyl catseye often has a shimmering blue tone. The silk in such gems, which creates the chatoyancy, is so fine a microscope is needed to resolve the fibers. Consequently the eye is the sharpest of any catseye gemstone. The optimum color is a honey brown, and light striking the stone obliquely usually creates a shadow effect within the gem, such that the side away from the light is a rich brown, while the side facing the light is yellowish white, creating the so-called milk and honey look characteristic of the finest chrysoberyls. This quality in a large (over 20 carats) stone creates a very high-value situation.

Alexandrite is well known today as a scarce and costly gem. Stones over 5 carats are very rare, especially if the color change is good. The quality of the color change with illumination conditions is the primary basis of alexandrite quality and value. Optimum colors are intense blue-green to green (daylight) vs. purple-red (in incandescent light). Brazilian gems tend to have a pale set of colors, pale mauve to pale blue-green, but finer gems have been found recently in limited quantity. Ceylon alexandrite is often deep olive green in sunlight, while Russian stones are bluish green in daylight. Rhodesian gems are fine emerald green in color in sunlight, but are usually tiny (under a carat) if clean. The color change in Rhodesian gems is among the best known, and it is a shame that large clean stones are virtually unobtainable from the rough from this locality.

Names: *Catseye* is named from the resemblance of the eye in the stone to the narrow iris in the eye of a cat. Another name for this gem, *cymophane*, is from Greek words meaning *appearing like a wave* because of the opalescent appearance of some crystals. *Alexandrite* is named after Czar Alexander I of Russia, on whose birthday the gem was found. Chrysoberyl is derived from the Greek *chrysos*, meaning *golden*, in allusion to the usual yellowish color of this mineral.

CHRYSOCOLLA

Formula: $(Cu, Al)_2H_2Si_2O_5(OH)_4 \cdot nH_2O$.

Crystallography: Monoclinic. Crystals are microscopic, in aggregates; cryptocrystalline, opalline.

Colors: Blue, green and blue-green in various shades. Mixed with matrix of quartz and oxides of Cu, Fe and Mn, adding brown and black colors.

Luster: Vitreous (if silicified), waxy, dull.

Hardness: 2–4 (as high as 7 if heavily silicified, or inclusions in quartz).

Cleavage: None. Fracture uneven to conchoidal. Very brittle.

Optics: $\alpha = 1.575 - 1.585$; $\beta = 1.597$; $\gamma = 1.598 - 1.635$. Biaxial (−).

Note: If material silicified or inclusions in quartz, readings may be those of quartz.

Birefringence: 0.023–0.040.

Luminescence: None.

Spectral: Not diagnostic.

Occurrence: In the oxidized zone of copper deposits. May be mixed with copper carbonates such as malachite and turquoise.

Western U.S., especially Arizona, New Mexico, Nevada, Utah, Idaho.

Mexico; Chile; U.S.S.R.; Katanga, Zaire; Israel.

Stone Sizes: Large masses of material, weighing several pounds, have been found.

Comments: Chrysocolla often forms as a gel mixed with silica and hardens to a blue material that is basically a chrysocolla-saturated quartz. This material is very hard (7), wears well, and is often seen in jewelry. Chrysocolla mixed with malachite is often sold as *Eilat Stone*, and comes from many localities; the color is blue to blue-green, S.G. = 2.8–3.2. Material of fine blue color but very little silica tends to be brittle and crumbles easily, making it impossible to cut stones for jewelry purposes.

Name: *Chrysos* means *golden* and *kolla* means *glue*, from the Greek; this name was applied to a material used by the Greeks in soldering metals, a function now fulfilled by borax. *Eilat Stone* takes its name from Eilat, Gulf of Aqaba, Red Sea.

CHRYSOLITE   See: olivine.

CHRYSOPRASE   See: Quartz.

CHRYSOTILE   See: Serpentine.

CINNABAR

Formula: HgS.

Crystallography: Hexagonal. Usually massive, fine grained; crystals are prismatic or rhombohedral and characteristically twinned, especially those from China.

Colors: Scarlet red, brownish red, brown, black, gray.

Luster: Adamantine to submetallic; massive varieties dull, earthy.

Hardness: 2–2.5.

Density: 8.09.

Cleavage: Perfect 1 direction. Fracture conchoidal to uneven. Brittle.

Optics: $o = 2.905$; $e = 3.256$. Uniaxial (+).

Birefringence: 0.351 (very large).

Dispersion: Strong: over 0.40.

Spectral: Not diagnostic.

Luminescence: None.

Occurrence: Cinnabar is a mineral of low temperature ore deposits; also in veins, igneous rocks and around hot springs. Crystals are very rare.
Utah; Nevada; California; Texas; Arkansas.
Mexico; Peru; Yugoslavia; Italy; Spain; U.S.S.R.; Germany.
Hunan Prov., China: source of the world's finest crystals.

Stone Sizes: Cut cinnabars are extremely small, less than 3 carats normally, and very rare. Some rough exists that might cut 10 carat stones; it is unlikely that fine Chinese crystals that might be transparent would ever be cut, since they are extremely valuable as mineral specimens. Cabochons of almost any size up to several inches could be cut from massive cinnabar.
DG: 2.68 (red, Mexico).

Comments: Faceted cinnabar is extremely rare, and only a handful of stones exist. It is cut primarily for collectors, and is extremely soft and fragile. This is unfortunate because it is also a magnificent red color. Cinnabar carved in China appears regularly on the market, but is not abundant. Note that cinnabar is used by the Chinese to make a red pigment, which is applied to wood in the form of lacquer, and this is the nature of most "cinnabar" carvings sold.

Name: The name is lost in antiquity, and is very old, but believed to be derived from an Indian word, since India was the country of origin.

CINNAMON STONE   See: Garnet.

CITRINE   See: Quartz.

CLEAVELANDITE   See: Feldspar.

CLINOCHRYSOTILE   See: Serpentine.

CLINOHUMITE   See: Chondrodite.

CLINOZOISITE   See: Epidote.

COBALTITE

Formula: CoAsS.

Crystallography: Isometric. Crystals usually cubes and pyritohedra, or combinations of forms; also massive; granular.

Colors: Silvery white to reddish, steel gray with a violet tinge; blackish gray.

Streak: Grayish-black.

Luster: Metallic; opaque.

Hardness: 5.5.

Density: 6.3.

Cleavage: Perfect 1 direction. Fracture uneven. Brittle.

Spectral: Not diagnostic.

Luminescence: None.

Occurrence: High temperature deposits, in metamorphosed rocks, and in vein deposits.
Colorado; Idaho; California.
Dashkesan, Ajerbaijan, U.S.S.R.; India; Sonora, Mexico; Tunaberg, Sweden; Norway; Germany; Cornwall, England; W. Australia.
Cobalt, Ontario: in masses and fine crystals.

Stone Sizes: Massive material would cut stones of any desired size.

Comments: Cabochons are interesting because of the lovely reddish metallic appearance of this mineral. Cut stones are infrequently seen, and are cut only as a curiosity by the collector who wants to have one of everything.

Name: From the composition.

COLEMANITE

Formula: $Ca_2B_6O_{11} \cdot 5H_2O$.

Crystallography: Monoclinic. Crystals are equant, prismatic, pseudorhombohedral; massive, cleavable; granular, and as aggregates.

Colors: Colorless, white, grayish, yellowish white.

Luster: Vitreous to adamantine.

Hardness: 4.5.

Density: 2.42.

Cleavage: Perfect 1 direction. Fracture subconchoidal to uneven. Brittle.

Optics: $\alpha = 1.586$; $\beta = 1.592$; $\gamma = 1.614$.
Biaxial (+), $2V$ ca 55°.

Birefringence: 0.028.

Pleochroism: None.

Spectral: Not diagnostic.

Luminescence: May fluoresce and phosphoresce strong yellowish white or greenish white in SW.

Occurrence: In saline lake deposits in arid regions. Widespread at localities in *California*, especially *Boron* and *Death Valley*.
Argentina; U.S.S.R.; Turkey.

Stone Sizes: Could be as much as 50−100 carats from large crystals or masses. Crystals are normally up to about 1 inch in size.
SI: ca 14 (Calif.).

Comments: Colemanite is cut only as a curiosity, as it has no attractive colors. Faceted gems are normally colorless, have a low dispersion (no fire) and are also brittle and fragile, as well as difficult to cut. They have no appeal except to collectors of the unusual, and material for cutting is potentially abundantly available, since transparent material is not extremely rare.

Name: After William T. Coleman, owner of the mine where the mineral was first found.

CORAL

Formula: $CaCO_3$. (Composed primarily of the mineral Calcite.)

Crystallography: Hexagonal (R).

Colors: White, flesh pink, pale to deep rose red, salmon pink, red to dark red, blue (rarely), black. May be banded or zoned and show a cellular structure.

Luster: Dull to vitreous.

Hardness: 3.5−4.

Density: 2.6−2.7. *Note:* Black coral, composed of conchiolin, is 1.34.

Cleavage: None.

Optics: 1.65 and 1.49 (calcite indices), not usually measurable. Black coral (conchiolin) has R.I. of 1.56.

Birefringence: 0.160.

Spectral: Not diagnostic.

Luminescence: Pale violet or dull purplish red.

Occurrence: Throughout the *Mediterranean Sea and Red Sea areas, So. Ireland, Spain, Mauritius, Malaysia, Japan, Australia, Hawaii.*

Stone Sizes: Branches may be several inches to feet long, but not always thick. Coral is usually fashioned into beads, cabochons, and cameos, and is also carved. Large fine carvings of rich-colored material are very rare and costly. Most of the Mediterranean coral is worked in Italy, but much is also sent to Hong Kong for cutting.

Comments: Coral is the axial skeleton of an animal called the *coral polyp*, a tiny (1 mm) almost plantlike animal that lives in warm oceans (13−16°C). The solid material we know as coral is the colony in which these tiny animals live. Coral is often branched and treelike.

Japanese coral is pink, white and red. Hawaii produces black coral. Black and blue corals also come from the coast off Cameroon. The best red coral comes from the Mediterranean. The darkest color is called *oxblood* and the light pink variety, *angel skin*. Some black coral is composed of conchiolin, a horny organic material, which looks like coral but is much tougher and less brittle.

Name: Latin *corallium*, from the Greek *korallion*.

CORDIERITE   Gem names: Iolite; Water Sapphire.
Dimorph of Indialite.

Formula: $(Mg, Fe)_2Al_4Si_5O_{18}$.

Crystallography: Orthorhombic. Crystals prismatic with rectangular cross section; also massive, granular; may be pseudohexagonal. *Note:* Indialite is hexagonal.

Colors: Blue, bluish violet, smoky blue; rarely greenish, gray, yellowish, brown.

Luster: Vitreous.

Hardness: 7−7.5.

Density: 2.53−2.78. Most gems are 2.57−2.61 (higher with higher Fe content).

Cleavage: Distinct 1 direction. Fracture conchoidal. Brittle.

Optics: $\alpha = 1.522-1.558$; $\beta = 1.524-1.574$; $\gamma = 1.527-1.578$.
Biaxial (+), $2V = 65-104°$. Frequently optically (−).

Birefringence: 0.005−0.018.

Dispersion: 0.017.

Pleochroism: Intense and distinctive. Fe-rich crystals: α = colorless; γ = violet.
Mg-rich crystals: pale yellow to green/pale blue/violet, violet-blue.

Spectral: Iron spectrum. Weak bands at 6451, 5930, 5850, 5350, 4920, 4560, 4360, 4260. Spectrum observed varies with direction in crystal.

Luminescence: None (quenched by Fe).

Inclusions: crystals of apatite and zircon, the latter with pleochroic haloes the outer edges of which are deep yellow. Frequently dustlike masses of tiny crystals. Also hematite plates in parallel orientation (from Ceylon) impart a red color, and gems are sometimes called *bloodshot iolite.*

Occurrence: In altered aluminous rocks; igneous rocks; alluvial gravels.
California; Idaho; Wyoming; South Dakota; New York; New Hampshire.
Great Slave Lake, Canada; Greenland; Scotland; England; Norway; Germany; Finland.
Connecticut: gemmy material that cuts up to 2 carats.
Madras, India: gem iolite in abundance.
Ceylon and Burma: gemmy material from the gem gravels.
Paraiba, Brazil: some gemmy material.
Babati, Tanzania: gem material.
Karasburg, S.W. Africa: gem material.
Madagascar; Japan; Australia.

Stone Sizes: Iolites are frequently in the 1−10 carat range, dichroic with blue to violet color. Large clean stones free of inclusions are not common at all.
BM: worked crystal fragment of 177 grams.
PC: 17.
SI: 15.6 (blue, Ceylon; 10.2 (indigo, Ceylon).

Comments: The crystal structure of cordierite has many similarities to that of beryl; indialite, the dimorph, in fact has the same structure as beryl. Iolite with hematite inclusions (bloodshot iolite) comes from

Ceylon. The inclusions sometimes yield a gem showing a 4-rayed star (quite rare). The blue color of iolite along one optical direction strongly resembles sapphire, and such gems, correctly oriented in settings, are often confused with sapphires. Iolite is not a very rare material, but stones that are completely clean over 10 carats are quite uncommon, and clean 15−20 carat gems are worthy of museum display.

Name: After Mr. Cordier, a French geologist who first studied its crystals. *Iolite* is from Greek *ios* (violet) + *lithos* (stone).

CORUNDUM (= RUBY, SAPPHIRE)

Formula: Al_2O_3 + Fe, Ti, Cr.

Crystallography: Hexagonal (trigonal). Crystals common, often barrel-shaped, prisms with flat ends sometimes bipyramidal; also massive, granular, in rolled pebbles.

Colors: Pinkish red, medium to dark red varieties are called *ruby. All* other colors are termed *sapphire*, including colorless, white, gray, blue, blue-green, green, violet, purple, orange, yellow, yellow-green, brown, golden amber, peachy pink, pink, black.

Luster: Vitreous to adamantine.
Hardness: 9.
Density: 3.99−4.1; usually near 4.00.
Cleavage: None. Fracture conchoidal; frequent parting. Slightly brittle, usually tough.
Optics: $o = 1.757-1.768$; $e = 1.765-1.776$ (usually 1.760, 1.768).
Uniaxial (−).
See table.
Birefringence: 0.008−0.009.
Dispersion: 0.018 (low).
Pleochroism: Very pronounced.
Ruby: strong purplish red/orangy red.
Blue sapphire: strong violet-blue/blue-green.
Green sapphire: intense green/yellow-green.
Orange sapphire: yellow-brown or orange/colorless.
Yellow sapphire: medium yellow/pale yellow.
Purple sapphire: violet/orange.
Luminescence: The luminescence of corundum is intense and distinctive in identification.
Ruby: Burma stones fluoresce intensely, red, in SW, LW and X-rays. Red fluorescence is, however, *not* diagnostic of country of origin or natural origin. Thai

Characteristics of Ruby and Sapphire from Various Localities

Locality	(stone)	Color	e	o	Birefringence	Density
Brazil Jauru, Matto Grosso	(sapphire)	dark blue	1.762	1.770	0.008	3.95−4.05
Burma	(ruby)	fine red	1.760−1.769	1.768−1.778	0.008−0.009	3.996
	(sapphire)	blue	1.762	1.770	0.008	4.002
Thailand	(ruby)	red	1.760−1.764	1.768−1.772	0.008	4.006
	(ruby)	dark red	1.768	1.776	0.008	3.999
Ceylon	(ruby)	red	—	1.772	—	3.999
	(sapphire)	blue	1.757	1.765	0.008	3.996
	(sapphire)	yellow	1.761	1.769	0.008	3.994
	(sapphire)	green	1.765	1.773	0.008	3.999
		green	1.770	1.779	0.009	4.009
Kashmir	(sapphire)	blue	—	—	—	3.994
Pakistan Hunza Valley	(ruby)	red	1.762	1.770	0.008	3.99
Tanzania Umba Valley	(sapphire)	orange	1.760−1.763	1.768−1.772	0.008−0.009	3.99
Australia	(sapphire)	blue	—	—	—	4.001
		yellow-green	1.767	1.775	0.008	3.994
Malawi	(sapphire)	various	1.760−1.761	1.770	0.009	—
	(ruby)	red	1.762−1.763	1.771−1.772	0.009	—
Yugoslavia Prilip	(ruby)	red		ca 1.765	—	3.8−3.98

Note: Usually green gems, more iron-rich, have higher indices among the sapphires. General observations: *Colorless:* $e = 1.759-1.761$; $o = 1.768-1.769$. *Blue and green:* $e = 1.762-1.770$; $o = 1.770-1.779$.
In the above table, omitted data indicates a lack of generalized published information.

ruby fluoresces weak red (LW), weak or none in SW. Ceylon ruby fluoresces strong orange-red in LW, moderate in SW.

Sapphire: Blue stones give no reaction, except some blue Thai gems, which fluoresce weak greenish white in SW. Ceylon blue sapphire fluoresces red to orange in LW. Green gems are inert. Ceylon yellow sapphire fluoresces distinctive apricot color in LW and X-rays, and weak yellow-orange in SW. The fluorescence in LW is proportional to depth of color of gem.

Pink sapphire: Strong orange-red in LW, weaker color in SW.

Violet or alexandrite-like sapphire: strong red in LW, weak light red in SW.

Colorless: moderate light red-orange in LW.

Orange: strong orange-red in LW.

Some Ceylon, Montana and Kashmir sapphires glow dull red or yellow-orange in X-rays.

Spectral: The spectrum of ruby and sapphire can be used diagnostically.

Ruby: A distinctive spectrum: a strong red doublet at 6942/6928 is notable, and this may reverse and become fluorescent. Weaker lines at 6680 and 6592. Broad absorption of yellow, green and violet. Additional lines seen at 4765, 4750, 4685. (The reversible fluorescent doublet is a sensitive test for the presence of chromium in a corundum. Even mauve and purple sapphires have a trace of Cr and show these lines.)

Sapphire: The ferric iron spectrum dominates these stones. In green and blue-green gems, rich in iron, see lines at 4710, 4600, *4500* in the blue-green region. Also lines at 4500 and 4600 may seem to merge and become a broad band. The three bands described are generally known as the 4500 complex and are very distinctive in sapphires. Some blue Ceylon sapphires also show a 6935 red fluorescent line and the 4500 line is very weak in these gems. Intermediate sapphire colors are a mixture of the various spectra discussed.

Occurrence: Corundum is a mineral of crystalline limestones and dolomites that have been metamorphosed, as well as other metamorphic rock types: gneiss, schist; also in igneous rocks such as granite and nepheline syenite. Gem corundums are often found in placer deposits. Non-gem corundum is abundant throughout the world, but gem material is more restricted in occurrence.

Burma: Ruby historically comes from the Mogok stone tract. The history of the mines here is long, complex, and turbulent. Gems occur in a gravel layer called *byon* at a depth of 20 to 100 feet, and are recovered by washing and screening with broad screens and then hand-picking of encouraging-looking pebbles. Corundum originates in metamorphic marbles that have largely weathered away. This is the source of the world's finest rubies.

Thailand (Siam)*:* The areas of major importance here

are Chantabun and Battambang. The corundum deposits have only been worked in a major way in modern times. Gems are found in a sandy layer within 6 to 20 feet of the surface and are recovered by washing. Thai rubies are important on the current marketplace because of the scarcity of Burmese gems.

Cambodia: Pailin in Cambodia is a source of some of the world's finest sapphires, but the country is not significant as a ruby producer.

Kashmir: In northern India in the NW Himalayas occur fine sapphires at an elevation of nearly 15,000 feet. The deposit is snowed under most of the year. Gems occur in a pegmatite and in the valley below, in surface debris. Kashmir sapphires have a cloudiness due to inclusions and an extremely good blue color, making them greatly desired, but they are extremely scarce.

Hunza Valley, Pakistan: On the Pakistan side of the Kashmir Valley occur ruby and spinel of fine quality. The red is comparable to the Burma ruby. This material is not much seen on the market and is very scarce.

Ceylon: Ceylon is a source of many colors of sapphire, as well as ruby and star gems. Gems occur here in a gravel layer known as *illam* at a depth of up to 50 feet. The material is washed and screened and gems recovered by hand picking. Ceylon ruby is not as good as Burma material, and the sapphires are often pale in color, but can be very large.

Australia: Anakie, Queensland is a source of sapphire in blue, green and yellow shades, as well as some ruby. All are in alluvial deposits; some fine green gems are known, as well as an occasional excellent blue gem. Other occurrences are noted in New South Wales, especially the Invernell district. Victoria is a location for green sapphire.

Montana: Yogo Gulch is a well-known locality for fine blue sapphire, very good color, that occurs in igneous dikes. The crystals are very flattened and waferlike, so it is difficult to cut large, full-cut gems from them. Crystals occur in many different colors and are usually quite small, but the blue stones are extremely fine. This material is often zoned and may have a curious metallic-like luster. Ruby is uncommon here.

North Carolina: At Cowee Creek, in Macon Co., small rubies and sapphires are found in stream gravels and soil. The quality is usually poor, but an occasional fine, small ruby is found.

South West Africa: At Namaqualand opaque ruby is found that is suitable for cabochons.

Tanzania: Large ruby of fine color and quality is found in green, massive chromiferous zoisite. The crystals are usually opaque, and the rock as a whole is cut as a decorative material, but occasionally some small areas of this ruby are transparent enough to facet. Many colors of sapphire are found in the vicinity of Morogoro, Tanga Province, along with some ruby. The Umba Valley is a source of fine orange colored sapphires.

Rhodesia: Sapphires of various colors are found, often zoned with a creamy-white core and blue outer zone, or vice versa. The crystals are well formed and usually up to 3 inches in diameter. At the Baruta Mine, N.E. Rhodesia, a crystal of 3100 carats was found, deep blue. Rhodesia is also a source of black star sapphire. Sapphires from here are not well known on the market.

Malawi: Sapphires were found about 1958 at Chimwadzulu Hill.

Kenya: Excellent ruby is known from Logido, a recently-discovered ruby mine. The ruby is pinkish, but of fine color, usually in small sizes.

Afghanistan: Ruby of fine color has come from Jagdalek, near Kabul. This is an ancient source of many of the fine stones of ancient times.

India: Mysore produces poor quality rubies, but a significant amount of star ruby. Some of the stones from this area are of excellent quality, but are not common.

Brazil: The Matto Grosso area has produced sapphires.

Gem corundum is occasionally found in the following places: *Colombia; Norway; Finland; Greenland; U.S.S.R.; Czechoslovakia; Pakistan.*

Inclusions:

In general: Burma, Thailand and Australian blue sapphires contain crystals plagioclase feldspars, orthoclase, niobite, columbite, calcite, monazite, zircon apatite, fergusonite, thorite.

Ceylon and Tanzania sapphires contain crystals of chlorapatite, pyrite, magnetite, biotite, graphite, phlogopite, zircon, spinel.

Brazil (Jauru, Matto Grosso): rounded gas-filled disks that resemble bubbles.

Burma (Mogok): Short rutile needles at 60° angles; silk consisting of hollow tubes plus crystals of rutile, spinel, calcite, mica, garnet; zircon crystals with haloes; color swirls known as *treacle.*

Thailand: feathers = canals and tubelike liquid inclusions; flat, brownish cavities; twin planes; crystals of niobite, almandine, apatite, pyrrhotite; plagioclase crystals in sapphires. Rutile is absent.

Ceylon: long rutile needles; healing cracks; zircon crystals with haloes; flakes of biotite mica; feathers with irregular liquid hoses inside; color zoning frequent.

Pakistan (Hunza Valley): phlogopite; chlorite; monazite; spinel; rutile; magnetite; pyrite.

Cambodia (Pailin): specks of uranian pyrochlore (ruby red color, very small).

Kashmir: Yellow and brown feathers and thin films; liquid-filled canals; veil-like lines at 60° and 120°; cloudy haziness; negative crystals, flat films; rods and tubes.

Tanzania (Umba Valley): apatite; graphite; pyrrhotite.

Australia: Dislocation and twin lamellae; rutile crystals; liquid-filled feathers, flat cavities; color zoning frequent.

Malawi (Chimwadzulu Hill): fine tubes; small black crystals and short rods; healed fissures; color zoning.

Kenya (Longido): pargasite; spinel; zoisite crystals.

Stone Sizes: Sapphires, in general, reach a far greater size than do rubies. A ruby of 30 carats is a great rarity, whereas sapphires in museum collections weighing hundreds of carats are not uncommon. The largest rubies come from the chrome-zoisite matrix in Tanzania, but these are not really of gem quality. Fine gem rubies of large size occur in the Ceylon gravels, with smaller ones from Burma and Thailand. Enormous sapphires of fine color and transparency have been found in the gem gravels of Ceylon and Burma, but most are from Ceylon. A 1400 gram ruby was found in Yugoslavia (Prilip) but not gemmy. Malawi material reaches a size of about 12 carats (sapphire). Large sapphires have been found in Australia; Montana sapphires over 1 carat are very rare, but the blue ones are magnificent in this size range. In general, a fine blue sapphire over 5–10 carats is very rare, as is a fine ruby over 3–4 carats on the current market.

Ruby:

Crown Jewels of England: Edwardes Ruby, 167 carats.

Cathedrale St.-Guy, Prague: ruby of 250 carats.

Narodni Museum, Prague: 27.11 (Burma).

BM: ruby crystal of 690 grams (Burma).

PC: 96 carats, fine 27 carats known.

Historical rubies include 400 carat Burmese rough that yielded 70 and 45 carat gems. Rough of 304 carats was found about 1890.

Iranian Crown Jewels: fine buckle of 84 Burma ruby cabs, up to 11 carat size.

SI: 138.7 Rosser Reeves star ruby (red, Ceylon); 50.3 (violet-red star ruby, Ceylon).

Sapphire:

SI: 423 (blue, Ceylon, "Logan sapphire"); 330 (blue star, Burma—"star of Asia"); 316 (blue, Ceylon, "Star of Artaban"); 98.6 (deep blue, "Bismarck sapphire"); 92.6 (yellow, Burma); 67 (black star, Thailand); 62 (black star, Australia); 42.2 (purple, Ceylon); 35.4 (yellow-brown, Ceylon); 31 (orange, Ceylon); 25.3 (colorless, Ceylon).

PC: Black Star of Queensland, oval, found 1948, 733 carats, world's largest star. A yellow crystal of 217.5 carats was found in Queensland in 1946.

Natural History Museum, Paris: le Raspoli, 135 carat brown, lozenge-shaped rough, clean.

Tested by the G.I.A.: 5600 carat sapphire cabochon; also Mysore (India) ruby cab of 1795 carats.

PC (tested by G.I.A.): Montana blue sapphire, cushion cut, 12.54 carats, believed largest stone from this locality.

Diamond Fund, Moscow: 258.8 (blue), fine lively gem.

ROM: 179.4 (golden yellow, Ceylon); 28.6 padparadscha, Ceylon); 43.95 (greenish yellow, Ceylon); 193.3 (blue star sapphire).

British mission to Burma, in 1929, saw 951 carat sapphire, which may be the largest ever found there.

AMNH: 100 (yellow, Ceylon); 100 (padparadscha, very

fine, Ceylon); 163 (blue, Ceylon); 34 (violet, Thailand); 563 carats (blue, "Star of India," Ceylon).

Iranian Crown Jewels: Hollow rectangular cabochon of 191.6 carats; oval, yellow gem of 119 carats. Also fine Kashmir blue oval, nearly clean, ca 75 carats.

Comments: Ruby is the most valuable of all gemstones, and sapphire one of the most popular. Despite the enormous size of these gems as seen in museum and Royal collections, corundums available on the marketplace are usually of more modest size. A 3–4 carat ruby is a rare and very expensive gem today, if of fine quality. Sapphires of good blue color over 5 carats, if clean, are similarly rare and also valuable. There is an abundance of good quality small sapphires, but not of rubies.

Star corundum is created by the inclusion of rutile needles within the host corundum crystal. The rutile needles orient themselves according to the hexagonal symmetry of the corundum, and reflections from these needles provide a chatoyancy. When such material is cut into a cabochon the sheen is concentrated along the top of the stone into three white lines crossing at 60° angles, creating a six-rayed star. Very rarely there are two distinct sets of needles oriented according to the first and second order prisms of the corundum (30° apart), resulting in a strong, 12-rayed star.

Corundum is the hardest mineral known, next to diamond, and is very compact and dense, with no cleavage. As a result, corundum is one of the best of all jewelry stones, especially star corundum, which is tough as well as scratch-resistant. Faceted gems are slightly brittle and can be chipped, though much less easily than other gems. Very few ruby deposits are known that can be actively worked, which creates ever greater strain on ruby supply on the marketplace. Many more sapphire deposits are in operation, so the situation here is not as critical.

Name: *Corundum* is from the Sanskrit word *kurivinda*. *Ruby* and *sapphire* come from Latin words meaning *red* and *blue*, respectively.

COVELLITE

Formula: CuS.

Crystallography: Hexagonal. Crystals are tabular; also massive and cleavages.

Colors: Light to dark indigo blue; purplish; commonly iridescent, yellow and red.

Streak: Shining gray-black.

Luster: Submetallic to resinous; opaque, except in thin slivers.

Hardness: 1.5–2.

Density: 4.68.

Cleavage: Perfect and easy 1 direction. Fracture uneven. Brittle. Thin sheets flexible.

Optics: $o = 1.45$. Uniaxial (+).

Pleochroism: Strong, but visible only in very thin sheets.

Luminescence: None.

Occurrence: Secondary enrichment zones of copper mines.

Butte, Montana; Wyoming; South Dakota; Colorado; Utah; California; Alaska.

Sardinia, Italy; Argentina; New Zealand; Philippines; Germany; Austria; Yugoslavia.

Stone Sizes: Cabochons are generally cut from massive or foliated material. The stones can be very large, up to several inches long.

Comments: Covellite is cut strictly as a collector curiosity. Cut gems have no great value, but the blue or iridescent colors can be very attractive. Covellite is much too soft to wear and difficult to cut—it can be scratched with a fingernail!

Name: After N. Covelli who discovered the mineral on Mt. Vesuvius, Italy.

CREEDITE

Formula: $Ca_3Al_2(SO_4)(F, OH)_{10} \cdot 2H_2O$.

Crystallography: Monoclinic. Crystals short, prismatic; also radial clusters.

Colors: Colorless, white, rose to lilac or purple.

Luster: Vitreous.

Hardness: 4.

Density: 2.71–2.73.

Cleavage: Perfect 1 direction. Fracture conchoidal. Brittle.

Optics: $\alpha = 1.461$; $\beta = 1.478$; $\gamma = 1.485$. Biaxial (−), $2V = 64°$.

Birefringence: 0.024.

Dispersion: Moderate.

Spectral: Not diagnostic.

Luminescence: Medium white to cream color (SW); bright white to cream (LW).

Occurrence:
Darwin, California; Granite, Nevada.
Colquiri, Bolivia.
In cavities in rock with fluorite and barite at *Creede, Colorado.*
Also occurs in a fluorite–barite mine at *Wagon Wheel Gap, Colo.*
Santa Eulalia, Chihuahua, Mexico: in crystals up to 1 inch long, gemmy.

Stone Sizes: Faceted gems very small, usually less than 1–2 carats.

Comments: Creedite is one of the very rare minerals known to collectors. It may well be that less than a dozen gems have ever been cut of this material. The mineral itself is rare, cuttable crystals even more so. These would be colorless and from the Mexican occurrence. The hardness is too low for wear—strictly a collector gem.

Name: Occurrence in the Creede Quadrangle, Colorado.

CRISTOBALITE See: Quartz.

CROCOITE

Formula: $PbCrO_4$.

Crystallography: Monoclinic. Crystals prismatic, sometimes hollow.

Colors: Red-orange, cherry red, orange, yellowish.

Streak: Orange-yellow.

Luster: Adamantine to vitreous.

Hardness: 2.5−3.

Density: 5.9−6.1.

Cleavage: Indistinct. Brittle.

Optics: $\alpha = 2.29-2.31$; $\beta = 2.36$; $\gamma = 2.66$. Biaxial (+), $2V = 57°$.

Birefringence: 0.270.

Dispersion: Strong.

Pleochroism: Orange-red to blood red.

Spectral: Distinct band at 5550 but seen only in thin fragments. Transmits mainly in the yellow-red region of the spectrum.

Luninescence: Weak reddish to dark brown (SW); weaker effect in LW.

Occurrence: Secondary mineral in oxidized zones of lead deposits.
Dundas, Tasmania: best crystals found in the world, some gemmy; large clusters.
Beresov Dist., U.S.S.R.: red crystals.
Tiger, Arizona: very tiny crystals.
California; Minas Gerais, Brazil.

Stone Sizes: Gems can be up to about 10 carats, but these are usually not transparent. Clean stones up to 1−2 carats are available in deep red-orange color from Tasmania.
DG: 14.5 (orange, Tasmania).

Comments: Crocoite is one of the loveliest of all collector stones. It s too soft and brittle for wear, but it is quite a rare mineral and relatively few stones have been cut. The dispersion is high but completely masked by the intense body color.

Name: From the Greek *krokos*, meaning *saffron*, in allusion to the color.

CRYOLITE

Formula: Na_3AlF_6.

Crystallography: Monoclinic. Crystals cuboidal and prismatic; usually massive, however.

Colors: Colorless, white, brownish, reddish; rarely gray to black.

Luster: Vitreous to greasy.

Hardness: 2.5.

Density: 2.97.

Cleavage: None. Fracture uneven. Brittle.

Optics: $\alpha = 1.338$; $\beta = 1.338$; $\gamma = 1.339$. Biaxial (+), $2V = 43°$.

Birefringence: 0.001; almost isotropic.

Dispersion: 0.024 (approx.).

Pleochroism: None.

Spectral: Not diagnostic.

Luminescence: None observed.

Occurrence: Occurs in alkalic rocks at *Ivigtut, Greenland.*
Also *Spain; U.S.S.R.; Colorado* (small amounts).

Stone Sizes: Large cabochons could be cut from the abundant material in Greenland. Facetable material is quite rare, however, and only tiny gems can be obtained.

Comments: Cut cryolite is somewhat translucent, and has a "sleepy" look. The cuttable material has a very low birefringence, is colorless, and very soft—not exactly an exciting-looking gem. However, there are very few cut stones in existence, because of the extreme scarcity of suitable rough. In addition, cryolite is only found abundantly at one locality (Ivigtut).

Name: From the Greek *kryos* (*frost*) + *lithos* (*stone*), hence *ice-stone*, in allusion to its appearance.

CRYSTAL See: Quartz.

CUPRITE

Formula: Cu_2O.

Crystallography: Isometric. Crystals cubes and octahedra, or combinations; also needle-like, in densely packed mats called *chalcotrichite* with no gem significance.

Colors: Brownish red, red, purplish red, nearly black.

Streak: Brownish red.

Luster: Adamantine to submetallic; earthy.

Hardness: 3.5−4.

Density: 6.14; S.W. Africa = 6.0−6.07.

Cleavage: Poor. Fracture conchoidal to uneven. Brittle.

Optics: $N = 2.848$.

Pleochroism: Sometimes anomalously pleochroic.

Luminescence: None.

Occurrence: Secondary mineral in copper deposits. Usually microscopic crystals.

Arizona; New Mexico; Pennsylvania; Colorado; Utah; Idaho.

Mexico; Bolivia; Chile; France; U.S.S.R.; Zaire; Japan; other locations.

Onganja, S.W. Africa: unique occurrence, with crystals up to more than 6 inches across, blood red and transparent; often coated with green malachite.

Stone Sizes: Largest mass of cuttable cuprite (*PC*) is completely transparent and weighs 2 kg. Before the amazing Onganja discovery the largest stones were less than 1 carat, as only tiny crystals had ever been found. Onganja stones have been cut up to 300 carats, flawless, and potentially could be much larger.

SI: 182 (round, S.W. Africa).

PC: 203.75 (octagon, S.W. Africa).

DG: 48.6 (red, S.W. Africa).

Comments: Cuprite is one of the rarest of all gems. Cuttable material comes from only one locality for all practical purposes. Only good crystals or pieces of crystals are cuttable, however, as other material from this mine is opaque. Mineral collectors do not wish to see their fine crystals cut, limiting the supply of available faceting material. Cut gems have a metallic appearance and magnificent deep red color. They are unwearable, but among the most beautiful of all gems, and someday may be extremely rare.

Name: From the Latin *cuprum* (*copper*) in allusion to the composition.

CYPRINE See: Idocrase.

D

DANBURITE

Formula: $CaB_2Si_2O_8$.

Crystallography: Orthorhombic. Crystals prismatic with wedge-shaped terminations, like topaz.

Colors: Colorless, white, pink, light to dark yellow, yellowish brown, brown.

Luster: Vitreous to greasy.

Hardness: 7.

Density: 2.97−3.03 (usually 3.00).

Cleavage: Indistinct. Fracture subconchoidal to uneven. Brittle.

Optics: $\alpha = 1.630$; $\beta = 1.633$; $\gamma = 1.636$.
Biaxial (−); $2V = 88°$ in red to green light; optically (+) at lower wavelengths.

Birefringence: 0.006.

Dispersion: 0.017.

Pleochroism: None.

Spectral: Sometimes shows rare earth spectrum, so-called didymium lines.

Luminescence: Sky blue to bright blue-green in LW. Also thermoluminescent (red).

Occurrence: In dolomites; in carbonate veins in granitic rocks.

Danbury, Connecticut: type locality.

Charcas, San Luis Potosi, Mexico: colorless, yellow, light pink (gemmy).

Mogok, Burma: yellow and colorless, sometimes large crystals (rolled pebbles).

Obira, Bungo, Kyushu, Japan: colorless crystals, sometimes gemmy.

Madagascar: yellow crystals at Mt. Bity, often gemmy.

Stone Sizes: Danburite is not a very rare mineral, but is scarce in large facetable pieces. The usual range is 1−5 carats, especially for colorless material from Mexico. The yellow Burmese gems are rare today, especially in the 7−10 carat range.

BM: Burma gem, step cut, flawless, wine-yellow color, 138.61 carats.

PC: 20 (Burma, peach color).

SI: 18.4 (yellow, Burma); 7.9 (colorless, Japan).

Comments: Danburite is a hard and durable stone with poor cleavage—an excellent choice for wear. The dispersion is quite low, so gems have no fire but are very bright when properly cut. Large ones are very rare, and sufficient material exists to allow almost every collector to have a colorless gem.

Name: After the type locality, Danbury, Connecticut.

DATOLITE

Formula: $CaBSiO_4(OH)$.

Crystallography: Monoclinic. Crystals prismatic or stubby; massive, granular.

Colors: Colorless, white, pale yellow, green, also pink, reddish, and brownish due to impurities; massive varieties can be white to orange-brown or pink.

Luster: Vitreous.

Hardness: 5−5.5.

Density: 2.8−3.0.

Cleavage: None; fracture uneven to conchoidal; brittle.

Optics: $\alpha = 1.622-1.626$; $\beta = 1.649-1.658$; $\gamma = 1.666-1.670$.
Biaxial (−), $2V = 75°$.

Birefringence: 0.044−0.047.

Dispersion: 0.016.

Pleochroism: None.

Spectral: Not diagnostic.

Luminescence: Blue in SW (attributed to the presence of Eu).

Occurrence: A secondary mineral in basic igneous rocks and traprocks.

Springfield, Massachusetts; Lane's Quarry, Westfield, Massachusetts; Paterson, New Jersey (and other localities in that state).

Tyrol, Austria; Habach, Austria; Cornwall, England.

Lake Superior Copper district, Michigan: nodules of massive datolite.

Stone Sizes: Brown or white massive material will cut cabochons up to several ounces. The colors in the Michigan material are due to copper staining. Cabochons are seldom seen in collections—collectors prefer to polish the faces of sliced-open nodules. These can be up to about 6 inches in diameter. The best faceting material comes from Massachusetts, with fine pale green material from New Jersey. The largest gems cut from this are in the 5 carat range. Larger stones are very rare.

SI: 5.4 and 5.0 (colorless, Mass.).

Comments: Datolite is a rather soft gemstone if wear is considered. The nodules come in very attractive colors. Faceted stones are extremely brilliant, though their dispersion (fire) is low. Most faceted gems are colorless, pale yellowish or pale green.

Name: From a Greek word meaning *to divide* because of the granular nature of the massive variety.

DEMANTOID See: Garnet.

36

DIAMOND

Diamond is the best known gemstone. Its history of use and great value extends thousands of years into the past. Diamond has been the center of intrigue, warfare, romance, and tradition on a scale unequaled by any other gem.

The history and lore of diamonds, diamond technology, and cutting are subjects so vast in themselves that they are far beyond the scope of this book. Several excellent books on these topics are listed in the Bibliography on page 139.

Formula: C (carbon).
Essentially pure with only minor traces of impurities.

Crystallography: Isometric. Crystals sometimes sharp octahedra, dodecahedra, and combinations with other forms. Crystals modified, often rounded and distinguished by the presence of triangular-shaped pits on octahedral faces (once believed due to etching, these "trigons" are currently believed a result of the growth process).

Colors: Colorless, gray, shades of yellow, brown, pink, green, orange, lavender, blue, black.

Luster: Adamantine.

Hardness: 10. Diamond is the hardest natural substance and easily scratches any other mineral. The difference in hardness between diamond and corundum (9) is very much greater than that between any other two minerals on the Mohs scale.

Density: 3.515; Carbonado 2.9–3.5.

Cleavage: Perfect 1 direction (octahedral). Brittle. In spite of its great hardness, diamond can be split easily along octahedral planes. This feature is useful in cutting, since cleaving a large diamond saves weeks of laborious sawing. The cleavage also makes it possible for diamonds to be chipped in wear.

Optics: Isotropic, index very constant; $N = 2.417$.

Dispersion: 0.044. This high dispersion in a colorless diamond creates the "fire" that is the source of the diamond's attractiveness.

Pleochroism: None.

Spectral: The absorption spectra of various colored diamonds are quite distinctive and useful, especially in distinguishing irradiation-colored diamond from natural colored stones. The colored diamonds can be grouped into several series:
Cape Series: Colorless to yellow diamonds that fluoresce blue. Strong lines at 4155, *4785*, 4650, 4520, 4350, 4230. Most lines are hard to see.
Brown Series: Brown, green, and greenish-yellow diamonds that fluoresce green. Strong line at 5040 plus weak lines at 5320 and 4980.
Yellow Series: Colorless, brownish-yellow or yellow and yellow-fluorescing diamonds. This series includes the true "canary" yellow diamonds. No discrete spectrum, but sometimes a weak line at 4155.
Type II-B Blue: No absorption spectrum.

Luminescence: Many diamonds fluoresce blue to violet, with the fluorescence sometimes in zones (often a result of twinning). The effect is sometimes strong enough to be visible in daylight. Yellow stones sometimes fluoresce yellow-green. Some pink diamonds from India fluoresce and phosphoresce orange. The famous Hope diamond, deep blue in color, phosphoresces deep red. Most fluorescence occurs in LW; the SW reaction is weaker and same as LW. Many diamonds fluoresce bluish-white in SW. Blue-fluorescing diamonds may phosphoresce yellow (an "afterglow" reaction). The various diamonds have been organized into types, with varying UV transparency.
Type I: Transparent to all wavelengths down to about 3000 Å; this type contains nitrogen, and is further subdivided into Types Ia and Ib. Type Ia represents the majority of all diamond, and the nitrogen is in the form of platelets. About 0.1% of Type I diamonds are Type Ib, in which the nitrogen is dispersed throughout the crystal.
Type II: Transparent all the way to 2250 Å; this type contains aluminum. Type IIa does not phosphoresce in SW, and contains little nitrogen. Type IIb has bluish phosphorescence in SW and is also electrically conductive. Nitrogen in these diamonds is absent or very scarce.

Inclusions: Diamond crystals frequently contain crystals of other minerals.
Olivine may look like bubbles (rounded crystals), present in single crystals or clusters, often on octahedral faces and aligned parallel to octahedral edges. These are pale green or colorless.
Garnet is present in single crystals or clusters; brown, orange, yellow, pink, violet-red, lilac, and purple colors have been observed. These are usually pyrope garnets and sometimes reach large size. They are seen frequently in S. African diamonds.
Graphite is present as black inclusions.
Pyrrhotite, *pyrite*, *pentlandite*, *ilmenite*, and *rutile* (dark colored ore minerals) may resemble graphite inclusions; these are typical of diamond from Ghana.
Diamond crystals are often seen as inclusions in other diamonds, usually in perfect crystal forms.
Chrome diopside is present as emerald-green, well-formed crystals. Also seen in S. African diamonds is chrome enstatite.
Chrome spinel in octahedra, sometimes distorted, usually reddish-brown or black; these are commonly seen in Russian diamonds.
Cloudlike inclusions are sometimes in the shape of a Maltese cross, are diagnostic of diamonds from India.

Occurrence: Diamond is a mineral formed at very high temperatures and pressures, deep within the earth. Synthetic diamond is produced at pressures as high as 100,000 atmospheres (equivalent to 200 miles of rock!) and temperatures around 5000° C; these conditions may approximate those of natural diamond formation.

Diamond formed at depth is apparently "exploded" to the surface in fissures that become circular near the surface and are known as "pipes." The mineralogy of the rocks in these pipes, known as *kimberlite*, is unusual and unique, and reflects high pressure of formation. Diamond is found in kimberlites, and also in alluvial deposits (streams, river channels, beaches, deltas, and former stream beds) derived from kimberlite weathering and erosion.

S. Africa: Diamonds were first discovered on the shores of the Orange River. After several "rushes," abundant "diamond fever," and a turbulent period of changing ownership, nearly all the deposits were under control of De Beers Consolidated Mines, Ltd., by 1888. De Beers is now part of Anglo American, a huge conglomerate that also owns the rich gold mines of the Rand in S. Africa. S. African diamonds are the world's most famous, and such mine names as Premier, Jagersfontein, Bultfontein, Dutoitspan, and Wesselton are famous for their output. South Africa is still a world leader in diamond production but large stones are becoming very scarce.

Other African countries: Diamonds are found in many parts of Africa. Rhodesia is noted for alluvial deposits. The huge production of very fine stones from *Angola* is now interrupted by political problems. *Ghana* produces diamond from gravel beds, mostly industrial; some are gem quality. The *Ivory Coast* and *Republic of Guinea* produce alluvial diamonds. A large deposit is known in *S.W. Africa* where the Orange River enters the Atlantic Ocean. Huge machines work enormous beach deposits in Namaqualand, and other spots along this coast. *Central African Republic* produces diamonds associated with gravel beds. Alluvial diamonds occur in *Zaire* and especially in *Sierra Leone.* The Sierra Leone diamonds are among the world's finest. They occur in river gravels, are often very large and of top gem quality. Occasional stones are found in *Tanzania;* John Williamson found a large pipe in 1935, and some fine diamond has been recovered from this deposit. Other African sources include *Lesotho* and *Guyana.*

India: The first major historical source of diamonds, and also the source of many of the largest and most famous gems (including the Hope diamond). Mine areas are in Golconda, Andhra Pradesh (Hyderabad), Kollur, and other spots. Indian diamonds are primarily alluvial, found in sandstones and conglomerates or gravel deposits.

Brazil: Produces a large quantity of diamond, but little of good gem quality. The Diamantina district was opened in 1725, and diamond also comes from Bahia, Minas Gerais, Matto Grosso, and other states. Diamond in Brazil occurs in a variety of rock types and also alluvial deposits. Most of the stones are small in size but an occasional large, fine gemstone is found. Bahia state produces black microcrystalline diamond known as *carbonado.* The largest of these found weighed 3078 carats.

Borneo and Indonesia: Small alluvial deposits. Most stones are small (less than 1 carat). Diamonds from Borneo have been reported to be harder than those from other deposits.

Venezuela: A substantial alluvial production, mostly of small, yellowish crystals.

U.S.S.R.: Russia is one of the leading world suppliers of diamonds. The country is rich in pipes (several hundred have been found), some of very large size (such as the famous "Mir" pipe). However, most Russian diamonds are very small, severely limiting the value of the production. A high percentage of crystals are of good color and transparency, and the production is substantial enough to be a major factor in the world diamond market. All the pipes are located in Siberia, where weather conditions make mining both difficult and expensive.

U.S.A.: The only significant diamond deposit in North America is at Murfreesboro, Arkansas. This is a very large pipe, which has never been systematically developed and might be extremely rich. It is on Government land and has been worked surficially only by tourists who pay a small fee for the privilege of digging. The largest crystal found here weighed 40.23 carats and was named the "Uncle Sam" diamond.

Alluvial diamonds have been found throughout the U.S., presumably carried south by waters flowing from Canadian glaciers thousands of years ago. The Canadian source pipes have never been discovered, however. Large diamonds found in Virginia include the "Dewey" (1885, 23.75 carats) and the "Punch Jones" (34.46 carats).

Stone Sizes: The largest rough diamonds ever found include the Cullinan (3106 carats, white, S. Africa, 1905); the Excelsior (995.2 carats, white, S. Africa, 1893), the Star of Sierra Leone (968.8 carats, white, Sierra Leone, 1972), and the Great Mogul (787.5 carats, white, India, 1650). A fine yellowish octahedron of 616 carats is on display at the Mine Museum in Kimberley, S. Africa, found in 1975.

The largest cut stones include: Cullinan I (530.2, white, pear shape, in the British Crown Jewels), Cullinan II (317.4, white, cushion, British Crown Jewels), Great Mogul (280.0, white, dome-shape, location unknown), Nizam (277.0, white, table cut, was in India in 1934), Jubilee (245.35, white, cushion, privately owned, Paris), and the Orloff 189.6, white, rose-cut, Russian Diamond Fund in the Kremlin).

Comments: Diamond is the most romanced and heavily marketed of all gemstones. Nearly every jewelry establishment handles diamonds, even if it has no other gemstones in stock. The annual world production of diamonds is on the order of 10 tons. Of course, only a small percentage of this is of gem quality, but diamond of very fine quality is nowhere near as scarce as equivalently high quality ruby or emerald.

Name: From the Greek word *adamas*, meaning the *hardest steel*, and hence the hardest gemstone.

DIASPORE *Dimorph of* Boehmite.

Formula: AlO(OH) + Mn.

Crystallography: Orthorhombic. Crystals are elongated plates or acicular; also massive, foliated.

Colors: Colorless, white, yellowish, pink, rose red to dark red (Mn), lilac, greenish, brownish.

Luster: Vitreous; pearly on cleavage.

Hardness: 6.5-7.

Density: 3.3-3.5.

Cleavage: Perfect 1 direction. Fracture conchoidal.

Optics: $\alpha = 1.702$; $\beta = 1.722$; $\gamma = 1.750$.
Biaxial (+), $2V = 85°$.

Birefringence: 0.048.

Pleochroism: Strong in manganiferous variety: violet-blue/pale green/rose to dark red.

Spectral: Not diagnostic.

Luminescence: Dull pale yellow (Chester, Massachusetts) in SW.

Occurrence: In metamorphosed limestones, chloritic schists, and altered igneous rocks; also in bauxite deposits.
Greenland; Cornwall, England; Norway; Sweden; France; Switzerland; Germany; Greece; U.S.S.R.; Japan; China.
Chester, Massachusetts: with corundum in emery deposit; some fragments cuttable.
Chester Co., Pennsylvania: fine transparent crystals up to 2 inches long and $\frac{1}{4}$ inch thick, colorless to brown, some cuttable.
Hungary: good crystals.
Postmasburg dist., S. Africa: manganiferous variety.

Stone Sizes: Diaspore may never actually have been cut, although there is mention of it as a potential gem material in the literature. The crystals from Massachusetts and Pennsylvania were, when found, apparently suited for cutting. A few stones may exist in especially complete collections.

Comments: Diaspore always occurs in small crystals, and gemmy ones are very rare. The material is hard enough to make a durable jewelry stone, and the colors are potentially very attractive. A cut gem would be one of the rarest of all collector items.

Name: From the Greek *diaspeirein*, meaning *to scatter*, because it falls apart in the hot flame of a blowpipe.

DICKINSONITE

Formula: $H_2Na_6(Mn, Fe, Ca, Mg)_{14}(PO_4)_{12} \cdot H_2O$.

Crystallography: Monoclinic. Crystals tabular, pseudorhombohedral; foliated, micaceous, radiating.

Colors: Oil green, olive green, yellowish green, brownish green, brownish.

Luster: Vitreous; pearly on cleavage.

Hardness: 3.5-4.

Density: 3.38-3.41.

Cleavage: Perfect and easy, 1 direction. Fracture uneven.

Optics: $\alpha = 1.648-1.658$; $\beta = 1.655-1.662$; $\gamma = 1.662-1.671$
Biaxial (+), $2V$ ca 90°.

Birefringence: 0.013-0.014.

Dispersion: Strong.

Pleochroism: Pale olive green to pale yellowish green.

Spectral: Not diagnostic.

Luminescence: None observed.

Occurrence: A secondary phosphate mineral in granite pegmatites.
Branchville, Connecticut; Portland, Connecticut; Poland, Maine.

Stone Sizes: Very tiny green gems, less than 1-2 carats, have been cut from Connecticut material.

Comments: This mineral is seldom even mentioned in the gem literature, because it is so rare and has been so rarely cut. Faceted gems are practically nonexistent, and would be among the rarest of all cut stones.

Name: After the Rev. William Dickinson in recognition of his interest in the locality where first found.

DINOSAUR BONE See: Quartz.

DIOPSIDE

Formula: $CaMgSi_2O_6$.
Complete series to $CaFeSi_2O_6 = $ *Hedenbergite*
Intermediate members = *Salite, Ferrosalite*
Ferrosalite rich in Mn and Zn = *Jeffersonite*
Diopside rich in Mn = *Schefferite*
Diopside rich in Mn and Zn = *Zinc Schefferite* (variety)
Diopside rich in Cr = *Chrome Diopside* (variety)

Crystallography: Monoclinic. Crystals often well formed, prismatic, stubby; also massive.

Colors: Colorless, white, gray, pale green, dark green, blackish green, brown, yellowish to reddish brown, bright green (Cr variety); rarely blue.
Schefferite is light to dark brown.
Hedenbergite always dark green, brownish green or black.

Luster: Vitreous.

Hardness: 5.5-6.5.

Density: Usually 3.29; range 3.22-3.38 for diopside, higher if more Fe present.

Cleavage: Perfect 1 direction. Fracture uneven to conchoidal. Brittle.

	Diopside	Hedenbergite	Jeffersonite	Schefferite	Cr-Diopside
Optics					
α	1.664–1.695	1.716–1.726	1.713	1.676	1.674
β	1.672–1.701	1.723–1.730	1.722	1.683	1.680
γ	1.695–1.721	1.741–1.751	1.745	1.705	1.702
$2V$	50–60°	52–62°	74°	60°	55°
Density	3.22–3.38	3.50–3.56	3.55	3.39	—
Birefringence	0.024–0.031	0.025–0.029	0.032	0.031	0.028
Pleochroism	None	pale green/ green-brown	dark/light brown		yellow/green

Intermediate compositions have intermediate properties in the diopside–hedenbergite series; increasing iron content results in higher properties. The pleochroism of salite is: pale green/blue-green/yellow-green.

Spectral: Chrome diopside has lines at: 5080, 5050, 4900, plus fuzzy bands at 6350, 6550, 6700 and a doublet at 6900.
Pale green diopside gives lines at 5050, 4930 and 4460.

Luminescence: Blue or cream white in SW, also orange-yellow; sometimes mauve in LW. May phosphoresce a peach color.

Occurrence: In Ca-rich metamorphic rocks; in kimberlite (Cr-diopside).
Burma: yellow faceted gems; also catseyes and pale green faceting material.
Madagascar: very dark green cutting material.
Ceylon: cuttable pebbles.
Ontario, Canada: green faceting material.
Quebec, Canada: red-brown material that cuts gems to 2 carats.
Ala, Piedmont, Italy: fine green diopside (*alalite* is local name).
St. Marcel, Piedmont, Italy: violet variety of diopside (*violane*).
Zillerthal, Austria: green fine crystals, some transparent.
Georgetown, California: green diopside. *Crestmore, California:* large crystals (non-gem).
DeKalb, New York: fine transparent green crystals up to several inches in length.
Slyudyanka, U.S.S.R.: green crystals (*baikalite* or *malacolite*).
Outokumpu, Finland: fine deep green Cr-diopside.
Nammakal, India: star stones and catseyes, also dark green facetable material.
Franklin, New Jersey: jeffersonite.
Långban, Sweden: jeffersonite.
Schefferite and Zn-schefferite also come from the last two localities.

Stone Sizes: New York material provides cutting rough of fine quality and large size. The Italian and Swiss and Austrian diopsides are usually smaller but of fine color. Madagascar diopside is very dark green and less attractive, up to about 20 carats. Chrome diopsides are known up to about 10–15 carats in general, and other locations provide material that cuts 2–10 carat gems.
AMNH: 38.0 (green, New York).
SI: 133.0 (black, star, India); 24.1 (black, catseye, India); 19.2 (green, Madagascar) 6.8 (yellow, Italy); 4.6 (yellow, Burma).

Comments: Violane has been used for beads and inlay—transparent material is always very tiny. The color of this material is deep violet or blue and is very rare. Catseye material cuts extremely sharp eyes, the best being from Burma. Faceted diopside is not extremely rare, but large clean stones are (over 15 carats). Colors are usually dark, so a bright and attractive gem is most desirable. Hedenbergite and the intermediate varieties tend to always be opaque except in very thin splinters.

Name: Greek words meaning *appearing double*.

DIOPTASE

Formula: $CuSiO_2(OH)_2$.

Crystallography: Hexagonal. Fine crystals are common in certain localities; stubby, elongated.

Colors: Rich emerald green; bluish green.

Streak: Pale blue-green.

Luster: Vitreous; greasy on fractures.

Hardness: 5.

Density: 3.28–3.35.

Cleavage: Perfect 1 direction. Fracture conchoidal to uneven. Brittle.

Optics: $o = 1.644–1.658$; $e = 1.697–1.709$. Uniaxial (+).

Birefringence: 0.053.

Dispersion: 0.036.

Spectral: Broad band at about 5500; strong absorption of blue and violet.

Luminescence: None.

Occurrence: Oxidized zone of copper deposits.
Zaire; Chile; U.S.S.R.
Arizona: microscopic crystals.
Guchab and Tsumeb, S.W. Africa: world's finest crystals, some transparent but mostly filled with cleavage

planes and fractures. These crystals are superb color, on matrix, and up to 2 inches long.

Stone Sizes: Crystals may be fairly large, but clean areas within such crystals are always very small, and stones are never larger than 1–2 carats. Cabochons are sometimes cut from translucent masses up to about 15 carats.

Comments: Dioptase is abundant in mineral collections throughout the world and is not considered a great rarity, but faceted gems are extremely rare due to a paucity of clean fragments. Clean stones over 1 carat are virtually nonexistent and few collections have stones at all. Cabochons are blue-green, translucent, and quite attractive, but are much too soft for wear.

Name: From Greek words meaning *to see through*, because the cleavage directions can be determined just by looking into the crystals.

DOLOMITE

Formula: $CaMg(Co_3)_2$ $\begin{cases} + Fe \\ + Mn, Zn, Pb, and Co. \end{cases}$
Note: $CaFe(CO_3)_2$ = Ankerite. $CaMn(CO_3)_2$ = Kutnahorite. There is complete series from dolomite, through ferroan dolomite, to ankerite.

Crystallography: Hexagonal (R). Crystals rhomb-shaped, sometimes with curved faces; saddle-shaped; massive or granular; twinning common.

Colors: Colorless, white, gray, green, pale brown, pink (Mn present). *Ankerite* is tan to brown, and *kutnahorite* is pink. *Dolomite* may also be pink due to Co.

Luster: Vitreous to pearly.

Hardness: 3.5–4; varies with direction in crystal.

Density: 2.85, as high as 2.93; ankerite, 2.93–3.10.

Cleavage: Perfect 1 direction. Fracture subconchoidal. Brittle.

Optics:
dolomite: o = 1.679–1.703; e = 1.500–1.520. Uniaxial (−).
ankerite: o = 1.690–1.750; e = 1.510–1.548. Uniaxial (−).
Indices increase from dolomite values with increasing substitution of iron.

Birefringence: 0.179–0.185. (Ankerite, 0.182–0.202).

Spectral: Not diagnostic.

Luminescence: Orange, blue, pale green, creamy white, weak brown in SW.
Orange, blue, pale green, creamy white in LW.

Occurrence: In sedimentary rocks; in Mg-rich igneous rocks that have been altered; geodes.
Quebec; Mexico; Brazil; Germany; Austria; Switzerland. Missouri, Oklahoma, Kansas: so-called Tri-State Mineral Region.

Keokuk, Iowa: in geodes.
New Mexico: transparent material, cuttable.
Eugua, Navarra, Spain: magnificent crystals and clusters, often large size and completely transparent, perfectly formed.
Cobaltian dolomite (pink) from *Pribram, Czechoslovakia.*
Kutnahorite from *Czechoslovakia and Hungary.*
Ankerite is a mineral of veins and hydrothermal or low-temperature deposits.

Stone Sizes: Massive material is generally carved; often it is stained pretty colors, and may be naturally color-banded. Facetable dolomite from New Mexico reaches a size of about 5 carats cut. Spanish material can provide stones over 100 carats.

Comments: Dolomite is a rarely seen gem with distinctive birefringence (as a carbonate), but is too soft and fragile for wear. Spanish crystals are widely sold to collectors so transparent material is fairly abundant.

Name: After Deodat Dolomieu, French engineer and mineralogist.

DOMEYKITE   See: Algodonite.

DRAVITE   See: Tourmaline.

DUMORTIERITE   See also: Holtite.

Formula: $Al_7O_3(BO_3)(SiO_4)_3$.

Crystallography: Orthorhombic. Crystals prismatic and very rare; usually massive, fibrous, granular.

Colors: Blue, violet, brown, pinkish.

Luster: Virtreous to dull.

Hardness: 8–8.5; massive varieties 7.

Density: 3.41 (but as low as 3.26).

Cleavage: Good 1 direction. Splintery or uneven fracture.

Optics: α = 1.686; β = 1.722; γ = 1.723. Biaxial (−), $2V$ = 13°.

Pleochroism: Black/brown/red-brown.

Luminescence: Blue in SW (France); also blue-white to violet in SW (Calif.).

Spectral: Not diagnostic.

Occurrence: In aluminous metamorphic rocks; in pegmatites.
California; Montana; Woodstock, Washington.
Champion Mine, Nevada: violet gem material.
France; Madagascar.
Ceylon: transparent and reddish-brown.

Stone Sizes: Massive blue and violet material occurs in pieces weighing several pounds. Only a small amount of facetable material has ever been found (Ceylon) and only a few cut stones may exist. These are all tiny (less than 2 carats).

Comments: Dumortierite is a beautiful and very hard material eminently suitable for jewelry in the form of cabochons. Arizona dumortierite is actually an impregnation of this mineral in quartz. Faceted gems are virtually unobtainable and absent from even the most comprehensive collections. Excellent catseyes have been cut from fibrous material.

Name: After M. Eugene Dumortier, a paleontologist.

E

EILAT STONE   See Chrysocolla.

EKANITE

Formula: (Th, U)(Ca, Fe, Pb)$_2$Si$_8$O$_{20}$.

Crystallography: Tetragonal. Crystals elongated parallel to long crystal axis; massive pebbles.

Colors: Green, dark brown.

Luster: Vitreous.

Hardness: 5–6.5.

Density: 3.28–3.32.

Cleavage: None.

Optics: $o = 1.573$; $e = 1.572$. Uniaxial (−).

Birefringence: 0.001

Spectral: May show lines at 6300 and 6580.

Luminescence: Not diagnostic.

Occurrence: Discovered in 1953 as waterworn, translucent green pebbles at *Eheliyagoda, near Ratnapura, Ceylon.* Occurs in the gem gravels. Some cut Ceylon stones have 4-rayed stars.
Mt. Ste. Hilaire, Quebec.
Also noted from *Central Asia.*

Stone Sizes: A stone was tested by the London Gem Labs in 1975: 43.8 carats, blackish color, S.G. = 3.288, R.I. = 1.595 (average); radioactive; 2 spectral lines seen.

Comments: Ekanite is metamict as a result of the U and Th content. The properties vary, depending on the degree of breakdown of the structure. Ekanite is one of the very rarest of all gems, and only a few are known. More undoubtedly exist, that have been sold as other Ceylon gems, but the total number of gems is a mere handful.

Name: After F. L. D. Ekanayake who first found it in a Ceylon gravel pit.

ELAEOLITE   See: Nepheline.

ELBAITE   See: Tourmaline.

EMERALD   See: Beryl.

ENSTATITE   *Orthopyroxene group:* Bronzite; Hypersthene; Ferrohypersthene; Ferrosilite.

Composition: This is a complex solid solution series involving Fe and Mg silicates. The series extends from enstatite: MgSiO$_3$, through bronzite: (Mg, Fe)SiO$_3$, hypersthene (Fe, Mg)SiO$_3$, to orthoferrosilite: FeSiO$_3$. Like the plagioclase feldspars, the series is arbitrarily broken into 6 regions of composition (numbers refer to % of orthoferrosilite molecule in formula):

0	10	30	50	70	90	100
Enstatite	Bronzite	Hypersthene	Ferrohypersthene	Eulite	Orthoferrosilite	

Crystallography: Orthorhombic. Crystals are prismatic and not common for most members of the series. Twinning is common, visible as lamellae in crystals; often crystals have interleaved lamellae of ortho- and clinopyroxenes.

Colors: *Enstatite* is colorless, gray, green, yellow, and brown. The same range applies to *bronzite.* *Hypersthene* is green, brown, grayish-black. *Orthoferrosilite* tends to be green or dark brown, somber tones.

Luster: *Enstatite* is vitreous. *Bronzite* is vitreous to submetallic. *Hypersthene* is vitreous, pearly or silky. *Orthoferrosilite* is vitreous.

Hardness: 5–6 for the whole series.

Cleavage: Good in 1 direction for all species in series.

Optic Sign: The optic sign changes along the series, from (+) to (−) and back to (+). The break points are at 12% and 88% orthoferrosilite:

0 (+) 12	(−)	88 (+) 100
Enstatite		Orthoferrosilite

Dispersion: Generally low, and becomes zero when $2V = 90°$ and $2V = 50°$.

Birefringence: In general, lower than that for the clinopyroxenes. (See table.)

	Enstatite	Bronzite	Hypersthene	Orthoferrosilite
Density	3.20–3.30	3.30–3.43	3.43–3.90	3.90–3.96
Optics				
α	1.650–1.665	1.665–1.686	1.686–1.755	1.755–1.768
β	1.653–1.671	(intermediate)		1.763–1.770
γ	1.658–1.680	1.680–1.703	1.703–1.772	1.772–1.788
sign	(+)	(−)	(−)	(+)
Birefringence	0.007–0.009	0.009–0.012	0.012–0.021	0.021–0.022

Pleochroism: The entire series has a characteristic pleochroism: pink to green.

α: pale red-brown/purplish/brown pink.

β: pale greenish-brown/pale reddish-yellow/pale brown/yellow.

γ: pale green/smoky green/green.

Spectral: All gems in this series show a strong line at 5060, and often at 5475.

Tanzanian gems: also diffuse lines at 4550, 4880, 5550.
Arizona gems: diffuse line at 4880.
Ceylon gems: diffuse line at 5550.
Brazil and Indian gems: diffuse lines at 4880, 5550
Other lines noted: 5090, 5025, 4830, 4590, 4490.

Luminescence: None.

Occurrence: Mg-rich members of the series are common in basic and ultrabasic rocks; also in layered intrusions; volcanic rocks; high-grade metamorphic rocks; regionally metamorphosed rocks and hornfels; meteorites.

Gem enstatite occurs in *Burma, Ceylon, Tanzania,* and *Arizona.*

Other noteworthy localities are *Norway, California,* and *Germany.*

India produces star enstatites, with 4-rayed stars.

Rare green gems come from *Kimberley, S. Africa.*

Bronzite comes from *Mysore, India* and *Styria, Austria*; 6-rayed bronzite stars have been found.

Hypersthene is noted from *Norway, Greenland, Germany,* and *California,* with gem material from *Baja California,* and *Mexico.*

Bastite is an altered enstatite, S.G. = 2.6, hardness = 3.5–4, opaque, from which cabochons are cut. Localities: *Burma* and *Harz Mountains, Germany.*

Stone Sizes: In general, gems from this series are small, because large ones are too dark in color to be attractive and crystals tend to be small. The exception is star stones, of which large examples exist. Enstatites and hypersthenes of 5–10 carats, if clean and lively in color, are very rare stones. Indian star enstatites over 50 carats are frequently encountered, but Indian faceted gems over 10 carats are rare.

ROM: 12.97 (Burma, enstatite).

SI: 11.0 (enstatite, brown, Ceylon); 3.9 (enstatite, brown, Austria).

PC: 4.5 (hypersthene, brown, Africa); 26.6 (enstatite, green, India).

Inclusions: In hypersthene have been noted tabular scales of hematite and goethite.

Comments: Most gem enstatites have indices in the range 1.663–1.673. The brown and green gems from Tanzania are enstatites, as are the brownish-green stones from Ceylon. Green and brown gems from India and Brazil tend to be in the bronzite composition range. The gems of the orthopyroxene series are usually very dark, slightly brittle because of cleavage, and generally not

appealing for jewelry purposes. The 4-rayed star gems are widely sold at very low cost, and the material is extremely plentiful. However, clean gems of hypersthene and enstatite are not abundant, except in very small (1–2 carat) sizes. Even in this size the colors tend to be dark and muddy. These are all true collector gemstones. Orthoferrosilite is included for completeness, and has no gem significance.

Names: *Enstatite* from the Greek for *an opponent* because of its high melting point. *Bronzite* is named for its bronzy color and luster. *Hypersthene* is from the Greek words for *very strong* or *tough. Orthoferrosilite* is named for its crystallography and composition.

EOSPHORITE *Series to* CHILDRENITE *if Fe exceeds Mn.*

Formula: $(Mn, Fe)AlPO_4(OH)_2 \cdot H_2O$.

Crystallography: Monoclinic (pseudo-orthorhombic). Crystals prismatic, often twinned.

Colors: Colorless, pale pink, pale yellow, light brown, reddish brown, black.

Luster: Vitreous to resinous.

Hardness: 5.

Density: 3.05 (pure Mn end member); 3.08 (Brazil).

Cleavage: Poor; fracture uneven to subconchoidal.

Optics: $\alpha = 1.638-1.639$; $\beta = 1.660-1.664$; $\gamma = 1.667-1.671$.
Biaxial (−), $2V = 50°$.

Birefringence: 0.029–0.035. (*Note:* less than childrenite.)

Pleochroism: Distinct: yellow/pink/pale pink to colorless.

Spectral: Strong line at 4100, moderate at 4900 (in brownish pink material).

Luminescence: None observed.

Occurrence: In granite pegmatites, usually associated with Mn phosphates.

Branchville, Connecticut; Maine; Keystone, South Dakota; North Groton, New Hampshire.

Hagendorf, Germany.

Minas Gerais, Brazil: excellent, flat, pink crystals up to 4 × 1 cm, at Itinga.

Stone Sizes: Cut eosphorites are always small, usually less than 3–4 carats. Cuttable crystals are usually very small and badly flawed, only from the Brazil localities.

Comments: Pink gems are extremely attractive when cut, especially as round brilliants. The hardness makes wear unrecommended; cutting presents no great problems. This is a very rare gemstone, seen only in a few collections.

Name: From Greek *eosphoros,* meaning *dawn-bearing,* in allusion to the pink color.

EPIDOTE GROUP

The epidote group consists of three related minerals that are fairly well-known to collectors and hobbyists, plus one popular gem mineral and three less common species. These minerals are monoclinic and orthorhombic.

Formula: The general formula of the epidote group is $X_2Y_3Z_3(O, OH, F)_{13}$, where X = Ca, Ce, La, Y, Th, Fe, Mn; Y = Al, Fe, Mn, Ti; Z = Si, Be.

Zoisite and *Clinozoisite:* $Ca_2Al_3Si_3O_{12}(OH)$.
Epidote: $Ca_2(Al, Fe)_3Si_3O_{12}(OH)$.
Piedmontite: $Ca_2(Mn, Fe, Al)_3Si_3O_{12}(OH)$
(also called *piemontite*).
Allanite: $(Ca, Ce, La, Y)_2(Mn, Fe, Al)_3Si_3O_{12}(OH)$.
Mukhinite: $Ca_2(Al_2V)Si_3O_{12}(OH)$.
Hancockite: $(Pb, Ca, Sr)_2(Al, Fe)_3Si_3O_{12}(OH)$.

Crystallography: All are Monoclinic, except *zoisite* which is Orthorhombic. Crystals prismatic and tabular; also granular, massive, fibrous; sometimes twinned, often striated.

Colors: *Clinozoisite* is colorless, pale yellow, gray, green, pink; often zoned.
Epidote shows shades of green, yellow, gray, grayish white, greenish black, black.
Piedmontite is reddish brown, black, rose red, pink.
Hancockite is brownish or black.
Allanite is light brown to black.
Zoisite is gray, green, brown, pink (*thulite*), yellowish, blue to violet (*tanzanite*).

Luster: Vitreous; pearly on cleavages; massive materials dull. Allanite resinous, pitchy.

Hardness: 6–7. Epidote sometimes slightly harder, piedmontite softer.

Luminescence: Usually none. Thulite (pink zoisite) from Nevada sometimes medium pale brown in SW. Also thulite from North Carolina is orangy-yellow in LW.

Cleavage: Perfect 1 direction in all (different orientation in zoisite). Fracture conchoidal to uneven. Brittle.

Pleochroism: None in clinozoisite. Distinct red to yellowish brown in hancockite.
Allanite: reddish brown/ brownish yellow/greenish brown;
light brown/brown/dark red-brown;
colorless/pale green/green.

Epidote: colorless, pale yellow or yellow-green/ greenish yellow/yellow-green.
Zoisite: deep blue/purple/green (tanzanite); pale pink/colorless/yellow *or* dark pink/ pink/yellow (thulite).
Piedmontite: yellow/amethystine violet/red.

Spectral: Most members of the group have non-diagnostic spectrum; epidote has very strong line at 4550, weak line sometimes seen at 4750. This spectrum is very sensitive to direction within the material and is not visible in certain orientations. Tanzanite has a broad absorption in the yellow-green centered at 5950, with faint bands also at 5280, *4550*, and a few weak lines in the red.

Occurrence: The minerals of the epidote group form at low temperatures, in low- to medium-grade metamorphic rocks. Allanite is more commonly found in igneous rocks such as pegmatites. Clinozoisite and epidote are also found in igneous rocks, and piedmontite in schists and manganese ore deposits. Zoisite occurs in calcareous rocks such as metamorphosed dolomites and calcareous shales subjected to regional metamorphism.
Epidote:
McFall Mine, Ramona, California; Idaho; Colorado; Michigan; Connecticut; Massachusetts; New Hampshire.
Baja California, Mexico; Arendal, Norway; Czechoslovakia; U.S.S.R.; Japan; Korea; Australia; Kenya; Madagascar.
Switzerland: many localities.
Bourg d'Oisans, France: fine crystals.
Italy: Piedmont, other localities.
Untersulzbachthal, Austria: main source of faceting rough.
Burma: at Tawmaw, a chrome-rich material, fine deep green color (tawmawite).
Outokumpu, Finland: chromiferous epidote (tawmawite).
Minas Gerais, Brazil: cuttable, yellowish-green crystals. (these are trichroic, low in iron; indices 1.722/1.737/ 1.743; birefringence 0.021, density 3.3–3.5)
Blue Ridge, Unaka Range, North Carolina (also in Virginia, Georgia): unakite, a granite consisting of pink feldspar and green epidote. A similar rock is also known from Rhodesia.
Clinozoisite:
Nevada; Colorado.

	Clinozoisite	Epidote	Piedmontite	Hancockite	Allanite	Zoisite
Density	3.21–3.38	3.38–3.49	3.45–3.52	4.03	3.4–4.2	3.15–3.38
Optics						
α	1.670–1.715	1.715–1.751	1.732–1.794	1.788	1.640–1.791	1.685–1.705
β	1.675–1.725	1.725–1.784	1.750–1.807	1.810	1.650–1.815	1.688–1.710
γ	1.690–1.734	1.734–1.797	1.762–1.829	1.830	1.660–1.828	1.697–1.725
2V	(+)14–90°	(−)90–116°	(+)2–9°	(−)50°	(±)40–123°	(+)0–60°
Birefringence	0.005–0.015	0.015–0.049	0.025–0.073	0.042	0.013–0.036	0.004–0.008

Timmons, Ontario, Canada; Ireland; Iceland; India; Italy; Switzerland; Austria; Czechoslovakia.
Kenya: gray-green crystals.
Gavilanes, Baja, Mexico: brownish, facetable crystals. crystals.
Piedmontite:
Pennsylvania; Missouri.
Scotland; Vermland, Sweden; Morbihan, France; Japan; Otago, New Zealand.
California and Arizona: many localities.
Piemonte, Italy: in sericite schists.
Egypt: in a porphyry, colored red by piedmontite.
Hancockite:
Franklin, New Jersey is only notable locality, in small crystals.
Allanite:
Various localities throughout the *U.S.*
Canada; Norway; Sweden; Greenland; U.S.S.R.; Madagascar.
Zoisite:
South Dakota; Massachusetts.
Wyoming: greenish gray material, sometimes tumble-polished for jewelry.
Washington: thulite.
California and Nevada: thulite.
North Carolina: thulite.
Baja, Mexico; Scotland; Austria; Finland; U.S.S.R.; Japan; Germany.
Longido, Tanzania: deep green crystals, colored by chromium, with ruby crystals.
Lelatema, Tanzania: fine blue-violet crystals, up to large size, often gemmy (tanzanite).
Norway: thulite.
Greenland: thulite.

Stone Sizes: Unakite occurs in huge blocks weighing many pounds, and is often cut into spheres as well as cabochons. Facetable epidote is rare over 5 carat sizes, and cut clinozoisite tends to be even smaller. Allanite is hardly ever cut except as cabochons, and piedmontite is opaque and massive, cut as cabochons only. Tanzanite is the only member of the epidote group that reaches large sizes in faceted gems. Rough tanzanite crystals weighing hundreds of carats have been found.
SI: 122.7 (blue, tanzanite, Tanzania); 18.2 (blue catseye tanzanite, Tanzania); 3.9 (epidote, brown, Austria).
DG: 7.30 (clinozoisite, brownish, Iran); 6.90 (epidote, brown).
PC: 220 (blue, tanzanite, Tanzania).

Comments: The epidote minerals are very interesting and span a wide range of the gem market.

Hancockite is very rare, from New Jersey, and if a faceted gem exists it would be extremely small (under 1-2 carats).

Epidote is usually so dark in color that a large faceted gem is nearly black, lifeless, and uninteresting; small

stones, under 3-4 carats, are often bright and lively, however.

Clinozoisite would be a better-looking gem, but is very rare in sizes over 5 carats. The only well known gem source of the latter is Baja, Mexico, though an occasional crystal from another locality yields a fine gem.

Allanite is very dark in color and seldom cut. The content of rare earth and radioactive elements causes it to become metamict with severe damage to the internal crystalline structure.

Unakite is a widely used and popular cabochon material that is exported throughout the world. It is best known from the U.S., but Ireland, Rhodesia, and probably other countries have similar rocks.

Mukhinite is a very rare mineral, in small grains from Gornaya Shoriya, U.S.S.R., and has never been cut.

Piedmontite is a distinct species, but is often confused with thulite,which is a pink manganiferous variety of the species zoisite; piedmontite is dark brown or reddish in color, seldom in large masses, while thulite can occur in large pieces and is often bright pink in color. Both materials can be cut and make lovely cabochons.

Pure clinozoisite is very rare; it usually contains some iron, and there is a complete solid solution series from it to epidote.

Tawmawite is a deep emerald-green epidote from Burma, the color of which is due to chromium. This material is very rare.

Tanzanite is the best known member of the epidote group, and is a variety of zoisite. The name was given by Tiffany & Co. in connection with a trade promotion, and the name stuck although it has no mineralogical significance. Tanzanite occurs in a variety of colors at the Tanzanian locality, but most crystals are heated to about 700° F. because they then turn a deep, intense blue color with violet dichroism. Tanzanite is quite soft and brittle, considering it is a popular ringstone, and great care should be exercised in wearing it. Inclusions that have been noted in tanzanite include actinolite, graphite and staurolite. (Tanzanite indices are 1.692/1.693/1.700; Birefringence 0.009.)

Epidote group minerals often contain fibrous inclusions that create a chatoyancy and yield catseye gems when cut into cabochons. Catseye clinozoisite and epidote are known. Catseye tanzanites are very rare, but have been found.

Names: *Zoisite* is named after Baron von Zois, who presented Werner, the great mineralogist, with the first specimens of the material. *Thulite* is after Thule, the ancient name for Norway. *Tanzanite* is the Tiffany & Co. tradename for blue zoisite, named after the country of origin, Tanzania. *Clinozoisite* is the monoclinic dimorph of zoisite. *Piedmontite (piemontite)* is after the locality in Italy, Piemonte (Piedmont). *Unakite* is named after the Unaka range of mountains in the U.S. *Allanite* is named after mineralogist T. Allan.

EUCLASE

Formula: $BeAlSiO_4(OH)$.

Crystallography: Crystals tabular or prismatic, often well developed.

Colors: Colorless, white, pale blue, pale green, violet, yellow.

Luster: Vitreous.

Hardness: 6.5–7.5. May be variable within a single crystal.

Density: 3.08 (colorless); 3.05–3.10.

Cleavage: Perfect 1 direction. Fracture conchoidal. Brittle.

Optics: $\alpha = 1.650–1.651$; $\beta = 1.655–1.658$; $\gamma = 1.671–1.676$.
Biaxial (+), $2V = 50°$.

Birefringence: 0.020–0.025.

Dispersion: 0.016.

Spectral: There are 2 vague bands at 4680 and 4550; if Cr is present it may display a characteristic spectrum in the red with a doublet at 7050.

Luminescence: Feeble or none.

Occurrence: Euclase is a mineral of granite pegmatites.
Colorado.
Bôa Vista, Minas Gerais, Brazil; Ireland; Austria; Norway.
Ouro Prieto, Minas Gerais, Brazil: fine gem material in good crystals up to a length of about 6 cm. Also at *Santana de Encoberto, Minas Gerais, Brazil (note:* material from this locality has a high birefringence).
Orenburg dist., So. Urals, U.S.S.R.: in cuttable crystals.
Tanzania: Morogoro district.

Stone Sizes: Crystals are more commonly found in small sizes, about 1 inch for colorless material. Most euclase is colorless, and colored crystals are very rare. Blue and green gems are very scarce over 2–3 carats, as are colorless stones over ca 5–6 carats.
SI: 12.5 (green, Brazil); 8.9 (yellow, Brazil); 3.7 (blue-green, Brazil).
PC: Violet crystals (Brazil) that would cut a gem ca 10 carats; 7.43 (blue, Brazil).
DG: 15.45 (colorless, Brazil); 14.0 (mint green, Brazil).

Comments: Euclase is a hard enough gem to be worn safely in jewelry. It is not terribly exciting to look at in colorless stones, but the colored gems are truly beautiful and exceedingly rare if over 1–2 carats. Stones can be very brilliant, but the cleavage makes cutting difficult.

Name: From the Greek *eu* (*easy*) and *klasis* (fracture), because of the easy cleavage.

EULITE See: Enstatite.

EUXENITE *Series to* POLYCRASE.

Formula: $(Y, Ca, Ce, U, Th)(Nb, Ta, Ti)_2O_6$;
Polycrase: $(Y, Ca, Ce, U, Th)(Ti, Nb, Ta)_2O_6$.

Crystallography: Orthorhombic. Crystals prismatic, stubby; as aggregates; massive.

Colors: Black, sometimes with a tinge of brown or green.

Streak: Grayish, yellow-brown.

Luster: Submetallic; vitreous to resinous.

Hardness: 5.5–6.5.

Density: 4.30–5.87 depending on the Ta content and hydration.

Cleavage: None. Fracture conchoidal. Brittle.

Optics: Isotropic due to metamictization. $N = 2.06–2.24$.

Luminescence: None.

Occurrence: In granite pegmatites; also as detrital grains.
California; Colorado; Pennsylvania; Maine.
Norway; Canada; Greenland; Brazil; Finland; Zaire; Madagascar; Australia.
Wyoming: large crystals.

Stone Sizes: Gems cut from euxenite are almost always small, as the material is seldom transparent.

Comments: Euxenite is a material seldom seen in collections. Most collectors would not regard the mineral as facetable, but transparent fragments and areas of crystals have been noted that could cut small gems. Sometimes cabochons are cut by collectors but these are not very striking. The colors of faceted stones would be too dark to make them appealing.

Name: From the Greek *euxenos* (hospitable) because of the many useful elements it contains. *Polycrase* is from the Greek, meaning *mixture of many*, also in allusion to the composition.

FAYALITE   See: Olivine.

FELDSPARS

Feldspars are the most common minerals at the earth's surface. In fact, if the entire composition of the earth's crust were regarded as a single mineral, it would calculate out almost exactly as a feldspar.

The feldspars are complex aluminosilicate minerals containing K, Na, and Ca, with some rarer types rich in Ba. The structures of these species are very similar. However, most feldspars crystallize from a melt in igneous rocks. The structures at high temperatures are different from those at low temperatures. In addition, the various compositions that may exist at high temperatures may not be stable at low temperatures. When a feldspar cools, it may segregate internally into separate mineral crystals, one type oriented within the other according to the symmetry of the host crystal. The specific type of intergrowth, composition of the minerals involved and the size of the included crystals all depend on the original high-temperature composition and the cooling history of the feldspar, which may be very complex. It is easy to see why it may take years for a mineralogist simply to understand the complexities of the feldspar group, let alone contribute new data.

These complications, while both troublesome and intriguing to mineralogists, are not critical to gemological discussions. We may therefore simplify the discussion to a summary of the basic feldspar species and their properties, insofar as these are relevant to gemstones.

Potassium Feldspars: These all have the composition $KAlSi_3O_8$ but differ in structure. *Orthoclase* is monoclinic; *Sanidine* and *Anorthoclase* are also monoclinic, but the distribution of atoms within the structure is distinctive and different from each other and orthoclase. *Microcline* is triclinic. The properties are summarized in the table below. Sanidine and anorthoclase contain appreciable sodium.

Plagioclase Feldspars: The term plagioclase indicates a solid solution series, ranging in composition from *albite:* $NaAlSi_3O_8$ to *anorthite:* $CaAl_2Si_2O_8$; for convenience the series was long ago divided into six distinct species (arbitrarily), as follows: *albite* (Ab); *oligoclase* (Og); *andesine* (Ad); *labradorite* (La); *bytownite* (By); *anorthite* (An). The series is divided according to the relative percentages of albite vs. anorthite:

	Ab	Og	Ad	La	By	An
Ab	100 90	70	50	30	10	0

The optical parameters vary nearly linearly with composition, but because of the structural complexities, X-ray diffraction work is usually advised in identification of a plagioclase feldspar. Most plagioclase crystals are twinned according to various laws which are related to the crystal structures and also the distribution of atoms in the structures. Zoning is common, and is due to variation in the growth history of the crystals and to the fact that, in a magma, the composition of the melt changes as crystallization proceeds and minerals are extracted from the molten mass. The properties of a plagioclase crystal

Properties of the Potassium Feldspars.

	Microcline	Orthoclase	Sanidine/Anorthoclase
Crystallography	Triclinic	Monoclinic	Monoclinic
Twinning	Lamellar twinning is not seen in the potassium feldspars		
Hardness	6–6.5	6–6.5	6
Density	2.54–2.63	2.55–2.63	2.56–2.62
Optics			
α	1.514–1.529	1.518–1.529	1.518–1.527
β	1.518–1.533	1.522–1.533	1.522–1.532
γ	1.521–1.539	1.522–1.539	1.522–1.534
sign	(−)	(−)	(−)
$2V$	66–103°	33–103°	18–54°
Dispersion	—	0.012	—
Spectral	none dist.	strong 4200 line; bands at 4450, 4200	none dist.
Luminescence	yellow-green in LW; inert SW; green in X-rays.	weak blue in LW or orange in SW; white to violet in X-rays.	N.D.

may therefore vary widely within a small grain. Plagioclases also are often clouded, i.e. contain dustlike particles of other minerals, including spinel, rutile, garnet, magnetite, clinozoisite, muscovite.

Compositions within the feldspar group are complicated by the fact that K may enter the plagioclase structure, or Na the orthoclase structure. The resulting compositions are known as ternary (3-component) feldspars. In addition, as in the plagioclase series itself, high temperature mixed feldspar compositions are stable, but at low temperatures unmixing occurs, i.e., a segregation of the potassic and sodic molecules into separate feldspar phases, one distributed within the other. This creates such oddities as *perthites* (mixtures of albite with oligoclase or orthoclase), *sunstone,moonstone*, and *peristerites*, which are albite—oligoclase mixtures. The presence of feldspar lamellae in another feldspar gives rise to the Schiller effect, an iridescence due to light refraction. In labradorites the Schiller is best developed, creating a lovely color play in shades of green, blue, gold and yellow. The color may be homogeneous or vary within a single feldspar crystal.

Most feldspar crystals are tabular and flattened, and are (in the case of plagioclase) usually complexly twinned. All the plagioclases are triclinic, and all the feldspars have excellent cleavage in 2 directions. The luster is vitreous, inclining to pearly on the cleavages. Feldspars are sometimes massive, cleavable or granular.

Microcline may be colorless, white, pink, yellow, red, gray or green to blue-green. The latter color is popular in gem circles, and the blue-green variety known as *amazonite* is widely cut into cabochons, beads, and carvings. Orthoclase is usually colorless, white, gray, yellow, reddish and greenish, while sanidine is colorless, pinkish or brownish. The plagioclases are all colorless, white or gray, though the drabness is often broken by spectacular Schiller effects. Moonstones may be colored by impurities such as goethite (brown).

Microcline
Occurrence: Microcline occurs in acidic alkali-rich plutonic rocks; also in rocks such as pegmatites, granites, syenites, and schists.
Pala, California; Maine; New York; North Carolina.

U.S.S.R.; Norway; Sweden; Germany; Italy; Japan; South Africa.
Colorado (Pike's Peak area): amazonite.
Amelia Courthouse, Virginia: finest amazonite in U.S.
South Dakota: perthite.
Canada: perthite, especially Ontario and Quebec.
Brazil: fine amazonite.
India (Kashmir district): amazonite.

Stone Sizes: Amazonite cabochons up to almost any sizes are available; the material is usually sold by the pound to hobbyists. The same applies to perthite. The Amelia material has fine color and translucency, but perfect cleavage adds fragility.

Comments: Microcline crystals associated with smoky quartz, are popular mineral specimens from the Pike's Peak area of Colorado. The color of amazonite ranges from pale green to dark green and blue-green. Often pinkish orthoclase is also present as an intergrowth.

Orthoclase
Occurrence: A component of many rocks, especially alkalic and plutonic acid rocks, also granites, pegmatites, syenites.
Many localities in the *U.S.*
Canada.
Switzerland: fine crystals, known as *adularia* (S.G. = 2.56), from the St. Gotthard Region; the material contains some Na.
Itrongahy, Madagascar: fine, transparent yellow orthoclase in large crystals, usually with rounded faces. (Indices 1.522/1.527; birefringence 0.005, S.G. 2.56.) Faceted gems may be very large and deep in color.
Greenland: brownish transparent crystals to more than 2 inches.
Tvedestrand, Norway: orthoclase *sunstone*, deep red-orange, in masses up to a few inches in size.
Ceylon: in the gem gravels.
Burma: gravels.

Stones Sizes: Madagascar produces by far the largest cuttable orthoclase known.
SI: 249.6 (yellow, Madagascar); 104.5 (pale green catseye, Ceylon); 22.7 (white star, Ceylon); 6.0 (North Carolina, colorless).

Properties of Plagioclase Feldspars.

	Albite	Oligoclase	Andesine	Labradorite	Bytownite	Anorthite
Hardness of all species = 6—6.5						
Density	2.57—2.69	2.62—2.67	2.65—2.69	2.69—2.72	2.72—2.75	2.75—2.77
Optics						
α	1.527	1.542	1.543	1.560	1.561	1.577
β	1.531	1.546	1.548	1.563	1.565	1.585
γ	1.538	1.549	1.551	1.572	1.570	1.590
sign	(+)	(−)	(+/−)	(+)	(−)	(−)
$2V$	77°	82°	76—86°	85°	86°	70°
Birefringence	0.011	0.007	0.008	0.012	0.009	0.013

Comments: Yellow and colorless catseye gems are known from Burma and Ceylon. Some of these (Ceylon) are also asteriated. Yellow faceted orthoclase is a handsome gemstone. Unfortunately, the cleavage makes it less advantageous for wear. Also, fine rough is hard to find, but large stones are displayed in museums. Orthoclase moonstone is also found and will be discussed with plagioclase moonstones.

Sanidine

Occurrence: A component of acid igneous rocks. *Oregon; California.*
Near Koblenz, Germany: brown transparent gems, S.G. 2.57−2.58, birefringence 0.007, indices: 1.516−1.520/ 1.521/1.525/1.522−1.526.
Ashton, Idaho: sanidine crystals in volcanic tuff, up to 1 cm, colorless, well formed. Indices: 1.516−1.519/ 1.520−1.522/1.521−1.523; $2V = 8-19°$; birefringence 0.003−0.005.

Stone Sizes: Sanidine is not a common mineral, and is hardly ever seen as a gemstone. Crystals tend to be colorless and nondescript, and are rare in cuttable sizes.

Comments: Sanidine is a mineral of volcanic rocks, with little gem significance.

Perthite

Occurrence: Perthite is an intergrowth of albite, oligoclase, plus orthoclase or microcline. The characteristic texture is produced by unmixing from high temperature. The appearance of the material depends on the cooling history, and hence the relative crystal sizes of the different feldspars in the mixture. Usually perthite consists of brown and white lamellae; the white feldspar often has a golden yellow or white Schiller. Perthitic intergrowths are very typical of the whole range of plagioclase compositions, and therefore must be considered one of the most abundant mineral associations in nature.

Fine perthite that is suitable for cutting comes from Dungannon Twp., Ontario in large pieces, as well as from various localities in Quebec, and from other countries.

Peristerite

Occurrence: Peristerite is well known from *Ontario, Canada,* where it is very abundant. It is also found in *Kenya:* S.G. 2.63, R.I. 1.535−1.544.

Comments: Compositions in the calcic oligoclase range (Ab_{76}) cool and unmix to an inhomogeneous mixture of two feldspars, producing a Schiller, which in the case of peristerites is white or bluish. The effect seems to emanate within the body of the feldspar, as a kind of glow.

Albite

Composition: $Ab_{100}-Ab_{90}$.

Crystallography: Triclinic. Twinned; platy crystals.

Colors: Colorless, white, yellow, pink, gray, reddish, greenish.

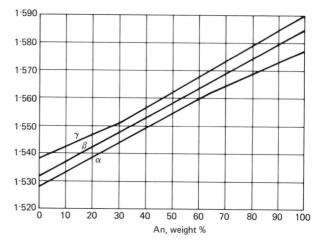

Luster: Vitreous to pearly.

Luminescence: None usually; may be whitish in LW, lime green in X-rays (Kenya).

Spectral: Not diagnostic.

Occur: Albite usually forms at low temperatures; it is common in pegmatites, granite and other igneous rocks, various metamorphic rocks, also marbles.
Essex Co., New York.
Ontario, Canada; Quebec, Canada; Madagascar; Austria.
Rutherford Mine, Amelia, Virginia: fine colorless albite, facetable, large; crystals are platy variety known as *cleavelandite.*
Upson Co., Georgia: moonstone.
South Dakota: cleavelandite.
Brazil: cleavelandite.
Kenya: colorless crystals, some with blue or yellow tinge. (indices: 1.535/1.539/1.544; S.G. 2.63).
Many other localities worldwide.

Stone Sizes: Clean gems are usually in the 1−3 carat range, from cleavelandite crystals. Catseye gems up to about 50 carats are known.
ROM: 12.25 (catseye, Burma).
DG: 11.13 (catseye, white).

Comments: Translucent albite is sometimes found that is colored a rich green by inclusions of chrome-rich jadeite. Albite is sometimes intergrown with emerald, especially in the strange hexagonal skeletal crystals known as *trapiche emeralds.* Facetable albite from Madagascar has indices: $\alpha = 1.530-1.531$; $\beta = 1.532-1.533$; $\gamma = 1.539-1.540$; birefringence 0.009−0.010; density 2.62. Small faceted gems are fairly rare, almost always from the tips of cleavelandite crystals. Albite gems are colorless in most cases, and not exciting to look at. Albite moonstones are known from many localities (discussed below).

Moonstone

Moonstone refers to feldspar of widely varying composition and from a wide variety of localities. The basic attribute is the presence of finely dispersed plates of one feldspar within another, as a result of unmixing on cooling.

Orthoclase moonstone consists of albite within an orthoclase matrix. A blue color is produced if the albite crystals are very fine; the sheen is white if the albite plates are thick. The color of the orthoclase may be white, beige, brown, red-brown, greenish or yellowish. Red coloration is due to goethite (iron oxide) inclusions. Some of this material cuts fine catseyes, where the sheen is concentrated into a narrow band. The sheen in moonstone is referred to as *adularescence.*

The density of such material is 2.56–2.59; material from Ceylon tends to be at the low end of this range, material from India at the higher end. The refractive index is usually 1.520–1.525, birefringence 0.005.

The moonstone from Burma and Ceylon is adularia and displays a white to blue sheen. The body colors may be white, blue, or reddish brown. The blue-sheen material, especially when the body of the moonstone is colorless and transparent, is very rare and greatly prized in large sizes (over 15 carats).

Grant Co., New Mexico produces a very fine quality sanidine moonstone with a blue sheen. Orthoclase moonstone from Virginia is of a quality comparable to the Ceylon material: indices 1.518–1.524, birefringence 0.006. Moonstone also comes from Tanzania and a variety of states in the U.S.

Inclusions: Moonstones are characterized by fissure systems, along incipient cleavages in the body of the material, created by exsolution pressures. Such fissure systems are short parallel cracks with shorter cracks emanating perpendicularly along the length of the parallel fissures. These resemble many-legged insects under the microscope and are known as *centipedes.* Moonstones also have rectangular dark areas due to stress cracking or negative crystals. Sometimes a cavity extends from such a rectangular dark area that creates an inclusion with a comma shape. Burmese moonstones are characterized by oriented needle inclusions.

Stone Sizes: Moonstone is rare in both large size and fine quality, but Indian material with strong body color is abundant and very inexpensive. This is fortunate because the material is well cut and very attractive. Moonstone with a blue sheen is the most valuable, and is rare in stones over 15–20 carats. Stones with a silvery or white adularescence are abundant and available in sizes up to hundreds of carats.

Oligoclase, Andesine, Bytownite, Anorthite

These feldspars are rarely encountered in gem form. Their occurrence is widespread throughout the world, in a great variety of rock types and environments. But in most cases transparent crystals are rare.

In many cases faceted gems are identified as a feldspar in the plagioclase series, but the finder does not have the instrumentation needed to pin down the species. This is accomplished by a combination of optical and X-ray analysis. A few plagioclase gems have been well characterized, however, and reported in the literature.

Occurrence:

Oligoclase is reported from the *Hawk Mine, Bakersville, North Carolina,* in colorless to pale green facetable crystals. The indices are 1.537–1.547, density 2.651. Oligoclase is also reported from *Kenya,* colorless grains, with indices as follows: $\alpha = 1.538-1.540$, $\beta = 1.542-1.544$, $\gamma = 1.549-1.550$; birefringence 0.010–0.011, S.G. 2.64. North Carolina gems up to about 1–5 carats, colorless to pale green, are reported.

Andesine is known from many localities, including *California; Utah; Colorado; South Dakota; Minnesota; New York; North Carolina; Colombia; Argentina; Greenland; Norway; France; Italy; Germany; S.Africa; India; and Japan.*

Bytownite is found in basic plutonic rocks, some metamorphic rocks, and meteorites. Localities include *Montana; South Dakota; Oklahoma; Minnesota; Wisconsin; Scotland; England; Sweden; Japan; S. Africa.* Bytownite is sometimes reddish in color and pebbles from *Arizona* and *New Mexico* have been faceted into small gems. Bytownite is also reported from *Plush, Oregon,* but this is a well known locality for labradorite in facetable crystals; it may be that some of the feldspar has a borderline composition and crosses over into the bytownite range.

Anorthite is the most calcic of the plagioclases, and sometimes makes up a distinctive rock known as *anorthosite,* which has been extensively studied. Localities for the mineral include *Pala, California; Grass Valley, Nevada; Italian Mountains, Colorado; Greenland; England; Sweden; Finland; Italy; Sicily; India; Japan.* Anorthite has been cut for collectors, but very rarely and faceted gems are always small.

Labradorite

Of all the feldspars, none besides orthoclase is as frequently encountered as a faceted gem as is labradorite. The material ranges in color from colorless to yellow, but inclusions of minerals such as hematite create a wide range of other body colors. These are best known from localities in Oregon. In addition, the phenomenon of Schiller is best developed in the labradorite range of plagioclase compositions. Labradorite that is translucent to opaque but which shows blue, green, and golden Schiller colors is widely cut by hobbyists. Labradorite with Schiller is also a component of many dark-colored igneous rocks that are used in building and construction as facing materials, and such rocks are very attractive when polished because the blue sheen of the labradorite grains flashes out at many different angles.

Inclusions: Zircon and magnetite; also ilmenite and rutile tablets (Madagascar). Hematite inclusions create an *aventurescence,* or sparkly effect due to reflection off of parallel included flakes. This reflection creates a rolling sheen of golden red spangles, leading to the name *sunstone.* Sunstone is also characteristic of oligoclase and is discussed below.

Pleochroism: Usually absent in feldspars, but most notable in labradorite from Oregon. It is better developed in darker-colored stones:

Stone color	Pleochroism
Yellow	colorless/light yellow
Red-orange and blue-green (multicolored)	bluish green/light red-violet/reddish orange
Bluish green	bluish green/light orange/colorless
Red orange	orange/light reddish purple
Orange	orange/reddish orange
Yellowish green	bluish green/light orange
Blue-green and violet	red-violet/reddish orange/bluish green

Other Effects: A labradorite moonstone is known from Madagascar. It has a blue sheen and the indices are: $\alpha = 1.550-1.553$, $\gamma = 1.560-1.561$. Birefringence $0.008-0.010$. S.G. 2.70.

Occurrence: Labradorite is best known from *Nain, Labrador:* crystals here are up to 2 feet long, but are badly cracked.
New York; Texas.
Oregon: facetable.
Modoc Co., California: facetable crystals to 1 inch.
Finland: fine Schiller, very intense; cut stones called *spectrolite.*
Clear Lake, Millard Co., Utah: facetable crystals.
Nevada: facetable crystals.
Madagascar: moonstone effect.
Australia: pale yellow, transparent material, indices $\alpha = 1.556$, $\gamma = 1.564$, S.G. 2.695.
Oregon labradorite has the following properties: $\alpha = 1.559-1.563$; $\gamma = 1.569-1.573$, birefringence 0.008, S.G. 2.71-2.73; material is $Ab_{32}An_{68}$.

Stone Sizes: Labradorite rocks are available in very large sizes, suitable for facings of office buildings! This material is sometimes cut into cabochons also. Labradorite in larger crystals, with uniform Schiller (rather than in smaller, randomly oriented grains) is frequently cut into cabochons by hobbyists. The best material for this purpose comes from Finland, but the material is not common and is fairly expensive compared to other feldspars.

Faceted gems up to about 100 carats are known. It is likely that somewhat larger material exists, but fracturing of rough prevents the cutting of larger stones.
SI: 11.1 (yellow, Utah); 5.8 (yellow, Nevada); 23.8 (yellow, Oregon) 39 (yellow, Oregon); 23.43 (yellow, Mexico).
PC: 37.8 (yellow, Mexico).

Comments: The Schiller in labradorite is similar to that in peristerite, but the color range includes blue, green, blue-green, gold, yellow, and purple. The color play is iridescent like the feathers of a peacock.

Faceted labradorite makes a handsome, although unusual jewelry stone. It is as hard as moonstone or any of the other feldspars that are worn regularly in jewelry, but the cleavage is always worth minding. Gems larger than 20 carats can be considered exceptional. Oregon material is abundantly available in the 2-10 carat range.

Sunstone

This is material containing hematite or goethite inclusions, which reflect light in parallel orientation, and create a sparkling sheen in gold to brown color shades. Sunstone may be oligoclase or labradorite in composition, and is much admired as a cabochon material among hobbyists. Very fine material is not abundant and is hard to obtain.

Occurrence:
New Mexico; New York; North Carolina; Maine; Pennsylvania; Virginia.
L. Baikal, U.S.S.R.; Labrador; Bancroft area, Ontario, Canada.
Tvedestrand and Hitterö, Norway: as masses in quartz veins.
Lake Huron (Canada side): brownish to pink color.
Kangayam, India.

Stone Sizes: Cabochons from Norwegian and Indian material may reach 100 carats or more. Most available material cuts smaller stones, however. This is because the rough is usually badly shattered and cracked.

Feldspar Names
Microcline is from Greek words meaning *small* and *inclined* because the cleavage is close to, but not quite 90°. *Amazonite* is named after the Amazon River basin in S. America. *Orthoclase* is from Greek words meaning *break straight* because the cleavages are at 90°. *Sanidine* is also from the Greek, *sanis*, meaning *board*, in reference to the tabular crystals. *Anorthoclase* is from Greek words for *not upright* because the cleavage is not 90°.

Feldspar itself is from the German word *Feldspath* and related to the German word for rock, *fels. Plagioclase* is from the Greek, meaning *oblique cleavage.*

Albite comes from the Latin *albus,* meaning *white,* because the mineral is usually white. *Perthite* is named for the locality, Perth, Ontario, Canada. *Adularia* is also a locality-derived name, from Adular-Bergstock, Switzerland, where the variety occurs. *Peristerite* is from the Greek word *peristera,* meaning *pigeon.* The name *moonstone* alludes to the lustrous sheen of this material, in the same way that *sunstone* derives its name.

Oligoclase comes from Greek words meaning *little break* because the cleavage was believed to be less perfect than in albite. *Andesine* is named after the Andes Mountains of South America. Bytown, Canada gave its name to *bytownite. Anorthite* is from the Greek words *an* plus *orthos,* meaning *not straight,* because the crystal faces meet at an oblique angle. *Labradorite* was, of course, named for its occurrence in Labrador.

FERGUSONITE *Series to* FORMANITE: YTaO₄.

Formula: YNbO₄ + Er, Ce, Fe, Ti.

Crystallography: Tetragonal. Crystals prismatic, pyramidal; usually masses.

Colors: Black, brownish black; surface altered brown, gray or yellow.

Streak: Greenish gray, yellowish brown, brown.

Luster: Vitreous; submetallic; alters to dull surface.

Hardness: 5.5−6.5.

Density: 5.6−5.8. Formanite: 7.03 (calculated).

Cleavage: Traces. Fracture subconchoidal. Brittle.

Optics: Isotropic due to metamictization. $N = 2.05-2.19$ (mean), variable.

Pleochroism: Weak.

Occurrence: Granite pegmatites rich in rare earths. *California; North Carolina; Virginia; Texas; Massachusetts.*
Norway; U.S.S.R.; Ytterby, Sweden; E. Africa; Rhodesia; Madagascar.
Formanite is from *W. Australia.*

Stone Sizes: Cabochons are cut to several inches from massive material. Faceted stones are extremely tiny (less than 1 carat).

Comments: This mineral is not abundant, and known from various localities. Cabochons are cut merely as curiosities, as they have no special features that would recommend them except rarity. There are reports of transparent grains or parts of crystals that have been cut by collectors, but these are merely curiosities and are seldom encountered.

Name: After Robert Ferguson, a Scottish physician.

FERROHYPERSTHENE   See: Enstatite.

FERROSALITE   See: Diopside.

FERROSILITE   See: Enstatite.

FERROTANTALITE   See: Manganotantalite.

FIBROLITE   See: Sillimanite.

FIRE AGATE   See: Quartz.

FLINT   See: Quartz.

FLOWSTONE   See: Calcite.

FLUORITE

Formula: CaF₂.

Crystallography: Isometric. Usually in good crystals, cubes, octahedra and other forms, often twinned; also massive, granular.

Colors: An extremely wide range is represented: colorless, purple (various shades), green (various shades), blue-green, blue, yellow to orange, brown (various shades), white, pink, red, brownish red, pinkish red, brownish black, black. Crystals are frequently color-zoned.

Luster: Vitreous.

Hardness: 4.

Density: 3.180; massive material with impurities, 3.0−3.25.

Cleavage: Perfect 4 directions. Quite brittle. Cleavage is octahedral, very easy.

Optics: Isotropic; $N = 1.432-1.434$.

Dispersion: 0.007 (very low).

Spectral: U and rare earths are often present; spectrum reflects their presence. Spectra usually vague, however. Green material has lines at 6340, 6100, 5820, 4450, and broad band at 4270.

Luminescence: Yellow, blue, white, reddish, violet, green in LW. Fluorescence likely due to U and rare earths, sometimes to organic inclusions (hydrocarbons). Some material is thermoluminescent; some is phosphorescent. Phosphoresces in X-rays. Subject of luminescence and fluorescence began with studies of fluorite.

Occurrence: In hydrothermal deposits; sedimentary rocks; hot springs; rarely in pegmatites; usually associated with sulfide ore deposits. There are many localities worldwide.
New Mexico; Colorado.
Italy; South Africa; Austria; Czechoslovakia; Germany; U.S.S.R.
England: Blue John or *Derbyshire Spar* used for more than 1500 years as decorative material, in vases, carvings, bowls, etc. It is banded in white and shades of blue, violet, and reddish-brown. *Derbyshire* deposits now exhausted. Also from *Cumberland* and *Cornwall.*
Chamonix, Switzerland: octahedral pink crystals, on quartz, very rare.
Illinois: best known, especially violet material from Rosiclare. Occurs in many colors in Illinois and *Missouri* (purple, blue, yellow, brown, colorless).
Westmoreland, New Hampshire: bright green fluorite in crystals up to 8 inches across.
Ontario, Canada: banded, violet material in calcite.
Columbia: (green).
Transparent material could be found in any of these occurrences.

Stone Sizes: Fluorites can be very large, because crystals of almost any color can be found in various localities, many large and transparent.

SI: 354 (pale yellow, Illinois); 124.5 (green, New Hampshire); 117 (Green, Africa); 11.2 (violet, Illinois); 85.4 (blue, Illinois); 32.7 (colorless, Illinois); 13 (pink, Switzerland).

PC: Over 100 (pink, S. Africa).

DG: 68 (deep blue, S.W. Africa); 23.7 (pink, Africa); 72.4 (green).

Comments: Fluorite is really too fragile for wear, because of the delicate nature of the material and the good cleavage. It is also rather soft. Fluorite occurs in a wide range of colors, many of them quite striking; faceted gems can be very bright if they are cut properly, despite the low refractive index. Most of the stones available are in the violet, blue, and green family. Pinks are rarer, as is the deep green Colombian material. Sometimes bicolor gems are cut from zoned crystals, and these are true collector items. Fluorite is difficult to cut, so a large stone free of cracks and blemishes is a very rare thing in the gem world.

Name: From the Latin *fluere* to flow, because it melts easily and is used as a flux in smelting.

FORMANITE See: Fergusonite.

FORSTERITE See: Olivine.

FRIEDELITE

Formula: $(Mn, Fe)_8Si_6O_{18}(OH, Cl)_4 \cdot 3H_2O$.

Crystallography: Hexagonal (R). Crystals are tabular, needle-like, hemimorphic, and very rare. Usually massive, fibrous aggregates, cryptocrystalline.

Colors: Pale pink to dark brownish red, red, brown, orange-red.

Luster: Vitreous.

Hardness: 4−5.

Density: 3.04−3.07.

Cleavage: Perfect 1 direction. Fracture unever. Brittle.

Optics: $o = 1.654-1.664$; $e = 1.625-1.629$. Uniaxial (−).

Usually refractometer shows shadow edge at about 1.645.

Birefringence: 0.030.

Spectral: Broad band at 5560 and also 4560 (indistinct); spectrum not diagnostic.

Luminescence: May be reddish in LW and SW. Some material green (SW) and yellow (LW).

Occurrence: In manganese deposits.
Örebro, Sweden; Adervielle, France.
Franklin, New Jersey: source of gem material. Usually brownish, cryptocrystalline and looks like a fibrous chalcedony. Seams at this deposit of the material were up to 2 inches wide.

Stone Sizes: Translucent stones up to 1−5 carats normal; cabochons to about 30×40 mm. The larger stones lose any transparency.

Comments: Friedelite is not abundant, and little material has been faceted. The cabochons cut from Franklin material are lovely and rich colored; this is usually translucent material. The faceted gems are exceedingly rare and true collector gems. Such stones are seldom seen even in large collections.

Name: After the French chemist and mineralogist, Charles Friedel.

ALGODONITE: Mohawk Mine, Keweenaw Peninsula, Michigan (each ca 1 inch across)

ADAMITE: Mapimi, Mexico (ca 1 inch across)

ACTINOLITE: Switzerland (0.94)

AMBER: Baltic Sea area (various cut gems and utility objects)

AMBER: Baltic Sea area (ca 1 inch across)

All numbers refer to carat weights, unless otherwise indicated. Sequential numbers refer to rows of gems, reading left to right. The term "ca" means "approximately".

AMBER: Baltic Sea area (ca 3 inches long)

ANHYDRITE: Germany (6.1)

ANATASE:
Switzerland (0.5)

AMBLYGONITE: Brazil (5.2, 6.3)

ANDALUSITE: Brazil (1.5, 3.0, 0.35, 2.6)

ANGLESITE: Tsumeb, S.W. Africa (16.1, 16.2)

APATITE: Canada (green, 8.05), Burma (white, 7.34), Mexico (yellow 7.9),
E. Africa (green, 2.25), Brazil (brown, 1.6), Burma (beige, 0.75),
Brazil (green, 2.87), Africa (green, 1.5), Maine (pink, 0.59), Brazil (blue, 0.51)

APATITE: Brazil (11.4)

APATITE: *Catseye apatite,*
India (ca 10)

3

APOPHYLLITE: India (1.3, 8.6, 2.4)

AXINITE: Baja, California
(ca 2, rough 1½ inches long)

AUGELITE: California (ca 1.5, rough ½ inch across)

AZURITE with MALACHITE: Bisbee, Arizona (ca 2.5 inches across)

ARAGONITE:
Czechoslovakia (5.35)

4

BARITE: South Dakota (4.7), Colorado (9.4, 1.9)

BARITE: France (65.1)

BERYL: *Emerald,* Lake
Manyara, Tanzania (1.50)

BENITOITE: San Benito Co., California.
Back row (1.21, 1.28, 3.53, 7.38). Front row (1.06, 2.45, 2.75, 0.33, 0.72)

BERYL: Brazil, except for red gem (Utah), from 4 to 45 carats (Utah= 0.5)

BERYL: *Emerald,* Colombia (1.06, 2.02, 0.95)

BERYL *Aquamarine catseye,* Brazil (18.37)

BERYL: *Aquamarine,* Brazil (9.16)

BERYL: *Aquamarine,* Idaho (16.0), Brazil (8.55)

BERYL: *Morganite,* Brazil (47.23)

BERYLLONITE: Maine (ca 2, rough 1 inch across)

BORACITE: Hanover, Germany (0.6)

BERYLLONITE: Stoneham, Maine (20.64)—one of the world's largest

BORNITE: Butte, Montana (specimens 2 inches across)

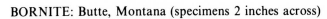

BRAZILIANITE: Brazil (3.0, 2.7)

BUSTAMITE: Broken Hill,
New South Wales, Australia (2.6)

BREITHAUPTITE: Hi Ho Silver Mine,
Cobalt, Ontario, Canada (ca 2 inches across)

BROOKITE: Magnet Cove, Arkansas (crystal, black, ca ½ inch across)

8

CALCITE: Spain, *Cobaltocalcite* (2.1, 2.8), Baja, California (15.7), Canada (2.0)

CALCITE: Mexico (65.0)

CALCITE: Italy, *Ruin Marble* (ca 4 inches long slab)

CANASITE: Bur'atskaja, Urals, Siberia, U.S.S.R.
(ca 2 inches across)

CALCITE: Spain, *Cobaltocalcite* (6.2, 12.2)

CANCRINITE: Bigwood Township,
Ontario (ca 3 inches across)

CASSITERITE: Bolivia (14.25, 3.5)

CASSITERITE: Bolivia (2.9, 4.6)

CELESTITE: Canada (1.5)

CELESTITE: Madagascar (16.3)

CERUSSITE: Tsumeb, S.W. Africa (4.1, 5.3)

CERULEITE: Arizona (specimens each ca 1 inch across)

CHAMBERSITE:
Texas (0.5)

CHILDRENITE: Brazil (1.37)

CHABAZITE: Nova Scotia (specimen ca 3 inches across)

CHIOLITE: Greenland (1.1)

11

CHONDRODITE: Tilly Foster Mine, Brewster,
New York (ca 2, rough 1 inch long)

CHROMITE: Nye, Montana
(ca 4 inches high, specimen)

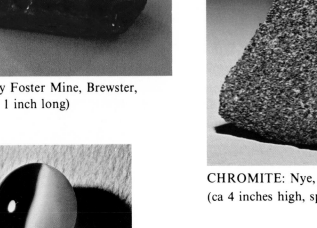

CHRYSOBERYL: Ceylon,
Catseye (ca 5)

CHRYSOBERYL: Brazil (6.4, 5.1, 6.6)

CHRYSOBERYL: Brazil (ca 12, 18, 18)

CHRYSOBERYL: U.S.S.R.,
Alexandrite (ca 6) incandescent
light (above); daylight (below)

CHRYSOCOLLA: Arizona and New Mexico
(large specimen ca 4 inches high)

CHRYSOCOLLA: Arizona (4.1)

CINNABAR: Charcas,
Mexico (1.37)

COLEMANITE: Boron,
California (26.50)

COBALTITE: Skutterud, Norway (crystals ½ to 1 inch diameter)

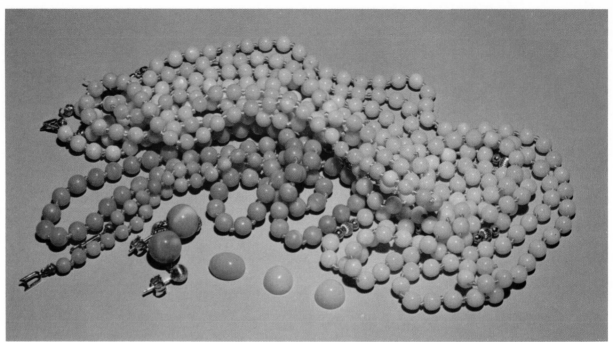

CORAL: Mediterranean Sea (reddish beads ca 5 mm size)

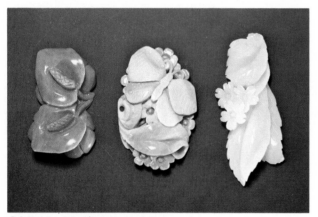

CORAL: Mediterranean Sea
(each carving ca 2 inches long)

CORDIERITE: *Iolite;* Ceylon (3.68),
Australia (2.70)

CORUNDUM: *Sapphire;* worldwide localities (ca 0.5 to 5)

CORUNDUM: *Sapphire,*
Ceylon (87.6)

CORUNDUM: *Sapphire,*
"padparadscha" color; Ceylon (29.25)

CORUNDUM: *Ruby,*
Burma (ca 2.5)

CORUNDUM: *Ruby,* Thailand (2.22, 3.68, 3.35)

CORUNDUM: *Star ruby;* Ceylon (2.75),
Burma (2.6, 0.62), India (8.4)

CORUNDUM: *Star sapphire;*
Ceylon (33.6)

CORUNDUM: *Star sapphire;* Ceylon (ca 2 to 7)

15

CRYOLITE: Greenland (2.5)

COVELLITE: Butte, Montana (ca 4 inches across)

CREEDITE: Santa Eulalia, Chihuahua, Mexico (ca 2 inches across)

CUPRITE: Onganja, S.W. Africa
(48.07)

CROCOITE: Dundas, Tasmania (3.4)

G

GADOLINITE

Formula: $Be_2FeY_2Si_2O_{10}$.

Crystallography: Monoclilnic. Crystals rough and coarse, often terminated; massive.

Colors: Black, greenish black, brown, very rarely light green.

Streak: Greenish gray.

Luster: Vitreous to greasy.

Hardness: 6.5−7.

Density: 4.0−4.65 (usually 4.4); metamict material ca 4.2

Cleavage: None. Fracture conchoidal. Brittle.

Optics: $\alpha = 1.77-1.78$; $\gamma = 1.78-1.82$.
Biaxial (+), $2V = 85°$. Usually metamict and amorphous, hence isotropic.

Birefringence: High, and variable 0.01−0.04.

Occurrence: Granites and granite pegmatites.
Colorado; Texas; Arizona.
Greenland; Sweden; Norway; U.S.S.R.; Japan; Switzerland; Australia.

Stone Sizes: Massive material cuts cabochons up to several pounds, because Norwegian crystals have been found up to 4 inches across. Texas has unearthed nodules up to 60 pounds. Faceted gems, however, would be very tiny and very rare, as the mineral is rarely transparent, even in thin splinters.

Comments: This is not a terribly attractive gemstone, but faceted gems would be a tremendous rarity. The material is quite brittle but there is no cleavage to cause problems in cutting. The author does not know of the whereabouts of a faceted gem at this writing.

Name: After the Swedish chemist, J. Gadolin.

GAHNITE   See: Spinel.

GALAXITE   See: Spinel.

GARNET FAMILY

Formula: $A_3B_2Si_3O_{12}$. A = Fe, Ca, Mn, Mg; B = Al, Fe, Ti, Cr.

The garnets are a complex family of minerals, all having very similar structures, but varying enormously in chemical composition and properties.

For convenience, garnets have in the past been grouped according to composition. Garnets containing Al in the B position in the formula are widely called *pyralspites* (acronym: PYRope, ALmandine, SPessar-tine) and garnets with Ca in the A position are called *ugrandites* (Uvarovite, GRossular, ANDradite).

There is complete solid solution between certain garnet species, but not between others, a fact due to specific differences in internal structure. Uvarovite is a fairly rare garnet with restricted occurrence; the other five garnets may be thought of as comprising a 5-component system (see diagram) illustrating the general scheme of chemical substitutions.

The formulas of the garnet species are listed here to show similarities.

Uvarovite: $Ca_3Cr_2Si_3O_{12}$ *Pyrope:* $Mg_3Al_2Si_3O_{12}$
Grossular: $Ca_3Al_2Si_3O_{12}$ *Almandine:* $Fe_3Al_2Si_3O_{12}$
Andradite: $Ca_3Fe_2Si_3O_{12}$ *Spessartine:* $Mn_3Al_2Si_3O_{12}$
Also note:

Goldmanite: $Ca_3V_2Si_3O_{12}$. Tiny, dark green crystals.

Hydrogrossular: $Ca_3Al_2(SiO_4)_{3-x}(OH)_{4x}$. May be a component of grossular.

Henritermierite: $Ca_3(Mn, Al)(SiO_4)_2(OH)_4$. Tetragonal, very garnetlike, often twinned.

Kimzeyite: $Ca_3(Zr, Ti)_2(Al, Si)_3O_{12}$.

Knorringite: $Mg_3Cr_2Si_3O_{12}$. Like a "chromiferous pyrope."

Majorite: $Mg_3(Fe, Al, Si)_2Si_3O_{12}$. Purple; found in a meteorite!

These are mostly rare species, but the fact that the garnet structure type can accommodate such a wide variation in composition indicates the range of substitutions possible in natural garnets. This accounts for the huge range of colors seen in the family as a whole.

Optical properties of garnets are very dependent on chemistry. Sometimes straight-line graphs are used to relate composition with refractive index or density. This type of graph assumes a simple additive relationship in chemical substitution, and is inadequate when several substitutions occur simultaneously. In many instances a chemical analysis is needed to identify a garnet positively.

Physical Properties

The garnets have no cleavage, but display a conchoidal fracture and are somewhat brittle and tend to chip easily. The luster is vitreous, inclining to resinous in grossular, andradite, and some almandines. The hardness is 6.5−7.5 in grossular and uvarovite, 6.5−7 in andradite, and 7−7.5 in the pyralspite series.

Garnets are all Isometric, and crystals show the common forms in this crystal system, such as the trapezohedron and dodecahedron. Interestingly, the most common isometric forms, the cube and octahedron, are extremely rare in garnet crystals. Garnets may also be massive, granular, and in tumbled pebbles.

Colors:

Uvarovite: dark green.

Grossular: Colorless, white, gray, yellow, yellowish green, green (various shades, pale apple green, medium apple green, emerald green, dark green), yellow, brown, pink, reddish, black.

Andradite: Yellow-green, green, greenish brown, brown, grayish black, black. The color is related to the content of Ti and Mn. If there is little of either element the color is light and may resemble grossular.

Pyrope: Purplish red, pinkish red, orangy red, crimson, dark red. *Note:* Pure pyrope would be colorless; the red colors are derived from Fe + Cr.

Almandine: Deep red, brownish red, brownish black, violet-red.

Spessartine: Red, reddish orange, orange, yellow-brown, reddish brown, blackish-brown.

A well-known commercial garnet is known, which is intermediate between pyrope and almandine. It is often said that such a garnet is a mixture of "molecules" of these garnets, whereas this really means its structure contains both Fe and Al. The intermediate garnet, known as *rhodolite*, usually has a distinctive purplish color.

The above variations make it easy to see why it is foolish to try to guess the identity of a garnet on the basis of color alone!

Stone Sizes: Garnet crystals are usually small, microscopic up to about 6 inches in the case of grossular. Rarely garnets in rock, with poor external forms, are much larger, such as the almandine from Gore Mountain, New York, which reaches a diameter of 60 cm. A few spessartines in Brazil have measured several pounds in weight while still retaining great transparency and fine color, but these are very rare. A typical garnet crystal is about half an inch to an inch in diameter.

Optics: These are very dependent on chemistry, as indicated previously; the pyralspites are generally isotropic, but the presence of the large Ca atom in the structure of the ugrandites makes them birefringent; this may be due to strain, but more probably has a structural explanation. Grossular and andradite are almost always zoned, often twinned, and are distinctly *not* isotropic in the microscope.

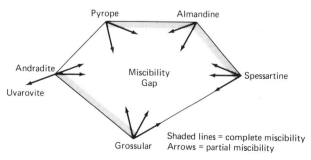

Chemical substitutions in garnet (after Mackowsky).

Uvarovite

Density: 3.4−3.8 (usually 3.71−3.77).

Optics: $N = 1.74-1.87$.

Occurrence: Chromites and serpentines, i.e., metamorphic environments where both Ca and Cr are present. *Oregon.*
Thetford, Quebec, Canada.
Outokumpu, Finland: best known locality, in large, fine, green crystals.
Norway. U.S.S.R.: fine crystals. *S. Africa.*
Northern California: in chromite deposits.

Stone Sizes: Faceted uvarovites are extremely rare, because crystals are always opaque. An occasional crystal may have a transparent corner that could yield a stone of less than 1 carat, even though crystals may reach a size of 1−2 inches.

Comments: The color of uvarovite is like that of emerald (deep, rich green), so it is a shame that crystals cannot be cut. Uvarovite is a rare mineral, prized by collectors. It is not generally regarded as a gem garnet.

Name: After Count S.S. Uvarov of Russia, one-time President of the St. Petersburg (Leningrad) Academy.

Grossular

Also known as *hessonite, essonite, cinnamon stone; rosolite* is a pinkish variety from Mexico.

Density: 3.4−3.71; usually near 3.65.

Optics: $N = 1.72-1.80$; usually 1.73−1.74.

Dispersion: 0.027.

Spectral: None in pale colored faceted gems; a trace of almandine may produce a faint chrome spectrum. A trace of Cr may also produce this spectrum in green varieties. Massive grossular may show a weak line at 4610, or a band at 6300. Green, massive grossular from Pakistan shows a line at 6970 (weak) with weak lines in the orange, plus a strong band at 6300 and diffuse lines at 6050, 5050.

Luminescence: Usually none in UV. All massive material glows orange in X-rays, as do many faceted gems.

Occurrence: In metamorphosed, impure calcareous rocks, especially contact zones; also in schists and serpentines; worldwide occurrence, widespread.
Eden Mills, Vermont: fine orange crystals, some gemmy, with green diopside.
California: many localities.
New England: many localities.
Asbestos, Quebec: fine orange to pinkish crystals, up to 2 inches across, gemmy.
Lake Jaco, Chihuahua, Mexico: large pinkish, white and greenish crystals; color zoned concentrically, usually opaque; crystals up to about 5 inches in diameter.
Ceylon: grossulars are found in the gem gravels.
Wilui River, U.S.S.R.: opaque green crystals with idocrase.
China: massive white grossular.

New Zealand: hydrogrossular.
Kenya and Tanzania: fine grossular in various colors, especially the dark green material being marketed as *tsavorite.*
S. Africa: massive green material that resembles jade.
Pakistan: some faceted green gems; also massive green grossular, various shades.
Brazil; Switzerland.

Stone Sizes: Hydrogrossular and massive varieties are cut as cabochons of large size, including green shades and also pink, translucent grossular. Massive white material from China has been carved. Orange and brown grossulars from the Ceylon gem gravels up to several hundred carats have been found; the fine cinnamon-colored stones from Quebec are clean only in small sizes, but good gems up to about 25 carats have been cut. Tsavorite is rare in clean gems over 1 carat; the largest known are in the 10–15 carat range.
SI: 64.2 (orange-brown, Ceylon).
PC: 13.89 (yellow, oval).
AMNH: 61.5 (cameo head of Christ, hessonite).

Comments: Grossular has a granular appearance under the microscope, sometimes referred to as *treacle,* a swirled look due to included diopside crystals and irregular streaks at grain boundaries. Zircon crystals are included in some grossulars, as well as actinolite and apatite (Tanzania material). So-called *Transvaal jade* is the green massive material from S. Africa. The color of grossular depends on the content of Fe and Mn. If there is less than 2% Fe, grossular is pale or colorless. Greater amounts of Fe produce brown and green colors, and a rich green shade is due to Cr. *Californite* is a mixture of idocrase and grossular, usually pale to medium green in color. It comes from California, Pakistan, and South Africa.

Hydrogrossular is a component of the massive grossulars. Material from New Zealand is known as *rodingite* ($N = 1.702$, density 3.35). Transvaal jade occurs in green, gray-green, bluish and pink colors, is compact and homogeneous, may have a splintery fracture and waxy luster. The gray material contains zoisite. Pink material, containing Mn, has $N = 1.675–1.705$, density 3.27. The green, jadelike material has $N = 1.728$, density 3.488. Pakistan massive grossular has $N = 1.738–1.742$, density 3.63, with a Cr absorption spectrum. Similar material from Tanzania has $N = 1.742–1.744$, density 3.68.

Colorless grossular from Georgetown, California has $N = 1.737$, density 3.506. Yellow garnet from Tanzania fluoresces orange in X-rays and also UV, $N = 1.734$, density 3.604. *Tsavorite* from Lualenyi, Kenya has $N = 1.743$, density = 3.61 (mean). It is inert in UV light, contains a trace of Cr and a significant amount of vanadium. The color of these tsavorites is therefore due to vanadium, not chromium as originally suspected.

The pinkish grossular in marble from Lake Jaco and Morelos, Mexico is variously known as *xalostocite, landerite* and *rosolite.*

Andradite

Melanite has 1–5% Ti oxide; *schorlomite* is rich in Ti also; *topazolite* is yellowish-green, from Italy; *demantoid* is rich green, colored by Cr.

Density: 3.7–4.1; melanite about 3.9; demantoid 3.82–3.85.

Optics: $N = 1.88–1.94$; melanite: ca 1.89; demantoid: 1.888; schorlomite: 1.935; topazolite (yellow): 1.887.

Dispersion: 0.057 (large).

Spectral: A strong band is visible at 4430, cutoff at the violet end of the spectrum. Sometimes (in demantoids) the Cr spectrum is visible, with a doublet at 7010, sharp line at 6930 and 2 bands in the orange at 6400 and 6220. Demantoid is red in the Chelsea filter.

Luminescence: None.

Inclusions: Demantoid is distinguished by so-called horsetail inclusions of byssolite (fibrous amphibole); these are diagnostic for this gem.

Occurrence: Andradite occurs in schists and serpentine rocks (demantoid and topazolite); also in alkali-rich igneous rocks (melanite and schorlomite); and in metamorphosed limestones and contact zones (brown and green colors).
California; Arizona; New Jersey; Pennsylvania.
Greenland; Norway; Sweden; Uganda.
Colorado: melanite.
Arkansas: schorlomite.
New Mexico: in metamorphic limestones and ore deposits.
U.S.S.R.: fine demantoid from the Urals.
Zaire: brown and green andradite, also some demantoid.
Ala, Piedmont, Italy: dark apple green demantoid garnet; also topazolite (yellow).
Korea: andradite, some with Cr and fine green.
Monte Somma, Vesuvius, and *Trentino, Italy:* melanite (black).

Stone Sizes: Andradite is seldom faceted, but brownish stones up to a few carats are known. Demantoid, however, is a fine and well known gem, and is one of the most valuable of all the garnets.
SI: 10.4 (U.S.S.R.); also 4.1, 3.4 and 2.3.
PC: 18 (sold in New York City); a California collector owns a huge topazolite (green color) that would yield faceted gems over 20 carats. This crystal weighs ca 1 ounce.
U.S.S.R.: many fine demantoids in museum collections.

Comments: Demantoid was once abundant in jewelry, but has become very scarce and is seen primarily in antique jewelry. Stones larger than 10 carats are very rare. Topazolite of fine yellow color is usually very small, and a cut gem over 2–3 carats would be rare. Black garnets have occasionally been used in mourning jewelry.

Brown andradite is not a well-known gem garnet. The dispersion of andradite is the highest of any garnet, and gems have tremendous fire, but this is usually masked by the body color. The fire is eminently visible in some paler demantoids, which makes them distinctive and much more attractive than comparably colored grossulars, which have much lower dispersion. The horse-tail inclusions are proof positive in identification.

Pyrope

Density: 3.65−3.87.

Optics: $N = 1.730 - 1.766$.

Dispersion: 0.022.

Spectral: The chromium spectrum of emission lines in the far red is absent in pyrope; however, the almandine (iron) spectrum is often visible. Otherwise, Cr masks the almandine spectrum and we see a narrow, weak doublet at 6870/6850, with possible weak lines at 6710, 6500. A broad band, about 1000 Å wide, may be visible at 5700.

Luminescence: None.

Inclusions: Pyrope contains small rounded crystals, circular snowballs of quartz crystals, and (from Arizona) octahedra and minute needles.

Occurrence: In peridotites, kimberlites and serpentine rocks, and sands and gravels derived from their weathering; also in eclogite and other basic igneous rocks.
Utah; New Mexico; Arkansas; North Carolina.
Czechoslovakia; Brazil; Argentina; Tanzania; Transbaikalia, U.S.S.R.; Bingara, N.S.W., Australia; Anakie, Queensland, Australia; Otterøy, Norway.
Arizona: a component of ant hills.
Umba Valley, E. Africa: shows color change (see below).
S. Africa: in kimberlite and eclogite associated with diamond; fine color.
The best known pyrope is from near *Trebnitz, Czechoslovakia*, the so-called Bohemian garnets. The garnets occur in volcanic breccia and tuffs, and conglomerates. These garnets provided a major local industry in the 19th Century, but the deposits are exhausted. An enormous quantity of pyrope from these mines was sold.

Stone Sizes: Pyropes of large size are extremely rare. Stones over 1−2 carats are usually very dark. Many large gems are in the Kunsthistorisches Museum in Vienna. There are stories about hen's-egg-sized gems in the former Imperial Treasury in Vienna. The Green Vaults of Dresden contain a huge gem said to be the size of a pigeon's egg. Reports of a 468.5 carat gem also appear in the literature.

Comments: A pure pyrope (end member in the series) is unknown in nature. Pyropes always contain some almandine and spessartine components. The almandine component can easily be detected spectroscopically. Large, clean pyropes of lively color are very rare and would be very expensive. Some pyropes show an interesting color change. Material from Norway ($N = 1.747$,

S.G. 3.715) is wine red in incandescent light, violet in daylight, but these stones are very small (about half a carat). Pyrope from the Umba Valley in E. Africa ($N = 1.757$, S.G. 3.816) are pyrope−spessartines (with some Ca and Ti); they are greenish blue in daylight and magenta in tungsten light. They have inclusions of plates of hematite and rutile needles. Gems sold as pyrope are usually almandines with a pyrope component, especially if they are of large size. The pyropes from S. Africa occur with diamonds, and sometimes pyrope crystals are inclusions within diamonds. The color of these is superb, blood red, but the sizes are always very small.

Almandine

Density: 3.95−4.3; usually 3.95 or above.

Optics: $N = 1.75 - 1.83$; usually above 1.78.

Dispersion: 0.027.

Spectral: The spectrum of almandine is distinctive and diagnostic: there is a band 200 Å wide at 5760 (strong) and also strong bands at 5260 and 5050. Lines may appear at 6170 and 4260. This pattern of 3 (or sometimes 5) bands is seen in all almandines, and most garnets with a significant almandine component.

Luminescence: None.

Inclusions: Almandine is usually included with a variety of minerals. There are zircon crystals with haloes due to radioactivity; irregular, dotlike crystals and lumpy crystals; rutile needles, usually short fibers, crossed at 110° and 70°; there are dense hornblende rods (especially from Ceylon); asbestiform needles of augite or hornblende that run parallel to the dodecahedral edges; also apatite; ilmenite; spinel; monazite; biotite; quartz.

Occurrence: Almandine is a widespread constituent of metamorphic rocks; also in igneous rocks, in contact metamorphic zones, and as an alluvial mineral.
Colorado; South Dakota; Michigan; New York; Pennsylvania; Connecticut; Maine.
Canada; Brazil; Uruguay; Greenland; Norway; Sweden; Ceylon; Austria; Japan; Madagascar; Tanzania; Zambia.
Fort Wrangell, Alaska: fine, well-formed crystals in slate. *California; Idaho:* star garnets.
Major gem almandine sources are as follows:
India: Jaipur (in mica schist); also Rajasthan and Hyderabad; some stars also.
Ceylon: at Trincomalee, fine color and large size.
Brazil: Minas Gerais; Bahia.
Idaho: star garnets.
Madagascar: large sizes.

Stone Sizes: Almandines of large size are known, such as the 60 cm crystals in rock at the Barton Mine, New York. This material is so badly shattered that stones up to only 1−2 carats can be cut from the fragments. Indian and Brazilian almandine constitutes the bulk of material on the marketplace.

SI: 174 and 67.3 (stars, red-brown, Idaho); 40.6 (red-brown, Madagascar).

Comments: Almandine is perhaps the commonest garnet. Gemstones always have some spessartine and pyrope components, and this creates a wide range of colors, including brown, red-brown, purplish red, wine red, purple, deep red. Inclusions of asbestiform minerals (pyroxene or amphibole) create a chatoyancy that yields, in cabochons, a 4-rayed star. Star gems come primarily from Idaho, and also from India. The Idaho material has $N = 1.808$, density 4.07 (up to 4.76 due to inclusions). Inclusions in faceted gems vary widely, but are usually not too obtrusive. This is especially true of the silk, which is often visible only under magnification.

Rhodolite

Rhodolite is intermediate in composition between almandine and pyrope, with a ratio of Mg to Fe of 2 to 1 (i.e., 2 pyrope + 1 almandine). The distinctiveness of rhodolite is in its color, which is always a purplish-red.

The absorption spectrum always shows almandine lines. Inclusions include apatite crystals (North Carolina) and any of the other inclusions found in almandine. The color of a garnet is misleading, and a chemical analysis is required to show whether a garnet is an almandine or pyrope, or a mixed crystal.

Density: 3.79–3.80 (Tanzania); 3.83–3.89 (Rhodesia); 3.84–3.89 (North Carolina).

Optics: $N = 1.750$–1.760 (Rhodesia); 1.76–1.761 (North Carolina); 1.745–1.760 (Tanzania).

Dispersion: 0.026.

Occurrence: *North Carolina:* rhododendron red, lilac, pinkish. *Ceylon; Madagascar; Tanzania; Rhodesia.*

Comments: The original locality for rhodolite was Cowee Creek, Macon Co., North Carolina. Stones from this locality are very small (under 1–2 carats), but new finds in Africa have yielded gems over 25 carats. Material from the N. Pare Mountains, Tanzania, may show a color change, blue in daylight to purplish-red in incandescent light, similar to alexandrite ($N = 1.765$, S.G. 3.88).

Spessartine

Density: 3.8–4.25; gems usually 4.12–4.20.

Optics: 1.79–1.81; Brazil 1.803–1.805; Amelia, Virginia 1.795.

Dispersion: 0.027.

Spectral: The Mn spectrum is evident: lines at 4950, 4850, 4620 (all weak) and strong lines at 4320, 4240 (weaker), 4120 (intense). Almandine may be present contributing lines at 4320 and 4120.

Luminescence: None.

Inclusions: Wavy feathers, due to liquid drops, that have a shredded look, especially in gems from Ceylon and Brazil.

Occurrence: In granite pegmatites; also gneiss, quartzite and rhyolite, and sometimes as a component in skarns. *Nevada; Colorado; New Mexico; Pennsylvania; North Carolina.*
San Diego Co., California: good crystals, especially at Ramona (fine orange gems).
Amelia Court House, Virginia: fine orange to deep brownish material, gemmy.
Norway; Tsializina, Madagascar.
Ceylon and Burma: in the gem gravels.
Brazil (Arassuahy and Ceara): large crystals (pounds), gemmy, fine color.

Stone Sizes: Gems weighing more than 100 carats have been cut from Brazilian and Madagascar gems. Amelia stones are fine color (orange) but small, up to about 15–20 carats, although crystals weighing several pounds have been found there.
SI: 109 (red, Brazil); 53.8 (red, Brazil); 40.1 (orange, Virginia).
AMNH: 96 (reddish, Brazil—not clean).

Comments: Spessartine is fairly rare as a gem garnet, and one of the most beautiful. Large stones are very rare, and usually quite dark. The finest color is an orangy red, as exemplified by the material from Ramona, California and Amelia, Virginia. A red-brown tint indicates a higher content of almandine, accompanied by higher refractive index; pale orange colors are closer to pure spessartine. Spessartine as a component of almandine tends to add a lively reddish tinge of color.

Garnet Names

Garnet is named from the Latin word *granatus*, meaning *grain*. This originated in the comparison of garnet grains in rock with the scattered dark seeds of the pomegranate fruit.

Uvarovite is named after Count S.S. Uvarov, one-time President of the St. Petersburg (Leningrad) Academy.

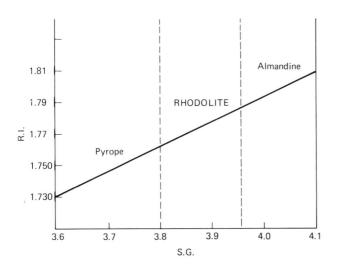

Grossular is named after *R. grossularia*, the botanical name for the gooseberry, because of the resemblance of the color (pale green) to that of the plant.

Californite is named after the original occurrence in California.

Andradite is named after the Portugese mineralogist d'Andrade, who described one of the subvarieties of this species. *Topazolite* is named after its resemblance to yellow topaz. *Demantoid* comes from the French *demant* (*diamond*) because of the brilliance and luster. *Melanite* comes from the Greek *melanos* (*black*).

Pyrope comes from the Greek words for *firelike*, in allusion to the red color.

Almandine is a corruption of the locality name Alabanda, in Asia Minor, from which place came the red garnets described by Pliny.

Rhodolite is named from the Greek *rhodon*, rose, in allusion to the color.

Spessartine is named after the locality Spessart, in N.W. Bavaria (Germany).

GAYLUSSITE

Formula: $Na_2Ca(CO_3)_2 \cdot 5H_2O$.

Crystallography: Monoclinic. Crystals elongated, flattened, and wedge-shaped.

Colors: Colorless, white, grayish, yellowish.

Luster: Vitreous.

Hardness: 2.5−3.

Density: 1.995.

Cleavage: Perfect 1 direction. Fracture conchoidal. Brittle.

Optics: $\alpha = 1.445$; $\beta = 1.516$; $\gamma = 1.522$.
Biaxial (−), $2V = 34°$.

Birefringence: 0.077.

Pleochroism: None.

Spectral: Not diagnostic.

Luminescence: Weak cream white in SW (Nevada). May be triboluminescent.

Occurrence: In evaporite deposits rich in borax or alkaline lakes.
California: Searles Lake, Owens Lake, China Lake, Borax Lake.
Wyoming; Nevada.
Mongolia, China.
Venezuela: in clay beds.
Kenya: in transparent crystals.

Stone Sizes: Crystals from Searles Lake have been found up to 2 inches long. Gems could be cut from such crystals up to about 20−30 carats.

Comments: This mineral is very hard to cut because of extreme softness and cleavage. Gaylussite dries out slowly in air and the surfaces may turn white. Stones in collections are therefore best stored in sealed containers to prevent dehydration. Gaylussite is seen only in collections, and relatively few stones have been cut. Transparent crystals are not terribly rare, but cut gems are relatively uninteresting.

Name: After the eminent French chemist, Prof. L. J. Gay-Lussac.

GLASS: See: Obsidian.

GOLDMANITE See: Garnet.

GOSHENITE See: Beryl.

GRANDIDIERITE

Formula: $(Mg, Fe)Al_3BSiO_9$.

Crystallography: Orthorhombic. Crystals elongated and not well formed; massive.

Colors: Blue-green; translucent.

Luster: Vitreous.

Hardness: 7.5.

Density: 2.97−3.0.

Cleavage: Perfect 1 direction, good 1 direction.

Optics: $\alpha = 1.590−1.602$; $\beta = 1.618−1.636$; $\gamma = 1.623−1.639$.
Biaxial (−), $2V = 30°$.

Birefringence: 0.037.

Pleochroism: Strong: dark blue-green/colorless/dark green.

Spectral: Not diagnostic.

Luminescence: None.

Occurrence: Generally in pegmatites.
Andrahomana, So. Madagascar: only well-known locality.

Stone Sizes: Cut as cabochons up to about 1 inch (1−10 carats). The material is translucent at best.

Comments: Grandidierite is a rather rare mineral, with a lovely blue-green color. It is never transparent, but cabochons from translucent material are quite attractive. The high hardness makes it suitable for wear, although the cleavage is good. Cut grandidierite is seldom seen in collections, because few collectors know it exists in cuttable form.

GROSSULAR See: Garnet.

GYPSUM *Also known as* Alabaster; *variety* Satin Spar.

Formula: $CaSO_4 \cdot 2H_2O$.

Crystallography: Monoclinic. Crystals often perfect and large; tabular; rosettes; lenticular; *helictites* are grotesque shapes found in caves; often twinned; massive; granular.

Colors: Colorless, white, gray; impurities make it yellowish, reddish, brownish, greenish. Sometimes banded and patterned, like marble.

Luster: Subvitreous; pearly on cleavages.

Hardness: 2.

Density: 2.32 (range 2.30−2.33).

Cleavage: Perfect and easy, 1 direction; distinct 2 other directions.

Optics: $\alpha = 1.520$; $\beta = 1.523$; $\gamma = 1.530$. Biaxial (+), $2V = 58°$.

Birefringence: 0.010.

Dispersion: 0.033.

Pleochroism: None.

Spectral: Not diagnostic.

Luminescence: Sometimes indistinct brownish or greenish white in UV. Inert in X-rays.

Occurrence: In sedimentary rocks and deposits; saline lakes; oxidized parts of ore deposits; volcanic deposits. *Utah; Michigan; Colorado; South Dakota; New Mexico; New York; Kansas; other states.*
California: many locations.
Mexico: at Naica, Chihuahua, in enormous crystals to 6 feet long.
Braden, Chile: crystals reported up to 10 feet long.
Alabaster from *England; Tuscany, Italy.*

Stone Sizes: Massive gypsum in any desired size (for cabochons and carvings). Fibrous material cut into large carvings, up to several pounds. Faceted gypsum could be up to hundreds of carats, as large transparent crystals exist.

Comments: Gypsum is one of the most abundant minerals and is found especially in evaporite environments. Alabaster, the massive, granular variety, has been used for thousands of years, made into vases, bowls and other useful and decorative objects. Today it is used in ashtrays, clock housings, paperweights, etc.

Gypsum can be scratched by the fingernail, so it is much too soft for hard use. Care must be taken in handling carvings and useful objects, but scratches can be polished out rather easily.
Selenite is the term applied to colorless, transparent crystals. *Satin spar* is used to describe massive fibrous varieties that are often cut into cabochons or carved into animal shapes. This material has a great chatoyancy, and brown colored satin spar makes lovely decorative items. Faceted gypsum is not often seen, because cut stones are unattractive and very difficult to fashion, due to the exceptionally perfect cleavage and low hardness of the material.

Name: *Gypsum* from the Greek *gypsos*, a name applied to what we now call plaster. *Satin spar* in allusion to the satiny luster of the fibrous material. *Selenite* from the Greek word for *moon*, due to the pearly luster on cleavage surfaces. *Alabaster* from the Greek word *alabastros*, a stone from which ointment-vases were made.

H

HACKMANITE   *See:* Sodalite.

HAMBERGITE

Formula: $Be_2BO_3(OH, F)$.

Crystallography: Orthorhombic. Crystals prismatic, flattened.

Colors: Colorless, white, grayish white, yellowish white.

Luster: Vitreous to dull.

Hardness: 7.5.

Density: 2.35−2.37.

Cleavage: Perfect 1 direction. Fracture conchoidal to uneven. Brittle.

Optics: $\alpha = 1.55$; $\beta = 1.59$; $\gamma = 1.63$.
Biaxial (+), $2V = 87°$.

Birefringence: 0.072.

Dispersion: 0.015.

Spectral: Not diagnostic.

Inclusions: Tubes.

Luminescence: None in most specimens; sometimes weak pink-orange in LW (Norway).

Occurrence: In syenite pegmatites and alkali pegmatites, in crystals up to 2×1 inch.
Anjanabanoana, Madagascar: large gemmy crystals.
Non-gem material from *Kashmir, India; Czechoslovakia; Ramona, California; Langesundsfjord, Norway.*

Stone Sizes: Hambergite is a fairly rare mineral, seldom transparent enough to facet. Cut gems over 5 carats are very rare. In 1968 a dealer offered a white stone of 28.86 carats, however.

Comments: Hambergite is a gem for collectors of the unusual, although it is hard enough for wear. The remarkable properties of this material are noteworthy— it has the lowest known density for any gem of such high birefringence. This combination of properties makes identification fairly easy. Stones have little fire and may resemble quartz, but the birefringence is much larger than that of similar-appearing gemstones. Usually cut stones are not clean, but are filled with cleavage traces.

Name: After Axel Hamberg, Swedish mineralogist, who called attention to the mineral.

HANCOCKITE   See: Epidote.

HAUYNE   *Sodalite group.* See Lazurite.
Formula: $(Na, Ca)_{4-8}(Al_6Si_6)O_{24}(SO_4, S)_{1-2}$.

Crystallography: Isometric. Crystals dodecahedral or octahedral; usually rounded grains.

Colors: Blue; also white, shades of gray, green, yellow and red. Translucent to semi-transparent.

Luster: Vitreous to greasy.

Streak: Slightly bluish to colorless.

Hardness: 5.5−6.

Density: 2.44−2.50.

Cleavage: Distinct 1 direction. Fracture conchoidal to uneven. Brittle.

Optics: $N = 1.496−1.505$.

Spectral: Not diagnostic.

Luminescence: Usually none; sometimes orange-red in LW (Germany).

Occurrence: Alkaline igneous rocks, associated with leucite and nepheline.
Montana; South Dakota; Colorado.
Quebec, Canada; France; Laacher See, Germany; Italy; Morocco.

Stone Sizes: Opaque material is cut into cabochons up to an inch or two, but faceted gems are exceedingly rare, and always small (under 1−2 carats).

Comments: Haüyne is one of the major constituents of lapis lazuli, a well-known and ancient gem material. It is, however, rarely seen as a distinct gem species. It is cut for collectors mainly as a curiosity, but faceted gems would be deep blue in color and extremely beautiful. Blue is the most sought after color in this material.

Name: After René Just Haüy, one of the great early mineralogists.

HAWK'S EYE   See: Quartz.

HEDENBERGITE   See: Diopside.

HELIODOR   See: Beryl.

HELIOTROPE   See: Quartz.

HEMATINE   See: Hematite.

HEMATITE

Formula: Fe_2O_3.

Crystallography: Hexagonal (R). Crystals in wide variety of forms, often lustrous or tarnished. Massive; compact; fibrous; reniform (kidney ore); micaceous; stalactitic; earthy.

Colors: Steel gray to black; blood red in thin slivers or crystals. Massive material is brownish red.

Streak: Deep red or brownish red.

Luster: Metallic, submetallic, dull; glistening in micaceous variety.

Hardness: 5–6.5.

Density: 4.95–5.26.

Cleavage: None. Fracture even to subconchoidal. Brittle.

Optics: $o = 3.22$; $e = 2.94$. Uniaxial (−).

Birefringence: 0.280.

Occurrence: A major ore of iron; usually in sedimentary deposits in thick beds; also in igneous rocks, metamorphic rocks, and lavas (deposited from vapor). *Lake Superior region, Minnesota; Michigan; Wisconsin; New York; Alaska; Tennessee; Pennsylvania; Missouri; South Dakota; Wyoming; Arizona.*
Elba, Italy. Canada; Mexico; Cuba; most European countries.
Brazil: fine crystals. *England:* kidney ore from Cumberland area.

Stone Sizes: Hematite is almost always opaque, usually cut into beads, cameos, intaglios, and carvings of any desired size. Massive material is available in very large pieces, solid, and good for cutting. Opaque submetallic gems are also sometimes faceted in the nature of marcasite, with a flat base and a few facets.

Comments: Hematite was used by the American Indians and others as a face paint (so-called red ochre). The polishing compound known as *rouge*, used widely on silver and gold, is powdered hematite. The streak is characteristic and diagnostic. Hematite is a weak electrical conductor, as opposed to psilomelane, a similar-appearing manganese oxide. Much hematite is cut in Idar-Oberstein, Germany, but the material comes from England. Hematite is simulated by a variety of materials. One of these is known as *hematine*, and consists of a mixture of stainless steel with sulfides of Cr and Ni. It has a red streak but is quite magnetic, whereas hematite is not. Hematine is made into intaglios and cameos. Hematite crystals that may be transparent are far too thin to cut, so faceted stones are unknown.

Name: From the Greek *hema* (*blood*), due to the red streak (powder) and appearance of some specimens.

HEMIMORPHITE

Formula: $Zn_4Si_2O_7(OH)_2 \cdot H_2O$.

Crystallography: Orthorhombic. Crystals tabular and thin, striated; fan-shaped aggregates.

Colors: White, colorless, pale blue, greenish, gray, yellowish, brown.

Luster: Vitreous; silky; dull.

Hardness: 4.5–5.

Density: 3.4–3.5.

Cleavage: Perfect 1 direction. Fracture even to subconchoidal. Brittle.

Optics: $\alpha = 1.614$; $\beta = 1.617$; $\gamma = 1.636$. Biaxial (+), $2V = 46°$.

Birefringence: 0.022.

Pleochroism: None.

Spectral: Not diagnostic.

Luminescence: None observed.

Occurrence: A secondary mineral in the oxide zones of ore deposits.
Found throughout the *southwestern U.S.* and *Mexico; various localities worldwide.*
Mexico: At Mapimi in Durango and at Santa Eulalia, Chihuahua are found crystals up to several inches in length; some of these are transparent and will yield stones up to ca 7–10 carats. Also found as blue crusts.

Stone Sizes: Blue massive material cut as cabochons to several inches in length. Colorless material from Mexico in faceted gems 1–3 carats; larger stones are very rare. *DG:* 1.90 (colorless, Mexico).

Comments: Hemimorphite is very rare as a faceted gemstone. Suitable material is known only from Mexico thus far. The massive blue material is a very delicate color, but is seldom cut because not very much has appeared on the market.

Name: In allusion to crystal forms.

HENRITERMIERITE See: Garnet.

HERCYNITE See: Chromite, Spinel.

HERDERITE

Formula: $CaBePO_4(F, OH)$.

Crystallography: Monoclinic. Crystals stout or prismatic; tabular; crusts.

Colors: Colorless, pale yellow, greenish white, pink, green.

Luster: Vitreous.

Hardness: 5–5.5.

Density: 2.95–3.02.

Cleavage: Interrupted. Fracture conchoidal. Brittle.

Optics: $\alpha = 1.591-1.594$; $\beta = 1.611-1.613$; $\gamma = 1.619-1.624$.
Biaxial (−), $2V = 67-75°$.
Note: Green gem from Brazil: $\alpha = 1.581$; $\beta = 1.601$; $\gamma = 1.610$. Birefringence 0.029. S.G. 3.02. Contains 7% F.

Birefringence: 0.029–0.030.

Dispersion: 0.017.

Pleochroism: None or weak.

Spectral: Not diagnostic.

Luminescence: Pale green in LW and SW; also pale violet in SW (Brazil, green gem) and stronger violet in LW. Orange fluorescence in X-rays with persistent phosphorescence.

Occurrence: Late stage hydrothermal mineral in granite pegmatites.
New Hampshire.
Germany; Austria; U.S.S.R.
Maine: colorless and pale yellow crystals.
Minas Gerais, Brazil: crystals up to nearly fist size, colorless and pink; some green.

Stone Sizes: Faceted gems from Maine are usually small (1−5 carats) and pale colored or colorless. Brazil gems, however, have stronger color and may be up to 25−30 carats from larger crystals.
SI: 5.9 (green, Brazil).
DG: 3.65 (blue, Brazil).

Comments: Herderite is a rare collector gem, especially in larger sizes. It is too soft for wear, but attractive when cut. Clean stones are very hard to find. There is always the possibility of new and larger material coming on the market from Brazilian sources.

Name: After S.A.W. von Herder, a mining official in Freiburg, Germany.

HESSONITE See: Garnet.

HETEROSITE See: purpurite.

HIDDENITE See: Spodumene.

HODGKINSONITE

Formula: $MnZn_2SiO_5 \cdot H_2O$.

Crystallography: Monoclinic. Crystals pyramidal or prismatic; massive; granular.

Colors: Bright pink to reddish brown, purplish pink.

Luster: Vitreous.

Hardness: 4.5−5.

Density: 3.91−3.99.

Cleavage: Perfect 1 direction. Fracture conchoidal. Brittle.

Optics: $\alpha = 1.720$; $\beta = 1.741$; $\gamma = 1.746$.
Biaxial (−), $2V = 52°$.

Birefringence: 0.026.

Pleochroism: Distinct: lavender/colorless/lavender.

Spectral: Not diagnostic.

Luminescence: Dull red in LW.

Occurrence: In metamorphosed limestone at Franklin, New Jersey with various other Zn and Mn minerals. Individual crystals reached $\frac{3}{4}$ inch in diameter, in veins up to several inches thick. The material was mined out years ago.

Stone Sizes: Cut gems are very small, less than 2 carats. This is an exceedingly rare material, available from only one locality, and only from older specimens.
PC: 0.89.

Comments: Hodgkinsonite is one of the rarest of all collector gems. Cut stones are bright and richly colored, but the crystals were never abundant and still fewer had transparent areas. Fewer than 10 cut stones may exist.

Name: After H.H. Hodgkinson of Franklin, New Jersey, who discovered the mineral.

HOLTITE

Formula: A *very complex* borosilicate of Al, Sb, and Ta, containing Fe, Be, Ti, Mn, and Nb.

Crystallography: Orthorhombic. Compact pebbles of acicular crystals, 2−15 mm diameter. Needles often in parallel arrangement.

Colors: Cream white, buff, olive green, brownish.

Luster: Dull to resinous.

Hardness: 8.5.

Density: 3.90.

Cleavage: Good 1 direction.

Optics: $\alpha = 1.743-1.746$; $\beta = 1.756-1.759$; $\gamma = 1.758-1.761$.
Biaxial (−), $2V = 49-55°$.

Birefringence: 0.015.

Pleochroism: Distinct: yellow/colorless/colorless.

Luminescence: Dull orange in SW, bright yellow in LW.

Occurrence: Alluvial tin deposit near *Greenbushes, W. Australia,* associated with cassiterite.

Stone Sizes: Could yield cabochons up to about 1 inch.

Comments: This mineral was first noted in 1937, but never described in detail before 1971. It has not yet been seen as a gem, but the high hardness would allow it to be worn with no risk of scratching. Holtite is now considered to be a variety of dumortierite. The mineral comes from the one locality and a cut stone would have to be considered a great rarity.

Name: After Harold E. Holt, Prime Minister of Australia from 1966 to 1967.

HOWLITE

Formula: $Ca_2B_5SiO_9(OH)_5$.

Crystallography: Monoclinic. Crystals tiny; usually nodular masses, chalky or porcellaneous.

Colors: White, opaque except in tiny grains.

Luster: Subvitreous.

Hardness: 3.5 or less.

Density: 2.45−2.58.

Cleavage: Smooth and even fracture.

Optics: $\alpha = 1.583-1.586$; $\beta = 1.596-1.598$; $\gamma = 1.605$. Biaxial (−), $2V$ large.

Birefringence: 0.022.

Pleochroism: None.

Spectral: Not diagnostic.

Luminescence: Brownish yellow in SW; some California material deep orange in LW.

Occurrence: Microscopic crystals or nodules occur in arid regions or borate deposits.
California: abundant nodules, up to a weight of several hundred pounds, as at Lang in Los Angeles Co.
Also occurs in the *Mohave Desert, California.*
Nova Scotia: small nodules.

Stone Sizes: Spheres up to about 8 inches in diameter have been cut; also seen as cabochons and tumble-polished stones.

Comments: Howlite is always opaque in nodules; it is an abundant material and easy to acquire. Sometimes it contains black, threadlike impurities resembling the veining in turquoise. Howlite is frequently dyed blue to resemble turquoise, and it makes a most convincing simulant. The white material is relatively unexciting in appearance.

Name: After H. How who described a mineral of approximately the same composition.

HUMITE See: Chondrodite.

HUREAULITE

Formula: $Mn_5(PO_4)_2[(PO_3)(OH)]_2 \cdot 4H_2O$.

Crystallography: Monoclinic. Crystals prismatic up to 3 cm, tabular; massive; compact.

Colors: Pale rose, violet-rose, yellowish, red-orange, orange-red, brownish orange, yellowish to reddish brown, gray, colorless.

Luster: Vitreous to greasy.

Hardness: 3.5.

Density: 3.19.

Cleavage: Good 1 direction. Fracture uneven. Brittle.

Optics: $\alpha = 1.637-1.652$; $\beta = 1.645-1.658$; $\gamma = 1.649-1.663$. Biaxial (−), $2V = 75°$.

Birefringence: 0.012.

Pleochroism: colorless/pale rose to yellow/reddish yellow-brown.

Spectral: Not diagnostic.

Luminescence: None.

Occurrence: In phosphate masses in granite pegmatites.
Branchville, Connecticut; North Groton, New Hampshire; South Dakota.
Haute Vienne, France; Portugal; Germany; Poland.
Pala, California: orange masses.

Stone Sizes: Massive material only suited for cabochons. No faceted gems have been reported to date, but facetable material likely exists and one day will be cut.

Comments: The colors are rich and lively, but the mineral is too soft for wear. Hureaulite is a rare collector gem, and very rare even in cabochon form.

Name: After the locality, Hureaux, France.

HYALITE See: Opal.

HYDROGROSSULAR See: Garnet.

HYPERSTHENE See: Enstatite.

I

ICELAND SPAR   See: Calcite.

IDOCRASE   *Alternative name:* Vesuvianite.

Formula: $Ca_{19}Al_4Fe(Al, Mg, Fe)_8Si_{18}O_{70}(OH, F)_8$ + Be, Cu, Cr, Mn, Na, K, Ti, B, H_2O, U, Th, Zn, Sn, Sb, rare earths.
Incredible array of elements substitute in the idocrase structure.

Crystallography: Tetragonal. Crystals often well formed, prismatic, pyramidal, often with complex modifications; granular, massive. Often intergrown with grossular.

Colors: Colorless, green (various shades), brown (various shades), white, yellow (various shades), red, brownish red, blue, blue-green, pink, violet. Sometimes color-zoned.

Luster: Vitreous to resinous.

Hardness: 6–7.

Density: 3.32–3.47.

Cleavage: None. Fracture conchoidal.

Optics: Variable depending on paragenesis and mineral associations.

Zillerthal, Tyrol, Switzerland: brown crystals; also at Zermatt, other locations.

Laurel, Quebec, Canada: bright yellow grains and masses.

Amity, New York (xanthite): brown crystals, large; seldom cut.

Telemark, Norway (cyprine): fine blue masses with pink thulite.

Asbestos, Quebec, Canada: superb crystal groups and masses, apple green, sometimes colored deep green by Cr or pink by Mn.

Kenya: green and brown crystal fragments suitable for faceting.

Sanford, Maine: brown and green crystals and masses.

Wilui River, U.S.S.R.: green crystals (known as *wiluite*).

Morelos, Mexico: green crystals associated with pink grossular in lake bed.

Quetta, Pakistan: fine green crystals; some transparent.

Stone Sizes: Crystals up to several inches in length occur at a few localities, but these are seldom transparent except in small areas. The maximum expectable size for a faceted idocrase in on the order of 10 carats (for brown material from Italy and Africa), perhaps 15 carats (Pulga, California, large crystals found) in green.

Environment	e	o	Birefringence
Serpentinites	1.705–1.750	1.702–1.761	0.018
Contact metamorphic rocks	1.655–1.733	1.674–1.737	0.015
Alkalic rocks	1.655–1.727	1.715–1.731	0.004
Regionally metamorphosed rocks	1.697–1.698	1.705–1.707	0.008

Uniaxial (+) or (−); sometimes anomalously biaxial (−) or (+); twinned.

Note: Antimonian idocrase from contact metamorphic rocks, greenish-yellow grains, $e = 1.758–1.775$, $o = 1.775–1.795$, birefringence 0.017–0.025; $Sb_2O_3 > 15\%$.

Dispersion: 0.019.

Pleochroism: Weak in color shades of crystal color.

Spectral: Strong line at 4610, weak at 5285.

Luminescence: None.

Occurrence: Serpentines and related rocks; contact metamorphic deposits, especially in limestones and dolomites; alkalic rocks; regionally metamorphosed rocks.

Finland; Japan; Korea.

Arkansas.

California: californite.

Ala, Piedmont, Italy: fine brown and green crystals.

SI: 3.5 (brown, Italy).

DG: 8.50 (brown, Africa).

Comments: *Idocrase* is one of the lesser known and more beautiful collector gems. When properly cut it is as bright and attractive as the garnets which it so strongly resembles (grossular). The complexities of its chemistry lead to a huge range in properties and colors. Cuttable material is known from Italy (brown and green), Quebec (pale green, bright yellow), New York (brown), Pakistan (green), Kenya (brown and green).

Californite is a massive idocrase–grossular mixture reported first from California and later found in various other localities, such as Africa and Pakistan. The density is 3.25–3.32, and has a strong 4610 band in its spectrum, which is easily distinguished from the chrome spectrum of jadeite.

Name: From the Greek words *idos* and *krasis*, meaning *mixed appearance,* because idocrase crystal forms resemble those seen on other species.

INDERITE *Also known as* Lesserite; *dimorph of* Kurnakovite.

Formula: $Mg_2B_6O_{11} \cdot 15H_2O$.

Crystallography: Monoclinic. Crystals prismatic, up to 10×1 cm; nodular; acicular crystals also.

Colors: Colorless; massive varieties white to pink.

Luster: Vitreous; pearly on cleavage.

Hardness: 2.5.

Density: 1.78−1.86.

Cleavage: Perfect 1 direction. Fracture uneven. Brittle.

Optics: $\alpha = 1.486-1.489$; $\beta = 1.488-1.493$; $\gamma = 1.504-1.507$.
Biaxial (+), $2V = 37-52°$.

Birefringence: 0.017−0.020.

Spectral: Not diagnostic.

Luminescence: None.

Occurrence: Borate deposits in arid regions.
Kern Co., California: large crystals, often transparent.
Inder borate deposit, Kazakhstan, *U.S.S.R.:* as nodules in red clay.

Stone Sizes: Gems over 50 carats or more could be cut from large transparent crystals.

Comments: Inderite is very soft and hard to cut, and only a few stones have been cut by collectors. There is plenty of cuttable material in existence, and although the material comes from only a few localities it is not considered a great rarity. The surface of cut stones may become white and cloudy after cutting; care must be taken in storage and to dry the stones after cutting.

Name: After the locality, Inder Lake, Kazakhstan, U.S.S.R.

INDICOLITE See Tourmaline.

IOLITE See: Cordierite.

J

JADE   See: Jadeite, Nephrite.

JADEITE (= JADE)   Pyroxene group.

Formula: $NaAlSi_2O_6$.

Crystallography: Monoclinic. Crystals very rare and tiny, usually granular with tough, interlocked crystals; fibrous; as alluvial boulders and pebbles.

Colors: Colorless, white, all shades of green, yellow-green, yellowish brown, brown, red, orange, violet (mauve), gray, black.

Luster: Vitreous.

Hardness: 6.5−7.

Density: 3.25−3.36; usually 3.34+.

Cleavage: None (massive). Fracture splintery. Very tough.

Optics: $\alpha = 1.640$; $\beta = 1.645$; $\gamma = 1.652-1.667$. Shadow edge usually 1.66.
Biaxial (+), $2V = 67°$.

Birefringence: 0.012−0.020.

Pleochroism: None.

Spectral: Jadeite has a distinctive spectrum useful in identification.

There is a strong line at 4375, weak bands at 4500, 4330. The 4375 line is diagnostic for jadeite but may not be seen in rich, deep green material, which has a Cr spectrum: strong line at 6915, weak at 6550, 6300.

Luminescence: Pale colors may show dim white glow in LW. No reaction in SW. X-rays may give intense blue-violet glow in pale yellow and mauve stones.

Occurrence: Jadeite occurs chiefly in serpentine derived from olivine rocks in Upper Burma. Also as alluvial boulders.
Mexico; near Manzanal, Guatemala.
San Benito Co., California: lenses and nodules in chert (discovered 1939); also mixture of nephrite and jadeite (see *nephrite*, page 80). Colors: white, gray-green, pale green, dark blue-green; semi-opaque.
New Zealand. Japan: not gem quality.
U.S.S.R.: apple-green colored jadeite occurs.
Maw-Sit-Sit, Upper Burma; jadeite mixed with albite, showing dark spots and green vein pattern. This jadeite may be rich in Cr (index 1.52−1.54, density 2.46−3.15, jade−albite mixture).

Stone Sizes: Translucent and colorless material occurs rarely and in very small pieces. Boulders may weigh up to several tons. Carvings 18 inches high are seen in many collections, in various colors. So-called *Imperial jade*, almost transparent and the deep green color of fine emerald, is occasionally seen in cabochons and small carvings up to about 50 carats. Stones over 5 carats are very rare.

Comments: *Jadeite* is usually marketed through Yunan Province, China. Green boulders may have a brown skin due to weathering, which is often utilized in carving. The best jade known is Burmese in origin and occurs in a wide range of colors. There are many simulants and imitations. *Imperial jade* is exceedingly rare and very costly. Another popular color is a fine apple green shade, as well as lavender (mauve). The rich green material from Burma is sometimes called *Yunan jade* and is extremely beautiful when light passes through it. *Chloromelanite* is opaque, dark green to black jade that is seldom seen in jewelry but is occasionally carved.

The value of a jade item is as much a function of the artistry of the carving or workmanship and the antiquity value as the color and quality of the jade itself. The complexities of evaluation caused by these factors make jade a very specialized gemstone and the market largely a collector market.

Name: *Jade* from the Spanish *piedras de ijada*, (*stone of the loins*); this is due to the healing powers for kidney ailments ascribed to jade, doubtless as a result of sympathetic magic because of the kidney or organ shapes of tumbled pebbles. Translated into French this was *pierre de l'éjade;* a printer's error when the name first appeared in French made it *pierre de le jade*, which the English people quickly chopped down to simply *jade*.
See also: Nephrite.

JASPER   See: Quartz.

JEFFERSONITE   See: Diopside.

JEREMEJEVITE

Formula: $Al_6B_5O_{15}(OH)_3$.

Crystallography: Hexagonal. Crystals elongated and tapering; small grains.

Colors: Colorless, pale blue-green, pale yellow-brown.

Luster: Vitreous.

Hardness: 6.5.

Density: 3.28−3.31.

Cleavage: None; fracture conchoidal.

Optics: $e = 1.640$; $o = 1.653$. Uniaxial (−).
Cores of crystals sometimes biaxial, $2V = 0-50°$.

Birefringence: 0.007−0.013.

Pleochroism: S.W. African material: light cornflower blue/colorless to light yellow.

Spectral: Vague absorbtion band at about 5000.

Luminescence: None.

Occurrence:
A few single crystals were found on *Mt. Soktuj, Nerchinsk dist., E. Siberia, U.S.S.R.*, in loose granitic debris under the turf.
Cape Cross, near Swakopmund, S.W. Africa: very long pyramidal crystals (up to 2 cm) of blue-green color: *e* = 1.639, *o* = 1.648, birefringence 0.007.

Stone Sizes: No gems cut from the U.S.S.R. material; however, the Swakopmund crystals have been cut, with gems up to about 5 carats possible. These are a lovely blue-green color, are relatively easy to cut, and hard enough for wear. A typical size for a clean gem is 1-2 carats.

Comments: Until the S.W. African find, jeremejevite was an exceedingly rare mineral available in almost microscopic grains. The African crystals are amazing in that they are both large and gemmy. At this writing few gems have been cut from the material and the extent of the find is not known. The crystals are not abundant at the locality, so jeremejevite is still an extremely rare collector gemstone.

Name: After Pavel V. Jeremejev, Russian mineralogist and engineer.

JET

Formula: C.
Carbon, plus impurities; *not a mineral.*

Crystallography: Amorphous. Usually in coal seams as black masses and lumps.

Colors: Black, brownish.

Luster: Dull; vitreous when polished.

Hardness: 2.4-4.

Density: 1.30-1.35.

Cleavage: None. Conchoidal fracture. Brittle.

Optics: Blurred shadow edge on refractometer at 1.66.

Other Tests: Burns like coal, and gives burning coal odor with hot needle.

Occurrence: Jet is fossilized wood, actually lignite, a form of brown coal.
Henry Mountains, Utah; Colorado; New Mexico.
Spain; Aude, France; Germany; U.S.S.R.
Whitby, England: jet in seams; classic locality.

Stone Sizes: Carvings and cabochons of any desired size could be cut.

Comments: Jet has been known since Roman times and has been the most popular of all black gems. It has been used for many years in mourning jewelry. It is less popular and widely used in modern times. It takes a very good polish, and is less brittle than the harder anthracite coal that it resembles. Jet is often faceted (the stones have a flat bottom) to add sparkle to the somber tones of jet jewelry.

Name: Originally from Gagas, the name of a town and river in Asia Minor.

JULGOLDITE See: Chlorastrolite.

K

KIMZEYITE   See: Garnet.

KNORRINGITE   See: Garnet.

KORNERUPINE

Formula: $Mg_3Al_6(Si, Al, B)_5O_{21}(OH)$.

Crystallography: Orthorhombic. Crystals prismatic; also fibrous, columnar.

Colors: Colorless, white, pink, greenish yellow, sea green, dark green, brown, black.

Luster: Vitreous.

Hardness: 6−7.

Cleavage: Perfect 2 directions. Fracture conchoidal. Brittle.

Density: 3.27−3.45; gems are 3.28−3.35.

Optics: varies with locality:

Locality	α	β	γ	Birefrin-gence	Density
Madagascar	1.661	1.673	1.674	0.013	3.28
Ceylon	1.669	1.681	1.682	0.013	3.35
Germany	1.675	1.687	1.687	0.014	3.37
Natal	1.682	1.696	1.699	0.017	3.45
East Africa	1.662	1.675	1.677	0.015	—

Biaxial (−), $2V = 3$−$48°$. Gems may be pseudo-uniaxial.

Dispersion: 0.018.

Pleochroism: Pronounced, and visible to the naked eye: green/yellow to reddish-brown.

Spectral: Weak band seen at 5030.

Inclusions: Zircon crystals.

Luminescence: none (Ceylon) or yellowish (Burmese green gems, stronger in E. African stones) in LW and SW.

Occurrence: First found in Greenland in radiating crystals (non-gem).
Gatineau Co., Quebec: large crystals, dark green to greenish yellow.
Itrongahy, Madagascar: large, gemmy, dark green crystals, also pale aquamarine-blue.
Betroka, Madagascar; Inanakafy, Madagascar: gray to brown prismatic crystals.
Matale dist., Ceylon: yellow-brown and reddish pebbles, as rolled grains in gravels.
Mogok, Burma: greenish brown material in gem gravels.

Kwale dist., Kenya: light green material, some large clean pieces; colored green by vanadium.
Tanzania: chrome variety with green color.

Stone Sizes: Canadian crystals (non-gem) are up to 2 inches across. Most gems are under 5 carats, but occasional large material from Ceylon or Burma yields a gem in the 25−30 carat class.
SI: 21.6 (brown, Ceylon); 10.8 (brown, Madagascar); 8.1 (green, Ceylon).
PC: 16.50 (golden, Ceylon), sold in 1968.
DG: 6.4 (Ceylon).

Comments: Star kornerupine also exists from Mogok, Burma, but is *very* rare. Some catseyes have also been found (indices 1.673/1.686/1.690). Kornerupine is generally dark brown or green and not very attractive because of the somber colors. The light green material from Kenya is very much more appealing, but the sizes are always small (under 3 carats as a rule). Despite the fact that many stones are in museums and collections, kornerupine is a rather rare gemstone and worth acquiring when available.

Name: After the Danish geologist Kornerup.

KUNZITE   See: Spodumene.

KURNAKOVITE   *Dimorph of* Inderite.

Formula: $Mg_2B_6O_{11} \cdot 15H_2O$.

Crystallography: Triclinic. Crystals large and blocky, often in clusters; large cleavable masses; aggregates.

Colors: Colorless, with a white surface coating.

Luster: Vitreous; pearly on cleavage.

Hardness: 2.5−3.

Density: 1.78−1.85.

Cleavage: Good 1 direction. Fracture conchoidal. Brittle.

Optics: $\alpha = 1.488$−1.491; $\beta = 1.508$−1.511; $\gamma = 1.515$−1.525.
Biaxial (+), $2V = 80°$.

Birefringence: 0.027−0.036.

Pleochroism: None.

Spectral: Not diagnostic.

Luminescence: None.

Occurrence: Borate deposits in arid areas.
Inder Lake, Kazakhstan, U.S.S.R.
Boron, Kern Co., California: crystals to 24 inches across and large masses.

DATOLITE: Paterson,
New Jersey (4.0)

DANBURITE: Charcas, Mexico (8.5)

DIAMOND: Africa (portion of A. V. Gumuchian's
"Spectrum Collection", New York City; ca ½ to 5)

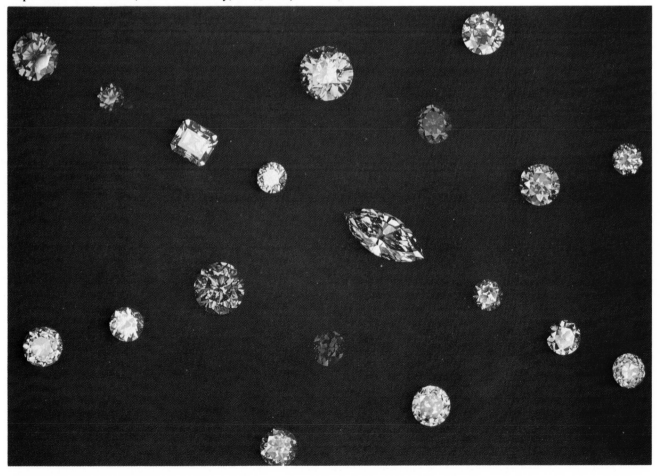

DIAMOND: S. Africa (ca 2)

DIAMOND: S. Africa; at sorting office of DeBeers Co., Kimberley
(ca 0.25 to 5, rough crystals)

DIOPSIDE: Burma (2.61), U.S.S.R. (1.04), New York (3.83)

DIOPSIDE: *Chrome diopside,* U.S.S.R (ca 1 each)

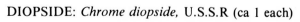

DIOPTASE: Tsumeb, S.W. Africa
(specimen ca 6 inches high)

DOLOMITE: New Mexico
(ca 2, rough 2 inches across)

DOLOMITE: Spain (4.5)

DOMEYKITE: Mohawk Mine, Keweenaw Peninsula, Michigan
(ca 2 inches across)

DUMORTIERITE: Nevada (ca 2 inches across),
Ogilby, California (1 inch across)

EKANITE: Ceylon (ca 0.5)

ENSTATITE: Burma (2.16), Africa (1.2), India (1.85)

ENSTATITE: Africa (1.8, 2.4), Burma (0.6, 0.47, 1.47 *catseye*)

ENSTATITE: India, *Star Enstatite* (ca 3 to 15)

HYPERSTHENE: Africa (ca 6)

EPIDOTE: Baja, Mexico (1.0),
Kenya (1.2)

CLINOZOISITE:
Mexico (1.18)

ZOISITE: Tanzania, *Tanzanite,*
unheated, showing natural color range (ca 0.5 to 5)

PIEDMONTITE: Adams, County, Pennsylvania
(ca 4 inches across)

ZOISITE: Norway, *Thulite*
(each specimen ca 2 inches across)

ZOISITE: Tanzania,
Tanzanite (18.9)

EUCLASE: Brazil (ca 0.3 to 1.3)

ORTHOCLASE (feldspar): Madagascar (4.98), Rhodesia (1.23), Ceylon (1.5) Madagascar (2.5)

ALBITE (feldspar): *Moonstone,* India and Ceylon (ca 5 each)

MICROCLINE (feldspar): *Amazonite,* Amelia Court House, Virginia (ca 1 inch), Ontario, Canada (ca 2 inches across)

ALBITE (feldspar): Ceylon (4.6), New Mexico (3.9)

LABRADORITE (feldspar): Oregon (2.2, 1.8), Madagascar (1.87), Mexico (5.1)

LABRADORITE (feldspar): Oregon (14)

LABRADORITE (feldspar): *Sunstone,* Oregon (ca 5)

LABRADORITE (feldspar): Finland (ca 2 inches across)

FRIEDELITE: Franklin,
New Jersey (1.74)

FERGUSONITE: Madawasca, Ontario, Canada (ca 1.5 inches long)

FLUORITE: Cumberland, England (203.35), Africa (52.6, 100+)

FLUORITE: Back row: Canada (6.14), Illinois (17.1)
Front row: Germany (4.35), Colombia (13.0), New Mexico (1.2), Switzerland (3.5)

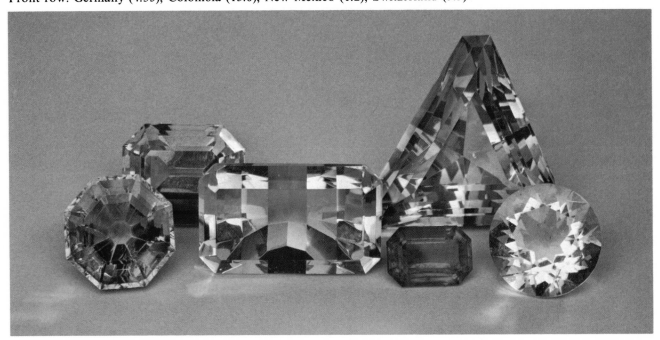

GROSSULAR (Garnet): S. Africa, cabochon (4.1);
all others Tanzania (ca 1 to 6.5)

GADOLINITE: Hitterö,
Southern Norway (2.21)

GROSSULAR (Garnet): Kenya, *Tsavorite* (pear shape 5.15;
front row 1.6, 1.4, 0.95, 3.0)

GROSSULAR (Garnet): *Hessonite:* Brazil (12.0), Quebec (5), Brazil (ca 7, 22)

ANDRADITE (garnet): Stanley Butte, Arizona (ca 3)

ANDRADITE (garnet): *Demantoid,* U.S.S.R. (1.93, 0.93, 4.37)

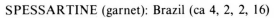

SPESSARTINE (garnet): Brazil (ca 4, 2, 2, 16)

ALMANDINE (garnet): Idaho (1.0), Africa (4.5, 9.0), Brazil (24.2), Africa, *rhodolite* (8.0, 3.5)

ALMANDINE (garnet):
Star garnet, Africa (ca 15)

GRANDIDIERITE:
Madagascar (1.1)

GYPSUM: Mexico (specimen ca 2 inches high)

27

HAMBERGITE:
Madagascar (1.5)

HEMIMORPHITE:
Mexico (0.75)

HEMATITE: Brazil (7.64)

HEMIMORPHITE: Zacatecas, Mexico (ca 3 inches high)

HERDERITE: Brazil (9.6, 3.65, 9.25)

HODGKINSONITE:
Franklin, New Jersey
(0.35)

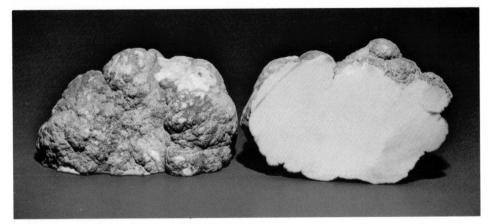

HOWLITE: California (nodule ca 3 inches across)

HUREAULITE: Pala, California
(ca 3 inches across)

IDOCRASE: Laurel, Quebec (ca 2)

INDERITE: Kern County, California (ca 2 inches long).
Exterior of specimen has dehydrated and opacified; interior is transparent.

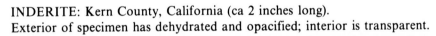

29

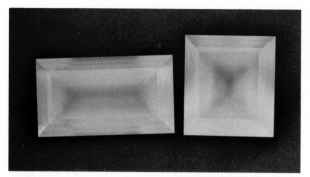

NEPHRITE (jade): Asia (1.9); JADEITE (jade): Burma (2.0)

NEPHRITE (jade): Siberia, U.S.S.R., (owl ca 2 inches tall)

JADEITE (jade): "*Imperial jade*", Burma (4.77)

JADEITE and NEPHRITE (jade): Asia, U.S.S.R., assorted carvings and beads (snuff bottles ca 2 inches high)

JADEITE (jade): Burma (ca 8 inches high)

NEPHRITE (jade): China,
"chicken-bone jade",
Ming Dynasty, 14th cent. (ca 8 inches high)

JADEITE (jade): *Chloromelanite*, Burma
(ca 3 inches long)

JEREMEJEVITE: Nerchinsk,
Siberia, U.S.S.R. (0.5, 0.4)

JET: Whitby, England (ca 3 carats each)

JADEITE (jade): Burma (fine lavender beads and carvings; large beads ca 10 mm)

KORNERUPINE: Kenya (0.55), Madagascar (1.23), Kenya (1.47)

KYANITE: Brazil (4.55, 7.80)

Stone Sizes: California material could yield stones of several hundred carats from large transparent masses or cleavages.

Comments: Kurnakovite is similar to inderite. Both are colorless and very uninteresting as faceted gems, which is why very few have been cut. The material is obtainable in large size, but softness and cleavage make cutting a real chore.

Name: After N.S. Kurnakov, Russian mineralogist and chemist.

KUTNAHORITE See: Dolomite.

KYANITE *Trimorphous with* Andalusite, Sillimanite.
Formula: Al_2SiO_5.

Crystallography: Triclinic. Crystals bladed, flattened and elongated; fibrous, massive.

Colors: Blue, blue-green, green; also white, gray, yellow, pink, nearly black. Color zoned in individual crystals.

Luster: Vitreous; pearly on cleavage.

Hardness: 4−7.5; varies with direction in single crystals.

Cleavage: Perfect 1 direction.

Density: 3.53−3.68; gems usually upper end of range.

Optics: $\alpha = 1.712-1.718$; $\beta = 1.721-1.723$; $\gamma = 1.727-1.734$.
Biaxial (−), $2V = 82-83°$.

Birefringence: 0.017.

Dispersion: 0.020.

Pleochroism: Pronounced: violet-blue/colorless/cobalt-blue.
Also pleochroic in all shades of yellow-green and green.

Spectral: One line observed in deep red at 7100, and 2 lines in deep blue, with dark edge at about 6000.

Luminescence: Variable fluorescence, mostly dim red in LW.

Occurrence: In schists, gneiss and granite pegmatites. Many localities are known.
Vermont; Connecticut; Virginia; Georgia; Massachusetts.
Various places in U.S., especially Yancy Co., *North Carolina:* deep blue or green crystals, up to 2 inches long, some facetable.
India; Italy.
Brazil: large blue and blue-green crystals.
Machakos Dist., Kenya: large blue crystals, banded with green; also colorless!
Switzerland: with staurolite in schist.
Kenya: fine blue color, facetable.

Stone Sizes: Gems have been cut up to about 20 carats, seldom completely clean over 5 carats, however. Many of these stones are Brazilian; some are African.
SI: 10.7 (blue, Brazil); 9.1 (green, Brazil); 4.9 (blue, Tanzania).
PC: 6.57 (blue-green, North Carolina).
DG: 14.0 (blue, Africa); 8.55 (bluish, Africa).

Comments: Kyanite is very rare in faceted gems, especially those free from inclusions and flaws. The material is extremely difficult to cut, because of its perfect cleavage and the extreme variability in hardness in different directions in the same crystal. A few catseye kyanites are known to exist.

Name: From the Greek *kyanos*, meaning *blue*.

L

LABRADORITE See: Feldspar.

LANDERITE See: Garnet.

LANGBEINITE
Formula: $K_2Mg_2(SO_4)_3$.

Crystallography: Isometric. Crystals are rare; usually massive, bedded; in nodules.

Colors: Colorless, white, gray, yellowish, greenish, pinkish, violet.

Luster: Vitreous.

Hardness: 3.5–4.

Density: 2.83.

Cleavage: None. Fracture conchoidal. Brittle.

Optics: $N = 1.536$.

Luminescence: Faint greenish white in LW (New Mexico).

Occurrence: Evaporite deposits from marine waters.
Saskatchewan, Canada; North Germany; Austria; India.
Carlsbad, New Mexico: beds up to 7 feet thick.

Stone Sizes: Colorless stones up to 10–15 carats potentially. Cabochons of any size.

Comments: This material is extremely nondescript, and is cut solely as a curiosity. The gems are soft, pale colored or colorless, with no fire. Few cut stones have been reported, but this may be due to a lack of interest rather than a lack of suitable rough.

Name: After A. Langbein of Leopoldshall, Austria.

LAPIS LAZULI See: Lazurite.

LAWSONITE
Formula: $CaAl_2Si_2O_7(OH)_2 \cdot H_2O$.

Crystallography: Orthorhombic. Crystals prismatic; massive, granular.

Colors: Colorless, white, gray, blue, pinkish.

Luster: Vitreous to greasy.

Hardness: 6+.

Density: 3.05–3.12.

Cleavage: Perfect in 2 directions.

Optics: $\alpha = 1.665$; $\beta = 1.674-1.675$; $\gamma = 1.684-1.686$. Biaxial (+), $2V = 84°$.

Birefringence: 0.019.

Dispersion: High.

Pleochroism: Blue/yellow-green/colorless *or* pale brownish yellow/deep blue-green/yellowish.

Spectral: Not diagnostic.

Luminescence: None.

Occurrence: Low-temperature metamorphic rocks; metamorphic schists; glaucophane schists.
Santa Clara, Cuba; Italy; Japan; New Caledonia; France; Italy; other locations.
Tiburon Peninsula, California: original material.
Covelo, Mendocino Co., California: 2 inch crystals.

Stone Sizes: The maximum likely is 2–3 carats. Gems are pale blue in color.

Comments: Lawsonite is extremely rare as a faceted stone, seldom reported and generally unavailable.

Name: After Prof. A.C. Lawson of the University of California.

LAZULITE *Series to* Scorzalite: $(Fe, Mg)Al_2(PO_4)_2(OH)_2$.
Formula: $MgAl_2(PO_4)_2(OH)_2$.

Crystallography: Monoclinic. Crystals acute pyramidal; massive, compact, granular.

Colors: Blue, blue-green, light blue, deep azure blue.

Luster: Vitreous to dull.

Cleavage: Indistinct to good in 1 direction.

	Lazulite	Scorzalite
Density	3.08 (Mg end)	3.38 (Fe end)
		(species boundary at 3.2)
Optics		
α	1.604–1.635	1.633–1.639
β	1.633–1.663	1.663–1.670
γ	1.642–1.673	1.673–1.680
sign	(−)	(−)
$2V$	69°	62°
Birefringence	0.031–0.038	0.040

Pleochroism: Strong: colorless/blue/dark blue.

Luminescence: None.

Spectral: Not diagnostic.

Occurrence: Quartz veins; granite pegmatites; metamorphic rocks, especially quartzites. *Note:* the Fe end member, scorzalite, is relatively rare. Lazulite localities are much better known, as follows.
Palermo Quarry, North Groton, New Hampshire; Graves Mountain, Georgia; South Dakota.
Potosi, Bolivia; Lobito Bay, Angola; Madagascar; Hörrsjoberg, Sweden.

Yukon, Alaska: fine gemmy blue crystals.

Champion Mine, Mono County, California: masses to 6 inches across.

Bhandara dist., India: gemmy crystals (indices 1.615/1.635/1.645; S.G. 3.17).

Minas Gerais, Brazil: fine blue gem crystals (indices 1.609/1.640).

Stone Sizes: The largest gemmy lazulite crystals yield stones up to about 5 carats. Most faceted gems are 1–2 carats, and even these tend to be badly flawed. The large California masses are not suited for faceting.

DG: 4.20 (blue, Africa).

Comments: Lazulite makes a magnificent, deep blue gemstone. Stones over 1 carat, if clean, are quite rare, and gems over 5 carats are exceedingly rare. The supply of rough is limited, although the mineral itself has widespread occurrence. Faceted lazulite strongly resembles blue apatite. The hardness is marginal for wearing in jewelry. Cabochons have been cut from massive lazulite, such as the material from New Hampshire and California.

Name: *Lazulite* from the German *lazurstein*, meaning *blue stone. Scorzalite* after E.P. Scorza, Brazilian mineralogist.

LAZURAPATITE   See: Apatite.

LAZURITE (= LAPIS LAZULI)   Sodalite group.

Formula: $(Na, Ca)_8(Al, Si)_{12}O_{24}(S, SO_4)$.

Crystallography: Isometric. Crystals very rare, dodecahedral, up to about 2 inches in size. Also massive, compact, disseminated, in veins.

Colors: Deep blue, azure blue, violet-blue, greenish blue.

Streak: Light blue.

Luster: Dull.

Hardness: 5–6 (depending on impurity content).

Density: Pure: 2.38–2.45; gem lapis: 2.7–2.9 or higher if much pyrite present.

Cleavage: Imperfect; none in massive material. Fracture uneven.

Optics: Isotropic. N ca 1.50.

Inclusions: Pyrite (brassy yellow) and white calcite in massive material.

Luminescence: Orange spots or streaks in LW (Afghanistan and Chile), dimmer and more pink in SW. X-rays cause yellowish glow in streaks. May fluoresce whitish in SW.

Chemical Test: A drop of HCl on lapis releases H_2S gas (rotten egg odor).

Occurrence: Contact metamorphic mineral in limestone, due to recrystallization of impurities; also in granites.

Italy; Labrador; Mogok, Burma; Pakistan.

California: blue-gray with white spots.

Colorado: stringers in limestone, dark color, much pyrite.

Badakshan, Afghanistan: among the oldest operating mines in the world (7,000 years). Lapis occurs in large blocks and crystals in white matrix. Source of the world's finest lapis.

Sludyanka R., Mongolia: light blue lapis, with pyrite.

Chilean Andes: gray and blue mixture, color inferior to Afghan material.

Stone Sizes: Rough blocks from Afghanistan, of fine color, are known up to 100 kg. One block of Chilean material, found in a Peruvian grave, was $24 \times 12 \times 8$ inches. In the Pitti Palace, Florence, Italy, is a 40.5 cm tall vase of fine blue material.

Comments: The gem known as lapis lazuli, or simply lapis, is actually a rock, composed of lazurite, haüyne, sodalite, and nosean, all members of the sodalite group of minerals. Lazurite itself may be considered a sulfur-rich haüyne. Also present in the rock are calcite and pyrite, in various percentages. The finest lapis is considered to be a solid, deep blue with no white calcite spots, and just a sprinkling of brassy yellow pyrite. Such material is found in Afghanistan and Pakistan only, in commercially interesting quantities.

Lapis is very well suited to men's jewelry, because it has a rich blue color and does not show wear easily. It is fairly tough, takes an excellent polish, and is dark enough not to be a problem in color coordination with clothes.

Name: From a Persian word, *lazhward*, meaning *blue*.

LEGRANDITE

Formula: $Zn_2(OH)AsO_4 \cdot H_2O$.

Crystallography: Monoclinic. Crystals prismatic, also in sprays and fans.

Colors: Yellow, colorless.

Luster: Vitreous.

Hardness: 4.5.

Density: 3.98–4.04.

Cleavage: Poor. Fracture uneven. Brittle.

Optics: $\alpha = 1.675-1.702$; $\beta = 1.690-1.709$; $\gamma = 1.735-1.740$.
Biaxial (+), $2V = 50°$.

Birefringence: 0.060.

Pleochroism: Colorless to yellow.

Spectral: Not diagnostic.

Luminescence: None.

Occurrence: In vugs in limonite. Only occurrence is in Mexico.

Flor de Pena Mine, Nuevo León, Mexico: first discovered locality.

Ojuela Mine, Mapimi, Mexico: best known locality, from which come magnificent crystal clusters, single crystals up to 6 cm long and 7.5 mm thick. This is the source of the only cuttable material.

Stone Sizes: The maximum to expect in a cut legrandite is about 2−4 carats. A larger stone would be a great rarity, and even 1 carat gems are very hard to find. Many mineral specimens exist, but transparent crystals are extremely rare even in the source locality.

Comments: This mineral was first described in 1932, and it has become a very popular specimen mineral among collectors, because of its intense yellow color and esthetic crystal groupings. It is too soft for wear, but the yellow color is unique among gems and very distinctive. This is one of the loveliest of all the rare collector gemstones.

Name: After a Belgian mine manager, Mr. Legrand, who collected the first specimens.

LEPIDOLITE   Mica family.

Formula: $K(Li, Al)_3(Si, Al)_4O_{10}(F, OH)_2$.

Crystallography: Monoclinic. Crystals tabular; also masses of plates, spheroidal masses.

Colorless: Yellow, pink, purplish, white, grayish.

Luster: Pearly on cleavage.

Hardness: 2.5−4.

Density: 2.8−3.3

Cleavage: Perfect and easy 1 direction.

Optics: $\alpha = 1.525-1.548$; $\beta = 1.551-1.585$; $\gamma = 1.554-1.587$.
Biaxial (−), $2V = O-58°$.

Birefringence: 0.018−0.038.

Pleochroism: Absorption stronger in the plane of the cleavage.

Spectral: Not diagnostic.

Luminescence: None.

Occurrence: Almost exclusively in granite pegmatites; also in tin veins.
San Diego Co., California; Gunnison, Colorado; Black Hills, South Dakota; Wyoming; Arizona; New Mexico; New England states, especially Maine.
Sweden; Germany; Finland; Czechoslovakia; U.S.S.R.; Madagascar; Japan; Bikita, Rhodesia.
Brazil: fine pink and reddish crystals.

Stone Sizes: Large nodules from California are up to 6 inches across or more. Lepidolite, like the other micas, is rarely transparent enough to facet, and then it is so difficult to cut that few people ever attempt the feat! Facetable lepidolite does exist, notably from Brazil.

Comments: Reddish granular or massive lepidolite is usually slabbed for ornamental purposes, such as ashtrays, paperweights and bookends. Faceted micas are virtually nonexistent, because of the extreme perfection of the cleavage and the variable hardness within crystals.

Name: From the Greek *lepis,* (*scale*), because of the scaly nature of the massive material.

LESSERITE   See: Inderite.

LEUCITE

Formula: $KAlSi_2O_6$.

Crystallography: Tetragonal (pseudocubic). Crystals trapezohedral; granular.

Colors: Colorless, white, gray, yellowish.

Luster: Vitreous; dull on some crystals.

Hardness: 5.5−6.

Density: 2.47−2.50.

Cleavage: Poor. Fracture conchoidal. Brittle.

Optics: Isotropic; N ca 1.50. Optically (+) if uniaxial.

Birefringence: Low to zero.

Luminescence: Medium-bright orange in LW (Italy), or none. Bluish glow in X-rays.

Occurrence: In potassium-rich basic lavas.
Wyoming; Montana; Arkansas; New Jersey.
British Columbia; France; Germany; Zaire; Uganda; Australia.
Alban Hills, near Rome, Italy: source of the world's only transparent leucite crystals. These are colorless, up to about 1 cm.

Stone Sizes: Italian material has been cut to about 3 carats. There is very little of this material, always small, and clean only in very tiny stones.

Comments: Leucite is abundant in various lava rocks, but is extremely rare in facetable crystals. The material has little appeal except for its extreme scarcity. Stones often have a slight milky or cloudy look, and anything over 3 carats is likely to be included.

Name: From the Greek *leukos,* meaning *white.*

LIDDICOATITE   See: Tourmaline.

LINARITE

Formula: $PbCu(SO_4)(OH)_2$.

Crystallography: Monoclinic. Crystals prismatic; also in druses and crusts.

Colors: Dark azure blue.

Streak: Pale blue.

Luster: Vitreous to subadamantine.

Hardness: 2.5.

Density: 5.30.

Cleavage: Perfect 1 direction. Fracture conchoidal. Brittle.

Optics: $\alpha = 1.809$; $\beta = 1.838$, $\gamma = 1.859$. Biaxial (−), $2V = 80°$.

Birefringence: 0.050.

Pleochroism: Pale blue/medium blue/Prussian blue.

Spectral: Not diagnostic.

Luminescence: None.

Occurrence: Secondary mineral in the oxidized zones of lead-copper deposits.
Blanchard Mine, Socorro Co., New Mexico; California; Montana; Utah; Idaho; Nevada.
England; Scotland; Spain; Germany; Sardinia; U.S.S.R.; Canada; Argentina; Peru; Chile; Japan; Australia; Tsumeb, S.W. Africa.
Mammoth Mine, Tiger, Arizona: large crystals of fine color.

Stone Sizes: Faceted gems over 1 carat are virtually unknown. Anything over $\frac{1}{2}$ carat is remarkably large for linarite. Crystals tend to be filled with fractures or translucent, and are usually very thin blades on rock.

Comments: The blue color of linarite is magnificent, and it is a shame that large facetable rough has not been found. Clean areas of crystals are usually very small, and breakage in cutting due to the softness and cleavage of the mineral further complicates the salvaging of a large gem. This is a lovely collector item, and an extremely rare one.

Name: After the locality, Linares, Spain.

LIZARDITE   See: Serpentine.

LUDLAMITE

Formula: $Fe_3(PO_4)_2 \cdot 4H_2O$.

Crystallography: Monoclinic. Crystals tabular, wedge-shaped; also granular.

Colors: Apple green, dark green, pale green, greenish white, colorless.

Streak: Pale greenish white.

Luster: Vitreous.

Hardness: 3.5.

Density: 3.19.

Cleavage: Perfect 1 direction. Fracture conchoidal. Brittle.

Optics: $\alpha = 1.650 - 1.653$; $\beta = 1.667 - 1.675$; $\gamma = 1.688 - 1.697$. Biaxial (+), $2V = 82°$.

Birefringence: 0.038 − 0.044.

Spectral: Not diagnostic.

Luminescence: None.

Occurrence: A secondary mineral in the oxidized zone of ore deposits; also due to the alteration of primary phosphates in granite pegmatites.
New Hampshire.
Cornwall, England; Hagendorf, Germany.
Blackbird Mine, Lemhi Co., Idaho: fine crystals up to $\frac{1}{2}$ inch across.
South Dakota: Crystalline masses to 12 inches in diameter with 7 mm crystals at Keystone, S.D.

Stone Sizes: Ludlamite is seldom cut, and transparent material is always small. The potential may exist for 5−10 carat gems, but most are in the 1−2 carat range.

Comments: Ludlamite has a lovely green color, but is too soft for wear. Large crystals are known from only a few localities, and cut stones are extremely rare.

Name: After a Mr. Ludlam of London.

M

MAGNESIOCHROMITE   See: Chromite.

MAGNESITE

Formula: $MgCO_3$.

Crystallography: Hexagonal (R). Crystals very rare (rhombs); massive, compact, fibrous.

Colors: Colorless, white, gray, yellowish to brown.

Luster: Vitreous to dull.

Hardness: 3.5−4.5.

Density: 3.0−3.12.

Cleavage: Perfect rhombohedral; brittle.

Optics: $o = 1.700-1.717$; $e = 1.509-1.515$. Uniaxial (−).

Birefringence: 0.022.

Luminescence: Blue, green, white in SW, often with greenish phosphorescence.

Other Tests: Effervesces in warm acids.

Occurrence: Alteration product of magnesium-rich rocks; sedimentary deposits; as a gangue mineral in hydrothermal ore deposits.
Norway; Austria; India; Algeria; Korea; Zaire; S. Africa.
Brumado, Bahia, Brazil: magnificent and large rhomb-shaped crystals, often transparent, colorless.

Stone Sizes: Largest known cut magnesite is 134.5 carats (*PC*) from Brazil material. Most other gems are under 10−15 carats.

Comments: Gems of magnesite that are completely transparent are both rare and beautiful. The huge birefringence is obvious even in small stones, and larger gems have a sleepy look, or fuzziness, due to the doubling of back facets as seen through the table. Faceted magnesite is rarely seen, and the material is relatively difficult to cut. Facetable crystals come only from Brazil.

Name: In allusion to the composition.

MAJORITE   See: Garnet.

MALACHITE

Formula: $CuCO_3(OH)_2$.

Crystallography: Monoclinic. Crystals are prismatic, usually small; also massive, sometimes banded; stalactitic; as crusts.

Colors: Green (various shades due to admixed clay in massive material), dark green.

Streak: Pale green.

Luster: Adamantine in crystals; vitreous; fibrous; dull.

Hardness: 3.5−4.5.

Density: 4.05 (as low as 3.6 in admixtures or when fibrous).

Cleavage: Perfect 1 direction. Fracture uneven. Brittle.

Optics: $\alpha=1.655$; $\beta=1.875$; $\gamma=1.909$. Biaxial (−), $2V = 43°$.
Mean index reading of 1.85 on massive material.

Birefringence: 0.254.

Pleochroism: Colorless/yellow-green/deep green.

Luminescence: None.

Other Tests: Effervesces in warm acids.

Occurrence: In the oxidized portions of copper ore bodies, with azurite and cuprite.
Arizona, at Bisbee and Gila, other localities; New Mexico; Utah; Tennessee.
Zambia; Broken Hill, N.S.W., Australia.
Tsumeb, S.W. Africa: magnificent large crystals.
Mednorudyansk, U.S.S.R.: immense masses, some up to 50 tons! Much good for cutting. Also mine at *Nizhne-Tagilsk.*
Zaire: banded material, also stalactitic, most familiar on marketplace.

Stone Sizes: Cabochons and carvings can be virtually any size from banded material. Stalactites have been found several feet long. In the U.S.S.R. there are place settings, including dinner plates and goblets, carved from fine malachite, as well as exquisite inlay work. Malachite slabs have also been used as paneling in palace rooms in the U.S.S.R. Facetable crystals are virtually nonexistent. Any cut gem would be very small, less than 2 carats.

Comments: Malachite is one of the most popular and beautiful of decorative stones. Its rich patterned coloration in shades of green is unique among gems. Malachite can (with great care) be turned on a lathe to make goblets and candlesticks. It is extensively used to make cabochons, beads, boxes and carvings of all kinds. Fibrous aggregates are packed masses of crystals, and these also take a high polish. Facetable crystals are microscopic in size, because larger ones are too opaque to let light through. A faceted gem larger than $\frac{1}{2}$ carat would be opaque.

Name: From a Greek word meaning *mallows* in allusion to the color.

MANGANOCOLUMBITE   See: Manganotantalite.

MANGANOTANTALITE *Series to* Manganocolumbite; Ferrotantalite; Columbotantalite.

Formula: $(Mn, Fe)(Ta, Nb)_2O_6$; Mn: Fe = 3:1.

Crystallography: Orthorhombic. Crystals short prismatic; massive.

Colors: Brownish black, reddish brown.

Streak: Dark red.

Luster: Vitreous to resinous.

Hardness: 6–6.5.

Density: 8.00 (calculated).

Cleavage: Distinct 1 direction. Fracture subconchoidal to uneven. Brittle.

Optics: $\alpha = 2.19$; $\beta = 2.25$; $\gamma = 2.34$. Biaxial (+), 2V large.

Birefringence: 0.150.

Dispersion: High.

Pleochroism: Shades of brown and red-brown.

Luminescence: None.

Spectral: Not diagnostic.

Occurrence: In granite pegmatites; sometimes in placer deposits.

Pala, California; Portland, Connecticut; Amelia, Virginia.

Andilana, Madagascar; Sanarka River, Urals, U.S.S.R.; Sweden; Wodgina, W. Australia.

Minas Gerais, Brazil: facetable crystals.

Alta Ligonha, Mozambique: gem quality crystals.

Stone Sizes: Cuttable crystals seldom reach 1 inch in size, and gems over 10 carats are rarities. However, the material is so dense that even a small stone is relatively heavy.

DG: 3.05 (red-brown, Brazil).

Comments: Manganotantalite makes a spectacular red-brown gem that is also a very rare collector's item. Transparent material is light enough in color to allow lots of light to enter and leave a cut gem, and properly cut stones are lively and brilliant. Cutting is difficult because of the cleavage.

Name: After the composition, a manganiferous tantalite.

MANGANPECTOLITE See: Pectolite.

MANSFIELDITE See: Scorodite.

MARBLE See: Calcite.

MARCASITE *Dimorph of* Pyrite.

Formula: FeS_2.

Crystallography: Orthorhombic. Crystals abundant, tabular, pyramidal, often with curved faces; also massive; granular; radial; globular; cockscomb-shaped aggregates.

Colors: Pale brassy yellow to whitish; may be iridescent.

Streak: Greenish black.

Luster: Metallic; opaque.

Hardness: 6–6.5.

Density: 4.85–4.92.

Cleavage: Distinct 1 direction. Fracture uneven. Brittle.

Occurrence: Marcasite forms at low temperatures, especially in sedimentary environments such as clays, shale, coal beds and in low temperature veins. Marcasite is abundant and widespread throughout the world.

Illinois; Oklahoma; Missouri; Kansas; Wisconsin.

Germany; Austria; Bolivia; France; Czechoslovakia.

England: in the chalk deposits along the coast and at Folkstone.

Stone Sizes: Massive material exists that could cut cabochons of any desired size. Marcasite is often faceted, the stones having flat backs. This type of jewelry was very popular in Victorian times. The cutting style is known as the *flattened rose cut.* Such gems were set in white-metal settings such as rhodium-plated silver.

Comments: Marcasite was used by the ancient Greeks, and it was also polished by the Incas of Central America, in large slabs. There have been surges of popularity for marcasite jewelry in the 18th Century and the Victorian era, but marcasite is seldom seen in modern jewelry. Marcasite is quite brittle, and a sharp blow can easily crack a stone or loosen it in its setting. Much of the "marcasite" in antique jewelry is actually the dimorph of marcasite, *pyrite* (see page 95). Steel is also used as an imitation marcasite, but is magnetic, whereas marcasite is not.

Name: Of Arabic or Moorish origin; it was applied to common crystallized pyrite by miners until about 1800.

MARIALITE See: Scapolite.

MEIONITE See: Scapolite.

MELANITE See: Garnet.

MELINOPHANE See: Meliphanite.

MELIPHANITE (= MELINOPHANE)

Formula: $(Ca, Na)_2Be(Si, Al)_2(O, OH, F)_7$.

Crystallography: Tetragonal. Crystals thin and tabular; also aggregates.

Colors: Colorless, shades of yellow, reddish.

Luster: Vitreous.

Hardness: 5–5.5.

Density: 3.0–3.03.

Cleavage: Perfect 1 direction. Fracture uneven. Brittle.

Optics: $o = 1.612$; $e = 1.593$. Uniaxial (–).

Birefringence: 0.019.

Pleochroism: Distinct in shades of yellow and red.

Spectral: Not diagnostic.

Luminescence: None.

Occurrence: Nepheline syenites and skarns.
Julienhaab dist., Greenland; Langesundsfjord, Norway; Gugiya, China.

Stone Sizes: Crystal clusters have been found up to several inches long. Clean, facetable material is very rare, however; the material is sometimes cut into small cabochons.

Comments: Meliphanite is an extremely rare gemstone, and perhaps fewer than 5–10 faceted stones have ever been cut.

Name: From Greek words meaning *appearing as honey*, in allusion to the color.

MELLITE

Formula: $Al_2C_6(COO)_6 \cdot 18H_2O$ (aluminum mellitate).

Crystallography: Tetragonal. Crystals prismatic, pyramidal; granular, nodular, massive.

Colors: Honey yellow, reddish, brownish, rarely white.

Streak: White.

Luster: Resinous to vitreous.

Hardness: 2–2.5.

Density: 1.64.

Cleavage: Indistinct. Fracture conchoidal. Sectile.

Optics: $o = 1.539$; $e = 1.511$. Uniaxial (–).
Sometimes anomalously biaxial.

Birefringence: 0.028.

Pleochroism: Weak; yellow/yellow-brown.

Spectral: Not diagnostic.

Luminescence: Dull white in SW, or medium light blue. Medium light blue in LW (Germany) or lemon yellow. May be weak brown in SW (U.S.S.R.).

Occurrence: A secondary mineral in brown coals and lignites.
Artern and Bitterfeld, Germany; Paris Basin, France; Czechoslovakia; Tula, U.S.S.R.

Stone Sizes: Mellites are always small (1–3 carats) and may be quite transparent.

Comments: Mellite is one of the most unusual of all gems, being an organic material formed by inorganic processes, just the reverse of the situation with pearls and coral. Crystals are additionally unusual in being pyroelectric (they generate an electric current when heated). Mellite is soft and very fragile, but is quite beautiful when cut. Truly this is one of the most interesting of the rare gemstones.

Name: From the Latin word *mel*, meaning *honey*, in allusion to the color.

MESOLITE See: Natrolite.

MICA See: Lepidolite.

MICROCLINE See: Feldspar.

MICROLITE Pyrochlore group.

Formula: $(Na, Ca)_2Ta_2O_6(O, OH, F)$.

Crystallography: Isometric. Crystals octahedral; also grains and masses.

Colors: Pale yellow to brown, reddish, green.

Streak: Pale yellow to brown.

Luster: Vitreous to resinous.

Hardness: 5–5.5.

Density: 4.3–5.7; usually 5.5.

Cleavage: Octahedral (not always evident). Fracture subconchoidal to uneven. Brittle.

Optics: $N = 1.93–1.94$ if slightly metamict; also 1.98–2.02.
Metamictization may cause anomalous birefringence.

Spectral: Not diagnostic.

Luminescence: None.

Occurrence: Primary mineral in granite pegmatites.
Connecticut; Maine; Massachusetts; South Dakota; Colorado; New Hampshire.
Greenland; Norway; Sweden; Finland; France; Madagascar; W. Australia.
Amelia, Virginia (Rutherford Mines); green and brown crystals, some gemmy ones up to a few inches in length.
Brazil: fine green crystals, some gemmy.

Stone Sizes: Cabochons can be cut to several inches in length (brownish or reddish massive material). Faceted gems are generally under 3–4 carats in weight; larger would be extremely rare. A crystal found in 1885 was garnet red in color, weighed 4.4 carats in the rough, and was cut into a stone that looked like a red zircon.
SI: 3.7 (brown, Virginia).

Comments: Microlite is usually opaque to translucent, and cut into cabochons by collectors. Faceted gems are very beautiful and extremely rare. Green Brazilian gems weighing less than 1 carat have appeared on the market, and the potential exists there for larger stones.

Name: From the Greek *mikros* (*small*), due to the small size of the crystals found at the original locality.

MICROSOMMITE See: Cancrinite.

MILARITE Osumilite Group.

Formula: $K_2Ca_4Be_4Al_2Si_{24}O_{60}\cdot H_2O$.

Crystallography: Hexagonal. Crystals prismatic and tabular; in grains.

Colors: Colorless, pale greeen, yellowish, yellowish green.

Luster: Vitreous.

Hardness: 5.5−6.

Density: 2.46−2.61.

Cleavage: None. Fracture conchoidal to uneven. Brittle.

Optics: $o = 1.532–1.551$; $e = 1.529–1.548$. Uniaxial (−).

Birefringence: 0.003.

Spectral: not diagnostic.

Luminescence: None.

Occurrence: In vugs in granites and syenites; hydrothermal veins.

St. Gotthard, Switzerland: green crystals.

Guanajuato, Mexico: yellow and yellow green crystals on matrix, flat, platelike.

Africa: occasional small facetable crystals found.

Stone Sizes: Crystals occur up to about 4 cm across, but facetable areas in such crystals are very small, and stones over 1 carat could be considered large for the species.

Comments: Milarite was originally known as a green mineral, until fine yellow crystals were discovered in Mexico in recent years (1968). Larger Mexican crystals have transparent areas and have been faceted into small gems, of pleasant appearance but great rarity.

Name: After the Val Milar, Switzerland, because the mineral was (mistakenly) thought to have occurred there.

MILLERITE

Formula: NiS.

Crystallography: Hexagonal. Crystals capillary or acicular; tufted; fibrous; also massive and cleavable.

Colors: Brassy and bronze yellow; tarnishes greenish gray.

Streak: Greenish black.

Luster: Metallic; opaque.

Hardness: 3−3.5.

Density: 5.3−5.6.

Cleavage: Perfect 2 directions. Fracture uneven. Brittle.

Occurrence: A low-temperature mineral in limestones and dolomites, serpentines and ore deposits in carbonate rocks.

Illinois; Wisconsin; Iowa.

Wales; Czechoslovakia; Germany.

Antwerp, New York: fine sprays of acicular crystals.

Gap Mine, Lancaster Co., Pennsylvania: acicular tufts.

Missouri: in geodes.

Hall's Gap, Kentucky: tufts of fibers in geodes.

Timagami, Ontario, Canada: large cleavable masses.

Stone Sizes: Cabochons of any size could be cut from massive material.

Comments: Massive millerite is sometimes cut into a cabochon by a collector or sliced into slabs for decorative purposes. The yellow color is very rich and attractive, and the cut gems are indeed curiosities. The mineral is too soft for wear. Massive millerite is of no great interest to mineral collectors, and therefore might be hard to obtain on the marketplace, although it is abundant at certain localities.

Name: After mineralogist W. H. Miller, who first studied the crystals.

MIMETITE   Apatite group, *Pyromorphite series.*

Formula: $Pb_5(AsO_4)_3Cl$.

Crystallography: Monoclinic (pseudo-hexagonal). Crystals acicular; globular; botryoidal.

Colors: Sulfur yellow, yellowsh brown, orange-yellow, orange, white, colorless.

Luster: Subadamantine to resinous.

Hardness: 3.5−4.

Density: 7.24, lower if Ca replaces Pb.

Cleavage: None. Fracture subconchoidal to uneven. Brittle.

Optics: $o = 2.147$; $e = 2.128$. Biaxial (−); optics may sometimes be uniaxial.

Birefringence: 0.019.

Pleochroism: Weak in yellow shades.

Spectral: Not diagnostic.

Luminescence: Orange-red in LW (Tsumeb, S.W. Africa).

Occurrence: A secondary mineral in the oxidized zone of lead deposits.

Pennsylvania.

Scotland; Sweden; France; Germany; U.S.S.R.; Czechoslovakia; Australia.

Southwestern U.S.: many localities.

Chihuahua, Mexico: fine globular orange and yellow masses.

Mapimi, Durango, Mexico: yellowish globular masses.

Cornwall and Cumberland, England: a variety called *campylite.*

Tsumeb, S.W. Africa: fine yellow transparent crystals, up to 1 inch long.

Stone Sizes: Cabochons up to an inch or two can be cut from globular orange and yellow masses from Mexico, and these make unusual and interesting stones. Tsumeb crystals are extremely rare (one pocket found) and most of the crystals are being preserved as specimens and will not be cut. Small broken crystals were cut, yielding some stones up to a few carats in weight, with a maximum of 5−7 carats.

Comments: Faceted mimetite is one of the rarest of all gems, since only one pocket of transparent crystals has ever been found (at Tsumeb) and few of these crystals have been cut. Orange and yellow cabochons are richly colored, but too soft for wear.

Name: From a Greek word meaning *imitator*, because of the resemblance to pyromorphite.

MOHAWKITE See: Algodonite.

MONAZITE

Formula: (Ce, La, Y, Th)PO_4.

Crystallography: Monoclinic. Crystals small, tabular, wedge-shaped; faces often rough or uneven; also massive, granular; detrital.

Colors: Brown, reddish brown, yellowish brown, pink, yellow, greenish, grayish white, white.

Luster: Vitreous to subadamantine; resinous; waxy.

Hardness: 5−5.5.

Density: 4.6−5.4.

Cleavage: Distinct 1 direction, sometimes perfect. Fracture conchoidal to uneven. Brittle.

Optics: $\alpha = 1.774-1.800$; $\beta = 1.777-1.801$; $\gamma = 1.828-1.849$.
Biaxial (+), $2V = 11-15°$.
Higher refractive index is accompanied by lower birefringence.

Birefringence: 0.049−0.055.

Pleochroism: Faint or none (yellowish shades).

Spectral: Extremely complex spectra observed, mostly rare earth types.

Luminescence: None.

Occurrence: An accessory mineral in igneous rocks and gneisses; sometimes in large crystals in granite pegmatites; as a detrital mineral in sands.
Petaca dist., New Mexico; Amelia, Virginia.
Norway; Finland.
Colorado: fine crystals.
Wyoming: crystals to several pounds.
Madagascar: in fine crystals.
Switzerland: excellent crystals in alpine vein deposits.
Callipampa, Bolivia: good crystals.
Deposits of alluvial material in *Australia, Ceylon, India, Brazil, Malaya, Nigeria.*

Stone Sizes: Faceted gems would normally be under 5 carats, either from Swiss crystals or from portions of crystals from other localities. Facetable material is very rare and cut stones are absent from all but a few private collections. Large cabochons could be cut from various large crystals that have been found.

Comments: Monazite may be partially metamict, with $N = 1.79$. Stones can be an attractive yellow or brown color but are usually small. Monazite would be a fine collector gem, but is very difficult to find.

Name: From the Greek *monazein, to be solitary,* because of the rarity of the mineral.

MONTEBRASITE See: Amblygonite.

MOONSTONE See: Feldspar.

MORDENITE Zeolite group.

Formula: $(Ca, Na_2, K_2)(Al_2Si_{10})O_{24} \cdot 7H_2O$.

Crystallography: Orthorhombic. Crystals prismatic; fibrous, cottony, compact.

Colors: Colorless, white; stained yellowish, pinkish.

Luster: Vitreous to silky.

Hardness: 4−5.

Density: 2.12−2.15.

Cleavage: Perfect 1 direction. Fracture conchoidal. Brittle.

Optics: $\alpha = 1.472-1.483$; $\beta = 1.475-1.485$; $\gamma = 1.477-1.487$.
Biaxial (+), $2V = 76-104°$. Also optically (−).

Birefringence: 0.005.

Pleochroism: None.

Spectral: Not diagnostic.

Luminescence: None.

Occurrence: In veins and cavities in igneous rocks; also forms as hydration product of natural glasses.
California; Idaho; Utah; Colorado; Wyoming.
Nova Scotia, Canada; Scotland; Yugoslavia; U.S.S.R.; Japan; New Zealand.

Stone Sizes: Cabochons can be cut from nodules that reach a size of about 1 inch. Faceted gems have not been reported.

Comments: Compact, fibrous material is cabbed, because the fibers provide a chatoyancy that sometimes yields weak catseyes. Coloration in the material is due to staining. This is a relatively unexciting mineral, and gems are equally uninspiring, but has been reported as being cut for collectors.

Name: From the locality at Morden, King's County, Nova Scotia, where first found.

MORGANITE See: Beryl.

MORION See: Quartz.

MOSS AGATE See: Quartz.

MUKHINITE See: Epidote.

N

NAMBULITE

Formula: $NaLiMn_8Si_{10}O_{28}(OH)_2$.

Crystallography: Triclinic. Crystals prismatic, flattened and wedge-shaped.

Colors: Reddish brown, orange-brown, orange.

Streak: Pale yellow.

Luster: Vitreous.

Hardness: 6.5.

Density: 3.51.

Cleavage: Perfect 1 direction, distinct 1 direction.

Optics: $\alpha = 1.707$; $\beta = 1.710$; $\gamma = 1.730$. Biaxial (+), $2V = 30°$.

Birefringence: 0.023.

Dispersion: Weak.

Pleochroism: Weak.

Spectral: Not diagnostic.

Luminescence: No data.

Occurrence: Nambulite is a rare mineral reported in crystals up to 8 mm long at the Tunakozawa Mine, N.E. Japan. These crystals are found in veins cutting manganese oxide ores. Much larger crystals, up to approximately 3 cm across, have recently been found in S.W. Africa, at the Kombat mine, near Tsumeb. The writer has seen a completely transparent crystal in a private collection that would yield about 20−25 carats of flawless faceted gems, the largest of these perhaps 10 carats in weight. As of this writing no gems have been cut from this material.

Stone Sizes: Gems up to about 10 carats could potentially be cut from S.W. African crystals.

Comments: The color of S.W. African nambulite is a striking orange-red, very intense, and not really like any other gem seen by the writer. Cut stones would be both extremely rare and quite magnificent, perhaps bearing some similarities to rhodonite.

Name: After Professor Matsuo Nambu of Tohoku University, Japan, for his studies of manganese minerals.

NATROLITE; MESOLITE; SCOLECITE *Solid solution series*, Zeolite group.

Formulas: *Natrolite:* $Na_2[AlSi_3O_{10}]\cdot2H_2O$. *Mesolite:* $Na_2Ca_2[Al_2Si_3O_{10}]\cdot8H_2O$ (intermediate in series). *Scolecite:* $Ca[Al_2Si_3O_{10}]\cdot3H_2O$.

All three minerals are fibrous or elongated zeolite minerals that ocur in single crystals or radial aggregates. Mesolite crystals are always twinned.

Colors: Colorless, white (natrolite sometimes gray, yellowish, reddish).

Luster: Vitreous; silky in fibrous varieties.

Cleavage: Perfect 2 directions. Fracture uneven. Brittle.

Luminescence: Some natrolite fluoresces yellow-orange in LW (Germany). Indian mesolite may fluoresce pink (LW); mesolite may fluoresce cream white to green in LW (Colorado). None observed in scolecite.

Occurrence: Cavities in basalts and other dark igneous rocks; sometimes volcanic rocks. Scolecite occasionally forms in schists and contact zones at limestones.
Colorado; New Jersey; Oregon; Washington.
Nova Scotia, Canada; Greenland; Scotland; Iceland.
California: natrolite in San Benito Co.; scolecite at Crestmore, Riverside Co.
India (Poona): large crystals of scolecite and natrolite, some facetable.
Brevig, Norway: natrolite.
U.S.S.R.: huge natrolite crystals.
Australia: mesolite.
Sicily: mesolite.
France: natrolite.
Germany: natrolite.
Rio Grande do Sul, Brazil: immense crystals of scolecite.
Mt. Ste. Hilaire, Quebec: large natrolite crystals (white, opaque).

	Natrolite	Mesolite	Scolecite
Crystallography	Orthorhombic, pseudo-tetragonal	Monoclinic, pseudo-orthorhombic	Monoclinic, pseudo-orthorhombic
Hardness	5	5	5
Density	2.2−2.26	2.26	2.25−2.29
Optics			
α	1.473−1.483	1.505	1.507−1.513
β	1.476−1.486	1.504−1.508	1.516−1.520
γ	1.485−1.496	1.506	1.517−1.521
sign	(+)	(+)	(−)
$2V$	58−64°	ca 80°	36−56°
Birefringence	0.012	0.001	0.007

So. Quebec: in asbestos mines, natrolite crystals to 3 feet long and 4 inches across (not of gem quality).

Bound Brook, New Jersey: one find of natrolite crystals, thousands of single crystals well terminated, up to 6 inches long, many transparent.

Stone Sizes: Natrolites were known only in stones under 1 carat until the Bound Brook New Jersey find. Some of these crystals cut gems over 20 carats, flawless.
SI: 9.31, 7.9 (colorless, N.J.).
DG: 7.95 (colorless, New Jersey) also scolecite, 0.98 (India).

Mesolite is never found in large transparent crystals. Faceted gems are thus very rare, although the possibility exists that larger crystals could be found one day. Fibrous material cuts fine catseye gems, but these also are small, and fragile.

Scolecite is also rare in facetable crystals; areas of some of the large Indian and Brazilian material might cut gems in the 5−10 carat range, but these specimens are in museums and will not be cut. Other stones would likely be in the 1−3 carat size range and colorless.

Comments: All three zeolites here discussed form elongated crystals; faceted gems are almost always, therefore, elongated emerald or step cuts. The New Jersey natrolites are by far the largest known faceted gems in this group. All three minerals are relatively fragile and soft, have good cleavage, and are white and more or less uninteresting, except for rarity. Compact masses, cut into cabochons, might be more durable due to interlocking of the fibers. The minerals can readily be distinguished on the basis of optical properties.

Names: *Natrolite* from the Latin *natron* (*soda*), because of the presence of sodium. *Mesolite* from the Greek *mesos*, an intermediate position, because of its position between natrolite and scolecite in chemistry and properties. *Scolecite* is from the Greek *skolex* (*worm*), because a borax bead of the mineral sometimes curls up like a worm.

NATROMONTEBRASITE See: Amblygonite.

NEPHELINE
Formula: $(Na, K)AlSiO_4$.

Crystallography: Hexagonal. Crystals stumpy, sometimes very large; massive, compact; in grains.

Colors: Colorless, white, gray, yellowish, greenish, bluish, dark green, brick red, brownish red.

Luster: Vitreous to greasy.

Hardness: 5.5−6.

Density: 2.55−2.66.

Cleavage: Indistinct. Fracture subconchoidal. Brittle.

Optics: $o = 1.529−1.546$; $e = 1.526−1.542$.
Uniaxial (−).

Birefringence: 0.004.

Dispersion: Low.

Spectral: Not diagnostic.

Luminescence: Medium light blue (Germany) or medium dull orange (Ontario) in LW.

Occurrence: Plutonic and volcanic rocks; pegmatites associated with nepheline syenites.
Julienhaab dist., Greenland; Langesundsfjord, Norway; Germany; Finland; U.S.S.R.; Burma; Korea.
Various localities in the U.S., especially *Maine; Arkansas.*
Ontario, Canada: crystals up to 15 inches long (nongemmy).
Vesuvius, Italy: small, glassy transparent grains.

Stone Sizes: Cabochons of nepheline have been cut in various sizes; crystals, especially those from Canada, can reach enormous size, but are not attractive. Faceting material is extremely rare and very small.

Comments: A variety called *elaeolite* is red, green, brown, or gray, massive or in crystals filled with minute inclusions. These inclusions produce a sheen that yields a catseye effect in cabochons. Facetable nepheline is a great rarity, and very few gems have been cut, always in the 1−2 carat range or smaller.

Name: From a Latin word meaning *cloud* because it becomes cloudy when immersed in acid. *Elaeolite* from a Latin word for *oil* because of its greasy luster.

NEPHRITE (= JADE) *Fibrous variety of* Actinolite.
Formula: $Ca_2(Mg, Fe)_5(Si_4O_{11})_2(OH)_2$.

Crystallography: Monoclinic. Masses of fibrous crystals, densely packed and very tough.

Colors: Creamy-beige (mutton fat jade) when rich in Mg. Green colors, due to Fe. Brown (oxidized Fe); sometimes a surface skin is dark brown. Also yellowish, grayish brown, yellow-green, black.

Luster: Vitreous to greasy; dull.

Hardness: 6−6.5.

Density: 2.90−3.02; usually 2.95.

Cleavage: None. Fracture splintery. Very tough.

Optics: $\alpha = 1.600−1.627$; $\gamma = 1.614−1.641$.
Biaxial (−). Usually refractometer shows a shadow edge at about 1.62.

Birefringence: 0.027.

Pleochroism: Strong dichroism, masked due to the fibrous nature of the material.

Spectral: Doublet at 6890, two vague bands at 4980 and 4600; sharp line at 5090.

Luminescence: None.

Occurrence: Nephrite is most frequently encountered in the form of rolled boulders.

Wisconsin: gray-green color, not too attractive.

Alaska: green colors, in very large masses, sometimes fibrous (chatoyant).

California: alluvial material, various green shades, in boulders up to 1000 pounds.

Lander, Wyoming: boulders mottled green with white—very distinctive material.

New Zealand: Maori Greenstone, in situ and in boulders, usually dark green to black.

Fraser River, British Columbia: dark-colored nephrite, little of which is very fine quality.

U.S.S.R. (at Lake Baikal): dark spinach-green color with abundant graphitic black inclusions or spots—very distinctive jade, fine color.

China (Sinkiang Province): generally light in color.

Poland: creamy white to gray-green, with green patches (near Jordansmuhl).

New South Wales, Australia. Taiwan: spinach green to pea green, in seams in rock; despite abundance of material on market, large pieces are very scarce.

Mashaba dist., Rhodesia; Italy; Germany.

Mexico: alluvial.

Stone Sizes: Alluvial boulders of several tons are not uncommon in certain localities. Large fine pieces are always carved, for example the sculpture *Thunder,* by Donald Hord, in Wyoming jade (145 pounds).

AMNH displays a huge block of nephrite from Poland weighing 4718 pounds.

SI displays boulder of several hundred pounds, sliced open, with thin slab backlit to show the color.

Comments: Nephrite colors do not match in either variety or intensity the colors of jadeite. Nephrite shades are usually dark and somber, with a few exceptions, and nephrite never attains the fine green of Imperial jade (jadeite). The Chinese long ago mastered the art of carving nephrite, and immense brush pots and statues grace many museums around the world. Of special note is the M.M. Vetleson jade collection that occupies an entire room at *SI.* Carvings have been done using only one side of a jade boulder, leaving the rough shape as a background. Fine use is also made of the weathering skin (brownish) of green nephrite, creating a cameo effect, sometimes of great detail and fine workmanship.

Name: From the Greek word *nephros,* meaning *kidney;* the rounded, organlike shape of nephrite boulders and pebbles undoubtedly stimulated men to regard these stones as magical cures for the organs they resembled, through sympathetic magic.

See also: Jadeite.

NICCOLITE

Formula: NiAs.

Crystallography: Hexagonal. Crystals very rare; massive.

Colors: Pale coppery red; tarnishes black.

Streak: Pale brownish black.

Luster: Metallic; opaque.

Hardness: 5–5.5.

Density: 7.78.

Cleavage: None. Fracture uneven. Brittle.

Luminescence: None.

Occurrence: In vein deposits in basic igneous rocks, usually associated with ores of Ag, Co and Ni.

Sonora, Mexico; Germany; France; Austria; Czechoslovakia; Japan.

California; Colorado; New Jersey.

Sudbury dist., Ontario: in large masses; also at *Cobalt, Thunder Bay* and the *Gowganda dist., Ontario.*

Stone Sizes: Cabochons of any desired size could be cut from massive pieces.

Comments: Niccolite is always cut as cabochons. The color is delicate peachy red and is extremely beautiful, especially in polished material. The metallic luster combined with this unusual color is very distinctive. Niccolite is hard enough to be worn on bola ties and pendants. It sometimes tarnishes to a darker color, and a coat of clear nail polish may prevent this.

Name: From *niccolum,* the Latin word for nickel.

NORBERGITE See: Chondrodite.

NOSEAN See: Lazurite.

O

OBSIDIAN (= VOLCANIC GLASS)

Formula: Variable composition: SiO_2 approximately 66–72% + oxides of Ca, Na, K, etc. Basaltic glass is ca 50% SiO_2.

Crystallography: Amorphous; usually as rounded masses ejected in volcanic eruptions, as small broken pieces, fine, hairlike filaments (e.g., Pelee's Hair), and as flows.

Colors: Black; gray, banded with brown streaks; rarely green, blue, red.
Basaltic glass is black, brown, gray, blue and blue-green. Iridescence noted: gold, silver, blue, violet, green and combinations of these colors, due to inclusions of minute bubbles that reflect light.

Luster: Vitreous.

Hardness: 5; 6 for basalt glass.

Density: 2.33–2.42 (2.70–3.0 in basalt glass).

Cleavage: None. Fracture conchoidal (best example). Very brittle. Basalt glass may be splintery, brittle.

Optics: Isotropic. $N = 1.48$–1.51 (usually 1.49). Crystals included in the glass may be birefringent.

Inclusions: Elongated, torpedo-shaped bubbles, round bubbles, teardrop-shaped bubbles. Bubbles are often in parallel arrangement. Needle-like inclusions may give a silvery sheen. Protogenic silica minerals crystallizing in obsidian may be white and resemble snowflakes, hence the term *snowflake obsidian*.

Luminescence: None.

Occurrence: Most occurrences of obsidian that are used in gems are in the U.S. Obsidian is found in areas of present and former volcanic activity.
Nevada; Hawaii.
Iceland; Japan.
Oregon: some iridescent material is known.

Wyoming: notably at Yellowstone Park.
New Mexico: Apache tears, small rounded obsidian lumps in white perlite shells.
Arizona; Colorado; California; several localities.
Utah: major source of snowflake obsidian.
Mexico: obsidian abundant, especially banded and sheen varieties.

Stone Sizes: Fragments range from microscopic to many inches across. Carvings up to 8–10 inches could be made. Larger pieces of obsidian are available in place in certain localities.

Comments: Obsidian is an attractive material and displays a wide variety of appearances. *Snowflake obsidian,* with spherulites of cristobalite, is widely used in jewelry as cabochons. *Apache tears,* which are cores of unaltered glass in nodular shells of decomposed obsidian, are popular among beginning hobbyists. Some of these have been faceted. Green, blue and reddish (transparent) obsidians are quite rare, and these are being faceted by gem cutters. Obsidian is heat-sensitive, so care must be used in cutting; it is also rather brittle, so is delicate in jewelry. Faceted gems tend to be vary dark and unattractive, except in small sizes, or in the blue and green varieties.

Name: The material was supposed to have been discovered in Ethiopia by a man named Obsius.

ODONTOLITE See: Vivianite.

OLIGOCLASE See: Feldspar.

OLIVINE (= PERIDOT) *Solid Solution Series:* Forsterite (Mg) *to* Fayalite (Fe).

Formula: Mg_2SiO_4–Fe_2SiO_4. Rarely Mn also present.

	%MgO	%FeO	α	β	γ	Birefringence	Density	2V
Forsterite	100	0	1.635	1.651	1.670	0.035	3.222	(+)82°
Mogok, Burma	57.8	1.11	1.654	1.671	1.689	0.036	3.22	86°
Ross Island, Antarctica	—	—	1.653	—	1.689	0.036	3.34	—
Arizona	49.5	9.1	1.653	1.669	1.690	0.037	3.35	—
New Mexico	49.4	8.7	1.652	1.671	1.688	0.036	3.33	—
Kenya: yellowish	($Fo_{90}Fa_{10}$)		1.650	—	1.686	0.036	3.45	—
Kenya: brownish			1.651	—	1.681	0.038	3.35	—
Norway	51.86	8.5	1.650	—	1.686	0.036	3.30	—
Fayalite	0	100	1.827	1.869	1.879	0.052	4.39	(−)134°

Greenish peridots have a density of ca 3.3–3.4; brownish peridots have a density of ca 3.5.

Crystallography: Orthorhombic. Crystals rare, usually striated prisms, corroded grains; often as rolled pebbles, or in nodules called *bombs* in volcanic areas.

Colors: *Forsterite:* green, pale lemon yellow. *Fayalite:* green, yellowish, amber brown, brown, olive green.

The color of olivine is idiochromatic and due to ferrous iron. The best green gemstones have an iron content of about 12–15%. More Fe than this results in an unattractive, muddy color. Very bright green colors may result from a trace of Cr.

Luster: Oily to vitreous.

Hardness: 6.5 (fayalite) to 7 (forsterite).

Cleavage: Imperfect to weak. Fracture conchoidal. Brittle.

Optics, Density: vary with composition:

Dispersion: 0.020.

Pleochroism: None in *forsterite*. *Peridots* weak, green to yellow-green. *Fayalite:* greenish yellow/orange-yellow/greenish yellow.

Luminescence: None.

Inclusions: Glass balls that look like bubbles in Hawaiian material; some U.S. localities contain inclusions of Cr-spinel (not magnetite as previously thought); also noted are biotite grains, and *lotus leaves*, which are petal-like liquid inclusions around Cr-spinel crystals.

Occurrence: *Forsterite* occurs in magnesian limestones that have been altered by heat and pressure from igneous intrusion; *fayalite* is rare, occasionally seen in lithophysae (balls of cristobalite) in obsidian. Intermediate olivines are a main constituent of basic igneous rocks, and concentrations in basalts and ultrabasic rocks can be mined for gem content.

California (Riverside, San Bernardino Co.); Bolton, Massachusetts.

Hawaii: in volcanic bombs.

New Mexico and *Arizona:* peridot occurs as grains used by ants to build large hills; these grains are all erosional fragments from a parent rock, now eroded away; this material is mined on the Navajo Indian Reservation, and stones cut from these fragments are usually small (under 5 carats), with an occasional larger gem.

Kenya: brown crystals.

Zebirget, Egypt (Isle of St. John): This is the most ancient source for peridot, and a source of some of the most confusing name mixups in gem literature. Zebirget (or Zebirged) is an island in the Red Sea, and is often shrouded in fog, making it hard to find by ancient navigators. The location had been lost, in fact, for centuries and was rediscovered about 1905. It is located 35 miles off the Egyptian coastal port of Berenica. Crystals of peridot are found in veins of nickel ore in an altered peridotite rock. Transparent masses up to 190

carats have been found. The color of the gem material is a medium green, not too dark, and very rich.

Burma: Peridot is found in masses on the slopes of Kyaukpon, near Mogok. The material yields dark green, oily gems of fine color, transparent, some of several hundred carats in size. This is the world's only major source of very large peridot.

Norway: Peridot is found in Norway at Ameklovdalen, Sondmore. The gems are paler than from other localities, and a lovely lime-green hue, because the material contains less Fe. Cuttable pieces are very rare in large size, and seldom cut stones over 5 carats.

Mexico: In northern Mexico, in the state of Chihuahua, is located one of the world's largest deposits of olivine. The material is similar to the Arizona peridot, but also occurs in brown grains, and in sizes that will cut gems over 20 carats.

Minas Gerais, Brazil; Queensland, Australia.

Emali, Kenya: gem quality.

Ross Island, Antarctica: some gem quality, cuttable.

U.S.S.R.; Finland; Italy; Germany; Greenland; New Caledonia.

Spectral: Peridot shows a strong iron spectrum, with three main bands: strong at 4930, narrow at 4730, broad at 4530; there are some vague bands also at 6530 and 5290, but the set of three evenly spaced bands is distinctive.

Stone Sizes: Burma material cuts the largest gems, followed by Egypt. The potential exists for some very large stones from Mexico, from the Chivera Mine. Peridot from Antarctica is limited to a few stones under 2 carats. Arizona material over 10 carats is very rare in cut form.

SI: 319 and 289 (green, Burma).

Diamond Treasury, Moscow: 192.

Geol. Mus., London: 136 (Burma).

Topkapi Museum, Istanbul: many large and fine cabochons.

ROM: 108 (Burma), also 87.1, 83.3 (Burma).

DG: 82.40, 24.7 (Burma).

Comments: Catseye and star peridots are known, but are very rare. The low hardness of peridot means that ringstones will show scratches rather rapidly, and may become badly chipped. The cleavage may allow an occasional stone to split if struck a sharp blow. Peridot is an ancient gem, often referred to as *chrysolite*, a term still used in referring to intermediate members of the olivine series. There is considerable variation in shade of green depending on the locality of origin. Brown gems rich in iron are not commonly seen, but can be very beautiful, especially when the color is more golden than brown.

Names: *Chrysolite* from the Greek, meaning *yellow stone. Forsterite* after J. Forster, a mineralogist. *Fayalite* is named after the Fayal islands in the Azores, because it was believed to occur there in volcanic rocks. *Olivine* from the Latin *oliva* (*olive*) because of the similarity in color.

ONYX   See: Calcite, Quartz.

OPAL

Formula: $SiO_2 \cdot nH_2O$. Water = 1–21% in opal, usually 6–10% in precious opal.

Crystallography: Amorphous. Recent work shows that opal is composed of an aggregate of tiny spherical particles, i.e., a solidified gel; often forms concretions; botryoidal; reniform; stalactitic.

Colors: Colorless, white, yellow, orange and red (various shades), yellowish brown, greenish, blue, gray, black, violet.

Luster: Vitreous, waxy, pearly.

Hardness: 5.5–6.5.

Density: 1.99–2.25; orange-red variety ca 2.00; black and white opal, 2.10.

Cleavage: None. Fracture conchoidal. Brittle.

Optics: Isotropic; $N = 1.44–1.47$.
Mexican opal as low as 1.37, usually 1.42–1.43.

Dispersion: Very low.

Spectral: None.

Luminescence: Green fluorescence in opal often due to included U minerals.

OPAL TERMINOLOGY

Siliceous sinter; geyserite: massive, glassy opal that forms around hot springs and geysers; no gem significance.

Diatomaceous earth; tripoli: fine-grained, powdery masses of opal or the siliceous remains of microscopic marine animals called diatoms. Often used as polishing agents, fillers.

Pseudomorphs: opal may, in percolating through the ground, replace (on a microscopic or even cellular basis) wood, bone and shells.

Hyalite: transparent, colorless or white to gray opal, glassy, occasionally faceted but generally no gem significance.

Common opal: opaque or glassy opal, in a wide range of colors, sometimes with a waxy luster; often fluorescent; seldom cut into gems.

Water opal: transparent, colorless opal which may have fire in it. *Note.* The term *fire* refers to the magnificent play of color displayed by opal, which is due to light diffraction from neatly stacked layers of the microscopic spheres of which opal is composed. Common opal is a jumble of spheres of random sizes, but in precious opal the spheres are the same size and they are layered in neat rows. The particular color seen depends on the size of the spheres, and the angle of viewing.

Fire opal: transparent to translucent red or orange opal, which may or may not have fire in it! The term fire opal refers to a *body color, not to play of color.*

Precious opal: opal of any color with fire, or play of colors displayed.

White opal: white body-color opal, usually with play of color.

Gray opal: light to dark body color, with play of color superimposed.

Black opal: black body color with fire, often spectacular against dark background. Body color also very dark bluish, greenish, or brownish.

Semiblack opal: another way of describing *gray opal.*

Milk opal: milk white, translucent, also yellowish or greenish in color.

Crystal opal: water opal or milk opal, generally rich in fire; transparent to translucent in transmitted light; colors seen by reflected light.

Contra-luz opal: very rare type, usually from Mexico, with color play in *both* transmitted and reflected light.

Hydrophane: light-colored, opaque, becomes iridescent and transparent when soaked in water.

Jasper opal: reddish-brown opal, opaque, that resembles jasper.

Cachalong: porcelaniferous, often bluish-white, very porous—adheres to the tongue.

Prase opal: translucent or opaque green opal; a common opal resembling prase.

Moss opal: white to brownish opaque opal that contains dendritic inclusions.

Locality	SW	LW
White Cliffs, Australia	—	medium blue; phosphorescent
Park, Wyoming	dull white; phosphorescent	strong white; phosphorescent
Queretaro, Mexico	dull white; phosphorescent	bright blue; phosphorescent
Virgin Valley, Nevada	bright green	medium green, blue-white; phosphorescent
Quartzite, Arizona	pale yellow	bright pale yellow

Opal may also fluoresce brownish. Black opal generally inert. Fire opal luminesces greenish brown. Common opal often fluoresces green.

LAZULITE: Brazil (4.55, 7.80)

LAZURITE (Lapis Lazuli): Back row (left), New York State (ca 2 inches across), (right), Afghanistan (ca 3 inches).
Front row: Afghanistan, Chile, Afghanistan.

LINARITE: New Mexico (0.39)

LAZURITE (Lapis Lazuli): Afghanistan (30 x 40 mm), Chile (20 mm), Afghanistan (30 x 40 mm)

LUDLAMITE: Idaho (ca 0.5)

LEGRANDITE: Mexico (ca 2, rough ca 1½ inches long)

LEUCITE: Italy
(crystals ca 1 inch across, rarely transparent)

LEPIDOLITE: California (ca 3 inches across)

MAGNESITE: Brazil (134.5)
This is the world's largest cut magnesite.

MALACHITE: Zaire (ca 4 inches high)

MANGANOTANTALITE:
Alta Ligonha,
Mozambique (5.5)

BISMUTOTANTALITE:
Madagascar (0.5)

MALACHITE with AZURITE:
Bisbee, Arizona (ca 4 inches high)

MANGANOTANTALITE: Brazil (1.2);
STIBIOTANTALITE: Brazil (2.25)

COLUMBOTANTALITE:
Brazil (2.9)

STIBIOTANTALITE:
Mozambique (1.0)

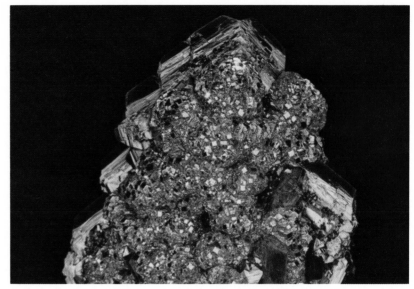

MARCASITE: Germany (ca 6 inches high)

MELLITE: Germany (0.42)

MILARITE:
Tsumeb, S.W. Africa (0.53)

STIBIOTANTALITE:
Africa (7.05)

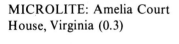

MICROLITE: Amelia Court
House, Virginia (0.3)

MIMETITE:
Tsumeb, S.W. Africa (2.81)

NATROLITE: Bound Brook, New Jersey (ca 5)

NICCOLITE: Cobalt, Ontario, Canada
(polished cab ca 1 inch long)

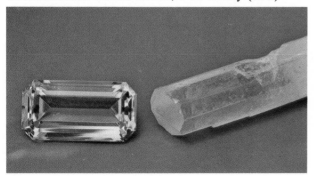

OBSIDIAN: Mexico (banded and sheen varieties), Utah
("snowflake obsidian", cabochon 30 x 40 mm).

OPAL: Australia (carvings ca 2 and 1½ inches tall)

OPAL: Australia,
gray-base crystal opal (10.35)

OPAL: Brazil (7.9)

OPAL: Mexico,
Fire Opal (22.45)

OPAL: Mexico (small stones ca 0.5)

OPAL: Australia,
Triplet, with ceramic
base and quartz top
(30 x 23 mm)

OPAL: Mexico, "*Contraluz*",
illuminated from front (ca 4)

OPAL: Mexico, "*Contraluz*",
illuminated from rear (ca 4)

OPAL: Back row: Mexico (5.85), Brazil (8.32), Mexico (8.94), Idaho (15.96)
Front row: Idaho (1.84), Mexico (1.1, 3.25)

PEARL: Persian Gulf (largest beads ca 8 mm)

PEARL: Worldwide localities, selected to show color variation

PECTOLITE: Jeffrey Mines, Asbestos, Quebec, Canada (transparent crystal ca ¼ inch)

PECTOLITE: Dominican Republic (largest cabochon ca 30 carats)

PERIDOT: Arizona (1.1, 2.1), St. John's Island, Red Sea (26), Burma (8.4)

PERIDOT: Norway (4.7), St. John's Island, Red Sea (2.25),
Arizona (2.3, 2.4), Burma (8.61)

PETALITE: Brazil (3.5)

PHOSGENITE: Monte Poni,
Sardinia (1.5)

PHENAKITE: Colorado (ca 2.5)

PHOSPHOPHYLLITE: Potosi, Bolivia (3.65)

PHOSPHOPHYLLITE: Potosi, Bolivia (8.1)

PROUSTITE: Germany (7.53)

POLLUCITE: Maine (ca 2)

PREHNITE: Mexico (2.47), Australia (7.65)

PUMPELLYITE: Isle Royale, Lake
Superior, Michigan (pebbles ca ¼ inch)

PURPURITE: Usakos, S.W. Africa (specimens ca 2 inches across)

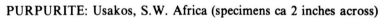

PYRITE: Butte, Montana (crystal group ca 3 inches across)

PYROPHYLLITE: Graves Mountain, Georgia (specimen ca 6 inches across)

PYROXMANGITE: Japan (0.55)

PYRRHOTITE: Sudbury, Ontario, Canada (polished specimen ca 4 inches long)

QUARTZ: Brazil, colorless, green and rose colors (ca 3 to 10)

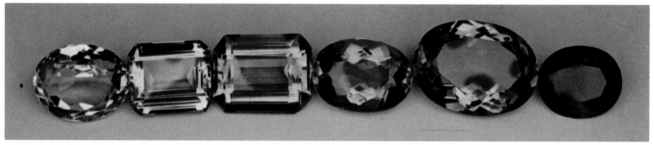

QUARTZ: *Amethyst,* Brazil (ca 5 to 8)

QUARTZ: *Citrine,* Brazil (ca 5 to 10)

QUARTZ: *Smoky Quartz,* Brazil (ca 5 to 20)

QUARTZ: *Chrysoprase,*
Australia (largest beads ca 8 mm)

QUARTZ: *Rutillated quartz,* Brazil
(ca 4 inches across)

QUARTZ: *Rock crystal,* Brazil, carved in Germany
(ca 3 inches long)

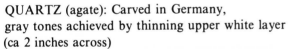

QUARTZ (agate): Carved in Germany,
gray tones achieved by thinning upper white layer
(ca 2 inches across)

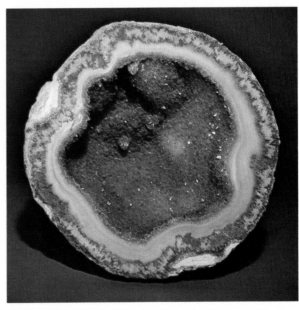

QUARTZ: *Geode,* Mexico (ca 5 inches across)

QUARTZ (agate): Moss agate, Montana (ca 15 x 20 mm)

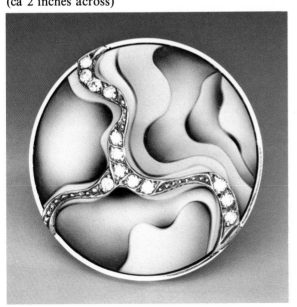

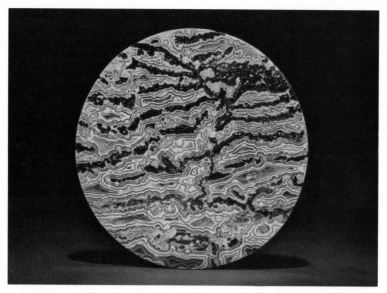

QUARTZ (agate): Mexico, *Lace agate* (disc ca 2 inches across)

QUARTZ (agate): Mexico, "fortification agate"
(slab ca 4 inches across)

QUARTZ (agate): Mexico, "fortification agate"
(slab ca 4 inches across)

QUARTZ (agate): India, "clamshell agate"
(slab ca 6 inches across)

QUARTZ (jasper): Idaho, *Bruneau jasper*
(slab ca 5 inches across)

QUARTZ (jasper): Oregon, "picture jasper"
(slab ca 6 inches across)

QUARTZ (jasper): Oregon, "picture jasper"
(cabochon ca 30 x 40 mm)

QUARTZ (jasper): Oregon, "scenic jasper" (slab ca 5 inches across)

QUARTZ (jasper): Mexico (slab ca 4 inches across)

QUARTZ: *Petrified wood,* Utah (slab ca 4 inches across)

QUARTZ: *Tigereye,* S. Africa
(rough mass ca 3 inches long; blue and red cabs are dyed)

QUARTZ (jasper): "Indian paint rock", California
(slab ca 4 inches across)

REALGAR: Washington (0.65)

RHODIZITE: Madagascar (0.49)

RHODOCHROSITE:
Alma, Colorado (2.4)

RHODOCHROSITE: Colorado
(8.48), Hotazel, S. Africa (2.45)

RHODOCHROSITE: Argentina, cross section of
stalactite, with cabochons (cabs ca 15 x 20 mm)

RUTILE: North Carolina
(ca 0.5, specimen ca 2 inches long)

RHODONITE: Australia (cabochon 30 x 40 mm, box ca 6 inches long)

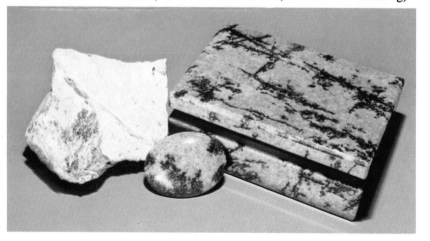

RHODONITE: Broken Hill, New
South Wales, Australia (4.5)

48

Menilite: opaque gray to brown opal with a concretionary structure.

Tabasheer: opaline silica occurring in the joints of bamboo.

Girasol: opal that is almost transparent and has a billowy light effect within it, resembling moonstone.

Chrysocolla in opal: blue material, with finely disseminated chrysocolla that gives the color.

Liver opal: term sometimes used for brown common opal.

Resin opal: yellowish brown common opal with a waxy luster.

TERMS FOR COLOR AND COLOR DISTRIBUTION IN OPAL

Onyx opal and agate opal: alternating layers of precious and common opal. In *catseye opal* the color play is concentrated in the form of an eye or band. *Matrix opal* consists of specks of precious opal in a rock matrix, usually sandstone; this type of opal is often dyed black to enhance the color play. *Ironstone opal* is in a brown and hard, compact type of sandstone. Matrix opal may also be layers or stringers of opal in a rock matrix.

Flame opal: sweeping reddish streaks and bands move across the gem, resembling flickering flames.

Flash opal: As the gem is moved back and forth, flashes of color appear and disappear at various spots.

Harlequin opal: the color display is in the form of angular, or quiltlike patches, all in contact with each other, like a mosaic.

Pinfire opal: the color is in the form of tiny dots or speckles, set close together.

Peacock opal: many colors appear in the same gem, resembling the display of the tail of the male peacock.

Also: Gold opal (gold fire), *blue opal* (bluish fire), *lechosos opal* (green colors).

Occurrence: In sedimentary rocks or where low-temperature solutions bearing silica can percolate through rocks.

Honduras: Deposits known since before 1843, perhaps much older than that. Occurs as veins in dark reddish to black trachyte rock. White opal contrasts strongly with the dark colored matrix. Pieces not large, seldom very spectacular.

Czechoslovakia: Source of opal known in Roman times, near the village of Czerwenitza (formerly in Hungary). Opal occurs as seams in grayish brown andesite rock. The opal is a mosaic of strong colors and is very attractive, against a milky-white background color. Much of this is harlequin opal.

Indonesia: Very little known material, as thin seams in dark rock. Much of it is water opal and resembles material from Mexico. The white opal resembles poor-grade Autralian. Some black opal is produced which is very unusual and consists of reddish flecks of color swimming in a translucent but very dark brown body.

Most gems are very small (less than 10 carats) from this locality, and production is very small.

Mexico: Mexican opal occurs in siliceous volcanic lavas, in cavities, and in many localities. Yellow and red fire opal comes from a trachyte porphyry at Zimapan in Hidalgo. At San Luis Potosí, Chihuahua, occurs hyalite and precious opal that is completely transparent, colorless, and rich in fire. Queretaro is a well known opal-producing locality. Fine Mexican opal is very rare in large sizes (over 50 carats), but among the most beautiful.

Virgin Valley, Nevada: in Humboldt Co., as cracks and seams in opalized wood. This was discovered about 1900. The opal is magnificent, but is very hydrous and has a strong tendency to crack due to loss of water when exposed to the air. This behavior is known as *crazing*, or, when on the surface, *checking*. Whole skeletons of extinct animals have been replaced by fine precious opal at this locality. Similar opal is found in Idaho.

Brazil: Opal occurs in sandstone in Piaui State, northern Brazil, and also near Manaus, northern Brazil. The material is white and fiery and sometimes resembles good-quality Australian white opal. It is perhaps the most durable opal, low in water and not heat-sensitive—the author has seen a cut gem held for half a minute over a candle flame with no adverse effects. The material seems to be abundant, and much of it is shipped to Australia where it is cut and sold, often as Australian opal.

Poland: Green-colored prase opal, colored by nickel.

Australia: The first discoveries were probably about 1850, but major finds were made in about 1872, in Queensland. Opal in Australia is in various types:

Boulder opal: shells of coarse, hardened, sandy clay with layers of opal in between.

Yowah nuts: walnut-sized concretions, in a regular layer, like a comglomerate. The opal is the central kernel and never reaches the outer edge.

Seam opal: thin to thick seams of white or black opal in sandstone matrix. Also known as sandstone opal. Large stones are very rare in this material.

Major finds of opal are best known in Australia from specific localities:

Lightning Ridge: black opal in nodules, world's finest of this material; first mined commercially in about 1905.

Coober Pedy, So. Australia: discovered about 1915; only white opals found here, in sandstone and claystone matrix, but some very fine.

Andamooka, So. Australia: opals found here about 1930; very distinctive opal, white and also brownish in color; may be artificially blackened to enhance the appearance of the fire in the matrix.

White Cliffs area: started about 1889, but the opal is usually small, with veinlets of precious opal within common opal.

Australia is the best known opal-producing area in the world, but the deposits have been worked so intensely that they are starting to become depleted. Many fewer miners are now working the opal fields than 10 years ago, and new discoveries are rare. This factor, plus worldwide demand, is putting tremendous pressure on opal prices.

Stone Sizes: Many large and fine stones have been given individual names, like diamonds. Only a few can be included here, others are described in books specifically about opal.

Olympic Australis: Coober Pedy; uncut was 127 oz.

Noolinga Nera: Andamooka; 86 oz. rough, cut 205 carat oval.

Roebling Opal: Nevada (Rainbow Ridge), 2610 (in *SI*).

Light of the World: Lightning Ridge, Australia, 252, partly cut.

Red Admiral, or Butterfly: Lightning Ridge, 40−50 in rough. Many regard this gem as the world's most beautiful opal.

Pride of Australia: Lightning Ridge, 226, partly cut.

Pandora: Lightning Ridge, 711, cut.

SI: Australian gems; 345, 155, 83 (all white); black opals of 58.8, 54.3, 44. Also 355 (black, Nevada); 143.2 (orange, precious, Mexico); 55.9 (colorless, precious, Mexico); 39 (pale yellow-orange, precious, Brazil).

Comments: Opal is one of the most popular of all gems. It is very rare in large sizes (over 30−40 carats); especially rare is black opal, which is the loveliest and most expensive of all opal varieties. The value of opal lies in the size of the stone, the colors it displays, and the pattern of the color. This is all subjective, and varies according to advertising and the fashion of the time.

Opal is hydrous, and when it dehydrates it tends to crack spontaneously. It may crack or craze immediately when it is taken from the ground, or at any time thereafter, even after a period of many years! Opals kept in jewel cases and drawers may suddenly be found to have minute, threadlike cracks in them. The only way to prevent this is to keep opals perpetually in a jar of water, which is inconvenient. Much of the value of an opal is lost when cracking occurs, as the cracks seriously impair the strength of the gem and may allow it to fall out of the setting.

The hardness of opal is only about 5.5, which is very low for a gem that is used in jewelry; opal is *not* a good ringstone, but people persist in wearing it as such. Many opals in rings are damaged beyond repair, or crack and fall out and are lost. Frequently an opal in a ring is found to be chalk-white and lifeless; this may be solely due to a network of scratches on the surface that destroys the polish and reduces the color play, and can be fixed by simple repolishing. Opal is usually very brittle, and heat sensitive, so great care must be used in cutting to prevent cracking. Opals (or any other gems, for that matter) should not be worn while washing dishes, because of the thermal shock of the hot water.

Opal may have excellent color play, but occur as very thin seams in rock or in white opal without fire. These seams have been utilized by cementing them to a backing material, such as potch opal (without fire), obsidian, or a ceramic, using a black epoxy cement. The black cement makes the colors appear stronger. Such a composite stone is known as a *doublet*. If a quartz cabochon is cemented on top of the opal layer, the stone is called a *triplet*, and is a three-layer sandwich with opal in the middle. Triplets are good ringstones because the quartz is hard and protects the opal from scratching.

Bits of precious opal are sometimes suspended in tiny glass or plastic spheres or tear-shaped vials, in water or (usually) glycerine so they float slowly and gently. These jewels are known as *floating opals*.

Many types of opal can be treated to enhance their appearance. A common technique is to immerse white or gray opal (especially from Andamooka) in sugar solution, and then in strong sulfuric acid. The acid carbonizes the sugar and leaves microscopic carbon specks in the opal, which effectively blacken the body color and make the spots of fire stand out better. Opal has also been synthesized by Pierre Gilson of France, and is imitated by a variety of other materials, including plastics and glass.

Name: *Opalus* was the ancient name of this gem.

ORBICULAR JASPER   See: Quartz.

ORTHOCLASE   See: Feldspar.

ORTHOFERROSILITE   See: Enstatite.

P

PAINITE

Formula: $Ca_4Al_{20}BSiO_{38}$.

Crystallography: Hexagonal. One pseudo-orthorhombic crystal is known. No cut gems.

Colors: Dark red, garnetlike in hue.

Luster: Vitreous.

Hardness: 8.

Density: 4.0.

Cleavage: Not determined.

Optics: $o = 1.816$; $e = 1.787$. Uniaxial (−).

Birefringence: 0.029.

Pleochroism: $o =$ deep ruby red; $e =$ pale brownish orange.

Spectral: Faint Cr spectrum.

Inclusions: Minute cavities in thin sheets; inclusions of tabular hexagonal crystals.

Luminescence: Weak red in LW, strong red in SW.

Occurrence: Burma, in the gem gravels of Mogok. One red crystal was discovered in 1951 and identified in 1957 as a new mineral.

Comments: No cut gems are known. The only existing specimen is the red crystal in the British Museum in London, weighing 1.7 grams. The color resembles garnet, and the density is that of garnet or ruby. This means that there might be cut gems in existence that have been misidentified as ruby or garnet. The refractive indices are unlike those for ruby, and the material is so clearly birefringent that it could not be confused with garnet, if tested. Also, a garnet of this color would display the almandine spectrum, a very definitive test.

This is perhaps the rarest of all gem species—not a single cut stone is known to exist, and only one specimen has ever been identified!

Name: After the discoverer, A.C.D. Pain.

PEARL

Formula: $CaCo_3$(aragonite)—about 82—86%; conchiolin—10—14%; water—2%.
These proportions are variable.

Crystallography: Orthorhombic (aragonite), with the minute crystals radially oriented and a concentric structure.

Colors: The color of a pearl is a result of a *body color* and an *overtone color* (known as *orient*) present (due to surface effects) as a lustrous sheen. The orient is the color seen as *reflected* by a diffuse light source. The rest of the color observed is due to the body color. There are sometimes two overtone colors, one seen on the surface in full view, the other at the edge.

Luster: Pearly, dull.

Hardness: 2.5–4.5.

Density: 2.6–2.78; conch pearls, 2.85; cultured pearls, 2.72–2.78, i.e., heavier than most natural pearls, but this is *not* a diagnostic test.

Cleavage: None. Fracture uneven. Toughness is variable.

Birefringence: 0.156 (aragonite).

Optics: $N = 1.53$–1.69, but not observed; usually vague shadow edge in this range.

Acids: Pearls will dissolve in all acids.

Luminescence: Natural pearls may be light blue, yellowish, greenish, or pinkish in LW, SW. Cultured pearls no reaction, or same as natural in LW. Freshwater pearls always glow yellowish white in X-rays.

Pearl Colors
The surface tone or orient is due to diffraction at the edges of overlapping plates of aragonite crystals at the surface. These edges cause a feeling of roughness when a pearl is rubbed across the teeth.

Body Colors:
White, as follows:
White (no overtone); cream (no overtone); light cream to light yellow; light rose (pinkish overtone on white background); cream rosé (cream background with deep rose overtone); fancy pearls (cream background, with overtone of rose; blue or green secondary overtone seen at edges of pearl).

Black: includes gray, bronze, dark blue, blue-green, green. Some have metallic overtones.

Colored Pearls: Neither black nor white, usually with a blue background color, plus red, purple, yellowish, violet, blue, green. More frequently seen in freshwater pearls.

Darker colors are apparently due to dark conchiolin in the core of a pearl showing through the thin layers of aragonite crystals.

Shapes of Pearls
Round; pear-shaped (squat = egg shape, elongated pear = drop shaped); button (flat back); half pearls (flat back), three-quarter pearls ($\frac{3}{4}$ round with flat area); seed pearls (unsymmetrical, less than $\frac{1}{4}$ grain); dust pearls (almost microscopic); blister pearls (attached to shell); baroque pearls (any irregular shape not mentioned); slugs (baroque pearls with a poor luster).

Occurrence: Salt-water pearls are the most important on the marketplace. These come principally from the species of oyster known as *Pinctada*.

Persian Gulf: This is the world's major pearl-producing area, especially close to the coasts of Iran, Oman, and Saudi Arabia. These waters have produced pearls for more than 2000 years.

Persian Gulf pearls are usually small (less than 12 grains). The diving season is roughly May–September and the waters are worked by hundreds of small boats. The diving depth is about 30–90 feet, but usually less than 60 feet. Pearls are recovered from oysters, washed, and then sold to Indian merchants in Bombay. Then follows a bleaching operation (using hydrogen peroxide and sunlight), sorting, grading, and drilling. Poor-quality pearls go to the Far East, in general. Better pearls mostly go to Paris and from there many reach the U.S. Bombay is chiefly a brokerage center.

Persian Gulf pearls are creamy white. Density 2.68–2.74.

Gulf of Manaar: This is an arm of the Indian Ocean, between Ceylon and India. The waters have been fished for pearls for more than 2500 years, but fishing now is sporadic. The government of Ceylon controls the fishing and auctions the oysters that are caught. The oysters are opened by leaving them on the ground to rot, and the decomposition products are searched for pearls, which then go to Bombay. Gulf of Manaar pearls are pale cream-white, sometimes with fancy overtones of blue, green, and violet. Density 2.68–2.74.

Red Sea: This area is not a major pearl producer today. The pearls are reputed tō be whiter than those from other sources.

Australia: Pearl oysters are fished off the west, northwest, and north coasts. Armored diving suits are now used. Recovery of the shells is as important as recovery of the pearls, because the shells provide a major industry. Australian pearls are silvery white to yellow. Density 2.67–2.78.

South Seas: Native fisheries operate around Micronesia and Polynesia. The pearls may be large (up to 7100 grains!) and are generally round. Tahiti is the major pearl center. The colors are usually white with little orient, but also can be yellow, gray, and black. A metallic, grayish cast is characteristic.

Japan: The Japanese waters are rapidly becoming too polluted for the existence of *Pinctada*. Cultured pearls now constitute a much bigger industry. Japanese pearls are white, often with a greenish tinge. Density 2.66–2.76.

Venezuela: Venezuelan oysters are usually small varieties, and the pearls vary in color from white to bronze, also black. White pearls from here may be very iridescent and almost glassy. Density 2.65–2.75.

Mexico; Panama: The fisheries here are small and not important commercially.

Florida; Gulf of California: Occasionally pearls are found, especially conch pearls, which are pink (from conch shells). Pearls are also found in abalone, and colors may be green, yellow, blue and other tones. California has produced black pearls. Density of Florida pearls (pink) is about 2.85; California 2.61–2.69. Abalone shells are often hollow inside with bright iridescent colors that make them very distinctive. Conch shells are often used to make cameos. Conch pearls are usually pink, with a very distinctive flamelike surface pattern.

Freshwater Pearls: These come from a mussel called *Unio*, rather than from oysters. Freshwater pearls are found in rivers throughout the world, including Europe, South America and the U.S. Notable occurrences are in:
Scotland; Wales; England; Ireland.
France; Germany; Austria.
Mississippi River and its tributaries.
Amazon River basin.
Nova Scotia.
E. Pakistan.

Cultured Pearls
Patents for processes to produce cultured pearls were granted in Japan about 1910. The basic work was done by Otokichi Kuwabara, Tatsuhei Mise, Tokichi Nishikawa, and Kokichi Mikimoto. The process developed involved the insertion of a bead of mother-of-pearl (shell) up to about 13 mm in diameter, along with a piece of tissue from a part of the oyster known as the mantle, into the body of the oyster. The oysters upon which the surgery has been performed are allowed to convalesce in sheltered waters for 4–6 weeks. They are then allowed to grow, in cages, for a period of 3–6 years at a depth of 7–10 feet. Nacre accumulates around the inserted bead to form a pearly layer. Japan is the world leader in cultured pearl production.

Cultured *blister pearls* are half-pearls formed by accumulation on a half-bead stuck to the shell of the oyster. Large-diameter beads can be used. After pearl growth the nacrous (pearly) dome is removed and cemented onto a mother-of-pearl bead. This product is called a *Mabe pearl*.

Some cultured pearls are grown in fresh water in Lake Biwa, Japan, using clams. As many as 30 insertions per clam can be tolerated without killing the animal. Growth requires about 3 years, and the pearls have excellent color and luster.

Externally, cultured and natural pearls are virtually identical. Identification *requires* skilled use of special tools, such as the pearl endoscope or X-ray apparatus. X-radiography offers the only positive proof of the origin of a pearl. Other tests are helpful but not conclusive.

Stone Sizes: The *Hope Pearl* in the *BM* is 2 inches long, 4.5 inches in circumference at the broad end, weighs 1800 grains (*Note:* one grain = 0.048 grams = 0.013 carats). This is a salt-water pearl.
The *Queen Pearl* is of freshwater origin, round, translucent, weighs 93 grains, and was found near Paterson, New Jersey!

Miracle of the Sea is pear-shaped, weighs 1191 grains. *La Pellegrina*, a very famous pearl from the Orient, weighs 111.5 grains.

The following table gives the approximate weights (in grains) of pearls of mm sizes:

mm diam:	1	2	3	4	5	6	7	8	9	10	11	12	13	14
weight:	.02	.25	.75	1.75	3.50	6.0	9.75	14.5	19.5	28.0	38.0	48.0	61.0	81.0

15mm = 101 grains

Comments: Maximum beauty is not usually found in large pearls. They form, basically, by encapsulation of an irritant by tissues of a mollusc. The value of pearls is a function of color, luster, orient, translucency, texture, shape, and especially size. Groups of pearls, such as beads, are complex valuation problems, because then degree of matching becomes an issue. The price of a group of pearls or a single pearl is determined by a complex formula involving a base price multiplied by the *square* of the weight in grains. The base rate is higher for higher-quality and for matched pearls. In addition, there are ways of averaging sizes to determine the overall size to use in the formula for groups of pearls. The base rate is a fluctuating market factor, determined by experience.

The introduction of cultured pearls early in this century caused a major depression in the prices of pearls, because high-priced, rare, natural pearls could not initially be distinguished from cultured ones. The market took many years to recover, and with unambiguous laboratory tests now available, fine pearls have recovered their original esteem. Cultured pearls are fully accepted, and occupy a larger share of the market than natural pearls. Large (over 12 mm) pearls of fine color and orient are very rare and costly, and even more so if available in matched groups.

Name: From the Latin word *perula*, meaning *pearl*.

PECTOLITE   *Series to* Serandite (*through* Manganpectolite).

Formula: $NaCa_2Si_3O_8(OH) + Mn$.

Crystallography: Triclinic. Crystals acicular, radial or globular masses; often terminated.

Colors: Colorless, white, gray.

Luster: Vitreous to silky.

Hardness: 4.5−5.

Density: 2.74−2.88.

Cleavage: Perfect 1 direction. Fracture splintery.

Optics: $\alpha = 1.595-1.610$; $\beta = 1.605-1.615$; $\gamma = 1.632-1.645$.
Biaxial (+), $2V = 50-63°$. Refractometer spot reading at about 1.60.

Birefringence: 0.036.

Spectral: Not diagnostic.

Luminescence: In LW, orange-pink (Bergen Hill, N.J.), cream white (Lendalfoot, Scotland). In SW, greenish yellow (Scotland), yellowish, orange with green areas (Magnet Cove, Arkansas and Lake Co., California), faint yellow with phosphorescence (Paterson, New Jersey).

Occurrence: In cavities in basaltic rocks, associated with zeolites; in lime-rich metamorphic rocks.
Scotland; Sweden; Czechoslovakia; U.S.S.R.; Morocco; S. Africa; Japan.
New Jersey: Paterson area, in fine radial sprays; also at Franklin and Sterling Hill.
Alaska: massive, jadelike (used as jade substitute); also fine-grained, pale blue-green.
Lake Co., California: dense material suited for cabochons.
Magnet Cove, Arkansas: pinkish manganiferous material.
Thetford Mines, Quebec; Asbestos, Quebec: magnificent prismatic crystals, some facetable, also twinned, up to 5 inches long; pale blue-green color, white.
Greenland: manganiferous.
Dominican Republic: compact, white and various shades of blue (sometimes dark) material capable of cutting cabochons with high polish.

Stone Sizes: Cabochons up to a few inches have been cut from dense, massive or fibrous material. A few small faceted gems have been cut from material found at Asbestos, Quebec about 1973. These are the only known faceted pectolite gems, and range in size up to about 3 carats.

Comments: Fibrous material has a chatoyancy that gives a catseye effect to cabochons. Pectolite is seldom cut, and is a curiosity for collectors. The fibrous aggregates are seldom cohesive enough to cut, and the material is too soft and fragile for wear, unless the fibers are intergrown. Such material could be jadelike in toughness as well as appearance. When sufficiently compact, cabochons take an excellent polish. The material from Quebec is extremely rare, and transparent crystals are usually tiny.

Dominican pectolite is the loveliest in the world; it is compact and takes a very high polish. It is colored in various shades of blue, and the finest is dark and translucent. The local trade name for the material is *Larimar;* it is mined on a mountainside 200 km west of Santo Domingo and, though locally abundant, this is a *rare* gem material.

Name: From the Greek *pektos*, meaning *congealed*, because of the translucent appearance the mineral sometimes has.

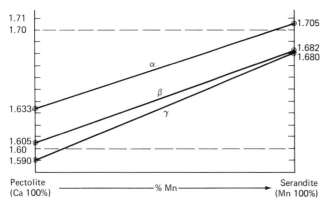

Refractive Index vs. composition in pectolite—serandite series.

PENTLANDITE

Formula; $(Fe, Ni)_9S_8$.

Crystallography: Isometric. Crystals extremely rare; massive, granular.

Colors: Light bronze yellow.

Streak: Bronze brown.

Luster: Metallic; opaque.

Hardness: 3.5−4.

Cleavage: None. Fracture conchoidal. Brittle.

Luminescence: None. Nonmagnetic.

Occurrence: Associated with pyrrhotite and other nickel ores in basic rocks.
Norway; Transvaal, S. Africa; Alaska; California; Nevada.
Sudbury, Ontario, Canada: major ore mineral, huge masses.

Stone Sizes: Cabochons of any desired size can be cut from massive material.

Comments: Pentlandite resembles other yellowish metallic minerals, and is cut by collectors as a curiosity. The cut stones are quite attractive, but too soft for hard wear. Pentlandite is usually intimately intermixed with pyrrhotite and chalcopyrite in Canadian ore bodies, creating an interesting, multicolored metallic appearance.

Name: After J.B. Pentland who first noted the mineral.

PERICLASE

Formula: MgO.

Crystallography: Isometric. Crystals octahedral, cubic; commonly as rounded grains.

Luster: Vitreous.

Hardness: 5.5.

Density: 3.56.

Cleavage: Perfect 1 direction. Fracture uneven. Brittle.

Optics: Isotropic; $N = 1.736$.

Luminescence: Pale yellow in LW (Terlingua, Texas).

Occurrence: Occurs in marbles, due to high-temperature contact metamorphism.
Texas; New Mexico.
Spain; Sardinia; Czechoslovakia.
Crestmore, Riverside Co., California: embedded grains.
Vesuvius, Italy: as glassy grains in the lava rocks.
Nordmark, Sweden: in the Mn mines.

Stone Sizes: The author has not seen any faceted gems, but they would be very small. Transparent grains from Vesuvius might be cuttable, but in general periclase is not known in transparent, large crystals.

Comments: Periclase has been synthesized in large masses in the laboratory, but these have no gem significance. A faceted natural periclase would be a great rarity due to the extreme scarcity of suitable faceting rough. The expected size would be less than 1 carat. This material might pop up sometime from a newly discovered contact deposit, in larger facetable masses.

Name: From the Greek *peri* plus *klastos, to break around*, in allusion to the cleavage.

PERIDOT   See: Olivine.

PERISTERITE   See: Feldspar.

PERTHITE   See: Feldspar.

PETALITE

Formula: $LiAlSi_4O_{10}$.

Crystallography: Monoclinic. Crystals rare, tabular; usually massive, cleavable.

Colors: Colorless, white, gray, yellow, sometimes reddish or greenish-white, pink.

Luster: Vitreous to pearly.

Hardness: 6−6.5.

Density: 2.3−2.5.

Cleavage: Perfect 1 direction. Brittle.

Optics: $\alpha = 1.503-1.510$; $\beta = 1.510-1.521$; $\gamma = 1.516-1.523$.
Biaxial (+), $2V = 83°$.

Birefringence: 0.012−0.014.

Spectral: Not diagnostic; may be vague band at 4540 in some stones.

Luminescence: In LW pale orange (Wyoming) or buff (Maine). May be orange in X-rays.

Occurrence: In granite pegmatites, in crystals and masses.
N. Bonneville, Wyoming; Greenwood, Maine; San Diego Co., California; Bolton, Massachusetts.
Uto, Sweden; Elba, Italy; U.S.S.R.
Londonderry, W. Australia: facetable material.
Arassuahy, Brazil: large, clean masses.

Bikita, Rhodesia: considerable material, mined for Li content.

Karibib, S.W. Africa: colorless, transparent and pinkish material.

Stone Sizes: Petalites are usually small, up to about 20 carats from Brazil crystals and smaller from other localities. Some Brazilian and S. African rough has yielded somewhat larger stones, in the 50 carat range.

SI: 55 (colorless, S.W. Africa).

DG: 14.8 (colorless, Australia).

Comments: Most faceted petalites are colorless and glassy looking. The desirability is in their rarity and if they are free of inclusions, especially in large sizes. A considerable number of 1−10 carat faceted gems from Brazil has been available on the market. Massive pink material from S. Africa is occasionally cabbed.

Name: From the Greek *petalos*, (*leaf*), in allusion to the cleavage. *Castorite*, the name applied to crystals, is after Castor, was one of the heavenly twins in Greek mythology (see Pollucite).

PETRIFIED WOOD   See: Quartz.

PHENAKITE

Formula: Be_2SiO_4.

Crystallography: Hexagonal. Crystals rhombohedral, prismatic, acicular; also granular, and in fibrous spherulites.

Colors: Colorless; also yellow, pink, brown, pinkish red, all due to surface stains; some crystals are colored by impurities.

Luster: Vitreous.

Hardness: 7.5−8.

Density: 2.93−3.00.

Cleavage: Indistinct, 1 direction. Fracture conchoidal. Brittle.

Optics: $o = 1.654$; $e = 1.670$. Uniaxial (+).

Birefringence: 0.016.

Dispersion: 0.005.

Pleochroism: Observed in strongly colored crystals; for example, in a greenish-blue stone: violet-red/intense blue.

Spectral: Not diagnostic.

Luminescence: Pale greenish or blue in UV light. Sometimes fluoresces blue in X-rays.

Inclusions: Crystals of aikinite; also mica (Brazil).

Occurrence: In granite pegmatites, often in good crystals.

Pala Co., California; Colorado (Pike's Peak area); New Hampshire; Lord's Hill, Maine.

Kragero, Norway; France; Switzerland; Czechoslovakia; Usugara dist., Tanzania; Klein Spitzkopje, S.W. Africa.

Virginia: crystals up to 2 inches across.

U.S.S.R.: reddish color.

San Miguel de Paracicaba, Brazil: large colorless crystals, often clean and cuttable.

Stone Sizes: Crystals up to $5 \times 10 \times 18$ cm have been found, though these are usually heavily flawed. The largest known rough was a pebble found in Ceylon that weighed 1470 carats and cut a 569 carat clean gem and several smaller stones. The large stone has many needle-like inclusions.

SI: 22.2 (colorless, U.S. location).

Comments: Phenacite is very hard and suited for wear in jewelry, but it is colorless and not exciting to look at. Cut gems have little fire but are very bright. Red gems cut from material from the U.S.S.R. are seldom seen, and very rare. The normal faceted gemstone is in the 1−5 carat range.

Name: From the Greek for *deceiver* because it had been mistaken for quartz.

PHOSGENITE

Formula: $Pb_2CO_3Cl_2$.

Crystallography: Tetragonal. Crystals prismatic, thick and tabular; massive, granular.

Colors: Colorless, white, yellowish white, gray, shades of brown, greenish, pinkish.

Luster: Adamantine.

Hardness: 2−3.

Density: 6.13.

Cleavage: Distinct 1 direction. Fracture conchoidal. Somewhat sectile.

Optics: $o = 2.114-2.118$; $e = 2.140-2.145$. Uniaxial (+).

Birefringence: 0.028.

Pleochroism: Very weak, reddish/greenish, only in thick pieces.

Luminescence: Strong yellowish fluorescence in UV and X-rays.

Occurrence: A secondary mineral in lead ore deposits. *California; Colorado; Arizona; New Mexico; Massachusetts.*

Matlocks, England; Tarnow, Poland; U.S.S.R.; Tasmania; Australia; Tunisia.

Monte Poni, Sardinia: fine yellow-brown crystals, up to 5 inches across; some have facetable areas.

Tsumeb, S.W. Africa: some cuttable.

Stone Sizes: Phosgenite is very rare as a faceted gem, almost always less than 2 carats, and usually yellowish brown in color (Sardinia). A few larger stones, up to about 10 carats, are known.

Comments: Massive material can be cut into interesting cabochons of various colors, up to the size of the rough (several inches). Phosgenite is too soft to wear. The strong fluorescence is of interest to specialists in fluorescent minerals.

Name: From *phosgene*, a name for the compound $COCl_2$ (carbonyl chloride), because the mineral contains C, O, and Cl.

PHOSPHOPHYLLITE

Formula: $Zn_2(Fe, Mn)(PO_4)_2 \cdot 4H_2O$.

Crystallography: Monoclinic. Crystals prismatic to tabular, well developed.

Colors: Colorless to blue-green.

Luster: Vitreous.

Hardness: 3–3.5.

Density: 3.08–3.13.

Cleavage: Perfect 1 direction. Fracture uneven. Brittle.

Optics: $\alpha = 1.595–1.599$; $\beta = 1.614–1.616$; $\gamma = 1.616–1.621$.
Biaxial (−), $2V = 45°$.

Birefringence: 0.021–0.033.

Pleochroism: None.

Spectral: Not diagnostic.

Luminescence: Fluoresces violet in SW.

Occurrence: In massive sulfide deposits (*Bolivia*) and in granite pegmatites (*Germany*).
Potosi, Bolivia: magnificent single crystals up to about 3×2 inches; refractive indices of this material 1.597–1.621, density 3.08, fine blue-green color, transparent.
Hagendorf, Germany: small crystals associated with secondary phosphate minerals.

Stone Sizes: Only Bolivian material has been cut, but some crystals have been found that could yield stones of about 75 carats or more. These are superb and very rare crystal specimens and will undoubtedly never be cut. Most stones are in the 1–10 carat range, cut from crystal fragments and broken crystals.
SI: 9, 5.04 (Bolivia).
PC: 74, flawless.
DG: 5.25 (Bolivia).

Comments: Phosphophyllite possesses a color almost unique in gems, a lovely blue-green shade enhanced by cutting. This is a *very* rare mineral, even rare in uncut form. Stones are seldom available because of lack of incentive to cut up good crystals. Few large stones exist; the material is quite brittle and fragile, and very difficult to cut, with an easily developed cleavage. This is one of the more desirable of the collector gems, and also one of the more expensive ones.

Name: After Greek words for *phosphorus-bearing* and *cleavable*.

PICOTITE   See: Spinel.

PICTURE JASPER   See: Quartz.

PIEDMONTITE   See: Epidote.

PLAGIOCLASE   See: Feldspar.

PLANCHEITE   See: Shattuckite.

PLASMA   See: Quartz.

PLEONASTE   See: Spinel.

POLLUCITE   *Series to* Analcime (Zeolite group).

Formula: $Cs_{1-x}Na_xAlSi_2O_6 \cdot xH_2O$; $x = $ ca 0.3. Also written: $(Cs, Na)_2(Al_2Si_4)O_{12} \cdot H_2O$.

Crystallography: Isometric. Crystals cubic, very rare; massive, fine-grained.

Colors: Colorless, white, gray; tinted pale pink, blue, violet.

Luster: Vitreous (slightly greasy).

Hardness: 6.5–7.

Density: 2.85–2.94.

Cleavage: None. Fracture conchoidal. Brittle.

Optics: Isotropic; $N = 1.518–1.525$.

Dispersion: 0.012.

Luminescence: Orange to pink fluorescence in UV and X-rays.

Inclusions: Usually whitish, resembling spikes or balls, very small; also very tiny snowflakes, bulging at the centers.

Occurrence: In granite pegmatites.
San Diego Co., California; Middletown, Connecticut. Bernic Lake, Manitoba; Elba, Italy; Finland; Kazakhstan, U.S.S.R.; Karibib, S.W. Africa.
Custer Co., South Dakota: massive material in thick seams.
Newry, Maine: gem material.
Various localities in *Maine and Massachusetts.*
Varutrask, Sweden: massive lilac to white material ($N = 1.518$, S.G. 2.90).

Stone Sizes: Masses in South Dakota reach 3–4 feet in thickness, opaque, whitish. Gems are usually colorless and very small; Maine material cut stones from masses that reached a size of 10 inches.
SI: 8.5 (colorless, Maine); 7.0 (colorless, Connecticut).
PC: 3.85 (pinkish, Maine).

Comments: Pollucite is essentially a very rare cesium mineral. In fact it is the *only* mineral in which Cs is an essential constituent. Gems are always very small, under 10 carats, despite the existence of large beds at some localities. It is colorless and lacks fire when cut, but is of interest for its great rarity.

Name: Pollux was, along with Castor, a brother of Helen of Troy in Greek mythology. This mineral was found in Italy in 1846, and named *pollux;* it was associated with another mineral, named *castor,* which was later studied and renamed *petalite.*

POLYCRASE   See: Euxenite.

PRASE   See: Quartz.

PREHNITE
Formula: $Ca_2Al_2Si_3O_{10}(OH)_2$ + Fe.
Crystallography: Orthorhombic. Crystals prismatic and tapering, rare; massive, in druses and crusts, stalactitic.
Colors: Pale green, dark green, yellow, yellowish green, gray, white, colorless.
Luster: Vitreous to pearly.
Hardness: 6−6.5.
Density: 2.80−2.95; gem material usually 2.88−2.94.
Cleavage: Distinct 1 direction. Fracture uneven. Brittle.
Optics: α = 1.611−1.632; β = 1.615−1.642; γ = 1.632−1.665.
Biaxial (+), 2V = 65−69° Usually refractometer gives shadow edge about 1.63.
Note: Faceted material from Australia, indices 1.618/1.625/1.648, birefringence 0.030. Values for optical constants increase with increasing iron content.
Birefringence: 0.021−0.033.
Pleochroism: None.
Spectral: Not diagnostic.
Luminescence: May be dull brownish yellow in UV and X-rays.
Occurrence: A low-temperature mineral occurring by deposition from groundwaters in basaltic rocks, associated with zeolites; hydrothermal crystals, in cavities in acid igneous rocks; in serpentine rocks due to late-stage mineralization.
California; Colorado; Michigan; Massachusetts; Connecticut.
France; Italy; Austria; Germany; U.S.S.R.; Czechoslovakia; S. Africa; Pakistan; New Zealand.
New Jersey: in basalts, associated with zeolites.
Fairfax Quarry, Centreville, Virginia: fine colored material (green).
Asbestos, Quebec, Canada: in acidic dikes, in crystals up to 3 inches long (colorless).
Scotland: facetable.
Australia: facetable.

Stone Sizes: Large masses, up to several tons in size, have been encountered in New Jersey traprocks. Single masses weighing 400 pounds have been collected. Australia and other localities produce translucent material that yields interesting faceted gems up to about 30 carats. *DG:* 38.20 (yellow, Australia).

Comments: Prehnite is popular as a cabochon material among hobbyists, because of its lovely green and blue-green to yellow colors. Completely transparent material is extremely rare, but might be found in crystals from Asbestos, Quebec. Yellowish to greenish translucent material from Australia has been faceted, and makes a striking cut gemstone with a rich color and interesting appearance, with a soft, velvety look. Material from Scotland is supposed to have yielded cuttable fragments, but such faceted gems would be rather small (under 5 carats).

Name: After Col. Prehn, who first found the material on the Cape of Good Hope.

PROSOPITE   See: Turquoise.

PROUSTITE   Dimorph of Xanthoconite.
Formula: Ag_3AsS_3.
Crystallography: Hexagonal (R). Crystals prismatic, rhombohedral; massive, compact.
Colors: Deep red, scarlet to vermilion red.
Streak: Bright red.
Luster: Adamantine to submetallic.
Hardness: 2−2.5.
Cleavage: Distinct 1 direction. Fracture conchoidal to uneven. Brittle.
Optics: o = 3.088; e = 2.792. Uniaxial (−).
Birefringence: 0.296.
Pleochroism: Strong in shades of red.
Spectral: Not diagnostic.
Luminescence: None.
Occurrence: Low-temperature ore deposits or the upper portions of vein deposits.
Idaho; Colorado; Nevada; California.
Sarrabus, Sardinia.
Cobalt dist., Ontario: small crystals.
Batopilas, Chihuahua, Mexico: small crystals.
Freiberg, Germany: fine crystals; other German localities, sometimes in very fine and large crystals, some cuttable.
Dolores Mine, Chanarcillo, Chile: world's finest proustite occurs here, in crystals of deep red color, often transparent, up to 6 inches long and very thick. The occurrence here is unique.
Stone Sizes: Most cuttable proustite is from Chile, but crystals for cutting are in private collections and mu-

seums and are not about to be cut up. Occasional fragments from Germany are transparent. Gems weighing several hundred carats could be cut from crystals on display in various museums. The finest proustites known are in the collection of the British Museum of Natural History, London.

SI: 9.9 (red, Germany).

Comments: Proustite is one of the most sought-after of all collector minerals, because of its magnificent color and the brilliance of good crystals. It is far too soft for wear, and exposure to light causes it to turn black (a photochromic effect due to the silver present) so the material should not be displayed in strong light. Faceted gems are deep red with a metallic surface that is both beautiful and distinctive. One of the rarest of all the better-looking collector gems.

Name: After J.L. Proust, a French chemist.

PSEUDOPHITE   See: Serpentine.

PUMPELLYITE (= CHLORASTROLITE)   Also note: Ferropumpellyite: contains ferrous iron. Julgoldite: contains both ferric and ferrrous iron.

Formula: $Ca_2MgAl_2(SiO_4)(Si_2O_7)(OH)_2 \cdot H_2O$.

Crystallography: Monoclinic. Crystals fibrous, flattened plates, in clusters or dense mats of randomly oriented fibers.

Colors: Green, bluish green, brown.

Luster: Vitreous; silky when fibrous.

Hardness: 6; chlorastrolite: 5−6.

Density: 3.18−3.33; chlorastrolite: 3.1−3.5.

Cleavage: Distinct in 2 directions. Fracture splintery. no cleavage in massive material.

Optics: $\alpha = 1.674-1.702$; $\beta = 1.675-1.715$; $\gamma = 1.688-1.722$.
Biaxial (+) and (−), $2V = 26-85°$. May show anomalous birefringent colors. Mean index ca 1.7.

Birefringence: Moderate.

Dispersion: Moderate.

Pleochroism: Distinct, as follows:
α: colorless/pale greenish yellow/pale yellowish green.
β: bluish green/pale green/brownish yellow.
γ: colorless/pale yellowish brown/brownish yellow.
Note: Pale colored pumpellyite has: low birefringence, weak dispersion, lower indices.
Dark colored pumpellyite has: higher values for all these properties.

Luminescence: None.

Spectral: Not diagnostic.

Occurrence: Pumpellyite occurs in a wide variety of igneous and metamorphic rocks and environments.

Scotland; Austria; Finland; U.S.S.R.; New Zealand; S. Africa; other localities.
Calumet, Michigan: in copper ores; also at *Isle Royale, Lake Superior, Michigan* (non-gem) and on the *Keweenaw Peninsula, Michigan* (non-gem).
Lake Superior: the periphery of the lake contains basic igneous rocks, containing spherical aggregates of green fibers of chlorastrolite, in masses. This material is sometimes cut, but is not homogeneous.
California: in glaucophane schists.
New Jersey: in basalts (traprocks).

Stone Sizes: Chlorastrolite is cut as cabochons approximately one to two inches long. Very fine deep green material occurs in small sizes, yielding stones less than one inch long.

Comments: The gem variety of pumpellyite, chlorastrolite, is best known as a gem from the Lake Superior district of the U.S. It typically forms aggregates of packed fibers that are mixed with other minerals, resulting in a green and white pattern that is reminiscent of tortoise shell. The effect is best observed when the fibers are in radial clusters that yield circular markings. The turtle-back pattern is considered most desirable and, because of the chatoyancy of the fibers, seems to move within the stone as the lighting is changed. Pumpellyite is a common mineral in many parts of the world, but fine green material is scarce and greatly prized by collectors. The best color is a very intense green resembling the color of fine emerald or Imperial jade. Good-quality chlorastrolite with strong pattern and color is now hard to obtain.

Name: *Pumpellyite* after Raphael Pumpelly, Michigan geologist who did pioneering studies of the Keweenaw Peninsula copper district of Michigan. *Chlorastrolite* is from Greek words meaning *green star stone.*

PURPURITE   Series to Heterosite.

Formula: $(Mn, Fe)PO_4$.

Crystallography: Orthorhombic. Crystals rare, in small masses and cleavages.

Colors: Deep rose to reddish purple; alters on outside to brown or black.

Streak: Reddish purple.

Luster: Dull, satiny.

Hardness: 4−4.5.

Density: 3.69.

Cleavage: Good 1 direction. Fracture uneven. Brittle.

Optics: $\alpha = 1.85$; $\beta = 1.86$; $\gamma = 1.92$.
Biaxial (+), $2V$ moderate.

Birefringence: 0.007.

Dispersion: Very strong.

Pleochroism: Strong; gray/rose-red; deep red/purplish red.

Spectral: Not diagnostic.

Luminescence: None.

Occurrence: A secondary mineral, due to the oxidation of phosphates in granite pegmatites.
South Dakota; California; North Carolina.
France; Portugal; W. Australia.
Usakos, S.W. Africa: rich purplish masses.

Stone Sizes: Cabochons up to several inches long can be cut from cleavages.

Comments: This material is never transparent, and too soft for wear. However, cabochons are a magnificent purplish rose hue that have essentially no counterpart in the gem world. The material is available from S.W. Africa in abundance and at low cost.

Name: After the Latin *purpura* (*purple*), in allusion to the color.

PYRITE Dimorph of Marcasite.

Formula: FeS_2.

Crystallography: Isometric. Crystals abundant and widespread, sometimes very large and displaying an immense variety of forms; also massive, granular.

Colors: Brassy yellow, sometimes with iridescent tarnish.

Streak: Greenish black.

Luster: Metallic; opaque.

Hardness: 6−6.5.

Density: 5.0−5.03.

Cleavage: Indistinct. Fracture conchoidal to uneven. Brittle.

Other Tests: Nonmagnetic; insoluble in HCl.

Occurrence: The most abundant of all sulfide minerals; occurs in nearly all rock types, and most geological environments. Localities too numerous to list in detail. Fine crystals are known from the following localities:
Leadville, Colorado; French Creek, Pennsylvania; Bingham, Utah.
Elba, Italy; Ambassaguas, Spain; England; Austria; Germany; Switzerland; Sweden; Peru; Bolivia.

Stone Sizes: Cabochons of any size could be cut from the large crystals that have been found. Pyrite is usually seen in inexpensive jewelry, faceted in rose-cut fashion with flat backs, similar to the older marcasite jewelry popular in Victorian times.

Comments: Pyrite is more commonly known as *fool's gold* and is familiar to nearly every mineral collector. It has been used for centuries both in jewelry and as an ore of iron. "Marcasite" stones in jewelry are frequently pyrite, since the latter is more stable. The material is very brittle and heat-sensitive, and requires some care in cutting. Cabochons are sometimes cut, but they have no special appeal.

Name: From the Greek word for fire, because pyrite emits sparks when struck like a flint.

PYROCHLORE See: Microlite.

PYROPE See: Garnet.

PYROPHYLLITE

Formula: $Al_2Si_4O_{10}(OH)_2$.

Crystallography: Monoclinic. Crystals tabular, often curved and deformed; foliated, radial, granular, compact.

Colors: White, yellow, pale blue, grayish green, brownish green.

Luster: Pearly to dull, greasy.

Hardness: 1−2.

Density: 2.65−2.90.

Cleavage: Perfect 1 direction. Sectile.

Optics: $\alpha = 1.534-1.556$, $\beta = 1.586-1.589$; $\gamma = 1.596-1.601$.
Biaxial (−), $2V = 53-62°$.
Vague shadow edge on refractometer at about 1.6.

Birefringence: 0.050.

Spectral: Not diagnostic.

Luminescence: Weak cream-white in LW (China)—variety called *agalmatolite*.

Occurrence: In schistose metamorphic rocks; also in hydrothermal veins with micas, quartz.
California; Arizona; Deep River, North Carolina; Pennsylvania; Georgia.
Minas Gerais, Brazil; Mexico; Sweden; Belgium; Switzerland; Japan; U.S.S.R.; Korea.
Transvaal, S. Africa: so-called *koranna stone*, which is dark gray and is about 86% pyrophyllite; R.I. ca 1.58, S.G. 2.72; also called *South African Wonderstone*.

Stone Sizes: Cabochons and carvings are cut from massive material, any practical size.

Comments: Pyrophyllite resembles talc in many ways, and is indistinguishable by eye from soapstone. Chemical tests are needed to distinguish them. North Carolina material is often used in carvings, as is the material from China known as *agalmatolite*.

Name: From the Greek words for *fire* and *leaf*, because of the sheetlike nature and thermal properties of the mineral. *Agalmatolite* means *figure stone*, in allusion to its use in carvings.

PYROXMANGITE

Formula: $(Mn, Fe)SiO_3$.

Crystallography: Triclinic. Crystals tabular; usually massive, in grains, cleavable.

Colors: Reddish brown, dark brown, pale to rose pink, purplish pink. The darker colors are due to alteration.

Luster: Vitreous to pearly.

Hardness: 5.5−6.

Density: 3.61−3.80.

Cleavage: Perfect 2 directions. Fracture uneven. Brittle.

Optics: $\alpha = 1.726-1.748$; $\beta = 1.728-1.750$; $\gamma = 1.744-1.764$.
Biaxial (+), $2V = 35-46°$.

Birefringence: 0.016−0.020.

Pleochroism: Slight in shades of pink and red.

Spectral: Not diagnostic.

Luminescence: None.

Occurrence: In metamorphosed rocks rich in manganese.
Kern Co, California; Iva, South Carolina; Boise, Idaho: pale pink.

Broken Hill, New South Wales, Australia: in fine crystals and grains, with rhodonite.
Scotland. Sweden: red-brown.
Finland: brown.
Honshu, Japan: gemmy material.

Stone Sizes: Faceted gems are always small, as the material is extremely scarce, and available only as small transparent grains. Large cabochons could be cut from cleavages and massive material. Collectors should expect to see stones up to about 2 carats.

Comments: Pyroxmangite is a very rare gemstone; grains are seldom clean enough to facet. The material resembles rhodonite and bustamite to a certain degree, but can be distinguished on the basis of optic sign and birefringence. Faceted gems are hard to cut because of the cleavages, but once completed they are extremely beautiful and rich in color.

Name: Originally thought to be manganiferous pyroxene, based on studies of the material from South Carolina.

Q

QUARTZ (= SILICA)

Formula: SiO_2.

Crystallography: Hexagonal (R). Occurs in a wide variety of crystal forms, up to large size; also as crystalline masses, cryptocrystalline, granular, in veins and stringers.

Colors: Colorless, white, gray (various shades) and many shades of yellow, orange, brown purple, violet, pink, green, and black.

Luster: Vitreous (crystalline varieties); greasy, waxy (cryptocrystalline varieties).

Hardness: 7.

Density: 2.651 (very constant); in chalcedonies, up to 2.91.

Cleavage: None or indistinct. Fracture conchoidal to uneven. Brittle. Cryptocrystalline varieties tough.

Optics: $o = 1.544$; $e = 1.553$ (very constant). Uniaxial (+).

Birefringence: 0.009 (some chalcedonies 0.004).

Dispersion: 0.013.

Pleochroism: None; weak in amethyst and citrine; strong (pink shades) in rose quartz.

Luminescence: Varies widely due to traces of impurities, usually in the cryptocrystalline varieties. Fluorescent colors include browns, greens, white, orange (LW, SW). Some material shows phosphorescence. X-rays produce faint blue glow in rose quartz.

Occurrence: Quartz is one of the most common minerals on earth, occurs in a wide variety of rock types and geological environments. Localities are too numerous to list but given in standard mineralogy texts.

Inclusions in Quartz

More than 40 types of minerals have been found as inclusions in crystalline quartz. Rock crystal frequently contains cavities or negative crystals with bubbles, creating what are known as two-phase inclusions. A network of cracks creates iridescent effects to produce what is called *iris quartz*. The minerals noted include:

Rutile: red, golden, silvery color.
Sagenite: any type of needle crystals.
Tourmaline: black, other colors.
Actinolite.
Chlorite: mossy, greenish inclusions.
Goethite: yellow and orange wisps, fibers, and crystals.
Hematite: blood-red platelets.
Chrysocolla: blue-green, finely disseminated.
Dumortierite: blue and violet colors.

scapolite; hornblende; epidote; anatase; brookite; chlorite; micas; ilmenite; calcite; gold; dufrenoysite; oil droplets;

Quartz *catseyes* have been found—the catseye effect is due to inclusions of fine asbestos. The colors are usually yellowish, brownish or pale green. This material is always cut into cabochons to bring out the effect. Occurrence: *India; Ceylon; Fichtelgebirge, Germany.*

Crocidolite (blue asbestos) may decompose and alter to quartz, retaining the fibrous structure. This can be further cemented by quartz and stained by iron oxides to yield a dense, siliceous, fibrous mateial called *tigereye*. The original blue crocidolite, if present, may add a blue tone and this is called *zebra tigereye*. If the material is unstained by iron and therefore solid blue, it is called *hawk's-eye*. Occurrence: *South Africa.*

Crystalline Quartz

Crystalline quartz is separated here from cryptocrystalline, or microcrystalline quartz. The crystalline varieties are those which occur in distinct, visible crystals.

amethyst, smoky quartz, citrine, rose quartz, milky quartz, blue quartz.

Quartzite is a granular variety that includes the gem *aventurine.* The color origins in crystalline quartz are complex and just now beginning to be fully understood.

The stable form of quartz below a temperature of 573°C is known as α-quartz. Between 573° and 870° another silica mineral forms, called *tridymite*. At 1470°, tridymite undergoes a structural rearrangement, resulting in the appearance of a new silica type called *cristobalite*, which is isometric. Finally, at 1710°, cristobalite melts to an extremely viscous liquid. If this liquid is chilled quickly, a glass forms (*silica glass*) which has many useful properties, but no regular internal structure.

Cristobalite has no gem significance but appears in some types of volcanic glass (see *obsidian*, page 000) as white globules and crystals resembling snowflakes. These form as a result of rapid cooling from high temperature.

The colored, crystalline quartz varieties generally occur in pegmatites and veins, having been deposited from water solutions over a long period of time. As a result of slow crystal growth, many such crystals achieve great internal perfection and yield enormous pieces of faceting rough. The only color varieties that do not form such large crystals are amethyst and rose quartz.

Rock Crystal: Used in faceted gems, beads, carvings, decorative objects, lamps. The material is common and has little intrinsic value, except in very large, flawless pieces. There are many types of mineral inclusions known. Occurrence: *Hot Springs, Arkansas; Herkimer, New York.*

Swiss Alps; Minas Gerais, Brazil; Japan; Madagascar; N. S. Wales, Australia; Upper Burma; Canada.

Milky Quartz: The milkiness is due to myriad tiny cavities and bubbles filled with CO_2 or water. Vein quartz is often white and frequently contains gold. This quartz is little used in gems, except cabs with milky quartz and yellow gold specks. Occurrence: *California; Colorado.*

Brown Quartz: The variety called *smoky quartz* is pale beige, tan, brown, or deep brown in color. Very dark brown material is known as *morion*, and also *cairngorm* from the locality in the Cairngorm Mountains, Scotland. The color appears to be caused by natural radioactivity.

Occurrence: *Minas Gerais, Brazil; Scotland; Madagascar; Switzerland; Korea.*
California; North Carolina.

Yellow Quartz: This variety is known as *citrine,* and ranges in color from pale yellow through yellow-orange to rich golden orange, very dark orange. A deep brown color is produced by heating certain types of amethyst. The name is from the old French *citrin* meaning *'yellow',* and the color is due to ferric iron. Occurrence: *Minas Gerais, Brazil; Madagascar.*

Amethyst: Amethyst is violet or purple colored quartz. The lightest color, a pale lilac shade, is known as *Rose of France.* The deepest color, especially with flashes of red against a purple background, is referred to as *Siberian.* The term today usually implies a color rather than a locality. The name *amethyst* is from the Greek *amethystos,* meaning *not drunken,* because the Greeks believed imbibing from an amethyst cup would prevent intoxication. Occurrence: *Brazil; Zambia; U.S.S.R.; S.W. Africa; India; Uruguay.*
Arizona; North Carolina.

Inclusions: Prismatic crystals and negative cavities, thumbprint marks, so-called rippled fractures, and twinning lines.

Transparent *green quartz* is produced by heating certain types of amethyst.

Rose Quartz: The color of rose quartz is due to Ti. The material is nearly always cloudy or translucent, rarely transparent. The color is pale pink to deep pink, rose-red. It is mainly used in cabochons, carvings, and decorative objects. Microscopic rutile needles may create a star effect. Occurrence: *Maine; South Dakota; New York.*
Brazil; Madagascar; India; Japan; S.W. Africa; U.S.S.R.

Quartzite: A rock made up of tightly packed quartz grains, formed at high temperature and pressure, due to metamorphism. Sometimes it contains small crystals that reflect light, and this material is called *aventurine.* Usually the included crystals are a green, chrome-rich mica called *fuchsite.* Other micas that may form aven-

turine include gray varieties or brown types (from Chile). The density is usually 2.64−2.69.
Occurrence: *Spain; U.S.S.R.; India; Chile.*

Dumortierite Quartz: A dense, deep blue to violet material made up of crystalline quartz colored by dumortierite, a complex borosilicate.

Cryptocrystalline Quartz

Cryptocrystalline quartz varieties are colored chiefly by mineral impurities in the growth environment, including oxides of Fe, Mn, Ti, Cr, Ni, and other elements. They form either as gelatinous masses that slowly dehydrate and crystallize, or by deposition from slowly percolating groundwaters, depositing silica over a long period of time. This latter type of deposition results in banding that is seen in certain types of agate. Deposition within a spherical cavity, such as a gas pocket in basalt or other volcanic rock, results in concentric banding also seen in agates.

Cryptocrystalline quartz varieties offer a huge diversity of patterns and colors. The most generally widespread of these materials is composed of tiny fibers of silica and is known as *chalcedony.* Names within the cryptocrystalline quartz family are generally based on colors and patterns. The solid-colored materials are mostly chalcedony stained by oxides, and are referred to as *jaspers.* Banded varieties, or materials with mosslike inclusions, are known as *agate.*

Chalcedony: Unstained material often grayish blue, compact form of silica. Occurrence: *India; U.S.S.R.; Iceland.*
California.

Carnelian: Translucent to semi-opaque, red or orange-red or brownish chalcedony. The color is due to iron oxide. Almost any chalcedony can be turned red by heating in an oven, since it contains finely disseminated iron compounds which are oxidized by heating. Occurrence: *Brazil; Uruguay; Egypt; India.*

Sard: Similar to carnelian, but is more brownish in color and more opaque. Occurrence: *Brazil; Uruguay.*

Plasma: Deep green; opaque because of densely packed actinolite crystals.

Prase: Green or yellowish green chalcedony.

Bloodstone: Also known as *heliotrope,* consists of dark green plasma with blood-red and orange spots of iron oxides. Occurrence: *India; Brazil; Australia; U.S.*

Onyx: Banded black and white chalcedony.

Sardonyx: Banded onyx, but with red and white layers.

Chrysoprase: Translucent green chalcedony colored by nickel. May resemble fine jade. Occurrence: *Australia; U.S.S.R.; Brazil.*
California.

Flint and Chert: Opaque, dull gray or whitish chalcedony, very compact and hard.

Patterned Chalcedony

Agate: Usually takes the form of colored layers or

bands, flat or concentric. Also mossy or dendritic inclusions, sometimes creating the impression of landscapes, vegetation, etc. *Banded agates* have regular color layers and bright colors. The *moss agates* have mossy inclusions of mineral oxides. *Scenic agates* have inclusions that look like pictures of scenery, with lakes, shorelines, trees and shrubs. *Lace agate* is banded with intricate swirls and loops. *Fire agate* has platy crystals of iron oxide layered with chalcedony, resulting in iridescence brought out by cutting and polishing. *Shell agate* is patterned by silicified shells in the rock. *Turritella agate* is composed mostly of shells and shell fragments of the gastropod *Turritella*, and certain other species. Occurrence:

Moss agates: *India; Scotland; U.S. Northwest.*
Scenic agates: *Yellowstone Park*, *Wyoming; Montana.*
Banded agate: *Brazil; Uruguay; Madagascar; Mexico.*
Lace agate: *Mexico; Arizona; S.W. Africa (blue).*
Fire agate: *Mexico.*

Jasper: Usually a mass of tiny silica crystals pigmented by impurities. The colors may be very strong, especially shades of brown, yellow, red, and green. Worldwide occurrence. *Orbicular jasper* has spherules of banded agate in a jasper matrix. *Scenic or picture jaspers* have fanciful patterns that may resemble scenery, such as ocean waves, shores and rolling hills. Occurrence: *Oregon; Idaho; Utah; Montana; Wyoming.*

Chrysocolla in Quartz: A tough, siliceous material consisting of blue chrysocolla in fine particles disseminated in silica, to produce a rich blue, hard material that takes an excellent polish. Occurrence: *Arizona; New Mexico; Mexico.*

Petrified Wood: Colorful agate that has replaced tree trunks and limbs; the woody structure is preserved in many cases and can be seen with a microscope. The colors may be very bright and strong. Occurrence: *Arizona; New Mexico; California; Washington; Oregon. Various European countries; many other localities.*

Dinosaur Bone: Silicified dinosaur bone! It has a lovely brownish color and interesting pattern. Occurrence: *Colorado; Wyoming; Utah.*

Names: *Rock crystal* is from the Greek *krystallos*, meaning *ice*, because the Greeks thought it was ice frozen forever hard by an unnatural frost created by the Gods. *Amethyst* comes from the Greek *amethystos*, as mentioned. *Citrine* is an allusion to the color citron (yellow). *Chalcedony* is an ancient name, perhaps from Chalcedon, a seaport in Asia Minor. *Agate* is from the Greek *achate*, the name of a river in southwestern Sicily where the material was found. *Onyx* is from the Greek word for *nail* or *claw*. *Sard* from Sardis, ancient locality reputed to be the origin of the stone. *Carnelian* is from the Latin *carnis (flesh)*, in allusion to the red color. *Plasma* is from

the Greek for *something molded or imitated*, because it was used for making intaglios. *Prase* is from the Greek *prason*, meaning *leek*, in allusion to the color. *Heliotrope* is from Greek words *helios (sun)* and *tropein (turn)*, because (according to Pliny) it gives a red reflection when turned to face the sun, while immersed in water. *Flint* and *chert* are of uncertain origin.

Stone Sizes:

Rock crystal reaches enormous size, as illustrated by the 12.75 inch diameter, 107 pound perfect sphere in *SI* of Burmese material, absolutely without flaws. This is the largest fine crystal ball in the world. Faceted gems of thousands of carats have been cut, such as the 7000 carat stone in *SI* and the 625 carat star quartz from New Hampshire.

Citrines in the thousands of carats are also known. *SI* has Brazilian stones of 1180, 783, 278, 265, and 217 carats, for example, and most large museums have similar baubles.

Smoky quartz is in the same size league as citrine, but larger stones get very dark and opague. *SI:* 4500 (California) and 1695 (Brazil) plus others.

Rose quartz gems are seldom transparent at all, and especially above 20–30 carats. Large spheres of rose quartz are milky at best.

Amethyst is rare in very large, transparent masses. The fine gems at *SI* are exceptional, such as the 1362 carat Brazilian stone and the 202.5 carat stone from North Carolina.

Quartzite and *milky quartz* are massive varieties available in large pieces. *Chalcedony* is usually nodular, but masses can be several pounds and many inches in diameter.

Star quartz is a rarity, but especially noted in rose quartz. *SI* has a sphere of Brazilian star material weighing 625 carats.

Comments: Quartz is composed of Si and O, the two most abundant elements in the crust of the earth. It displays a hugh variety of colors and shapes (when in crystals), and the cryptocrystalline varieties offer an almost endless spectrum of color and pattern. The basic properties of crystalline quartz are very constant despite color variation.

Many silica varieties can be treated by heating, irradiation, and dyes to alter their color. *Chalcedony* is frequently dyed with aniline dyes to many rich colors. The quartz gems vary in scarcity, with amethyst the rarest color, especially in large clean pieces. Cryptocrystalline varieties are so abundant that they offer a rich selection of decorative stones for wear at very modest cost.

QUARTZITE see: Quartz.

R

REALGAR

Formula: AsS.

Crystallography: Monoclinic. Crystals prismatic, striated; compact, powdery.

Colors: Dark red, orange-red.

Streak: Orange-yellow.

Luster: Resinous to greasy.

Hardness: 1.5–2.

Density: 3.56.

Cleavage: Good 1 direction. Fracture conchoidal. Sectile.

Optics: α=2.538; β=2.684; γ=2.704.
Biaxial (−), $2V = 40°$.

Birefringence: 0.166.

Dispersion: Strong.

Pleochroism: Strong: colorless to pale yellow.

Spectral: Not diagnostic.

Luminescence: None. May decompose on strong exposure to light.

Occurrence: Low-temperature hydrothermal vein deposits, especially with ores of lead and silver.
Getchell Mine, Nevada; Manhattan, Nevada; Mercur, Utah; Boron, California.
Romania; Czechoslovakia; Germany; Switzerland; Japan.
Washington: fine crystals, up to 2 inches long, some gemmy.

Stone Sizes: Occasional fragments of Washington crystals will cut gems to about 3 carats.

Comments: Realgar is very seldom transparent, although the mineral is widespread in occurrence throughout the world. It is extremely soft and fragile, difficult to cut, impossible to wear. It is cut only for collectors, but is extremely rare in cut form and stones are a fine red color and very lovely.

Name: From the Arabic *Rahj-al-ghar*, meaning *powder of the mine.*

RHODIZITE

Formula: $CsAl_4Be_4B_{11}O_{25}(OH)_4$.

Crystallography: Isometric. Crystals dodecahedral or tetrahedral, up to 2 cm size; massive.

Colors: Colorless, white, yellowish white, yellow, gray, rose red.

Luster: Vitreous to adamantine.

Hardness: 8.5.

Density: 3.44.

Cleavage: Difficult. Fracture conchoidal. Brittle.

Optics: Isotropic; $N = 1.694$.
Anomalously birefringent (may not be truly isotropic).

Dispersion: 0.018.

Spectral: Not diagnostic.

Luminescence: Weak yellowish glow in SW; strong greenish and yellowish, with phosphorescence in X-rays.

Occurrence: A pegmatite mineral, with few noteworthy localities.
Antandrokomby, Madagascar (and other localities in that country): yellowish and greenish crystals, some gemmy.
Near Mursinsk, U.S.S.R.: rose red color.

Stone Sizes: Madagascar material in fragments clean enough to cut has provided stones up to about 3 carats.
SI: 0.5 (Madagascar).

Comments: Rhodizite is quite a rare mineral, and only Madagascar has produced gem-quality crystals. Faceted gems are extremely rare and usually pale in color. The mineral is rather hard and stones would be excellent for jewelry, especially because there is no cleavage.

Name: From the Greek for *to be rose-colored* because it imparts a red color to the flame of a blowpipe.

RHODOCHROSITE *Series to* Siderite (*with Fe substitution*); *series to* Calcite (*with Ca substitution*).

Formula: $MnCO_3$ + Fe, Ca.

Crystallography: Hexagonal (R). Crystals rhombs and elongated; massive, compact, stalactitic.

Colors: Pale pink, rose red, deep pink, orangish red, yellowish, gray, tan, brown.

Luster: Vitreous to pearly.

Hardness: 3.5–4.

Density: 3.4–3.6 (pure = 3.7).

Cleavage: Perfect rhombohedral. Brittle.

Optics: $o = 1.786-1.840$; $e = 1.578-1.695$. Uniaxial (−).
Ca in formula reduces indices and density; Fe and Zn increase them. This also applies to the birefringence. Single crystals may be zoned and the refractive index varies up to 0.01 within a space of one inch in some material.

Birefringence: 0.201–0.220.

Pleochroism: Faint in deep red varieties.

SAMARSKITE: Colorado (specimen ca 1 inch across)

SARCOLITE: Italy (0.33)

SCAPOLITE: Brazil (24.0), Kenya (2.30)

SCAPOLITE: Kenya (73.31, crystal ca 3 inches long)

SCAPOLITE: Burman (6.65), Brazil (5.77), Kenya (1.93), Burma (9.0)

SCAPOLITE: *Catseye scapolite*, Burma (7.0)

SCHEELITE: California (2.2), Mexico (2.4)

SCHEELITE: California (15.05), Arizona (11.90)

SCHEELITE: Korea (7.5), Mexico (4.0), Arizona (2.0)

SCOLECITE: India (1.15)

SERANDITE: Mt. Ste. Hilaire, Quebec, Canada
(ca 1.5, rough ca 2 inches long)

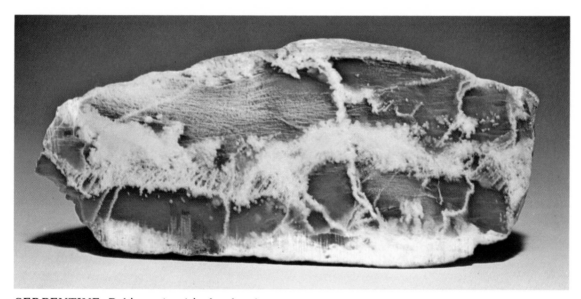

SERPENTINE: Pakistan (ca 4 inches long)

SERPENTINE: *Williamsite,*
Maryland (2.3)

SCORODITE: Tsumeb,
S.W. Africa (1.0)

SHATTUCKITE: Bisbee, Arizona
(ca 1 inch long)

SHORTITE: Wyoming (0.5)

SIDERITE: Portugal (1.40)

SILLIMANITE: *Fibrolite;* Kenya (0.34), Burma (2.44)

SINHALITE: Ceylon (15, 11.5)

SIMPSONITE: Brazil (0.27)

SMITHSONITE: Tsumeb,
S.W. Africa (3.16)

SMITHSONITE: Tsumeb, S.W. Africa
(cabochon ca 50, faceted gems 18, 12)

SMITHSONITE: Kelly Mine, New Mexico (blue, ca 5 inches), Mexico (other colors)

SODALITE: Bancroft, Ontario, Canada
(ca 1 inch long stones)

SODALITE: S.W. Africa (ca 2 each)

53

HACKMANITE: Ontario, Canada (0.8, 4.7)

SPHALERITE: Spain (ca 6)

SPHALERITE: Spain (25.5)

SPHALERITE: Baja, Mexico (ca 4, rough ca 1 inch across)

SPHENE: Baja, Mexico (6.0, 6.4, 6.75)

54

SPHENE: Baja, Mexico (2.62, 1.01, 2.6, 3.5, 2.13, 1.75, 1.75, 1.25)

SPHENE: Baja, Mexico (center stone ca 5)

SPINEL: Ceylon (7.44, 6.82)

SPINEL: Mostly Ceylon, showing range of colors (ca 1 to 15)

SPINEL: *Gahnite,* Brazil
(1.56)

SPODUMENE: Brazil (ca 12, 19.3, 1.7, 6.4)

STAUROLITE: Brazil (0.5)

STICHTITE: Argent Hill,
Tasmania, Australia
(specimen ca 2 inches across)

SULFUR: Girgenti, Sicily
(specimen ca 4 inches across)

STRONTIANITE: Austria
(2.1)

SPODUMENE: Pakistan (ca 170)
—largest known gem of this color.

SPODUMENE: *Kunzite,* Brazil (137)

TEKTITE: *Moldavite,* Czechoslovakia
(6.4)

TEKTITE: *Libya Glass,* Libya (4.12);
Moldavite, Czechoslovakia (6.05)

THAUMASITE: Paterson, New Jersey
(specimen ca 1 inch across)

THOMSONITE: New Mexico (cabochon, ca 23 x 47 mm);
Isle Royale, L. Superior, Michigan (pink stones)

TOPAZ: Back row, Brazil (12, 42, 37, 15)
Front row: Brazil (4), Mexico (8), Brazil (5, 18), Pakistan (12.5)

TOPAZ: Brazil (3.27, 3.14, 4.65, 6.7, 10.2)

TOPAZ: Pakistan (36, in ring)

TOPAZ: Brazil, heated and irradiated (115)

TOPAZ: Brazil (10.45, 28.7, 112, 12.7, 6.2)

TOURMALINE: *Rubellite;* Back row: Pala, California (15), Brazil (22, 18), Pala (26), Africa (11)
Front row: Pala (4), Brazil (5), Africa (8), Brazil (4, 4)

TOURMALINE: *Indicolite:* Back row: Maine (26), Brazil (22), Africa (10), Brazil (12)
Front row: Africa (1.5, 3), Brazil (3, 7, 7, 6)

TOURMALINE: *Bicolor;* Brazil (12, 6, 10), Pala, California (12.13)

TOURMALINE: Worldwide localities, color suite (ca 3 to 12)

TOURMALINE: Brazil (15.4)

TOURMALINE: *Catseye tourmaline*, Brazil (20.85)

TOURMALINE: *Rubellite;*
Pala, California (ca 10, in ring)

TOURMALINE: *"Watermelon tourmaline"*, Brazil (large slice ca 1 inch across)

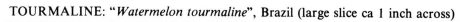

TREMOLITE: *Hexagonite,* Balmat, New York
(ca 1, crystal 1 inch long)

TUGTUPITE: Illimassauk, Greenland
(specimen ca 1 inch across)

TUGTUPITE: Illimassauk,
Greenland (0.51)

TURQUOISE: Arizona and New Mexico
(right, rear nugget ca 2 inches long)

TURQUOISE: Arizona and New Mexico (in silver jewelry)

TURQUOISE: Iran (superb matched beads, ca 15 mm)

TURQUOISE: Iran
(ca 0.5 carat cabochons in pin)

VANADINITE: Mibladen, Morocco
(crystals ca 2 inches across)

ULEXITE: Boron, California (ca 1 inch across, looking through
2-inch thickness along length of fibers)

VARISCITE: Fairfield, Utah
(slab ca 6 inches across, with other phosphates)

VARISCITE: Fairfield, Utah (cabochon ca 1 inch long)

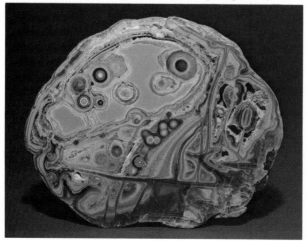

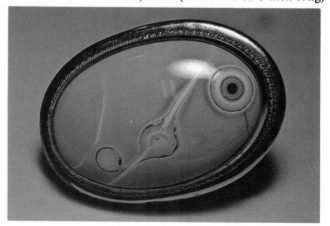

WAVELLITE: Hot Springs, Arkansas
(specimen ca 1 inch across)

WHEWELLITE: Burgk, Germany
(crystals in vug ca ¼ inch high)

WILLEMITE: Franklin, New Jersey (0.5, 6.94, 0.6)

WOLLASTONITE: Sunnyside Mine, Santa Fe, New Mexico
(specimen ca 4 inches high)

WITHERITE: England (1.89)

63

WULFENITE: Tsumeb,
S.W. Africa (21+)

WULFENITE: Arizona
(ca 1.5, crystal 1 inch long from the Red Cloud Mine)

ZINCITE: Franklin, New Jersey (ca 1, rough 2 inches long)

ZIRCON: Australia (5.2, 3.7), Cambodia (15.6, 4.25), Australia (2.35)

ZIRCON: Ceylon, Thailand and Tanganyika, showing range of colors (ca 1 to 4)

Spectral: Band at 5510 and at 4100, plus vague lines at 5350 and 5650.

Other Tests: Effervesces in warm acids.

Luminescence: Fluoresces medium pink in LW (Michigan), also dull red to violet in SW (Argentina and Colorado).

Occurrence: A gangue mineral in hydrothermal veins and a secondary mineral in ore deposits.
Colorado: spectacular crystals, pink to deep red, small to 3 inches on an edge. The world's finest rhodochrosite comes from *Alma, Colorado;* some is facetable (red) and pink faceting rough also exists from other localities.
Butte, Montana: crystal groups (non-gem).
Magdalena, Mexico: sometimes in cuttable pieces.
Hotazel, S. Africa: facetable, deep reddish crystals.
San Luis, Catamarca Province, Argentina: massive and banded material, also stalactitic, with growth to 4 feet long! These have concentric structures that cut interesting bullseyes when cross-sectioned. Some Argentina material is translucent and has been faceted.

Stone Sizes: Massive material from Argentina occurs in large pieces and has been carved, cut into beads, boxes, cabochons, and useful objects. Faceted, translucent pink material cuts stones up to about 20 carats. South African rhodochrosite is rich rose red in color, and rare in facetable crystals. The largest cut gems are in the 60 carat range. *SI* has a South African gem 9.5 carats. Colorado pink gems are perhaps the loveliest of all, and have been cut up to about 15 carats flawless. Most stones are under 5 carats.
DG: 5.95 (red, S. Africa).
PC: 59.65 (red oval, S. Africa).

Comments: Rhodochrosite is basically very rare in faceted form. The specimens are in such demand among mineral collectors that it would be an outrage to most to cut up a good crystal. Hotazel gems of large size have been available, but larger clean stones are very scarce and expensive. Colorado pink rhodochrosite in clean gems is also expensive, and anything over 2−4 carats is considered very large today. Argentinian material is translucent at best and much less costly, but few gems have appeared on the market. Mexican gem material resembles Colorado material, but is generally quite small.

Name: From the Greek for *rose-colored*, in allusion to the color.

RHODOLITE See: Garnet.

RHODONITE *Pyroxene group.*

Formula: $MnSiO_3$ (+ Ca to max. of 20%).

Crystallography: Triclinic. Crystals tabular; massive, cleavable, granular.

Colors: Rose red, pink, brownish red; often veined by black Mn oxides.

Luster: Vitreous; massive material dull.

Hardness: 5.5−6.5.

Density: 3.57−3.76 (massive); 3.67 in crystals.

Cleavage: Perfect 1 direction. Fracture conchoidal. Brittle (crystals); tough if compact.

Optics: Biaxial (+), $2V = 63-76°$. Shadow edge at 1.73 in massive varieties.

Pleochroism: Weak, but may be distinct: yellowish red/pinkish red/pale yellowish red.

Spectral: Broad band at 5480, strong narrow line at 5030, diffuse weak band at 4550. May also see lines at 4120, 4080.

Luminescence: Medium dull red in SW (Hungary), dull deep red in LW (Langban, Sweden).

Occurrence: In manganese-bearing orebodies, or in their vicinity.
California; Colorado; Montana; Franklin, New Jersey.
Cornwall, England; Mexico; South Africa.
U.S.S.R.: massive pink and rose colored material, very fine and rich (Sverdlovsk).
Australia: fine transparent crystals and massive material at Broken Hill, N.S.W.
Vermland, Sweden: good-colored gem material.
Honshu, Japan: facetable material.
Daghazeta, Tanzania: fine-quality massive material.
Mexico; South Africa.

Stone Sizes: Massive rhodonite from various localities is available in large pieces, often with attractive black veining of manganese oxides. This material is cut into cabochons, goblets, vases and other decorative objects, including figurines and boxes. Faceted gems are extremely rare, and are derived primarily from crystals found in Australia and Japan. The maximum size of such stones is in the 2−3 carat range, but a few larger stones may exist.

Comments: Rhodonite is a popular and useful decorative material, ranging from pink to a fine rose-red color. Faceted gems have an intense and beautiful color, but are delicate due to perfect cleavage. This cleavage is extremely easy to develop and rhodonite has the

	α	β	γ	Birefringence	Density	2V
Honshu, Japan	1.726	1.731	1.739	0.013	3.57	64°
Pajsberg, Sweden	1.720	1.725	1.733	0.013	3.62	75°
Broken Hill, New South Wales, Australia	1.723−1.726	1.728−1.730	1.735−1.737	0.011−0.013	3.68−3.70	74°

reputation of being perhaps one of the most difficult of all gems to facet. Most available rough is very small; the grains of gemmy rhodonite embedded in galena (lead sulfide) at Broken Hill, N.S.W. are distinctive. Rhodonite occurs with pyroxmangite, a related mineral, at this locality.

Name: From the Greek *rhodos*, in allusion to the color.

RICOLITE See: Serpentine.

ROCK CRYSTAL See: Quartz.

ROSOLITE See: Garnet.

RUBELLITE See: Tourmaline.

RUBY See: Corundum.

RUTILE

Formula: TiO_2 + Nb, Ta, Fe.

Crystallography: Tetragonal. Crystals prismatic, vertically striated, well developed, often twinned into a series of contact twins with up to 8 individuals, sometimes looping to form a complete circle! Also massive; granular.

Colors: Black, deep red, brownish red. Greenish (if Nb present), also bluish and violet. A variety rich in Cr is deep green.

Streak: Pale brown to yellowish; grayish or greenish black.

Luster: Metallic to adamantine.

Hardness: 6–6.5.

Density: 4.23; ferroan variety = 4.2–4.4; with Nb and Ta = 4.2–5.6.

Cleavage: Distinct 1 direction. Fracture conchoidal to uneven. Brittle.

Optics: o = 2.62; e = 2.90. Uniaxial (+). Sometimes anomalously biaxial.

Birefringence: 0.287.

Dispersion: 0.280.

Pleochroism: Distinct: shades of red, brown, yellow, green.

Spectral: Not diagnostic.

Luminescence: None.

Occurrence: Commonly seen as needles in quartz (*rutillated quartz*) and in agate (*sagenite*). Also present as fibers in corundum, creating stars in these gems. Present as needle inclusions in a wide variety of gem minerals.

Also occurs as a high-temperature mineral, in gneiss and schist, also in Alpine-type veins; found in igneous rocks, pegmatites, regionally metamorphosed rocks, including crystalline limestones, and as detrital grains. *Virginia; North Carolina; South Dakota; California. U.S.S.R.; Switzerland; France. Graves Mountain, Georgia:* in quartz veins, fine crystals, up to several pounds in size. *Magnet Cove, Arkansas:* in huge rough crystals. *Brazil:* large, fine crystals.

Stone Sizes: Large crystals often have transparent areas that can provide stones for faceting. However, a cut rutile above 2–3 carats is so dark it looks opaque, and this effectively limits the size of cut gems. *DG:* 3.70.

Comments: Rutile is often cut as a curiosity, and the finished gem is disappointing because it is so dark. The gems are usually deep red in color, but the color is so intense that it cannot be easily seen in stones larger than 1 carat. Cabochons of rutile might show reddish reflections in cracks and along imperfections. Swiss rutile seems a bit more transparent than material from other localities.

Name: From the Latin *rutilus* (*red*), in allusion to the color.

S

SALITE   See: Diopside.

SAMARSKITE   See also: Euxenite, Fergusonite.

Formula: $(Y, Ce, U, Ca, Pb)(Nb, Ta, Ti, Sn)_2O_6$.

Crystallography: Monoclinic. Crystals rough, tabular; massive, compact.

Colors: Velvety black, yellowish brown on exterior.

Streak: Black to reddish brown.

Luster: Dull after alteration; resinous; vitreous, submetallic.

Hardness: 5–6.

Density: 5.25–5.69 (variable)—usually near upper end of range.

Cleavage: Indistinct. Fracture conchoidal. Brittle.

Optics: Isotropic; $N = 2.20$ (variable).
Isotropic nature caused by metamictization.

Pleochroism: None.

Luminescence: None.

Occurrence: A pegmatite mineral, widespread in occurrence.
North Carolina; Colorado.
U.S.S.R.; Norway; Madagascar; Zaire; Japan; Minas Gerais, Brazil; Madras, India.

Stone Sizes: Large cabochons can be cut from masses found at various localities. This material is essentially opaque.

Comments: Samarskite is a very heavy material from which lustrous black to brownish cabochons are sometimes cut as a curiosity. The material is rather brittle and is not intended for wear. It is rarely seen or displayed, because black stones are not terribly attractive. Sometimes a stone is faceted in the nature of jet or marcasite.

Name: In honor of Col. Samarski, a Russian mining official.

SANIDINE   See: Feldspar.

SAPPHIRE   See: Corundum.

SARCOLITE

Formula: $(Ca, Na)_4Al_3(Al, Si)_3Si_6O_{24}$.

Crystallography: Tetragonal. Crystals equant, grains.

Colors: Reddish, rose red, reddish white.

Luster: Vitreous.

Hardness: 6.

Density: 2.92.

Cleavage: None. Fracture conchoidal. Very brittle.

Optics: $o = 1.604–1.640$; $e = 1.615–1.657$.
Uniaxial (+).

Birefringence: 0.011–0.017.

Occurrence: In volcanic rock at *Mt. Vesuvius, Italy*—this is the only locality (Monte Somma).

Comments: Tiny gems have been faceted from crystals found at the only known locality at Monte Somma. These stones are all very small (under 1–2 carats) and are extremely rare.

Name: From the Greek words for *flesh* and *stone*, in allusion to the color.

SARD   See: Quartz.

SATELITE   See: Serpentine.

SATIN SPAR   See: Gypsum.

SCAPOLITE   (= WERNERITE)   Solid solution series: Marialite to Meionite.

Formulas: *Marialite:* $3Na(AlSi_3)O_8 \cdot NaCl$.
Meionite: $3Ca(Al_2Si_2)O_8 \cdot CaCO_3$.

Crystallography: Tetragonal. Crystals prismatic, often large and coarse; massive, granular, cleavages.

Colors: Colorless, white, bluish gray, pale greenish yellow, yellow, pink, violet, brown, orange-brown.

Luster: Vitreous, resinous, pearly on cleavages.

Hardness: 6.

Density: 2.50–2.74; varies with composition.

Cleavage: Distinct 2 directions. Fracture uneven to subconchoidal. Brittle.

Dispersion: 0.017.

Pleochroism: *Pink and violet stones:* dark blue/lavender blue.
Colorless and pale yellow stones: colorless to pale yellow/yellow.

Spectral: Pink and violet stones: Bands in the red at 6630, 6520, due to Cr. Strong absorbtion in the yellow part of the spectrum.

Luminescence:
Burma: yellow to orange in LW (U spectrum), also pink in SW.
Tanzania: strong yellow in LW.

	Color	o	e	Birefringence	Density
Marialite	—	1.546–1.550	1.540–1.541	0.004–0.008	2.50–2.62
Entre Rios, Mozambique	yellow	1.568	1.548	0.020	2.70
Umba R., Tanzania	yellow-gold	1.567	1.548	0.019	2.671
Umba R., Tanzania	yellow-gold	1.562	1.543	0.019	2.659
Rio Pardo, Brazil	golden yellow dark	1.574	1.552	0.021	2.70
Rio Pardo, Brazil	golden yellow	1.570	1.549	0.021	2.68
Burma	colorless	1.560	1.544	0.016	—
Madagascar	—	1.568–1.571	1.550–1.552	0.018–0.020	—
Mozambique	—	1.554	1.540	0.014	—
Burma Catseye	violet	1.560	1.544	0.016	2.634
—	pink, white	1.549	1.540	0.009	2.63
Tanzania	yellow-white	1.579	1.553	0.026	2.74
Tanzania	golden yellow	1.553	1.539	0.014	2.63
Meionite	—	1.590–1.600	1.556–1.562	0.024–0.037	2.78

Quebec: massive material fluoresces yellow in LW (+ phosphorescence).
Some yellow faceted gems fluoresce lilac in SW, strong orange in X-rays.

Occurrence: in contact zones; regionally metamorphosed rocks; altered basic igneous rocks.
Madagascar: yellow, facetable crystals.
Espirito Santo, Brazil: pale yellow crystals sometimes large, facetable.
Burma: white, yellow, pink to violet; also catseyes in blue, pink, white.
Kenya and Tanzania: facetable golden yellow material; also pink to purple (rare).
Quebec: lemon yellow, opaque scapolite, some with silky luster.
Ontario.

Stone Sizes: White, yellow gems from Burma have been found in large sizes. Catseyes are usually under 10 carats, but larger ones are known. Kenya produces the finest golden yellow scapolite ever found. The largest stone, privately owned, is a magnificent deep orange oval of 73 carats. Pink Burmese step cut gems to 70 carats have been known. Brazilian yellow scapolite is cuttable to about 30 carats, smaller if clean.
ROM: 28.4 and 57.6 (yellow, Brazil); 7.91 (pink, Burma); 65.63 (colorless, Burma); 18.8 (gray, catseye); and 18.3 (pink, catseye).
SI: 288 (colorless, Burma); 29.9 (catseye, colorless, Burma); 29 (yellow, Brazil); 17.3 (catseye, pink, Ceylon); 12.3 (pink, Burma).
DG: 3.34 (blue catseye, Burma); 21.25 (white catseye, India).

Comments: Catseye scapolites from Burma are very rare and possess an unusually sharp eye, and occur in various colors. Cabochons from opaque Quebec and Ontario material are very lovely and often fluoresce brightly. The golden scapolite from Kenya is fairly new and is much darker than the Brazilian material. The pink to purple Kenya scapolite is also newly discovered and is extremely rare in sizes over about 3 carats. Most gems are in the 1–2 carat range. Faceted Burmese stones have appeared on the market from time to time, but very large ones are very rare.

Name: *Scapolite* from the Greek *skapos* (*shaft*), due to the stumpy nature of its prismatic crystals. *Marialite* named after Maria Rosa, wife of G. vom Rath. *Meionite* from Greek *meion* (*less*), because pyramidal form is smaller than that of idocrase from Vesuvius, which it resembles. *Mizzonite* from Greek *meizon* (*greater*) because the axial ratio is larger than that of meionite.

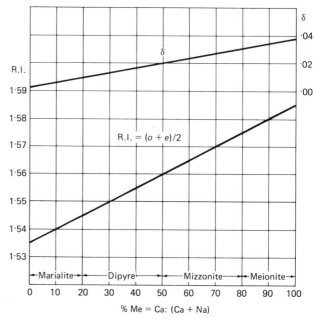

Adapted from Deer, W.A., Howie, R.A. and Zussman, J. (1962) *The Rock Forming Minerals*, 5 volumes, New York, John Wiley & Sons.

Refractive index and birefringence (δ) as related to chemical composition in the scapolite group. Chemistry is expressed as (molecular) percent meionite, which reflects the ratio Ca/(Ca + Na) in the formula. Refractive index is plotted as a mean index = (o + e)/2.

SCHEELITE

Formula: $CaWO_4 + Mo$.

Crystallography: Tetragonal. Crystals octahedral-shaped, tabular; massive, granular.

Colors: Colorless, white, gray, yellowish white, brownish, orange-yellow, greenish, violet, reddish.

Luster: Vitreous to adamantine.

Hardness: 4.5−5.

Density: 5.9−6.1.

Cleavage: Distinct 1 direction. Fracture subconchoidal to uneven. Brittle.

Optics: $o = 1.918-1.920$; $e = 1.934-1.937$. Uniaxial (+).

Birefringence: 0.016.

Dispersion: 0.038.

Spectral: Faint "didymium" lines in the yellow and green, especially 5840.

Luminescence: Brilliant bluish white in SW; inert LW.

Occurrence: In contact metamorphic deposits; hydrothermal veins; pegmatites; placer deposits.
Connecticut; South Dakota; Nevada; New Mexico.
Finland; Switzerland; France; England; Italy; Czechoslovakia; Germany; Japan; Australia; Canada; Bolivia; Peru.

Arizona: brown, large crystals, sometimes gemmy.
California: colorless gemmy crystals.
Near Milford, Utah: orange crystals, octahedral, some with clear tips.
Korea: white, grayish crystals; sometimes very large, cuttable in portions.

Stone Sizes: Crystals from Korea, Arizona, and other localities may be very large (4 inches on an edge) and are cuttable in sections. California gems may reach 70 carats; Mexican and Arizona stones are usually up to about 10 carats. Utah crystals rarely cut stones over 7 carats. Crystals from Korea up to 13 inches have been found, but none of these has been cuttable.
SI: 37, 18.7 and 15.8 (colorless, California); 12.4 (golden yellow, Mexico).
ROM: 14.0 (colorless, California).
AMNH: 20.65 (near Bishop, California).
PC: 17.58 (yellow, Mexico).
DG: 8.70 (Cohen Mine, Nevada).

Comments: Large scheelites are very rare, but are among the most beautiful of all the collector gems. The dispersion approaches that of diamond, and properly cut gems can have tremendous fire and brilliance. Crystals in museums could yield stones over 100 carats. Smaller clean gems are available on the marketplace.

Name: After Karl Wilhelm Scheele, Swedish chemist, who proved the existence of tungsten in scheelite in 1781.

SCHEFFERITE   See: Diopside.

SCHORL   See: Tourmaline.

SCHORLOMITE   See: Garnet.

SCOLECITE   See: Natrolite.

SCORODITE   *Series to* Mansfieldite: $AlAsO_4 \cdot 2H_2O$.

Formula: $FeAsO_4 \cdot 2H_2O$.

Crystallography: Orthorhombic. Crystals pyramidal, tabular, prismatic; massive, crusts.

Colors: Pale grayish green, yellowish brown to brown, colorless, bluish green, blue, violet.

Luster: Vitreous to resinous.

Hardness: 3.5−4.

Density: 3.28−3.29.

Cleavage: Imperfect. Fracture subconchoidal. Brittle.

Optics: Biaxial (+), variable 2*V*.

	α	β	γ	Birefringence	2*V*
Durango, Mexico	1.784	1.795	1.814	0.030	75°
Idaho	1.738	1.742	1.765	0.027	60°
Oregon	1.741	1.744	1.768	0.027	40°
Tsumeb, S.W.A.	1.785	1.796	1.812	0.027	75°

Pleochroism: Intense: purplish/bluish (Tsumeb).

Spectral: (Tsumeb) One line at 4500, broad absorption in the green.

Luminescence: None. Soluble in HCl.

Occurrence: A secondary mineral resulting from the oxidation of arsenious ores.
Utah; South Dakota; California; Washington; Idaho; Nevada; Wyoming.
Ontario, Canada; Japan; England.
Durango, Mexico: fine blue crystals.
Ouro Preto, Minas Gerais, Brazil: good crystals, some gemmy.
Tsumeb, S.W. Africa: pleochroic blue crystals, to 25 mm long, some gemmy.

Stone Sizes: Cut gems are always small, mostly from Tsumeb material. The maximum to expect is about 5 carats, but even this would be very large for the species.
SI: 2.6 (purplish, S.W. Africa).

Comments: Gems of scorodite are extremely rare (usually Tsumeb), but cut stones have a lovely color and intense pleochroism. Too soft to wear, the stone is suited for collectors of the rare and unusual.

Name: From the Greek for *garliclike* because the material emits the typical garlic odor of arsenic when heated.

SCORZALITE   See: Lazulite.

SELENITE   See: Gypsum.

SENARMONTITE   Isomorphous with Valentinite.
Formula: Sb_2O_3.

Crystallography: Isometric. Crystals octahedral, up to 3 cm on edge; massive.

Colors: Colorless to grayish white.

Luster; Resinous.

Hardness: 2–2.5.

Density: 5.5.

Cleavage: Traces. Fracture uneven. Very brittle.

Optics: Isotropic; $N = 2.087$.

Luminescence: None.

Spectral: Not diagnostic.

Occurrence: A secondary mineral formed by the alteration of stibnite (Sb_2S_3).
Inyo Co., California; South Dakota.
Quebec, Canada; Algeria; France; Germany; Sardinia; Italy.

Stone Sizes: There are reports of very tiny gems having been cut from transparent crystal fragments. Stones up to 1–2 carats seem possible.

Comments: Senarmontite is a rare mineral, restricted in occurrence to the presence of antimony sulfide ores. It is much too soft to wear, and the colors are usually nondescript. However, a faceted senarmontite would be a great rarity, in any size.

Name: After Henri de Senarmont, Professor of mineralogy at the School of Mines in Paris, who first described the species.

SERANDITE   *Series to* Pectolite.
Formula: $Na(Mn, Ca)_2Si_3O_8(OH)$.

Crystallography: Triclinic. Crystals prismatic in appearance, stubby, well formed.

Colors: Rose red, pinkish, salmon red.

Luster: Vitreous, pearly on cleavage.

Hardness: 4.5–5.

Density: 3.32.

Cleavage: Perfect 1 direction. Fracture uneven. Brittle.

Optics: $\alpha = 1.660$; $\beta = 1.664$; $\gamma = 1.688$.
Biaxial (+), $2V = 35°$.

Birefringence: 0.028.

Spectral: Not diagnostic.

Luminescence: None.

Occurrence: In nepheline syenite rocks at *Mt. Ste. Hilaire, Quebec, Canada.* Also known from *Los Islands, Guinea.*

Stone Sizes: Cut serandite over 2–3 carats is very rare, and cut gems of any size, in fact, are very rare. Cutting material only comes from Quebec, and even large crystals seldom have facetable areas.

Comments: This is essentially another one-locality mineral, where very small gems have been cut from an occasional crystal fragment that is not always even transparent.

SERPENTINE   A group of minerals.
Serpentine is a group of essentially four species with the same composition, but different properties: *antigorite, chrysotile, clinochrysotile,* and *lizardite.* All may form rocks that are cut and polished.

Formula: $Mg_3Si_2O_5(OH)_4$ + Ni.

Crystallography: Monoclinic. Usually flaky or masses of fibers, never in crystals; fibers usually too small for good optical readings.

Colors: White, yellowish, shades of green, yellowish green, brownish green, bluish white to bluish green, brownish red.

Luster: Resinous; greasy; pearly; waxy; earthy.

Hardness; 2.5; bowenite, 4–6.

Density: Variable, 2.44–2.62 is gem range; bowenite, 2.58–2.62.

Cleavage: Perfect 1 direction. Fibrous.

Spectral: Bowenite gives bands at 4920 and 4640—*not* diagnostic.

	Antigorite	Chrysotile	Clinochrysotile	Lizardite
Optics				
α	1.56	1.532–1.549	1.569	1.538–1.554
β	1.566	—	—	—
γ	1.571	1.545–1.556	1.570	1.546–1.560
Birefringence	0.014	0.013	0.001	0.008
Density	2.61	2.55	2.53	2.55
Hardness	2.5–3.5*	2.5	—	2.5

Bowenite, a variety of antigorite, has S.G. 2.58–2.62; hardness 4–6.

Luminescence: Williamsite may glow weak whitish green in LW.

Occurrence: Serpentine forms due to the alteration of basic and ultrabasic rocks. In some instances it may be mistaken for nephrite jade.

Bowenite:
New Zealand: dark bluish green, S.G. 2.67.
Delware River, *Pa.:* dark green.
Smithfield, Rhode Island: dark green.
China: light yellowish green.
Afghanistan: green.
S. Africa (*Transvaal*): banded in green shades.

Williamsite (a very translucent variety of antigorite): apple green color.
Rock Springs, Maryland: best-known locality; may contain Cr and be deep green in color; R.I. (mean) 1.56, S.G. 2.6–2.62, hardness 4.5.

Lizardite:
Kashmir, India. Scotland: gray, green,.S.G. 2.51.
Lizard Peninsula, Cornwall, England: veined various colors; S.G. 2.45.
South Africa; Austria; Anglesey, Wales.
Ireland: mixture of serpentine and carbonates, locally known as *Connemara marble*; mean R.I. 1.56, S.G. 2.48–2.77; abs. line 4650.

Antigorite: Faceted gem found of material from *Pakistan*, yellowish-green, nearly transparent; indices 1.559–1.561, birefringence 0.001–0.002.

Verd Antique: a green serpentine veined with calcite and other minerals. Found in *Greece; Italy; Egypt; Vermont.*

Stone Sizes: Serpentine is always massive, and usually cut as beads, cabochons, or carved into various useful and decorative objects. Occasionally, it is translucent enough to be faceted (especially williamsite), and such gems are indeed interesting and quite lovely.

Comments: *Bowenite* is usually blue-green, yellow-green, or dark green and translucent; it is used for carving, knife handles, etc., and in jewelry. *Williamsite* contains dark octahedral crystals of chromite, and patches of white brucite (magnesium hydroxide). *Ricolite* is a banded serpentine from Rico, New Mexico. *Satelite* is a serpentine pseudomorph after asbestiform tremolite from Maryland and California, grayish to greenish blue. *Pseudophite* or *styrian jade* is from Austria, and is an aluminous serpentine, with hardness 2.5, refractive index 1.57, density 2.69. *Chrysotile*, in fibrous form, is best known as *asbestos*, and is widely used in industry for its physical properties.

Names: *Serpentine* from the serpent-like markings seen in a serpentine marble; *chrysotile* is from the Greek *chrysos* (golden) and *tilos* (fibrous), aptly describing the properties of this mineral. *Antigorite* and *lizardite* are named after the type localities, Antigorio Valley, Piedmont, Italy and Lizard, Cornwall, England.

Bowenite is after G.T. Bowen, who studied material from Rhode Island (though he misidentified the material as nephrite). *Williamsite* is named after L. W. Williams, who first found it.

SHATTUCKITE

Formula: $Cu_5(SiO_3)_4(OH)_2$.

Crystallography: Orthorhombic. Crystals slender prismatic; massive, granular; fibrous.

Colors: Blue of various shades.

Luster: Vitreous to silky.

Hardness: Not determined.

Density: 3.8–4.11.

Cleavage: Very good in 2 directions. Fracture uneven to splintery.

Optics: $\alpha = 1.752–1.753$; $\beta = 1.782$; $\gamma = 1.815$. Mean refractive index 1.75.
Biaxial (+), $2V = 88°$.

Birefringence: 0.063.

Spectral: Not diagnostic.

Luminescence: None.

Occurrence: An alteration product of secondary copper minerals.
Shattuck Mine, Bisbee, Arizona: dense blue massive material; also psuedomorphous after malachite.
Ajo, Arizona: with other copper minerals.
Katanga, Zaire: masses of light blue crystals; fibrous, radial aggregates, sometimes resembling a pale blue pectolite.

Stone Sizes: Only cabochons can be cut, up to several inches in length.

Comments: Shattuckite is often mixed with quartz, and data measured on properties may be erroneous. The cabochons are rich blue in color and very popular, but the material is not abundant and seldom seen on the market.

Name: From the Arizona locality, the Shattuck Mine. Recent studies have shown that plancheite, a mineral similar to and often confused with shattuckite, is a distinct species. The formula of plancheite is: $Cu_8(Si_4O_{11})_2(OH)_4 \cdot xH_2O$.

SHORTITE

Formula: $Na_2Ca_2(CO_3)_3$.

Crystallography: Orthorhombic. Crystals wedge-shaped, to maximum size of 155 mm.

Colors: Colorless to pale yellow.

Luster: Vitreous.

Hardness: 3.

Density: 2.60.

Cleavage: Distinct 1 direction. Fracture conchoidal. Brittle.

Optics: $\alpha = 1.531$; $\beta = 1.555$; $\gamma = 1.570$. Biaxial (−), $2V = 75°$.

Birefringence: 0.039.

Spectral: Not diagnostic. Pyroelectric.

Luminescence: pinkish orange to orange-brown in SW (Green R., Wyoming).

Occurrence: Occurs in clays from an oil well, 20 miles west of Green River, Wyoming. Also in clay from oil well in Uintah Co., Utah.

Stone Sizes: Very small, less than 1 carat.

Comments: Shortite is an exceedingly rare mineral, and not overly attractive. Cut gems are among the rarest of all faceted stones. The material is a carbonate and therefore is fragile and soft.

Name: After Maxwell N. Short, professor of mineralogy at the University of Arizona.

SIDERITE *Series to* Rhodochrosite ($MnCO_3$) *and* Calcite ($CaCO_3$).

Formula: $FeCO_3$.

Crystallography: Hexagonal (R). Crystals rhombshaped; also massive, granular; globular; oolitic.

Colors: Pale yellowish brown, pale yellowish, pale green, greenish gray, yellowish gray, grayish brown, reddish brown, blackish brown; rarely almost colorless.

Luster: Vitreous, pearly, silky, dull.

Hardness: 3.5−4.5.

Density: 3.83−3.96.

Cleavage: Perfect rhombohedral. Brittle.

Optics: $o = 1.873$; $e = 1.633$. Uniaxial (−).

Birefringence: 0.240.

Spectral: Not diagnostic.

Luminescence: None.

Occurrence: A widespread mineral in sedimentary deposits; hydrothermal ore veins; also in pegmatites; basaltic rocks.
Colorado; Connecticut; Idaho.
Austria; France; Germany; Italy.
Minas Gerais, Brazil: large and fine crystals.
Mt. Ste. Hilaire, Quebec: brown rhombs up to 15 inches on edge.
Panesqueira, Portugal: fine light brown crystals, some transparent.
Ivigtut, Greenland: rich brown, gemmy-looking crystals in cryolite.
Cornwall, England: greenish crystals, some transparent, known as *chalybite.*

Stone Sizes: The massive material is not attractive and is not usually cut as cabochons, also because the perfect cleavage makes cutting very difficult. Faceted siderite is rare and stones are usually small (1−5 carats).

Comments: Siderite is a difficult stone to facet, but cut gems of great beauty have been fashioned, especially from Portugese rough.

Name: From the Greek *sideros (iron)* in reference to the composition. *Chalybite* is from the Greek *of steel*, referring to the Fe and C content.

SILICA See: Quartz.

SILLIMANITE (= **FIBROLITE**) Trimorphous with Kyanite, Andalusite.

Formula: Al_2SiO_5.

Crystallography: Orthorhombic. Crystals prismatic, rare; usually fibrous masses.

Colors: Colorless, white, gray, yellowish, brownish, greenish, bluish, violet-blue.

Luster: Vitreous to silky.

Hardness; 6.5−7.5.

Density: 3.23−3.27; compact varieties 3.14−3.18.

Cleavage: Perfect 1 direction. Fracture uneven. Brittle.

Optics: $\alpha = 1.654-1.661$; $\beta = 1.658-1.662$; $\gamma = 1.673-1.683$.
Biaxial (+), $2V = 21-30°$.

Birefringence: 0.020.

Dispersion: 0.015.

Pleochroism: May be strong:
α: pale brown, pale yellow to green;
β: brown or greenish;
γ: dark brown or blue.

Luminescence: Weak reddish fluorescence in blue Burma material.

Occurrence: A mineral of metamorphic rocks, such as schists and gneiss; also granites.
Idaho; South Dakota; Oklahoma; Pennsylvania; New York; Connecticut; Delaware; North Carolina; South Carolina.
Canada; Ireland; Scotland; France; Germany; Czechoslovakia; Brazil; India; Madagascar; Korea; S. Africa; Tanzania.
Ceylon and Burma: green, blue, violet-blue facetable material; also from Ceylon, grayish green, chatoyant fibrolite.
Kenya: facetable crystals, pale bluish color to colorless, S.G. 3.27.

Stone Sizes: Faceted gems are usually small (under 5 carats), and quite rare. Catseye gems are generally in the same size range, up to 10 carats, may be black.
SI: 5.9 (black catseye, South Carolina). *BM:* 35 (fibrolite).
Geol. Museum, London: 17 (fibrolite).

Comments: The fibrolite from Burma and Ceylon is well-known to gem collectors, and highly prized because of its great scarcity. Blue and greenish gems are lovely, though very difficult to cut. Chatoyant material sometimes yields catseye fibrolites, which are also very rare The newer material from Kenya is just as attractive as Burma fibrolite, but seems to be somewhat smaller in size.

Name: After Benjamin Silliman, mineralogist, of Yale University. *Fibrolite* is in allusion to the fibrous nature of this variety.

SIMPSONITE

Formula: $Al_4Ta_3O_{13}(OH)$.

Crystallography: Hexagonal. Crystals tabular, prismatic; also in crystalline masses.

Colors: Colorless, pale yellow, cream white, light brown, orange.

Luster: Vitreous, adamantine.

Hardness: 7–7.5.

Density: 5.92–6.84

Cleavage: None. Fracture conchoidal. Brittle.

Optics: $o = 2.034$; $e = 1.976$. Uniaxial (−).

Birefringence: 0.058.

Pleochroism: None.

Spectral: Not diagnostic.

Luminescence: In SW, bright blue-white (W. Australia), bright pale yellow (Bikita), medium pale yellow (Ecuador) or light blue (Paraiba, Brazil).

Occurrence: In granite pegmatites, usually with biotite.
Bikita, So. Rhodesia; Alto do Giz, Ecuador; Kola Peninsula, U.S.S.R.
Onca and Paraiba, Brazil: facetable material.
Tabba Tabba, W. Australia: facetable yellowish crystals.

Stone Sizes: Crystals have been found up to 5 cm, but only tiny stones have been cut from available rough. In general, stones are only seen from Brazil and Australia. A typical size is $\frac{1}{2}$–1 carat.

Comments: Simpsonite is an extremely rare gemstone. The material from W. Australia is bright yellow-orange and very beautiful. The mineral is hard and durable, with no cleavage, and could easily become a popular gemstone if it were more abundant. Gems over 1 carat could be considered extremely rare, because clean material is a very small percentage of the limited supply of simpsonite that has been found.

Name: After Dr. E. S. Simpson, former government mineralogist of W. Australia.

SINHALITE

Formula: $MgAlBO_4$.

Crystallography: Orthorhombic; found only as grains and rolled pebbles.

Colors: Yellowish, yellow-brown, dark brown, greenish brown, light pink, brownish pink.

Luster: Vitreous.

Hardness: 6.5–7.

Density: 3.475–3.50.

Cleavage: Not determined.

Optics: $\alpha = 1.665$–1.676; $\beta = 1.697$; $\gamma = 1.705$–1.712. Biaxial (−), $2V = 56°$.

Pleochroism: Distinct: pale brown/greenish brown/dark brown.

Spectral: Very distinctive, and similar to but distinct from peridot: bands at 4930, 4750, 4630 (absent in peridot), and 4520; general absorption of the violet end of the spectrum.

Luminescence: None.

Occurrence: A contact metamorphic mineral in limestones at granite contacts; alluvial.
Warren Co., New York: no gem value.
N.E. Tanzania (in a skarn): pink to brownish pink, some gemmy areas.
Burma: one rolled pebble noted.
Ceylon: major source of gem sinhalite, as rolled pebbles in gem gravels.

Stone Sizes: Interestingly, sinhalite, though quite rare, occurs in large sizes in the Ceylon gravels. The normal range is 1–20 carats, but gems over 100 carats have been found from time to time.
SI: 109.8 (brown, Ceylon); 43.5 (brown, Ceylon).
PC: 158 (Ceylon)—this is the largest known sinhalite gem.
DG: 24.76 (Ceylon).

Comments: Long thought to be brown peridot, sinhalite was investigated in 1952 and found to be a new mineral. When cut it is richly colored, bright, and attractive, and resembles citrine, peridot, or zircon. Large gems are very rare, but smaller stones are available on the marketplace. Some people have reported that it was easier at times to find a large sinhalite for sale than a small one, however, as rough pebbles from Ceylon are often large.

Name: From the old Sanskrit word for Ceylon, *sinhala*.

SKUTTERUDITE   see: Smaltite.

SMALTITE

Formula: $(Co, Ni)As_{3-x}$. Considered to be an arsenic-deficient *Skutterudite*.

Crystallography: Isometric. Crystals cubic to octahedral; massive, fine-grained.

Colors: Silver gray to tin white; may tarnish gray to iridescent.

Luster: Metallic; opaque.

Streak: Black.

Hardness: 5.5–6.

Density: ca 6.1.

Cleavage: Distinct 2 directions. Fracture uneven to conchoidal. Brittle.

Luminescence: None.

Occurrence: Occurs in medium- to high-temperature veins, with Ni and Co minerals.
California; Colorado.
Cobalt dist., Ontario, Canada; British Columbia.
Chile; Switzerland; Germany.

Stone Sizes: Cabochons could be cut to any size from massive material.

Comments: Smaltite is a collector's oddity, cut only as cabochons. It is seldom seen, because it is not especially distinctive, with a color resembling other metallic sulfides and arsenides.

Name: From its use as a source of cobalt for the pigment *smalt*, which is blue.

SMITHSONITE

Formula: $ZnCO_3$ + Fe, Ca, Co, Cu, Mn, Cd, Mg, Pb.

Crystallography: Hexagonal (R). Crystals rhombohedral; massive, botryoidal, compact, stalactitic.

Colors: White, gray, pale to deep yellow, yellowish brown to brown, pale green, apple green, blue-green, blue, pale to deep pink, purplish, rarely colorless.

Luster: Vitreous to pearly, earthy, dull.

Hardness: 4–4.5.

Density: 4.3–4.45.

Cleavage: Perfect rhombohedral. Brittle.

Optics: $o = 1.848$; $e = 1.621$. Uniaxial (−).

Birefringence: 0.227.

Dispersion: 0.037.

Spectral: Not diagnostic.

Other Tests: Effervesces in warm acids.

Luminescence: In SW, medium whitish blue (Japan), blue-white (Spain), rose red (England), and brown (Georgia, Sardinia). In LW, greenish yellow (Spain) and lavender (Calif.)

Occurrence: Smithsonite is a secondary mineral in the oxidized zone of ore deposits.
Colorado; Montana; Utah.
Germany; Austria; Belgium; France; Spain; Algeria; Tunisia.
Kelly, Socorro Co., New Mexico: blue and blue green, massive crusts, fine color.
Marion Co., Arkansas: yellow, banded crusts.
Laurium, Greece: fine blue and green crystals.
Sardinia, Italy: banded yellow material.
Tsumeb, S.W. Africa: yellowish and pinkish crystals, also green—facetable.

Broken Hill, Zambia: transparent crystals to 1 cm.
Australia: yellow.
Mexico: pink and bluish crusts much variation in color.

Stone Sizes: Beautiful cabochons up to many inches may be cut from the massive material from New Mexico, Sardinia and other localities. Crusts in some localities are several inches thick. The pink material from Mexico is especially lovely. Facetable crystals are rare, known only from the African localities, and stones over 10 carats could be considered exceptional.

Comments: The blue-green smithsonite from New Mexico has been popular with collectors for many years. Pinkish colors are due to cobalt, yellow to cadmium. The low hardness of smithsonite makes it unsuited for jewelry, but properly cut faceted gems are magnificent. The dispersion is almost as high as diamond, and faceted stones have both rich color and lots of fire. Among the most beautiful are the yellowish stones from Tsumeb, S.W. Africa.

Name: After James Smithson, the benefactor whose bequest founded the Smithsonian Institution in Washington, D.C.

SOAPSTONE See: Talc.

SODALITE Variety: Hackmanite (rich in S); Sodalite group.

Formula: $Na_4Al_3(SiO_4)_3Cl$.

Crystallography: Isometric. Crystals rare (dodecahedral); massive, granular.

Colors: Colorless, white, yellowish, greenish, reddish; usually light to dark blue.

Luster: Vitreous; greasy.

Hardness: 5.5–6.

Density: 2.14–2.4; massive blue ca 2.28.

Cleavage: Poor. Fracture uneven to conchoidal. Brittle.

Optics: Isotropic; $N = 1.483–1.487$.

Dispersion: 0.018.

Spectral: Not diagnostic.

Luminescence: In LW, usually orangy red to violet; also dull pink in SW (Guinea).
Hackmanite, from Dungannon Twp., Ontario, Canada: bright pale pink in SW, bright yellow-orange in LW. Mineral is white, may turn raspberry red after exposure to SW; color fades rapidly in sunlight, and cycle is repeatable.

Occurrence: In nepheline syenites and related rock types.
Montana; South Dakota; Colorado; Arkansas; Maine; New Hampshire; Massachusetts.
Greenland; Langesundsfjord, Norway; Rajasthan, India;

Bahia, Brazil; U.S.S.R.; Scotland; Ruma, French Guinea.

Bancroft, Ontario, Canada: massive, deep blue material, reddish streaks.

Dungannon Twp., Ontario: hackmanite; also sodalite from *British Columbia,* other locations.

Ohopoho, northern S.W. Africa: extremely intense, solid blue material, sometimes very translucent, almost transparent ($N = 1.486$).

Stone Sizes: Massive blue material provides blocks for carvings, decorative objects and cabochons or spheres to almost any desired size, from Canada and S.W. Africa especially. Much sodalite is carved in Idar-Oberstein, Germany, made into boxes and beads. Faceted gems are sometimes cut from very translucent S.W. African material, but these gems are very dark and not very transparent, except in tiny sizes (under 1 carat).

Comments: Sodalite is extremely rich in color, also quite tough and easy to cut, making it very desirable among hobbyists. Faceted gems are very lovely in spite of their lack of transparency, because the color is so beautiful. Sodalite group minerals are also responsible for the fine color of lapis lazuli, another blue gem.

Name: In allusion to the sodium content.

SPESSARTINE   See: Garnet.

SPHAEROCOBALTITE   See Calcite.

SPHALERITE (= BLENDE)   dimorph of Wurtzite.
Formula: ZnS + Fe.

Crystallography: Isometric. Crystals widespread, in various shapes; massive, cleavable, granular.

Colors: Colorless (very rarely); black (rich in Fe), brown, orange, yellow, green, orange-red, white, gray.

Streak: Pale brown to colorless.

Luster: Resinous to adamantine.

Hardness: 3.5–4.

Density: 3.9–4.1.

Cleavage: Perfect dodecahedral. Brittle.

Optics: Isotropic; $N = 2.37$–2.43 (Spanish material 2.40).

Dispersion: 0.156 (extremely high).

Spectral: Sometimes 3 bands seen in the red at 6900, 6670, 6510, due to cadmium.

Luminescence: Bright orange-red to red in LW, SW, from many localities.
Material from Otavi, S.W. Africa is triboluminescent.

Occurrence: Sphalerite is the chief ore of zinc, the most abundant zinc mineral, and is abundant in low-temperature ore deposits, especially in limestones; also in sedimentary rocks; hydrothermal ore veins.
Wisconsin; Montana; Colorado; Idaho; Arizona.

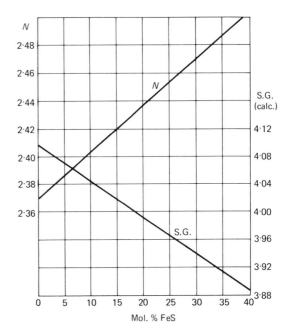

Adapted from Deer, W.A., Howie, R.A. and Zussman, J. (1962) *The Rock Forming Minerals,* 5 volumes, New York, John Wiley & Sons.

Refractive index (N) and specific gravity plotted against chemical composition in sphalerite, in which Fe substitutes for Zn, in the formula (Zn, Fe)S.

Canada; Tsumeb, S.W. Africa; England; Scotland; Sweden; France; Germany; Czechoslovakia; Romania; Australia.

Missouri, Oklahoma, Kansas: so-called Tri-State Region, heavily mineralized by lead and zinc, with many localities and operating mines.

Tiffin, Ohio: (red).

Franklin, New Jersey: almost colorless to pale green, transparent variety known as *cleiophane.*

Santander, Spain: major gem locality, large cleavages of red-orange color.

Cananea, Sonora, Mexico: fine green transparent material, often pale colored and color zoned, sometimes yellow.

Stone Sizes: Gems of hundreds of carats could easily be cut from the large reddish material from Spain. This material is also sometimes cut as cabochons. Green cleiophane from New Jersey has yielded faceted gems as large as 15 carats. Mexican gems could be cut to 50 carats.
SI: 73.3 (yellow-brown, Utah); 59.5 (yellow-green, N.J.); 48 (yellow, Mexico); 45.9 (yellow, Spain).

Comments: Sphalerite is one of the most beautiful of all cut gems. It occurs in shades of green, yellow, orange, brown and fiery red (all colors due to Fe), that are enhanced by faceting. The luster can be adamantine, like diamond, so cut gems with a good polish are very bright, and the dispersion is about 4 times that of diamond. Consequently, faceted gems are alive with fire and color, which is strong enough to be seen even against the rich body color. Pale-colored or colorless sphalerite is extremely rare, but gems of the other colors are easily available, as there is no shortage of facetable rough. Sphalerite, for all its beauty, is too soft and fragile to wear in jewelry. It has dodecahedral cleavage (6 directions) and the material is rather brittle and easily scratched. It could be a very important gem if harder and less fragile. Larger stones (over 20 carats) usually have some inclusions, as well as veils and flaws, so a completely transparent stone is also considered rare. Cutting is all-important, and the appearance of a cut gem depends largely on the quality of the surface polish.

Black sphalerite is called *marmatite*, and the word for sphalerite in European schools is *blende*.

Name: From the Greek *sphaleros*, meaning *treacherous*, because it often resembles galena (lead sulfide) but yielded no lead when first smelted. In Europe sphalerite is called *blende*, from the German *blenden*, meaning *to dazzle*. *Marmatite*, the black variety, is named after the locality at Marmato, Italy.

SPHENE (= TITANITE)

Formula: $CaTiSiO_5$.

Crystallography: Monoclinic. Crystals often wedge-shaped, well-formed, flattened, prismatic; also massive, compact.

Colors: Colorless, yellow, green, gray, brown, blue, rose red, black. Often zoned. Color correlates with Fe content: green and yellow = low in Fe; brown, black = high.

Luster: Adamantine to resinous.

Hardness: 5–5.5.

Density: 3.45–3.55.

Cleavage: Distinct 1 direction. Brittle.

Optics: $\alpha = 1.843–1.950$; $\beta = 1.870–2.034$; $\gamma = 1.943–2.110$.
Biaxial (+), $2V = 17–40°$: lower indices with lower Ti content.

Birefringence: 0.100–0.192.

Dispersion: 0.051 (strong).

Pleochroism: Moderate to strong: α = pale yellow; β = brownish-yellow; γ = orange-brown.
Sometimes (blue crystals): colorless/blue.

Spectral: Sometimes see "didymium" or rare earth spectrum.

Luminescence: None.

Occurrence: Sphene occurs as an accessory mineral in igneous rocks, and in metamorphic rocks such as schist and granite, often in fine crystals.
New York; Canada: brown and black crystals.
Madagascar: green crystals, some large.
Zillerthal, Austria; Grisons, Switzerland: both gem localities in past years.

Pakistan; Burma: some gemmy material found.
Mettur, India: about 30 miles from *Salem, Tamilnadu, So. India*—yellow, brown.
Baja, Mexico: yellow-brown, brown, green, dark green (Cr-bearing) gemmy crystals. This may be one of the world's major sphene deposits, with gemmy crystals to 4 inches.
Minas Gerais, Brazil: twinned yellowish to greenish crystals, often gemmy.

Stone Sizes: Sphene is very rare in clean stones over 5–10 carats. Even a 5 carat flawless gem is considered a rare and fine stone. Indian material cuts to about 10 carats, Madagascar material to perhaps 15 carats, and Brazilian yellow stones over 5 carats are scarce. Burma stones over 20 carats are known, but Baja has the potential for producing some of the largest faceted gems. Chrome sphene of fine color is extremely rare, especially over 2–3 carats.
SI: 9.3 (golden, Switzerland); 8.5 (brown, New York); 5.6 yellow-brown, Mexico).
PC: 63 carats (green).
DG: 4.95 (red!).

Comments: Sphene is a magnificent gemstone, rich in fire and with superb, intense body colors. The hardness is, unfortunately, low, and gems are brittle and easily scratched. The best-looking stones are round brilliant cut. Chrome sphene from Baja is the color of fine emerald, and very rare, especially if clean and larger than 1 carat. The Brazilian yellow gem material has a sleepy look and is not as bright as that from Baja.

Name: *Sphene* is from the Greek *sphenos* (*wedge*), in allusion to the characteristic wedge-shaped crystals. *Titanite* alludes to the dark brown to black color of the original specimens, rich in titanium.

SPINEL   Spinel Group.

Formula: $MgAl_2O_4$ + many replacing elements.

Crystallography: Isometric. Crystals octahedral; also as grains, massive.

Colors: Various shades of red, blue, green; also brown, black, gray, lilac, purple, orange, orange-red, rose, nearly colorless.

Luster: Vitreous.

Hardness: 7.5–8.

Density: 3.58–3.98; gems 3.58–3.61; see table below.

Cleavage: None. Fracture conchoidal.

Dispersion: 0.020.

The spinel group is fairly large, with widely varying chemistry and properties. All are isometric oxides of Mg, Fe and Zn with aluminum and traces of other elements.

	Formula	R.I.	Density	Color
Spinel	$MgAl_2O_4$	1.719	3.55–3.63	various (above)
Gahnite	$ZnAl_2O_4$	1.805	4.0–4.62	deep green
Gahnospinel	$(Mg, Zn)Al_2O_4$	1.725–1.753+	3.58–4.06	blue, dark blue
Hercynite	$FeAl_2O_4$	1.835	4.40	black, dark colors
Ceylonite (*pleonaste*)	$(Mg, Fe)Al_2O_4$	1.77–1.78	3.63–3.90 esp. 3.80	very dark colors
Picotite	$Fe(Al, Cr)_2O_4$	—	4.42	dark green to black
Galaxite	$MnAl_2O_4$	1.92	4.04	deep red to black

Refractive index variation with color, as generally observed in gems:
red: 1.715–1.735;
blue: 1.715–1.747;
others: 1.712–1.717 (normal).

Spectral: Very distinctive spectra, useful in identification.
Red and pink: Chromium spectrum, broad band at 5400 + absorption of violet; group of fine lines in the red may be fluorescent "organpipe" lines.
Blue: Iron spectrum, lines in blue especially at 4580 + narrow line at 4780 and weak lines at 4430, 4330; two strongest = 6860, 6750, plus 6350, 5850, 5550, 5080. (*Note:* This iron spectrum is distinctive vs. the cobalt blue of synthetic spinel.)
Mauve and pale blue: Similar spectrum to blue, but weaker.

Luminescence: *Reds and pinks:* crimson in LW, also SW; red in X-rays; no phosphorescence.
Blue: Inert in UV.
Deep purple: red in LW, essentially inert SW, lilac in X-rays.
Pale blue and violet: green in LW, X-rays, essentially inert in SW.

Inclusions: Spinels are generally very free of inclusions, but other inclusions are distinctive. Silk, as in sapphires and ruby, is seldom seen in spinel. Angular inclusions known as *spangles* are seen; distinctive are rows and swirls of tiny octahedra of another spinel, such as magnetite ($FeFe_2O_4$). Also characteristic are iron-stained films and feathers, especially at edges of gems. Also zircon inclusions and darkened surrounding areas *zircon haloes*, (due to radioactivity), accompanied by feather around zircon, due to stress cracking.
Mogok, Burma: calcite, apatite, dolomite, olivine.
Ceylon: zircon, sphene, baddeleyite, titanite (sphene).

Occurrence: Spinels are found in metamorphic rocks and their weathering products. Especially found in contact deposits (marbles and limestones).
California; Montana; New York; Colorado; New Jersey; Massachusetts; Virginia.
Canada; France; Italy; Germany; Finland; U.S.S.R.; India.
Sweden: gahnite.
Australia: gahnite.
Japan: galaxite.
New Zealand: gahnite.
Afghanistan: fine red spinel, source of many large gems of ancient world.
Ceylon: worn pebbles in wide variety of colors, especially blues; all the blue ones have a trace of Zn; many are black from Ceylon.
Burma: spinels from the gem gravels, often as perfect octahedra.
Cambodia and Thailand: spinels in alluvial gravels.

Stone Sizes: Spinels are known up to hundreds of carats, in various colors.
SI: 45.8 (pale purple, Ceylon); 36.1 (indigo blue, Burma); 34 (red, Burma); 29.7 (pink-violet, Ceylon).
BM: Deformed red octahedron from Ceylon, 520; another crystal, 355.
Louvre, Paris: fine red gem, 105.
AMNH: 71.5 (red, Ceylon).
Crown Jewels of England: Black Prince's Ruby, red spinel, estimated at 170; *Timur ruby*, red spinel, 361.
Diamond Fund, Moscow: fine red spinel, over 400.
Banque Markazi, Teheran: red stone over 500, another over 200, one about 225.

Comments: Spinel is an important gem, historically, because it has been confused with other gemstones, especially ruby. Large red gems such as the *Black Prince's Ruby* and the *Timur Ruby* in the Crown Jewels of England have proven to be fine large red spinels (*ruby spinel*). In ancient times this material was known as *Balas ruby.*
Star spinels have occasionally been cut, with 4-rayed stars, and colored gray or grayish-blue to black (from Burma); a six-rayed star can be seen in such material if oriented along the 3-fold symmetry axis of the crystal, i.e., parallel to the edges of an octahedral face.
Fine red spinels over 3 carats are very difficult to obtain, because of political upheaval in southeast Asia, which has made gem dealing very difficult. Large spinels of other colors are available from time to time. The value of fine red spinels is sure to increase because of scarcity and a general interest in colored stones among the gem-buying public.
Alexandrite-like spinels are known, that are grayish

blue when viewed in daylight and amethystine color in incandescent light. These are quite rare, and usually small.

Names: The name *spinel* is of doubtful origin; it may come from the Latin *spina*, alluding to spine-shaped crystals, but this is not a common habit for spinel. *Ceylonite* is named after the locality, Ceylon, and *gahnite* after the Swedish chemist, J. G. Gahn. *Galaxite* is named after the plant of the same name, which grows in an area where the mineral was first discovered, near Galax, Virginia.

SPODUMENE   Color varieties: Kunzite, Hiddenite. Older name: Triphane.

Formula: $LiAlSi_2O_6$.

Crystallography: Monoclinic. Crystals prismatic, flattened, often corroded; massive.

Colors: Colorless, gray, pale to dark yellow, pink, violet, pale green, deep green, blue-green, blue.

Luster: Vitreous.

Hardness: 6.5–7.5.

Density: 3.0–3.2; gems usually 3.18.

Cleavage: Perfect 1 direction. Fracture conchoidal. Brittle.

Optics: $\alpha = 1.653-1.670$; $\beta = 1.660-1.669$; $\gamma = 1.665-1.682$.
Biaxial (+), $2V = 55-68°$.

Birefringence: 0.014–0.027.

Dispersion: 0.017.

Pleochroism: Pronounced:
pink crystals: purple-violet/colorless;
green crystals: green/blue-green/colorless to pale green.

Spectral: Not diagnostic in kunzite.
Hiddenite shows a chromium spectrum, with doublet at 6905/6860 and weaker lines at 6690, 6460, broad absorption at 6200.
Yellow-green spodumene shows a distinct band at 4375 and weaker band at 4330.

Luminescence: *Kunzite:* golden pink to orange in LW, weaker in SW, orange in X-rays (with phosphorescence); X-irradiated kunzites may change color to blue-green, but this color disappears in sunlight.
Yellow-green spodumene: orange-yellow in LW, weaker in SW., strong in X-rays but no color change in body of material.
Hiddenite gives orange glow in X-rays, with phosphorescence.

Occurrence: A mineral of granite pegmatites.
King's Mountain, North Carolina; Maine; Connecticut; Massachusetts.
Etta Mine, South Dakota: immense white to gray crystals, up to 40 feet long, in rock.

Pala dist., California: fine kunzite, gem quality, plus yellow-green spodumenes.
Hiddenite, North Carolina: type locality for emerald green spodumene; also at *Stony Point, N.C.;* This material contains Cr and shows Cr spectrum.
Madagascar: kunzite, green and yellow spodumene, gem quality.
Minas Gerais, Brazil: major gem locality for kunzite, yellow spodumene, some green.
Material from Brazil contains no Cr, and green varieties are *not* hiddenite.
Pakistan: all colors, some very large crystals; gem quality.
Burma: gem quality.

Stone Sizes: Very large spodumene crystals exist, as in South Dakota, but these are not gem quality. Kunzite crystals do reach a size of many pounds while retaining fine color and transparency, and very large cut gems have been cut from nearly all the colors.
PC: ca 137 (deep yellow, Pakistan).
SI: 327 (yellow, Brazil); 71.1 (yellow, Madagascar); 68.8 (yellow-green, Brazil); 880 (kunzite, Brazil); 336 (deep violet, Brazil); 177 (kunzite, California); 11.6 (kunzite, North Carolina).
Harvard: kunzite crystals from Pala, Calif.—2200 grams.
Naturhistorisches Museum, Vienna: hiddenite crystals, 3 × 0.6 cm.
Denver Museum: 296.7 (kunzite, Brazil).

Comments: Spodumene is a very attractive gemstone and occurs in some pleasing colors. The pink variety, *kunzite,* is the best known, but yellow gems from Brazil and Pakistan are also lovely (Pakistan produces *much* deeper yellow material) as are the light blue-green stones from Pakistan and Brazil. *Hiddenite* is known only from North Carolina and is extremely rare and costly; the color is a medium-deep green, never the intense dark green of fine emerald, and crystals are always very small.

The perfect cleavage of spodumene makes cutting extremely difficult, and most hobbyists have some trouble with the material. Spodumene should be worn with some caution to prevent breakage. The pleochroism is intense, and cut stones should be oriented with the table perpendicular to the long axis of the crystal for the best effect. Kunzites of jewelry size are abundant and inexpensive.

Name: Spodumene is from the Greek *spodumenos* (*burnt to ashes*), in describing the common gray color of the mineral. *Kunzite* is named after G. F. Kunz, noted author and gemologist for Tiffany and Co. *Hiddenite* is named after A. E. Hidden, one-time superintendent of the mine in North Carolina where it was found.

STAUROLITE

Formula: $(Fe, Mg, Zn)_2Al_9Si_4O_{23}(OH) + Zn, Co$.

Crystallography: Monoclinic (pseudo-orthorhombic).

Crystals prismatic, typically twinned at 60 or 90°, the latter termed *fairy crosses;* massive.

Colors: Dark brown, reddish brown, yellowish brown, brownish black.

Luster: Vitreous to resinous.

Hardness: 7−7.5.

Density: 3.65−3.83.

Cleavage: Distinct 1 direction. Fracture conchoidal. Brittle.

Optics: $\alpha = 1.739-1.747$; $\beta = 1.745-1.753$; $\gamma = 1.752-1.761$.
Biaxial (+), $2V = 82-90°$.
Indices increase with iron content.

Birefringence: 0.011−0.015.

Dispersion: 0.023.

Pleochroism: Distinct: colorless/yellow or red/golden yellow.

Spectral: Not diagnostic. Weak band at 5780, strong at 4490.
Zincian staurolite: strong broad bands at 6100 and 6320, narrow weaker bands at 5315; spectrum absorbed beyond 4900.

Luminescence: None.

Occurrence: Staurolite is a mineral of metamorphic rocks, such as schists and gneiss.
New Hampshire; Maine; Vermont; Connecticut.
Canada; France; U.S.S.R.; Zambia; Scotland.
Virginia, North Carolina, Georgia: abundant "fairy crosses and twinned crystals. *New Mexico;* fine twinned crystals.
Brazil: facetable crystals rarely found.
Switzerland: occasionally a facetable crystal is encountered in schists.
Lusaka, Northern Rhodesia: (cobaltian)

Stone Sizes: Staurolite is almost never transparent, and then is very dark. Cut stones are always tiny, less than 2 carats in general, faceted from Brazilian or Swiss crystals.
SI: 3.0 (dark brown, Brazil).

Comments: Faceted staurolites are extremely rare and always small and dark in color. Staurolite forms very interesting crystals, but cut gems are too dark to be attractive, and lack fire. Nonetheless they are true rarities and prized for ther scarcity.
     Zincian staurolite, though very rare, is lighter in color and more attractive as a cut gem; S.G. 3.79, indices 1.721−1.731; trichroic: green/red/yellow. May be red-brown in incandescent light, yellow-green in daylight.

Name: From the Greek *stauros + lithos*, meaning *stone cross.*

STEATITE   See Talc.

STIBIOTANTALITE   Series to Tantalite.

Formula: $Sb(Ta, Nb)O_4$.

Crystallography: Orthorhombic. Crystals prismatic, striated, often twinned, massive.

Colors: Dark brown to light yellowish brown, reddish-yellow, yellowish gray, reddish brown, greenish, yellow. Often zoned.

Streak: Yellow-brown.

Luster: Vitreous to resinous.

Hardness: 5−5.5.

Density: 7.34−7.46.

Cleavage: Distinct 1 direction. Fracture subconchoidal. Brittle.

Optics: $\alpha = 2.37$; $\beta = 2.40$; $\gamma = 2.46$.
Biaxial (+), $2V = 75°$.

Birefringence: 0.090.

Dispersion: 0.146.

Spectral: Not diagnostic; may show "didymium" lines.

Luminescence: None.

Occurrence: In granite pegmatites, often in good crystals.
Topsham, Maine. San Diego Co., California: gemmy crystals.
Varuträsk, Sweden. W. Australia, (Wodgina dist): as rolled pebbles.

Stone Sizes: This material is virtually unknown in cut stones over 10 carats. The material is fairly rare, but transparent specimens are extremely rare.
DG: 4.65 (Brazil).

Comments: Cut stibiotantalite strongly resembles sphalerite, but the luster is much less brilliant (sphalerite can be adamantine), and stibiotantalite is usually more heavily included, as well as strongly birefringent. This birefringence gives the cut gems a *sleepy* look due to doubling of back facets as seen through the table. Cut gems over 2−3 carats are among the rarest of collector items.

Name: In allusion to the composition.

STICHTITE   Dimorph of Barbertonite.

Formula: $Mg_6Cr_2(CO_3)(OH)_{16} \cdot 4H_2O$.

Crystallography: Hexagonal (R). Massive, foliated, fibrous, lamellar, scaly.

Colors: Lilac to rose pink.

Streak: White to lilac.

Luster: Pearly, waxy, greasy.

Hardness: 1.5−2.5; greasy feel.

Density: 2.16 (Quebec)−2.22 (S. Africa).

Cleavage: Perfect 1 direction. Friable, flexible laminae (inelastic).

Optics: $o = 1.545$; $e = 1.518$. Uniaxial (−).

Shadow edge seen at about 1.53.

Birefringence: 0.027.

Pleochroism: Light to dark red.

Spectral: Typical Cr spectrum: 3 lines in the red at 6655 to 6300.

Luminescence: None.

Occurrence: In serpentine rocks, usually associated with chromite.

Black Lake, Quebec, Canada.

Dundas, Tasmania: mixed with green serpentine.

Transvaal, S. Africa; Algeria.

Stone Sizes: Massive material is sometime cut into cabochons, but the material is usually used to carve decorative objects such as ashtrays and bookends. The color is usually lilac to purplish, often veined with green serpentine, and the color combination is quite handsome. Blocks weighing several pounds are obtainable.

Comments: Stichtite is not facetable, but the pink color is quite striking in cabochons. Cut stones are especially beautiful when there are other minerals present to add splashes of green and yellow. This material somewhat resembles a pink, granular material from the U.S.S.R. referred to as *canasite*.

Name: After Robert Sticht of Tasmania, General Manager of the Mt. Lyell Mining and Railway Co.

STRENGITE See: Variscite.

STRONTIANITE Aragonite Group. Series to Aragonite ($CaCO_3$), Witherite ($BaCO_3$).

Formula: $SrCO_3$.

Crystallography: Orthorhombic. Crystals prismatic, often in tapering crystals in sprays and fans; massive, granular.

Colors: Colorless, white, gray, yellowish, yellowish brown, greenish, reddish.

Luster: Vitreous to resinous.

Hardness: 3.5.

Density: 3.63−3.785, depending on Sr content (vs. Ca).

Cleavage: Perfect 1 direction. Fracture uneven. Brittle.

Optics: $\alpha = 1.52$; $\beta = 1.66$; $\gamma = 1.67$. Biaxial (−), $2V = 7°$.

Birefringence: 0.150.

Dispersion: 0.008−0.028.

Spectral: Not diagnostic.

Luminescence: In SW and LW, may be white, olive green, bluish green, with phosphorescence. Both fluorescent and phosphorescent in X-rays.

Occurrence: A low-temperature mineral, in veins, geodes, marls and sulfide veins.

San Bernardino Co., California; Schoharie, New York;

Ohio; New Mexico; Texas; Louisiana; South Dakota; Washington.

Scotland; Mexico; India; Austria.

Carleton Co., Ontario; British Columbia; Germany: major deposits.

Pennsylvania: small crystals.

Stone Sizes: Very small faceted gems have been cut from small, pale colored crystals from various localities, especially Germany and Austria. The maximum size is about 2−4 carats, but an occasional larger stone might be encountered.

Comments: Strontianite is a collector's oddity, with no spectacular properties to recommend it. Colors are usually pale and there is little fire; in addition the high birefringence doubles back facets and kills the brilliance of the stone. Cut strontianites are, however, decidedly uncommon and worth pursuing for their scarcity value.

Name: From the town in Scotland where the mineral was first found.

SUCCINITE See: Amber.

SULFUR Alpha modification.

Formula: S + Se.

Crystallography: Orthorhombic. Crystals tabular and pyramidal, often well formed; massive; powdery.

Colors: Yellow, yellowish brown, yellowish gray, reddish, greenish.

Streak: White.

Luster: Resinous to greasy.

Density: 2.05−2.09.

Hardness: 1.5−2.5.

Cleavage: Imperfect. Fracture conchoidal. Sectile. Very brittle.

Optics: $\alpha = 1.958$; $\beta = 2.038$; $\gamma = 2.245$. Biaxial (+), $2V = 68°$.

Birefringence: 0.291.

Dispersion: 0.155.

Pleochroism: Distinct in shades of yellow.

Spectral: Not diagnostic.

Luminescence: None.

Occurrence: Sulfur is usually in combination with metals as sulfides; it occurs in native form in volcanic and hot spring areas (deposited from vapor); sedimentary rocks, and in huge quantities at salt domes.

Wyoming; Nevada; California.

Chile; Mexico.

Girgenti, Sicily: fine, large crystals.

Cianciana, Sicily: good crystals.

Louisiana and Texas; salt domes.

Stone Sizes: Transparent crystals exist that could yield stones over 50 carats, but these are specimens and not for cutting. Broken crystals have occasionally been faceted.

Comments: Sulfur has no use as a gem. It is so heat-sensitive that a crystal held in the hand may crack due to thermal shock. A crystal dropped from a height of several inches would most likely chip or crack—not ideal properties for jewelry stones! Cutting sulfur is enormously difficult, but the challenge has been met by cutters who have succeeded in fashioning stones of small size. Facetable sulfur is actually not very common, so cut gems do have some scarcity value.

Name: An ancient name for this mineral.

SUNSTONE   See: Feldspar.

T

TAAFEITE

Formula: $BeMgAl_4O_8$.

Crystallography: Hexagonal. Known only as cut gemstones and rounded masses.

Colors: Colorless, greenish, pinkish, lilac to purple.

Luster: Vitreous.

Hardness: 8−8.5.

Density: 3.60−3.61.

Cleavage: Not determined.

Optics: $o = 1.721-1.724$; $e = 1.717-1.720$. Uniaxial (−).

Birefringence: 0.004.

Pleochroism: None observed.

Spectral: Not diagnostic.

Luminescence: Distinct green in UV and X-rays.

Occurrence: Metamorphosed limestones and skarns; rolled pebbles.
China: reported in dolomitized limestone in Hunan Province.
Ceylon: rolled pebbles, assumed origin of known cut gems.
Note: Polytype of taaffeite discovered in 1966 in Musgrave Ranges, Central Australia: $o = 1.739$; $e = 1.735$; S.G. 3.68.

Stone Sizes: The originally discovered taaffeite came out of a lot of mauve spinels and weighed 1.419 carats; part of this was analyzed and the remainder was recut into a gem of 0.55 for the discoverer, Count Taaffe, a Dublin gemologist. The second stone found was 0.86 carats and is now in the *Geological Museum, London.* A third stone weighed 0.84 carats found at the G. I. A. offices in New York, and is now in the *SI* collection. A dark brownish gem of 5.34 carats was discovered and privately sold by George A. Bruce of North Carolina. Other stones may exist, misidentified as spinel.

Comments: Taaffeite reacts to most tests like mauve-colored spinel, but can be distinguished on the basis of birefringence. Additional stones will undoubtedly be found in lots of spinels or in jewelry. Taaffeite is one of the rarest of all gems as well as minerals, as fewer than 5 stones have been reported in the literature.

Name: After the discoverer, Count Taaffe of Dublin, who first noted the gem in 1945.

TALC (= SOAPSTONE = STEATITE)

Formula: $Mg_3Si_4O_{10}(OH)_2$.

Crystallography: Monoclinic, triclinic. Tabular crystals up to 1 cm size; usually massive, foliated, fine-grained, compact.

Colors: Pale green, dark green, greenish gray, white, gray, silvery white, brownish. Colors are due to impurities.

Luster: Greasy, pearly, dull.

Hardness: 1; greasy feel.

Density: 2.20−2.83.

Cleavage: Perfect 1 direction. Flexible and elastic lamellae. Sectile.

Optics: *Monoclinic:* $\alpha = 1.539-1.550$; $\beta = 1.589-1.594$; $\gamma = 1.589-1.600$.
Triclinic: $\alpha = 1.545$; $\beta = 1.584$; $\gamma = 1.584$.
Biaxial (−), $2V = 0-30°$ in monoclinic.
Shadow edge at 1.54.

Birefringence: *Monoclinic:* 0.050. *Triclinic:* 0.039.

Spectral: Not diagnostic.

Luminescence: Usually none. Some is pinkish in LW (Silver Kale, California).

Occurrence: In hydrothermally altered ultrabasic rocks and thermally altered siliceous dolomites. Worldwide occurrence, sometimes in large beds, often associated with serpentines.
Many localities in U.S., especially *Vermont, New Hampshire, Massachusetts, Virginia, North Carolina, Georgia, California.*
Lake Nyasa, Central Africa; India; China; Australia; Rhodesia; Canada; U.S.S.R.
Egypt: ancient deposit.

Stone Sizes: Steatite and soapstone are known in massive pieces that will yield large carvings, up to several pounds.

Comments: Steatite may be slightly harder than talc, due to impurities. *Talc* itself is often pseudomorphous after other minerals. Massive talc is easy to carve and is widely used for this purpose.

Name: *Talc* is from the Arabic word *talk* or *talq*, the name of the mineral. *Steatite* is from the Latin *steatis*, a type of stone, derived from the Greek word *steatos*, meaning *fat*.

TANTALITE *Series to* Columbite: $(Fe, Mn)(Nb, Ta)_2O_6$.

Formula: $(Fe, Mn)(Ta, Nb)_2O_6$.

Crystallography: Orthorhombic. Crystals tabular, prismatic, in aggregates; massive, compact.

Colors: Black, brownish black, reddish brown; may tarnish iridescent.

Streak: Black, brownish black, reddish brown.

Luster: Submetallic to vitreous.

Hardness: 6−6.5.

Density: 8.2; decreases with Ta content (columbite, 5.2).

Cleavage: Distinct 1 direction. Fracture uneven. Brittle.

Optics: $\alpha = 2.26$; $\beta = 2.30-2.40$; $\gamma = 2.43$. Biaxial (+), $2V$ Large. Usually opaque, indices measured on powders or thin splinters.

Birefringence: 0.160.

Pleochroism: Strong: brown/red-brown.

Spectral: Not diagnostic.

Luminescence: None.

Occurrence: In granite pegmatites.
Colorado; Wyoming; New England.
Canada; Brazil; Madagascar; France; Sweden; Finland; U.S.S.R.; Rhodesia; W. Australia.
South Dakota: various localities.
California: various localities.

Stone Sizes: Very large crystals have been found, weighing many pounds. The material is usually dark-colored, opaque, and of interest only for cabochons.

Comments: Tantalite is too dark to be of use as a faceted gem, but is cut sometimes as a collector curiosity, either faceted or in cabochons. These could be of any desired size.

Name: After the mythical character Tantalus, because it is difficult to dissolve the mineral in acids prior to analysis.

TANZANITE   See: Epidote.

TEKTITE

Formula: Silica (75%) + Al, Fe, Ca, Na, K, Mg, Ti, Mn.

Crystallography: Amorphous−a glass.

Colors: Black, green, greenish brown, brown in moldavites; other tektites black, colorless to brown; usually opaque.

Luster: Vitreous.

Hardness: 5.5.

Density: 2.21−2.96 (see table).

Cleavage: None. Fracture conchoidal. Brittle.

Optics: Isotropic; $N = 1.46-1.51$.

Spectral: Not diagnostic. Moldavites may show two vague bands in the blue and orange.

Inclusions: Often see numerous rounded or torpedo-shaped bubbles; also swirl striae which are *unlike* those seen in paste (glass used to imitate gemstones).

Luminescence: None in UV. Yellow-green in X-rays.

Occurrence: Tektites have worldwide occurrence, in fields in which the glass bits are literally strewn over the ground, and covering a very wide area. Tektites are found throughout the world (see table).

Stone Sizes: Faceted gems are usually cut from moldavites, because the color of these tektites is lighter

Tektites

Name	Locality	Max. Size	Density	Refractive Index	Color
*Moldavite**	Czechoslovakia	235 grams	2.30−2.36	1.48−1.49	bottle green
*Australite**	Australia	218 grams	2.38−2.46	1.50−1.52	black, brown edge
Darwin glass	Tasmania	—	2.75−2.96	1.47−1.48	green, black
Javaite	Java	—	2.43−2.45	1.509	black
Billitonite	Billiton Island (near Borneo)	—	2.46−2.51	1.51−1.53	black
*Indochinite**	Indochina	3200 grams	2.40−2.44	1.49−1.51	black
Philippinite (*rizalite*)	Philippines, esp. Luzon	—	2.44−2.45	1.513	black
Ivory Coast tektite	Ivory Coast	—	2.40−2.51	1.50−1.52	black
*Libyan Desert Glass**	Libya	10 pounds	2.21	1.462	pale greenish yellow
*Bediasite**	Gonzales Co., Texas	91.3 grams	2.33−2.43	1.48−1.51	black
*Georgia tektite**	Georgia	—	2.33	1.485	light olive-green
*Massachusetts tektite**	Martha's Vineyard, Mass.	—	2.33	1.485	light olive-green

*Have been faceted.

than most others. The color is a bottle green resembling diopside, and gems up to about 25 carats have been cut, although very large moldavites have been found. Various other U.S. tektites have been cut as curiosities, mostly small.

Comments: Tektites were first discovered in 1787 in Czechoslovakia (then Moravia) near the River Moldau, hence the name *moldavite*. It has been argued that tektites originated as a result of violent explosive activity on the moon, and were thrown all the way to the earth's surface. Other scientists, who currently are in the majority, argue that tektites are of terrestrial origin. The issue is being debated in a lively way and does not appear to be near solution.

Name: *Moldavite* from the River Moldau; other tektite names are from the localities where they occur.

THAUMASITE
Formula: $Ca_3Si(CO_3)(SO_4)(OH)_6 \cdot 12H_2O$.

Crystallography: Hexagonal. Crystals acicular; usually massive, compact.

Colors: Colorless, white.

Luster: Vitreous, silky, greasy.

Hardness: 3.5.

Density: 1.91.

Cleavage: Indistinct. Fracture subconchoidal. Brittle.

Optics: $o = 1.500-1.507$; $e = 1.464-1.468$. Uniaxial (−).

Birefringence: 0.036.

Spectral: Not diagnostic.

Luminescence: White in SW (Paterson, New Jersey) with phosphorescence.

Occurrence: Associated with zeolites; in lime-rich metamorphic rocks.
Crestmore, California; Beaver Co., Utah; Cochise Co., Arizona.
Paterson, New Jersey: fine crystals.
Centreville, Virginia: in masses.
Långban, Sweden.

Stone Sizes: Found as relatively compact fibrous masses up to a few inches in size. Facetable material does not exist, but cabochons have been cut from some of the more compact material.

Comments: Massive thaumasite cuts interesting cats-eye cabochons, especially if it is chatoyant, but the effect is relatively weak. The mineral is rather soft but seems to harden after exposed to the air.

Name: From the Greek *thaumasein* (*to be surprised*), because of its rather unusual chemical composition.

THOMSONITE   Zeolite group.
Formula: $NaCa_2Al_5Si_5O_{20} \cdot 6H_2O$.

Crystallography: Orthorhombic. Crystals prismatic or acicular, and very rare; usually compact, or in radial or fibrous aggregates.

Colors: Colorless, white, yellowish, pink, greenish, grayish. A translucent green variety has been called *lintonite*.

Luster: Vitreous to pearly.

Hardness: 5−5.5.

Density: 2.25−2.40.

Cleavage: Perfect 1 direction. Fracture uneven. Brittle.

Optics: $\alpha = 1.497-1.530$; $\beta = 1.513-1.533$; $\gamma = 1.518-1.544$.
Biaxial (+), $2V = 42-75°$.
Shadow edge at 1.52−1.54.

Birefringence: 0.021.

Spectral: None. Pyroelectric.

Luminescence: Patches of brown and white in LW.

Occurrence: Thomsonite is a secondary mineral in lavas and basic igneous rocks.
Oregon; California; Colorado; New Jersey.
Nova Scotia, Canada; Greenland; Ireland; Scotland; Italy; India; Czechoslovakia; Germany.
Thomsonite Beach, Isle Royale, Lake Superior: patterned pebbles.
Stockly Bay, Michigan: lintonite; also at *Grand Marais, Minnesota.*

Stone Sizes: Cabochons up to several inches in length have been cut from material recovered in Michigan and at Isle Royal, the best known locality. Large pieces are not abundant, especially with good patterns. Faceted gems are exceedingly rare. Gems up to 5 carats have been reported to the author as coming from a German locality.

Comments: *Thomsonite* cabochons take a high polish but are somewhat brittle. These are especially lovely when a pinkish gray eyelike pattern is present, but such material is rare. *Lintonite*, from Michigan, is translucent and green, and sometimes is mistaken for jade. A faceted thomsonite would have to be considered a great rarity.

Name: After Mr. R. D. Thompson. *Lintonite* is after a Miss Linton.

TIGEREYE   See: Quartz.

TINZENITE   See: Axinite.

TITANITE   See: Sphene.

TOPAZ
Formula: $Al_2SiO_4(F,OH)_2$.

Crystallography: Orthorhombic. Crystals prismatic, stumpy, sometimes very large, often well-formed; also massive, granular, as rolled pebbles.

Colors: Colorless, white, gray, pale to medium blue, greenish, yellow, yellow-brown, orange, pale pink, deep pink, tan, beige, red.

Luster: Vitreous.

Hardness: 8.

Cleavage: Perfect basal (1 direction). Fracture conchoidal. Brittle.

Dispersion: 0.014.

Density: There is a rough correlation between color and density, as follows:

> *Pink:* 3.50−3.53; *Yellow:* 3.51−3.54;
> *Colorless:* 3.56−3.57; *Blue:* 3.56−3.57.

New Hampshire: Crystals.

Texas: colorless and blue, some facetable to large size.

Pike's Peak area, Colorado: fine blue crystals in granitic rocks; also colorless, reddish, yellow some facetable.

Thomas Range, Utah: sherry colored terminated crystals in rhyolite; facetable.

Minas Gerais, Brazil: fine yellow to orange crystals, facetable to large size; also colorless and pale yellow crystals up to several hundred pounds in size; mostly transparent; pale blue crystals and rolled pebbles, much facetable; some orange crystals contain Cr and when heated (burned) turn pink and show a Cr spectrum.

Locality	α	β	γ	Birefrin-gence	Density	Color	Other
U.S.S.R.	1.609	—	1.619	0.010	3.53	bluish pale yellow	F-rich
Thomas Range, Utah	1.607	1.610	1.618	0.011	3.56	sherry	
Ouro Preto, Brazil	1.629	1.631	1.637	0.008	3.53	brownish	rich in (OH) + Cr
Pakistan	1.633	—	1.643	0.010	—	colorless	
Mardan, Pakistan	1.632	1.636	1.641	0.009	3.53	pink	
Tarryall Mountains, Colo.	1.610	—	1.620	0.010	3.56	blue	

The refractive indices and density of topaz have been linearly correlated with the ratio of (OH) to (OH + F) in the formula.

Pleochroism: Varies with color of material:

Dark yellow: citron yellow/honey yellow/straw yellow.

Pale blue: bright blue/pale rose/colorless.

Dark rose-red: red to dark red/yellow to honey yellow/rose red.

"Burned" pink: rose/rose/colorless.

Brown: yellow-brown/yellow-brown/weak yellow-brown.

Green: colorless to blue-green/green to bright blue-green/ colorless to bright green.

Inclusions: Usually planes of tiny liquid inclusions, each containing a gas bubble. Some three-phase inclusions have been noted also.

Spectral: Not diagnostic. Heated pink gems contain Cr, and may show a Cr spectrum with a weak line at 6820. As in ruby, this line may reverse and become fluorescent.

Luminescence: *Blue and colorless:* weak yellow-green in LW, weaker in SW, greenish white to violet-blue in X-rays, and gems turn brown due to irradiation. *Sherry brown and pink:* orange-yellow in LW, weaker in SW, sometimes greenish white in SW. This material fluoresces brownish yellow to orange in X-rays.

Occurrence: In pegmatites and high-temperature quartz veins; also in cavities in granite and rhyolite; in contact zones; in alluvial deposits as pebbles.

Mardan, Pakistan: fine pink crystals, terminated, cuttable, in limestone matrix.

San Luis Potosí, Mexico: fine brownish to sherry colored crystals; also colorless, many excellent forms, cuttable, some yellowish; can be darkened by irradiation but color fades in sunlight.

Urals, U.S.S.R.: fine blue crystals, often cuttable; also green, magenta colors (gemmy).

Jos, Nigeria: fine blue crystals, also white, many cuttable.

Madagascar: various colors in crystals and pebbles, often cuttable.

Ceylon and Burma: from the gem gravels, colorless, yellow, and blue gemmy masses.

Queensland and Tasmania, Australia: blue, colorless and brownish gem crystals.

Tingha, New South Wales, Australia: green, gemmy.

Klein Spitzkopje, S.W. Africa: colorless and blue crystals from pegmatites, gemmy.

Rhodesia; Cornwall, England; Scotland; Japan: crystals and pebbles.

Stone Sizes: Crystals of topaz reach a weight of hundreds of pounds, often quite gemmy at this size. Gems up to 20,000 carats have been cut from material of various colors. Museums seem to delight in obtaining monster-sized topaz gems for display. Pink gems are rare, however, over 5 carats (Pakistan), and a deep orange gem from Brazil weighing more than 20 carats is considered large. A 30 carat stone would be exceptional. The gem giants exist in blue, colorless and pale yellow colors. Red topaz from the tips of some Brazilian crystals is exceedingly rare, the largest about 70 carats.

SI: 7725 (yellow, Brazil); 3273 (blue, Brazil); 2680 (colorless, Brazil); 1469 (yellow-green, Brazil); 398 (pale blue, U.S.S.R.); 325 (colorless, Colorado); 170.8 (champagne, Madagascar); 146.4 (pale blue, Texas); 93.6 (orange, Brazil); 50.8 (colorless, Japan); 34 (deep pink, Brazil); 24.4 (blue, New Hampshire); 17 (blue, California).

AMNH: 71 (red, Brazil); 308 (pale blue, Brazil); 258 (deep blue, Brazil); 1463 (deep blue, egg-shaped, Brazil); 241 (pale orange-brown, Burma).

BM: 137 pounds (crystal, Norway); 1300 (colorless, Brazil); 614 (blue, Brazil).

ROM: 3000 (blue, Brazil); 365 (pale brown, Burma).

PC: 173 (blue, Texas).

Comments: Topaz is a popular and durable gem, occurring in a wide range of colors. The rarest colors are natural pink, from Pakistan and (rarely) from Brazil; red; and fine golden orange, sometimes with a pink tone. Some colorless blue topaz can, through irradiation plus heat treatment, be turned a deep blue color unknown in natural topaz. This is appearing on the market as a substitute for the much higher-priced dark aquamarine, and no detection test exists for the irradiation treatment. A very dark blue topaz should have its origin questioned if sold at a very high price, as this color in nature would be a great rarity.

Name: Topaz may derive from the Sanskrit word *tapas*, meaning *fire*, in allusion to the orange color; alternatively, it comes from the name of the island in the Red Sea called *topazos*, meaning *to seek*.

TOPAZOLITE See Garnet.

TOURMALINE GROUP

Tourmaline is a name applied to a family of related minerals, all having essentially the same crystal structures, but varying widely in chemical composition, colors and properties. The nomenclature of tourmalines is complex because there are six distinct mineral species in the group, as well as a wide variety of names that have been applied to specific color varieties. Tourmaline crystals are abundant worldwide, are sometimes large and well terminated, and often are cuttable.

Formulas:
Dravite: $NaMg_3Al_6B_3Si_6O_{27}(OH)_3(OH, F)$
Uvite: $CaMg_3(Al_5Mg)B_3Si_6O_{27}(OH)_3(OH, F)$
Schorl: $Na(Fe, Mn)_3Al_6B_3Si_6O_{27}(OH)_3(OH, F)$
Elbaite: $Na(Li, Al)_3Al_6B_3Si_6O_{27}(OH)_3(OH, F)$
Liddicoatite: $Ca(Li, Al)_3Al_6B_3Si_6O_{27}(OH)_3(OH, F)$
Buergerite: $NaFe_3Al_6B_3Si_6O_{30}F$

Crystallography: Hexagonal (trigonal). Crystals common, usually long prismatic, heavily striated along length, various terminations; also equant, acicular.

Colors: All colors are represented by tourmalines, from colorless to black. Crystals are frequently color-zoned along their length (bicolor, tricolor, particolor, etc.) or concentrically zoned (*watermelon tourmaline*). Dravite is usually black to brown, may be colorless. *Uvite* is black, brown, and green, usually dark colors. *Schorl* tends to be black, blue, or blue-green. *Buergerite* is always dark brown to black, with a bronze-colored iridescence or Schiller under the crystal surface. The gem tourmaline, *elbaite*, occurs in a huge range of colors and shades. *Liddicoatite* is a newly described species that was for years considered to be elbaite from Madagascar, but when investigated turned out to be a calcium analog of elbaite.

Certain color varieties of tourmaline have widely used names. *Achroite* is colorless tourmaline; *rubellite* refers to pink and red shades, and blue tourmaline is generally referred to as *indicolite*.

Luster: Vitreous.

Hardness: 7–7.5.

Spectral: Not diagnostic; usually weak spectra observed.

Dispersion: 0.017

Pleochroism: *Pink and red crystals:* pink/medium pink to red. *Light pink crystals:* colorless/light pink. *Blue and green crystals:* green or light green/yellow or blue-green. The absorption of the *o*-ray in tourmaline is strong enough to plane-polarize light. Sometimes this ray is totally absorbed and a tourmaline may appear to be isotropic, because it shows only one absorption edge on

	Dravite	Uvite	Schorl	Elbaite	Liddicoatite	Buergerite
Optics						
o	1.635–1.661	1.632–1.638	1.655–1.675	1.640–1.655	1.637	1.735
e	1.610–1.632	1.612–1.621	1.625–1.650	1.615–1.620	1.621	1.655
Birefringence	0.021–0.026	0.017–0.020	0.025–0.035	0.017–0.024	0.016	0.080
Density	3.03–3.15	3.05	3.10–3.25	3.03–3.10	3.02–3.08	3.31
Cleavage	poor	poor	poor	poor	poor	Distinct—prismatic
			Fracture conchoidal in all species in this group. Brittle.			
Pleochroism	strong	strong	strong	distinct	distinct	yellow-brown/ pale yellow

the refractometer. Pleochroism is especially strong in dark green and brown tourmalines. Pale colors have weak dichroism. Light traveling along the length of a prismatic crystal always shows a deeper color than at right angles to this direction.

Density: Differentiated according to tourmaline color (approximate values):
Pink and red: 3.01−3.06.
Pale green: 3.05.
Brown: 3.06.
Dark green: 3.08−3.11.
Blue: 3.05−3.11.
Yellow-orange: 3.10.
Black: 3.11−3.2.

Inclusions: Tourmaline displays elongated or thread-like cavities, sometimes with two-phase inclusions. The tubes usually run parallel to the length of crystals, and when densely packed may produce a chatoyant effect that yields catseye gems when cut into cabochons. There may be gas-filled fractures in red tourmalines; also flat films that reflect light and appear black. Hornblende. Mica crystals.

Luminescence: Tourmalines are usually weak to inert in UV light. May be chalky blue to strong blue in SW (Newry, Maine). Pink gems from Brazil may be blue or lavender in SW, and gems from Tanzania (golden yellow, brown and green stones) are strong yellow in SW.

Optics: Uniaxial (−).

Occurrence: Tourmaline occurs in crystalline schists; in granites and granite pegmatites (especially elbaite); in gneiss, marbles and other contact metamorphic rocks (especially dravite, uvite). Tourmaline is also found as inclusions in quartz.
Ceylon: Yellow and brown crystals; this is the original source of gem tourmaline, recently shown to be uvite rather than dravite.
Burma: The Mogok area produces red tourmalines, also some pink (elbaite).
Mursinka, Urals, U.S.S.R.: Also at Nerchinsk, blue, red, and violet crystals in a decomposed granite.
Brazil: In Minas Gerais and other states, usually elbaite, in a huge variety of colors and sometimes large crystals; also bicolor, catseye, watermelon tourmaline.
Kashmir, India: Green elbaite crystals (refractive indices 1.643, 1.622; S.G. 3.05, birefringence 0.021).
Usakos, S.W. Africa: Fine elbaite of rich green color (chrome tourmaline).
Klein Spitzkopje, Otavi, S.W. Africa: Tourmaline in many shades of green and other colors (elbaite).
Rhodesia: In the Somabula Forest area, fine elbaite.
Mozambique: At Alta Ligonha, pale colored elbaite in various shades; bicolors.
Madagascar: Liddicoatite (previously thought to be elbaite) in huge range of colors, shades; crystals often concentrically zoned with many color zones, triangular in outline; many crystals very large.
Tanzania: Elbaite containing Cr and V, resulting in rich green shades.
Kenya: Fine, deep red and other colors; the red is dravite; also yellow shades.
California: Elbaite in abundance at Pala and other localities, in both fine crystals and gemmy material. The pink elbaite from here is a unique pastel shade.
Maine: At Newry, recently discovered huge deposit of fine elbaite, with exquisite gem material in green, blue-green, blue, and pink to red colors.
Connecticut: At Haddam, elbaite in small but fine crystals, color-zoned.
Mexico: Buergerite occurs in rhyolite at San Luis Potosí.
New York; New Jersey: At Franklin, New Jersey, Hamburg, New Jersey, and at Gouverneur and DeKalb, New York, uvite crystals, some with gem potential. This material had always been regarded as dravite.

There are many other tourmaline localities, but the above are the major gem-producing localities.

Stone Sizes: Tourmalines weighing hundreds of carats have been cut, using material from various localities. Brazil and Mozambique produce some of the largest stones, but Maine and California crystals of very large size have been discovered. Most larger museums have fine tourmaline collections, and display very large gems. A representative collection of tourmaline colors would have to encompass well over 100 stones.
SI: 172.7 (champagne color, Mozambique); 122.9 (green, Mozambique); 117 (green, Brazil); 110.8 (pink, U.S.S.R.); 62.4 (pink, Brazil); 18.4 (pink, Maine); 103.8 (rose, Mozambique); 60 (blue-green, Brazil); 41.6 (brown, Ceylon); 23.5 (pale brown, Brazil); 17.9 (green, S. Africa); 17.7 (yellow-green, Elba, Italy).

Comments: Tourmaline is one of the most popular of gems among collectors, because it is usually inexpensive and occurs in such a huge range of colors. The colors are due to an almost unbelievable complexity of chemical composition, to which John Ruskin's quip still applies (1890): "the chemistry of it is more like a mediaeval doctor's prescription than the making of a respectable mineral." *Schorl*, the black tourmaline, was used in the Victorian era in mourning jewelry, a practice little used today. Such material is seldom seen in jewelry at all in modern times. Tourmaline crystals are often cracked and flawed, which puts a premium on clean gemstones expecially over about 10 carats in size. The only acceptable type of inclusions are the tubes that, when densely packed, produce a chatoyancy and catseye effect in cabochons. The eye in *catseye tourmalines* can be very strong, set against a richly colored gem. Tourmalines occur in a wide enough range of colors to satisfy just about any fashion requirement. There is no cleavage and the slight brittleness of the material is not a major problem in wear. Small tourmalines (under 5 carats) are fairly easy to obtain, and at modest cost. Very large, fine-colored stones are both rare and costly, however.

Names: *Tourmaline* is from the Singhalese word *turamali*, meaning *mixed colored stones*, because tourmalines were often confused with other gems. *Dravite* is named after the Carinthian district of Drave. *Schorl* is an old German mining term for unwanted minerals associated with ore. *Elbaite* is after the Isle of Elba, Italy. *Buergerite* is named after Professor Martin J. Buerger, crystallographer and well known research scientist. *Liddicoatite* is named after Richard T. Liddicoat, Director of the Gemological Institute of America.

TRANSVAAL JADE   See: Garnet.

TRAPICHE EMERALD   See: Feldspar.

TRAVERTINE   See: Calcite.

TREMOLITE   Variety: Hexagonite. *Series to* Actinolite. *Amphibole group.* See also: Jade, Nephrite.

Formula: $Ca_2Mg_5Si_8O_{22}(OH)_2$ + Fe.

Crystallography: Monoclinic. Crystals prismatic or bladed; fibrous, massive, granular.

Colors: White, colorless, gray, pale greenish, pink, brown.

Luster: Vitreous.

Hardness: 5-6.

Density: 2.9-3.2 (catseye gem, Ontario, 2.98; hexagonite, 2.98-3.03).

Cleavage: Good 2 directions. Fracture uneven. Brittle.

Optics: Variable with composition (see figure). $\alpha = 1.560-1.562$; $\beta = 1.613$; $\gamma = 1.624-1.643$. Biaxial (−), $2V = 81°$.
Note: Tanzania, green crystals: 1.608−1.631, S.G. 3.02.

Birefringence: 0.017−0.027; hexagonite 0.019−0.028.

Pleochroism: *Hexagonite:* bluish red/ deep rose/deep red-violet.
Tanzanian green crystals: light yellowish green/ light green/ green.

Spectral: Not diagnostic. Some tremolite shows a line at 4370 typical of jadeite. Chromiferous material may display chromium spectrum.

Luminescence: Hexagonite shows orange, medium pink to pinkish red fluorescence in LW, SW. Also, medium greenish white in SW (Lee, Massachusetts) and dull yellowish in LW.

Occurrence: Tremolite occurs in contact and regionally metamorphosed dolomites, in magnesian limestones, and in ultrabasic rocks.

California; Arizona; Utah; Colorado; Connecticut; South Dakota; Massachusetts.
Italy; Switzerland; Austria.
Fowler, New York: hexagonite, some cuttable; also at *Edwards and Balmat, New York.*
Ontario and Quebec, Canada: gray, green and blue crystals; a chatoyant greenish variety found in Ontario cuts interesting catseye gems.
Burma: green catseye gems discovered.
Lelatema, Tanzania: green facetable crystals found, up to 25 mm.
Sierra Leone: Cr-rich tremolite, deep green with Cr spectrum displayed.

Stone Sizes: Small colorless and transparent tremolite crystals are very rare, and cut gems are true collector items. The largest of these is in the 5−10 carat range. Larger crystals exist, but are usually badly fractured. *Hexagonite* is known only from New York in facetable material, and these pieces yield gems to only about 1 carat. Chrome tremolite is also very rare and cut gems are tiny.

Comments: It is possible to misidentify tremolite and mistake it for other amphiboles. Hexagonite is the rarest of the gem varieties of tremolite. If tremolite occurs in very tiny fibrous crystals, densely matted and interlocked, it is then known as *nephrite (jade).* Material containing more or less parallel fibers is somewhat chatoyant and yields weak catseyes. These are sometimes called *catseye jades,* but have been tested and are actually tremolite or (if more iron-rich) actinolite.

Name: From the Tremola Valley on the south side of St. Gotthard, Switzerland. *Hexagonite* was so named because it was thought to be a hexagonal mineral when first described.

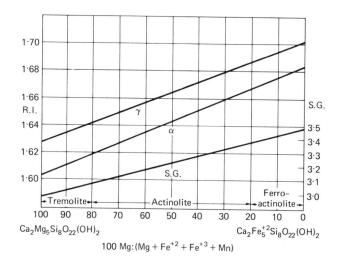

Refractive index and specific gravity variations with chemical composition in the tremolite-ferroactinolite series. Composition is expressed as $Mg/(Mg + Fe^{2+} + Fe^{3+} + Mn)$.

Adapted from Deer, W.A., Howie, R.A. and Zussman, J. (1962) *The Rock Forming Minerals*, 5 volumes, New York, John Wiley & Sons.

TRIDYMITE   See: Quartz.

TRIPHANE   See: Spodumene.

TSAVORITE   See: Garnet.

TUGTUPITE

Formula: $Na_4AlBeSi_4O_{12}Cl$.

Crystallography: Tetragonal. Only massive and compact form.

Colors: White to pink, rose red, bluish, greenish; mottled.

Luster: Vitreous to greasy.

Hardness: 4–6.5 reported.

Density: 2.3–2.57.

Cleavage: Distinct. Fracture conchoidal. Brittle.

Optics: $o = 1.496$; $e = 1.502$. Uniaxial (+) or (−). May be anomalously biaxial with $2V$ from 0°–10°.

Birefringence: 0.006–0.008.

Pleochroism: Strong: bluish-red/orange-red.

Spectral: Not diagnostic.

Luminescence: Very distinctive for this mineral. Generally redder in SW than LW.
Taseq, Greenland: SW, pastel orange-red; LW, bright orange; phosphoresces bright cream or orange-cream, better reaction in SW.
Kvanefjeld, Greenland: LW, bright orange to orange-red; SW, cerise red, and very intense; phosphoresces dull red to medium cream white.
The material darkens in color when exposed to UV light, and slowly bleaches.

Occurrence: Veins in nepheline syenite pegmatite, in Greenland.
Tugtup, Illimaussaq, Greenland: from the Taseq and Kvanefjeld areas.
Also noted on the *Kola Peninsula, U.S.S.R.*

Stone Sizes: Only a few faceted gems have been cut, all very small, and not completely transparent. A typical gem size would be 1–2 carats. Translucent material can also be faceted, but is usually cut into cabochons. Decorative objects were carved from some larger pieces when it was first found.

Comments: Tugtupite was discovered in 1960 and has been used sporadically in jewelry. The material has a rich color and has been sought after by collectors of fluorescent minerals because of its intense reaction in UV. Tugtupite seems to have diminished in abundance and is somewhat hard to obtain, especially in cuttable pieces, and it seems that the material was quite scarce at the source locality. Clean faceted gems are great rarities.

Name: After the locality. *Tugtup* means *reindeer*, hence, *reindeer stone*.

TURQUOISE   *Series to* Chalcosiderite.

Formula: $CuAl_6(PO_4)_4(OH)_8 \cdot 5H_2O + Fe$.

Crystallography: Triclinic. Crystals extremely rare and microscopic; microcrystalline, massive; concretionary; veins and crusts.

Colors: Crystals blue. Massive materials dark blue–pale blue, green, blue-green, apple green, grayish green.

Luster: Crystals vitreous; massive waxy or dull, earthy.

Hardness: 5–6.

Density: Crystals 2.84; massive in the range 2.6–2.9.
Persia, 2.75–2.85;
U.S.A., 2.6–2.7;
Eilat, Israel, 2.56–2.70;
Sinai Peninsula, 2.81;
Tibet, 2.72.
Bahia, Brazil, 2.40–2.65.

Cleavage: None in massive. Fracture even, sometimes conchoidal.

Optics: Massive material gives shadow edge (mean refractive index) of 1.62.
Crystals: $\alpha = 1.61$; $\beta = 1.62$; $\gamma = 1.65$.
Biaxial (+), $2V = 40°$.

Birefringence: 0.040.

Pleochroism: Weak: colorless/pale blue or pale green.

Spectral: can be distinctive; lines at 4600 (vague) and 4320—these are usually seen in light reflected from the turquoise surface.

Luminescence: Greenish yellow to blue in LW, inert in SW and X-rays.

Occurrence: Turquoise is formed by the action of percolating groundwaters in aluminous rocks where Cu is present, as in the vicinity of copper deposits.
Lynch Station, Virginia: the only occurrence of crystals that is well known. Such crystals are microscopic, but an occasional larger one could be tempting to a cutter, and some very tiny faceted gems might exist (under 1 carat).
Iran: The district of Nishapur, on Ali-mersai Mountain. Turquoise is found in porphyry and trachyte rocks, cemented by brown limonite. The color is uniform and a lovely sky blue, sometimes veined by thin lines of limonitic matrix. The blue is often very intense. The mines have been worked for centuries, and Persian turquoise is almost synonymous with material of the highest quality.
Tibet: Turquoise is the national gem of this country, and green is the most prized color. Very little material is available today.
China: Reports are scattered in the literature about turquoise in China, but they have not been substantially verified. Some mines appear to have operated there in ancient times.
Egypt: On the Sinai Peninsula, turquoise is mined at

Serâbît el Khâdim and Maharâh. These mines operated as early as 1,000 B.C., and were used by the Pharaohs. The producing area extends along the Suez Gulf, where the material occurs in sandstone. Earth movements have brecciated the turquoise and matrix, and there is considerable limonite present. The color is blue to greenish blue; some may fade in the sun.

U.S.S.R.: Turquoise is reported from the Uzbek Republic.

Chile: At the Chuquicamata copper mine turquoise of very fine color is found. Not much has reached the marketplace.

Australia: Dense, compact turquoise of fine blue color has been found in large deposits. This material is solid, takes a high polish, and is uniform in color. The nodules in which it occurs may reach a size of hundreds of pounds. The material has a slight tendency to shear along planes of weakness. The color resembles that of Persian turquoise.

Mexico: Some turquoise has been reported from Zacatecas.

Pau a Pique, *Bahia*, *Brazil:* Porous and cryptocrystalline material, RI ca 1.618.

U.S.A.: There are many turquoise localities in the U.S. Connoisseurs can tell the actual mine of origin of many cut gemstones because of distinctive nuances in color and matrix. The variation in these characteristics is enormous. Most of the mines are in *Nevada*, some are in *Arizona*, and others are in *Colorado and New Mexico*. Among the better known localities are: *Fox Mine* huge production; active since 1915.

Blue Gem Mine (*Nevada*): large variation in color, noted for blue and green colors in the same stone.

Stormy Mountain Mine (*Nevada*): dark blue, hard material with black chert matrix.

Lander Blue Mine (*Nevada*): finely divided spiderweb, with tiny turquoise specks; this is rare and highly valued today.

Bisbee (*Arizona*): intense dark blue material, wispy matrix.

Kingman (*Arizona*): some deep blue material has been treated to improve color.

Leadville (*Colorado*): small stones, deep blue with a tinge of green.

Santa Rita (*New Mexico*): pale to deep blue colors.

Other notable locations in Nevada are the following mines: *Papoose, Zuni, Montezuma, Crow Springs, Carlin, Red Mountain, Godber*.

Comments: Massive turquoise is always opaque, and the less porous varieties take a good polish. Turquoise is used in beads, carvings and other jewelry. It often has a brownish matrix, which is cut along with the turquoise and provides color contrast and pattern. Turquoise is frequently simulated by other materials, both natural and man-made, and pale turquoise is extensively treated to improve the color. It is *very* difficult to tell that such treatments have been performed without detailed knowledge and testing equipment, and some of the imitations are very realistic. *Spiderweb turquoise* is veined with black matrix, in a pattern that looks like crocheted lace. Higher values in turquoise are generally associated with darker shades and less green tint in the blue color.

Several turquoise-like materials have been discovered recently, which may well be circulating in the marketplace labeled turquoise. One of these is yellow-green in color, a more intense shade than that of variscite, with a density in the turquoise range. A chemical analysis showed more than 8% zinc oxide; the mineral is named *faustite* and is a zinc analog of turquoise.

Another turquoise-like material was found to have a mean R.I. of 1.50−1.51, S.G. 2.88, hardness 4−5, bluish color. This material gave a chemical analysis that matches the mineral *prosopite*: $CaAl_2(F, OH)_8$, and in addition there were large amounts of Cu and yttrium.

Name: *Turquoise* is of ancient derivation and means *Turkish*, because it was originally brought to Europe and Persia via Turkey.

U

ULEXITE

Formula: $NaCaB_5O_9 \cdot 8H_2O$.

Crystallography: Triclinic. Acicular crystals, nodules of fibers, tufts (*cottonballs*), and veins of parallel fibers.

Colors: Colorless, white.

Luster: Vitreous to silky.

Hardness: 1–2.5.

Density: 1.65–1.95.

Cleavage: Perfect 1 direction. Brittle.

Optics: $\alpha = 1.496$; $\beta = 1.505$; $\gamma = 1.519$.
Biaxial (+), $2V = 78°$.

Birefringence: 0.023.

Luminescence: Blue-green in SW, some phosphorescence.

Occurrence: In playa deposits and dry lakes associated with other borates.
Nevada.
Argentina; Peru; Chile; U.S.S.R.
California: world's major source; also source of TV stone and cabochon material.

Stone Sizes: Nodules occur up to several pounds. The material is always cut as cabochons for jewelry purposes. Faceting material has never been found.

Comments: The fibrous material cuts interesting catseye cabochon gems, but they are curios only, because they are much too soft and fragile for wear. The eye can be very strong, however. Sometimes ulexite occurs in seams, consisting of tightly packed parallel fibers. These are transparent along their length, and the packed aggregates act like an array of parallel glass fibers, displaying the property of fiber optics. If the material is polished perpendicular to the fiber direction, a piece of ulexite will transmit an image from the bottom of the slab to the top. For this reason the material has been nicknamed *TV stone*, and is popular among mineral enthusiasts.

Name: After the German chemist George L. Ulex, who first presented a correct chemical analysis of the species.

UNAKITE   See: Epidote.

UVAROVITE   See: Garnet.

UVITE   See: Tourmaline.

V

VALENTINITE   See: Senarmontite.

VANADINITE

Formula: $Pb_5(VO_4)_3Cl + P$, As.

Crystallography: Hexagonal.   Crystals hexagonal prisms, also tabular, filiform, skeletal.

Colors: Red, orange, orange-red, brownish red, pale yellow, yellow, brownish. Rarely colorless; zoned.

Streak: White to yellowish.

Luster: Resinous to subadamantine.

Hardness: 2.5−3.

Density: 6.88; range 6.5−7.1.

Cleavage: None. Fracture conchoidal. Brittle.

Optics: $e = 2.350$, $o = 2.416$. Uniaxial (−).

Birefringence: 0.066.

Dispersion: 0.202.

Pleochroism: Very slight, shades of orange and yellow.

Spectral: Not diagnostic.

Luminescence: None.

Occurrence: Secondary mineral in the oxidized zone of ore deposits, especially lead deposits. *Arizona (Apache Mine, Mammoth Mine, elsewhere); New Mexico; California; Utah; South Dakota; Colorado.*
Chihuahua, Mexico; Algeria; Scotland; Argentina; Tunisia; U.S.S.R.; Austria; Sardinia.
Mibladen, Morocco: large red to brown crystals.

Stone Sizes: Faceted gems are extremely rare and always small (less than 1 carat). The material is not normally cut into cabochons because it is almost always in good crystals which are prized by collectors. Potential faceting material would most likely come from Arizona or Morocco.

Comments: A faceted vanadinite would be a tremendous rarity. As few as 10 such gems may have been cut, perhaps even fewer. This is unfortunate, because the color is rich and beautiful. Arizona crystals tend to be very small, but the ones from Morocco reach a size of several inches.

Name: In allusion to the composition.

VARISCITE   *Series to* Strengite: $FePO_4 \cdot 2H_2O$.

Formula: $AlPO_4 \cdot 2H_2O$.

Crystallography: Orthorhombic. Crystals octahedral and very rare; also massive, crusts, nodules.

Colors: Colorless, pale green, dark green, yellowish green, blue-green.

Luster: Crystals vitreous; massive waxy to dull.

Hardness: 3.5−4.5.

Density: 2.2−2.57.

Cleavage: *Crystals:* good 1 direction; fracture conchoidal; brittle.
Massive: none; fracture splintery to uneven.

Optics: $\alpha = 1.563$; $\beta = 1.588$; $\gamma = 1.594$.
Shadow edge at about 1.56.
Biaxial (−), $2V$ moderate.

Birefringence: 0.031.

Spectral: Not diagnostic. Strong line at 6880, weaker line at 6500.

Luminescence: Dull green (Lewiston, Utah) or green (Fairfield, Utah) in SW; whitish green in LW from these localities.

Occurrence: Forms by the action of phosphate-bearing waters on aluminous rocks.
Arkansas; California; Nevada; Arizona; Pennsylvania. Germany; Czechoslovakia; Austria; Queensland, Australia; Brazil; Spain.
Fairfield Co., Utah: rich-colored nodules up to 12 inches across, mixed with other complex phosphates.
Tooele, Utah: massive, rich green nodules, suitable for cutting.

Stone Sizes: Nodules of variscite may weigh many pounds and have been found up to a diameter of about 24 inches. The material is suitable only for cabochons, but variscite mixed with other phosphates is sometimes also cut into spheres or used in decorative displays.

Comments: Variscite has ocasionally been used as a turquoise imitation. It is very popular among hobbyists as a cabochon material because of the interesting patterns in the Utah material. Variscite mixed with quartz from Ely, Nevada has been named *Amatrix* (for *American-matrix*).

Name: Named after Variscia, the old name of the Voigtland district in Germany where it was first found.

VERD ANTIQUE   See: Serpentine.

VESUVIANITE   See: Idocrase.

VILLIAUMITE

Formula: NaF.

Crystallography: Isometric. Crystals tiny; usually massive, granular.

Colors: Deep carmine red, lavender pink to light orange; becomes colorless if heated to 300°C.

Luster: Vitreous.

Hardness: 2–2.5.

Density: 2.79.

Cleavage: Perfect 1 direction. Brittle.

Optics: Isotropic; $N = 1.327$.

Birefringence: Sometimes anomalous.

Pleochroism: Anomalous, strong: yellow/pink to deep carmine red.

Spectral: Not diagnostic.

Luminescence: None.

Occurrence: In alkalic rocks, such as nepheline syenites.
Kola Peninsula, U.S.S.R.
Los, Guinea: Los is an island off the Guinea coast; facetable villiaumite occurs in nepheline syenite in reddish crystals, R.I. 1.330–1.332, S.G. 2.79.

Stone Sizes: Los material might facet gems up to 1–2 carats. Other facetable material has not been reported.

Comments: Villiaumite is never really discussed in connection with rare gems, because until recently facetable material was not known. The material from Los, reported in 1976, has been cut into very tiny gems of deep red color. Such gems are obviously among the rarest of all collector stones, despite their small size.

Name: After M. Villiaume, a French explorer in whose collections of rocks from Guinea the material was first found.

VIRIDINE See: Andalusite.

VISHNEVITE See: Cancrinite.

VIVIANITE

Formula: $Fe_3(PO_4)_2 \cdot 8H_2O$.

Crystallography: Monoclinic. Crystals prismatic, tabular, equant; in clusters, radial groups. Also massive, bladed, fibrous; crusts, earthy masses.

Colors: Colorless (fresh); darkens to shades of green and blue, then dark green, dark bluish green, dark purplish, bluish black.

Streak: Colorless, then dark blue after a time.

Luster: Vitreous, pearly on cleavage; also dull, earthy.

Hardness: 1.5–2.

Density: 2.64–2.68.

Cleavage: Perfect 1 direction. Fracture fibrous. Thin pieces are flexible and sectile.

Optics: $\alpha = 1.579–1.616$; $\beta = 1.602–1.656$; $\gamma = 1.629–1.675$.
Biaxial (+), $2V = 63–83°$.

Birefringence: 0.040–0.059.

Pleochroism: Intense: blue/pale yellowish green/pale yellowish green: *or* deep blue/pale bluish green/pale yellow green; *or* indigo/yellowish green/yellowish olive-green.

Luminescence: None.

Spectral: Not diagnostic.

Occurrence: A secondary mineral in ore veins; also occurs as an alteration product of primary phosphate minerals in granite pegmatites; forms as sedimentary concretions.
Colorado; California; New Jersey; Delaware; Maryland; Florida.
Canada; Australia; Japan; Germany; U.S.S.R.; France; England.
Lemhi Co., Idaho: fine crystals.
Bingham Canyon, Utah: crystals to 5 inches in length.
Richmond. Virginia: good crystals.
Black Hills, South Dakota: in pegmatites.
Llallagua and Poopo, Bolivia: fine cuttable crystals to 6 inches long.
N'gaoundere, Cameroon: massive crystals up to 4 feet long, dark in color, cuttable.

Stone Sizes: Faceted gems are rarely cut, because the material is so soft and fragile. The cleavage is almost micaceous, making it very difficult to polish gems. The Bolivian material, for example, could cut stones up to 75–100 carats (indices are 1.585/1.603/1.639, S.G. 2.64).

Comments: Vivianite is so fragile and soft that cut gems would be difficult to handle safely, let alone wear. The material darkens spontaneously, so the color of an attractive stone might disappear after a time, making it less enticing to spend the time cutting such material. The color of vivianite is very rich, and a few stones have been cut anyway.
Odontolite is a fossil material, a phosphate (actually fossil bone and teeth) that has been stained by vivianite and may resemble turquoise.

Name: After J. G. Vivian, an English mineralogist who discovered the species.

W

WARDITE

Formula: $NaAl_3(PO_4)_2(OH)_4 \cdot 2H_2O$.

Crystallography: Tetragonal. Crystals pyramidal; as crusts, aggregates, fibers, spherules.

Colors: Colorless, white, pale green to bluish green.

Luster: Vitreous.

Hardness: 5.

Density: 2.81–2.87.

Cleavage: Perfect 1 direction. Fracture conchoidal. Brittle.

Optics: $o = 1.586-1.594$; $e = 1.595-1.604$. Uniaxial (+). Sometimes anomalously biaxial.

Birefringence: 0.009.

Pleochroism: None.

Spectral: Not diagnostic.

Luminescence: None.

Occurrence: In phosphate masses in sediments, and in pegmatites.

Keystone, South Dakota; Pala, California.

Fairfield, Utah: in large nodules with variscite and other phosphates. Also at *Amatrice Hill, Lucin, Utah.*

Montebras, France: as an alteration of amblygonite.

W. Andover, New Hampshire: in crystals to 1 cm.

Piedras Lavradas, Paraiba, Brazil: greenish white crystals to about 1 inch.

Stone Sizes: Faceted gems are very rare, cut from Brazilian material. Cabochons are cut of white wardite mixed with green variscite from Utah. Faceted gems would all be under 2–3 carats in size.

Comments: Wardite is another of the many phosphates that have been cut by collectors. It is pale-colored and not terribly attractive, as well as fairly soft and fragile. It is far more frequently seen in cabochons than in faceted stones.

Name: After Henry A. Ward, American naturalist and collector.

WATER SAPPHIRE   See: Cordierite.

WAVELLITE

Formula: $Al_3(OH)_3(PO_4)_2 \cdot 5H_2O$.

Crystallography: Orthorhombic. Crystals very tiny; usually as radial aggregates of acicular crystals; often spherical crystal clusters; crusts; stalactitic.

Colors: White, greenish white, green, yellowish green, yellow, yellow-brown, brown to brownish black. Very rarely colorless, bluish.

Luster: Vitreous; also resinous to pearly.

Hardness: 3.5–4.

Density: 2.36.

Cleavage: Perfect 1 direction. Fracture subconchoidal to uneven. Brittle.

Optics: $\alpha = 1.520-1.535$; $\beta = 1.526-1.543$; $\gamma = 1.545-1.561$.
Biaxial (+), $2V = 71°$.

Birefringence: 0.025.

Spectral: Not diagnostic.

Luminescence: Occasionally bluish in LW (various localities).

Occurrence: A secondary mineral in hydrothermal veins; also in aluminous and phosphatic rocks.

Chester Co., Pennsylvania; Alabama; Florida; Colorado; California.

Bolivia; England; Ireland; France; Portugal; Germany; Czechoslovakia; Bulgaria; Romania; Tasmania.

Hot Springs, Arkansas: in fine, spherical and radial groups of acicular crystals.

Stone Sizes: Cabochons up to several inches in length can be cut from Arkansas material. No faceted gems have yet been reported.

Comments: Wavellite is a very attractive mineral, well-known to collectors. It is not generally regarded as cabochon material, but its radial aggregate crystal clusters can be cut into extremely interesting stones. These gems are very difficult to cut because of the splintering of the radiating crystal clusters. The individual crystals of wavellite in the clusters are very small, and a faceted gem would be a tremendous rarity.

Name: After William Wavell, a physician in England, who discovered the mineral.

WERNERITE   See: Scapolite.

WHEWELLITE

Formula: $CaC_2O_4 \cdot H_2O$ (calcium oxalate).

Crystallography: Monoclinic. Crystals prismatic or equant, also in twins.

Colors: Colorless, white, yellowish, brownish.

Luster: Vitreous to pearly.

Hardness: 2.5–3.

Density: 2.21–2.25.

Cleavage: Good in 1 direction, 2 others distinct. Fracture conchoidal. Brittle.

Optics: $\alpha = 1.489$; $\beta = 1.553$; $\gamma = 1.649-1.651$. Biaxial (+), $2V = 80°$.

Birefringence: 0.159−0.163.

Dispersion: 0.034.

Spectral: Not diagnostic.

Luminescence: None.

Occurrence: Coarse crystals occur in coal seams and concretions (organic origin). Also as a hydrothermal mineral in ore veins.
Czechoslovakia; France; Hungary; U.S.S.R.
Havre, Montana: in septarian concretions.
Burgk, Germany: crystals up to several inches in length.

Stone Sizes: Crystals are usually very small, colorless. Faceted gems from these will reach a maximum of about 2 carats.

Comments: Whewellite is one of the most unusual of minerals, because of its chemical composition and occurrence. It is seldom seen by collectors, and even less thought of as a faceted gemstone. It is really just a curiosity, and there is nothing intriguing about it except its rarity. The dispersion is fairly high, but hard to appreciate because of the usual small size of cut gems.

Name: After William Whewell, English natural scientist and philosopher.

WILKEITE   Apatite group.

Formula: $Ca_5(SiO_4, PO_4, SO_4)_3(O, OH, F)$,

Crystallography: Hexagonal. Crystals rounded; granular; massive.

Colors: Pale pinkish, yellowish, rose red.

Luster: Vitreous to resinous.

Hardness: 5.

Density: 3.12−3.23.

Cleavage: Imperfect; very brittle.

Optics: $o = 1.640-1.650$; $e = 1.636-1.646$. Uniaxial (−).

Birefringence: 0.010.

Spectral: Not diagnostic.

Luminescence: None reported.

Occurrence: In metamorphosed marbles.
Kyshtym, Urals, U.S.S.R.; Laacher See, Germany.
Crestmore, California: in marble.

Stone Sizes: Cuttable crystal fragments have been encountered, but the author knows of no faceted gems.

Comments: Wilkeite is a rare silicate−sulfate apatite that has not been encountered as faceted gems; however the author has seen cuttable crystals that would yield stones in the 1−5 carat range. These would be extremely rare stones.

Name: After R. M. Wilke, mineral collector and dealer of Palo Alto, California.

WILLEMITE

Formula: Zn_2SiO_4.

Crystallography: Hexagonal (R). Crystals prismatic, short and stubby or long needles; massive compact; granular.

Colors: Colorless, white, gray, various shades of green, yellow, orange, red-brown.

Luster: Vitreous to resinous.

Hardness: 5.5.

Density: 3.89−4.10 (usually the latter).

Cleavage: Poor. Fracture conchoidal. Brittle.

Optics: $o = 1.691$; $e = 1.719$. Uniaxial (+).

Birefringence: 0.028.

Pleochroism: Dichroism variable.

Spectral: Weak bands at 5830, 5400, 4900, 4420, and 4320; strong band at 4210.

Luminescence: Intense green or yellow-green in SW (Franklin, New Jersey), also in LW. Sometimes intensely phosphorescent (green).

Occurrence: In zinc ore bodies or metamorphic deposits where Zn is present.
Greenland; Belgium; Algeria; Zaire; Zambia.
Franklin and Sterling Hill, New Jersey: the foremost willemite occurrence; stubby green crystals and greenish orange masses to several inches in length. Also massive brown material and crystals to 6 inches long, called *troostite.*
Inyo Co., California; Utah; Arizona: microcrystals at various localities.
Tsumeb, S.W. Africa: small colorless crystals and bluish masses.
Mt. Ste. Hilaire, Quebec: blue, gemmy crystals.

Stone Sizes: Faceted gems are known to a maximum size of about 10 carats, all from the Franklin, New Jersey occurrence. Cabochons to several inches are frequently cut from massive Franklin material.
SI: 11.7 and 11.1 (yellow-orange, Franklin, N.J.).

Comments: Cabochons of massive brown troostite from New Jersey are attractive, as are cabochons of willemite with black franklinite and red zincite in white calcite. These latter stones fluoresce vividly in UV light. Faceted willemite is extremely rare and stones larger than 1−2 carats are worthy of museums. Most such stones are pale green, yellow-orange or brownish green. Gems are hard to polish, and the material is too soft and fragile for use in jewelry.

Name: After King William I of the Netherlands. *Troostite* after an early American mineralogist, Troost.

WILLIAMSITE   See: Serpentine.

WITHERITE   *Series to* Strontianite: $SrCO_3$.

Formula: $BaCO_3$.

Crystallography: Orthorhombic. Crystals twinned to yield pseudohexagonal dipyramids; prismatic; globular, botryoidal; granular; fibrous.

Colors: Colorless, white, gray with a tinge of yellow, green or brown.

Luster: Vitreous to resinous.

Hardness: 3–3.5.

Density: 4.27–4.79.

Cleavage: Distinct 1 direction. Fracture uneven. Brittle.

Optics: $\alpha = 1.529$; $\beta = 1.676$; $\gamma = 1.677$. Biaxial (−), $2V = 16°$.

Birefringence: 0.148.

Spectral: Not diagnostic. Effervesces in acid.

Luminescence: Green and yellow in SW (England) with phosphorescence. Yellowish, with phosphorescence, in LW. Fluoresces in X-rays.

Occurrence: A low-temperature mineral in hydrothermal vein deposits.
Lockport, New York; Kentucky; Montana; Arizona; California.
Austria; Germany; Czechoslovakia; France; Japan; U.S.S.R.; England.
Minerva Mine, Rosiclare, Illinois: large yellowish crystals.

Stone Sizes: Witherite is not normally cut into cabochons because the color is too pale to be attractive. Faceted gems, even those under 5 carats, are usually more translucent than transparent.

Comments: Witherite is very rarely faceted, and in such cases is quite rare. Stones are not especially beautiful, and they are soft and fragile as well. Their only major attribute is rarity. Witherite is fairly easy to cut but somewhat difficult to polish.

Name: After William Withering, an English physician and mineralogist, who first noted the mineral.

WOLLASTONITE

Formula: $CaSiO_3$.

Crystallography: Triclinic. Crystals tabular; massive, cleavable, fibrous, granular.

Colors: White, colorless, gray, pale green.

Luster: Vitreous to pearly; silky if fibrous.

Hardness: 4.5–5.

Density: 2.8–3.09.

Cleavage: Perfect 1 direction. Fracture splintery. Brittle.

Optics: $\alpha = 1.616–1.640$; $\beta = 1.628–1.650$; $\gamma = 1.631–1.653$.
Biaxial (−), $2V = 38–60°$.
Shadow edge in refractometer about 1.63.

Birefringence: 0.015.

Spectral: Not diagnostic.

Luminescence: Fluoresces blue-green and phosphoresces yellow in SW, same in LW, from California, Alaska, Pennsylvania.

Occurrence: Metamorphosed limestones and alkalic igneous rocks.
California (various localities); Willsboro, New York; Alaska; Pennsylvania; New Mexico.
Ontario and Quebec, Canada; Chiapas, Mexico; Norway; Italy; Romania; Finland.
Isle Royale, L. Superior: compact, pale red material, good for cutting.

Stone Sizes: Cabochons up to several inches in length can be cut from fibrous and massive material. No faceted gems have been reported.

Comments: Interesting cabochons have been cut from wollastonite, especially from the fibrous material (which yields catseye stones) and the reddish material from Lake Superior's Isle Royale. Wollastonite is strictly a curiosity and as a mineral is not especially rare. It resembles other white fibrous minerals, however, and is sometimes difficult to identify without using X-ray techniques.

Name: After W. H. Wollaston, British mineralogist and chemist.

WULFENITE

Formula: $PbMoO_4$.

Crystallography: Tetragonal. Crystals commonly tabular with square outline; also pyramidal; massive, granular.

Colors: Orange, (various shades), brownish orange, yellow, brownish yellow, yellow-orange, red, brown, yellowish gray, tan, greenish brown.

Luster: Resinous to adamantine.

Hardness: 2.5–3.

Density: 6.5–7.0.

Cleavage: Distinct 1 direction. Fracture uneven to subconchoidal. Brittle.

Optics: $o = 2.405$; $e = 2.283$. Uniaxial (−).

Birefringence: 0.122.

Dispersion: 0.203.

Pleochroism: Weak, in orange to yellow tints.

Spectral: Not diagnostic.

Luminescence: None.

Occurrence: Secondary mineral in the oxidized zone of ore deposits.

Arizona (Glove Mine, Rowley Mine, Red Cloud Mine, Mammoth Mine, others); New Mexico; Nevada; Utah; Wheatley Mines, Chester, Pennsylvania; Loudville, Massachusetts.
Mexico: Los Lomentos, many other locations; Polana; Yugoslavia; Austria; Czechoslovakia; Germany; Sardinia; Algeria; Morocco; Australia.
Tsumeb, S.W. Africa: yellowish tan crystals up to 5 inches on edge, some facetable.

Stone Sizes: Most wulfenite crystals, especially those from U.S. localities, are too thin for the cutting of gemstones. However, an occasional crystal is both thick and transparent enough for faceting, notably from the Red Cloud Mine, the Seventynine Mine, and others. Some of these have yielded gems up to about 5 carats. Tsumeb, S.W. Africa has produced wulfenite crystals several inches across, from which gems up to 50 carats have been faceted.
PC: 54 (yellow, Tsumeb).
DG: 15.25 (yellow, Tsumeb); 9.44 (red, Arizona).

Comments: The red of wulfenite, especially from the Red Cloud Mine in Arizona, is one of the richest colors in nature. Specimens of wulfenite are esthetically magnificent and are greatly prized by collectors. The crystal habit is tabular and the individual crystals are usually very thin, so it is difficult to find a suitable cutting fragment. Gems are then hard to cut because of the softness of the material and its sensitivity to heat and vibration. These characteristics make wulfenite totally unsuited for jewelry, but it makes a spectacular collector gem, and also one of great rarity. A red wulfenite over 1 carat is extremely scarce, likewise a yellowish or orange one over 1–2 carats. The only larger stones come from Tsumeb material, but the facetable crystals from this locality were extremely uncommon and very few stones have been cut from them.

Name: After the Austrian mineralogist, Franz Xavier Wülfen, who wrote a lengthy monograph in 1785 on the lead ores of Carinthia.

WURTZITE   See: Sphalerite.

X

XALOSTOCITE   See: Garnet.

XANTHITE   See: Idocrase.

XANTHOCONITE   See: Proustite.

Z

ZINCITE

Formula: ZnO + Mn.

Crystallography: Hexagonal. Crystals hemimorphic and very scarce; massive, cleavable, compact, grains.

Colors: Dark red, brownish red, deep yellow, orange-yellow; colorless if pure.

Streak: Orange-yellow.

Luster: Subadamantine to adamantine.

Hardness: 4–4.5.

Density: 5.68.

Cleavage: Perfect 1 direction but difficult. Fracture conchoidal.

Optics: $o = 2.013$; $e = 2.029$. Uniaxial (+).

Birefringence: 0.016.

Dispersion: 0.127.

Pleochroism: None.

Luminescence: None.

Occurrence: In metamorphosed limestone and zinc ores.

Franklin, New Jersey: only major locality; massive red ore, also in crystals up to 4 inches long, but these were found only in secondary calcite veins.

Poland; Spain; Tasmania.

larger masses have been encountered in the ore bodies, weighing several pounds. These are not especially interesting, but cabochons with red zincite, green willemite, and white calcite, peppered with black franklinite, are unique to the Franklin occurrence and are extrememly beautiful as well as highly fluorescent. Spheres have also been cut from this material. Cut zincite is one of the rarest of all gemstones, and seldom completely transparent. Usually it is slightly cloudy or translucent.

Name: In allusion to the composition.

ZIRCON

Formula: $ZrSiO_4$ + Fe, U, Th, Hf.

Crystallography: Tetragonal. Crystals prismatic, pyramidal; often twinned; rounded pebbles.

Colors: Reddish brown, yellow, gray, green, red, colorless; various other colors induced by heating.

Luster: Vitreous to adamantine; sometimes greasy.

Cleavage: Imperfect. Fracture conchoidal. Very brittle.

Zircon crystals usually contain traces of radioactive elements such as U and Th. These decay within the crystals, and over a period of thousands of years result in severe damage to the crystal structure of the host zircon. The damage can be severe enough to destroy the lattice

	Low Zircon	Intermediate Zircon	High Zircon
Colors	green; also brown, orange	brownish green, dark red	colorless, blue, brownish orange
Optics			
o	1.78–1.815 (almost isotropic)	1.83–1.93	1.92–1.94 (often 1.925)
e		1.84–1.970	1.97–2.01 (often 1.984)
Birefringence	0 to 0.008	0.008–0.043	0.036–0.059 (usually the latter)
Density	3.95–4.20 (usually about 4.0)	4.08–4.60	4.6–4.8 (usually about 4.70)

Stone Sizes: Cabochons have been cut from granular zincite in white calcite from Franklin. Faceted gems of Franklin material are very rare, maximum about 20 carats. Most of the few faceted zincites are in the 1–3 carat range.

SI: 20.1 and 12.3 (red, New Jersey).

AMNH: 16.27 (red, Franklin, New Jersey).

Phildelphia Acad. of Nat. Sci.: 12.7 (red, New Jersey).

Comments: Zincite is a very rare mineral, essentially restricted to one important locality. Well terminated crystals were only found up to about 3–4 inches, but

itself, ultimately decomposing the zircon internally into a mixture of quartz and zirconium oxide that is essentially amorphous. This damaged, nearly isotropic zircon is called *low zircon*, while the undecayed material is called *high zircon*. Material slightly damaged by radiation is called *intermediate zircon*, and a complete transition exists between the low and high type.

Birefringence: 0.008–0.069. Optically Uniaxial (+).

Dispersion: 0.039 for all zircon types.

Spectral: Zircon spectra are very distinctive and useful in identification. The strongest pervasive line is at 6535, seen even in types where a strong spectrum is absent. There are many narrow lines and strong bands across the whole spectrum, ranging from more than 40 lines (Burma green stones) to only a few lines (orange gems from New South Wales, Australia). Heat-treated stones and low types have a weak spectrum. Colorless, blue, and golden-brown (all heat-treated) stones display one fine line at 6535, and perhaps also a line at 6590. The complex spectrum of other zircons includes lines at *6535*, *6910*, 6830, 6625, 6605, 6210, 6150, 5895, 5625, *5375*, 5160, *4840*, 4600, 4327. Red zircons may display no spectrum at all.

Inclusions: Angular zoning and streaks are sometimes seen in the low type. Some silk is seen occasionally, as well as tensions cracks and epigenetic cracks stained with iron oxides. Metamict crystals may have bright fissures known as *angles*.

Heating Effects: Heating helps recrystallize partially metamicted zircons and results in a higher specific gravity; the absorption spectrum also sharpens. Heating green Ceylon zircon makes it paler in color. Red-brown Ceylon material becomes colorless. Red-brown Thai stones turn colorless, blue, or golden.

Luminescence: The fluorescence of zircon is variable. Some material is inert, other crystals glow intensely. Mustard yellow is a typical fluorescent color (SW), also yellow-orange. Some zircons glow dull yellow in LW and may phosphoresce. Zircon may be whitish, yellow, greenish, or violet-blue in X-rays.

Pleochroism: Distinct in *blue stones*: deep sky blue/colorless to yellowish gray. *Red:* red/clove brown. *Brown:* reddish brown/yellowish brown.

Occurrence: In igneous rocks worldwide, especially granites.
South Dakota; Colorado; Oklahoma; Texas; Maine; Massachusetts; New York; New Jersey.
U.S.S.R.; Korea; Germany; Brazil.
Ceylon: one of the most important zircon areas, material of all colors, in gravels.
Burma: yellowish and greenish stones found in gem gravels with ruby, complex absorption spectrum in these stones.

Thailand: most important commercial source of zircon for gem purposes.
France: red crystals at *Espaly, St. Marcel.*
Quebec and Ontario, Canada: dark, opaque crystals up to 15 pounds, yield only tiny gems.
Arendal, Norway; New South Wales, Australia: fine gem material (orange).
Emali, Tanzania: white zircon pebbles.

Stone Sizes: The largest zircon gems are from S.E. Asia gem gravels.
SI: 118.1 (brown, Ceylon); also Ceylon: 97.6 (yellow-brown), 23.5 (green), 23.9 (colorless) 75.8 (red-brown, Burma); 105.9 (brown, Thailand); 103.2 (blue, Thailand).
Geol. Museum, London: 44.27 (blue); 22.67 (golden); 14.34 (red); 21.32 (white).
ROM: 23.8 (brown); 17.80 (blue); 61.69 (blue, step cut).
AMNH: 208 (greenish-blue, Ceylon).

Comments: Zircon is an often underrated, but magnificent gemstone. When it is properly cut it rivals diamond in beauty, but often the cutting is not correct and the gem is relatively dull and lifeless. The dispersion is very high, close to that of diamond. Zircon is very brittle and edges of stones are easily chipped and abraded. Zircon must be worn carefully to prevent damage. The range of color in the material is wide, and many additional colors are produced by heating.

High zircon is fully crystalline and has the highest properties, whereas the low type is metamict, due to bombardment of the internal crystal structure by alpha particles released by U and Th. In cases of extreme damage to the structure, the material may appear isotropic, with lower refractive indices and less brilliance when cut. Interestingly, the dispersion is the same for both the high and low types. The popular blue color can be produced only by heating zircon; the same is true for the colorless and golden yellow shades. The crystals that yield these lovely colors are usually reddish-brown. Large, fine-colored zircons are very rare stones, and even smaller fine ones are seldom seen in jewelry today.

Name: *Zircon* is from the Arabic *zargun*, from the Persian *zar* (*gold*) plus *gun* (*color*). The name is very ancient.

ZOISITE See: Epidote.

BIBLIOGRAPHY

General

Arem, Joel E., *Gems and Jewelry*. New York, Bantam Books, 1975.

Bank, Hermann, *From The World of Gemstones*. Innsbruck: Pinguin, 1973.

Bauer, Max, *Precious Stones*. Charles Griffin & Co., Ltd., 1904; reprinted in 2 volumes, New York: Dover Publications, 1968.

Cavenago-Bignami, Speranza, *Gemmologia,* Second Ed. Milan: Editore Ulrico Hoepli, 1965.

Desautels, Paul E., *The Gem Kingdom*. New York: Random House, 1970.

Gübelin, Edward J., *Internal World of Gemstones*. Zurich: ABC Edition, 1974.

Kraus, Edward H., and Slawson, Chester B., *Gems and Gem Materials*. New York, McGraw-Hill, 1939.

Kunz, George F., *Gems and Precious Stones of North America*. Scientific Publishing Co., 1892; reprinted New York: Dover Publications, 1968.

Liddicoat, Richard T., Jr., *Handbook of Gem Identification*. Los Angeles: Gemological Institute of America, 1972.

Parsons, Charles J., *Practical Gem Knowledge For The Amateur*. San Diego: Lapidary Journal, Publisher, 1969.

Schubnel, Henri-Jean, *Pierres Precieuses Dans Le Monde*. Paris: Horizons de France, 1972.

Shipley, Robert, *Dictionary of Gems And Gemology*. Los Angeles, Gemological Institute of America, 1974.

Sinkankas, John, *Gemstones of North America*. Princeton, N. J.: D. Van Nostrand Co., 1959.

Sinkankas, John, *Gem Cutting*. New York: Van Nostrand Reinhold Co., 1962.

Sinkankas, John, *Van Nostrand's Standard Catalog of Gems*. Princeton, N. J.: D. Van Nostrand Co., 1969.

Sinkankas, John, *Gemstone And Mineral Data Book*. New York: Winchester Press, 1972.

Sinkankas, John, *Gemstones of North America*, vol. 2. New York: Van Nostrand Reinhold Co., 1976.

Smith, G.F. Herbert, *Gemstones,* 13th Ed. New York: Pitman, 1958.

Vargas, Glenn, and Vargas, Martha, *Descriptions Of Gem Materials*. Published by the authors at Palm Desert, California, 1972.

Webster, Robert, *Gems,* Third Ed. England: Butterworth & Co., Ltd., 1975.

Jewelry

Black, J. Anderson, *The Story of Jewelry*. New York: William Morrow & Co., 1974.

Evans, Joan, *A History of Jewellery, 1100–1870*. Boston: Boston Book & Art, 1970.

Heiniger, Ernst A., and Heiniger, Jean, *The Great Book Of Jewels*. Boston: N.Y. Graphics Soc., 1974.

Grigorietti, Guido, *Jewelry Through The Ages*. New York: American Heritage Press, 1969.

Meen, V.B., and Tushingham, A.D., *Crown Jewels Of Iran*. Toronto: University of Toronto Press, 1968.

Menzhausen, Joachim, *The Green Vaults*. Germany: Edition Leipzig, 1970.

Sitwell, H.D.W., *The Crown Jewels And Other Regalia In The Tower Of London*. London: W.S. Crowell, Ltd., 1953.

Diamonds

Argenzio, Victor, *Diamonds Eternal*. New York: David McKay Co., Inc. 1974.

Bruton, Eric, *Diamonds*. Philadelphia: Chilton Book Co., 1970.

Copeland, Lawrence L., *Diamonds . . . Famous, Notable And Unique*. Los Angeles: Gemological Institute of America, 1974.

DeBeers Consolidated Mines, Ltd., *Notable Diamonds of the World,* approx. 1972.

Grodzinski, Paul, *Diamond Technology*. London: N.A.G. Press, Ltd., 1942, 1953.

Tolansky, S., *The History And Use Of Diamond*. London: Methuen & Co., Ltd., 1962.

Specific Gemstones

Kunz, George F., and Stevenson, Charles H., *The Book Of The Pearl*. New York: The Century Co., 1908.

Dickinson, Joan Younger, *The Book Of Pearls*. New York: Crown Publishers, Inc., 1968.

Leiper, Hugh (ed.), *The Agates Of North America*. San Diego: The Lapidary Journal, 1966.

Easby, Elizabeth K., *Pre-Columbian Jade From Costa Rica*. New York: Andre Emmerich, Inc., 1968.

Gump, Richard, *Jade: Stone Of Heaven*. New York: Doubleday & Co., Inc., 1962.

Hansford, S. Howard, *Jade*. New York: American Elsevier Co., Inc., 1969.

Laufer, Berthold, *Jade—A Study In Chinese Archaeology And Religion*. Publ. 154, Anthropological Series, Vol. X, Field Museum of Natural History, Chicago. Reprinted (1974) Dover Publications, New York.

Palmer, J.P., *Jade*. London, Spring Books. 1967.

Kalokerinos, Archie, *In Search Of Opal*. Sidney, Ure Smith, 1967.

Leechman, Frank, *The Opal Book,* Fifth Ed. Sidney, Ure Smith, 1973.

Pogue, Joseph E., *Turquoise*. Memoirs of the National Academy of Sciences, Vol. XII, part 2, Mem. 2,3. Reprinted 1974, New Mexico, Rio Grande Press.

Mineralogy

Arem, Joel E., *Rocks and Minerals*. New York, Batam Books, 1973.

Barth, Tom F.W., *Feldspars*. New York, John Wiley & Sons, Inc., 1969.

Bloss, F. Donald, *An Introduction To The Methods Of Optical Crystallography*. New York: Holt, Rinehart & Winston, 1961.

Dana, James D., *The System Of Mineralogy,* Sixth Ed. New York, John Wiley, & Sons, 1898.

Deer, W.A., Howie, R.A., and Zussman, J., *Rock-Forming Minerals,* Vol. 1 (1962), Vol. 2 (1963), Vol. 3 (1962), Vol. 4 (1963), Vol. 5 (1962). New York, John Wiley & Sons, Inc.

Evans, R.C., *An Introduction To Crystal Chemistry,* Second Ed. Cambridge: The University Press, 1964.

Fleischer, Michael, *Glossary of Mineral Species.* Bowie, Md.: The Mineralogical Record, 1975.

Frondel, Clifford, *The System Of Mineralogy, Vol. 3—The Silica Minerals.* New York: John Wiley & Sons., Inc., 1962.

Gleason, Sterling, *Ultraviolet Guide to Minerals.* Princeton, N.J.: D. Van Nostrand, 1960.

Hey, Max, *An Index Of Mineral Species And Varieties Arranged Chemically,* Second Ed., with Appendix (1963). London: Trustees of the British Museum, 1962.

Hurlbut, Cornelius, *Dana's Manual Of Mineralogy,* 18th Ed. New York: John Wiley & Sons, Inc., 1972.

Palache, C., Berman, H., and Frondel, C., *The System Of Mineralogy,* Vols. 1 and 2. New York, John Wiley & Sons, Inc., 1944, 1951.

Roberts, W.L., Rapp, G.R., and Weber, J., *Encyclopedia Of Minerals.* New York: Van Nostrand-Reinhold Co., 1974.

Journals

Journal of Gemmology (London, Gemmological Association of Great Britain; quarterly).

Lapidary Journal (San Diego, California; monthly).

Gems & Gemology (Los Angeles, Gemological Inst. of America; quarterly).

Zeitschrift der Deutsche Gemologische Gesellschaft (Idar-Oberstein, Germany; quarterly).

American Mineralogist (Mineralogical Society of America; monthly).

MINERAL GROUPS OF GEMOLOGICAL INTEREST

(NOTE: only species of gemological interest have been listed)

AMPHIBOLE GROUP
Actinolite   Hornblende   Tremolite

APATITE GROUP
Carbonate-hydroxylapatite   Carbonate-fluorapatite
Fluorapatite   Mimetite   Pyromorphite   Vanadinite

ARAGONITE GROUP
Aragonite   Cerussite   Strontianite   Witherite

CALCITE GROUP
Calcite   Magnesite   Rhodochrosite   Siderite   Smithsonite

EPIDOTE GROUP
Allanite   Clinozoisite   Epidote   Hancockite   Piedmontite   Zoisite

FELDSPAR GROUP
Albite   Oligoclase   Andesine   Labradorite   Bytownite   Anorthite
Anorthoclase   Celsian   Hyalophane   Microcline   Orthoclase

GARNET GROUP
Almandine   Andradite   Grossular   Hydrogrossular   Kimzeyite
Pyrope   Schorlomite   Spessartine   Uvarovite

HUMITE GROUP
Chondrodite   Clinohumite   Humite   Norbergite

OLIVINE GROUP
Fayalite   Forsterite   Tephroite

PYROXENE GROUP
Acmite   Augite   Clinoenstatite   Clinohypersthene   Diopside   Enstatite
Hypersthene   Jadeite   Spodumene

RUTILE GROUP
Cassiterite   Rutile

SODALITE GROUP
Hauyne   Lazurite   Nosean   Sodalite

SPINEL GROUP
Chromite   Franklinite   Gahnite   Galaxite   Hercynite
Magnesiochromite   Magnetite   Spinel

TOURMALINE GROUP
Buergerite   Dravite   Uvite   Elbaite   Schorl   Liddicoatite

ZEOLITE GROUP
Analcime   Chabazite   Gmelinite   Heulandite   Mesolite   Natrolite
Pollucite   Scolecite   Stilbite   Thomsonite

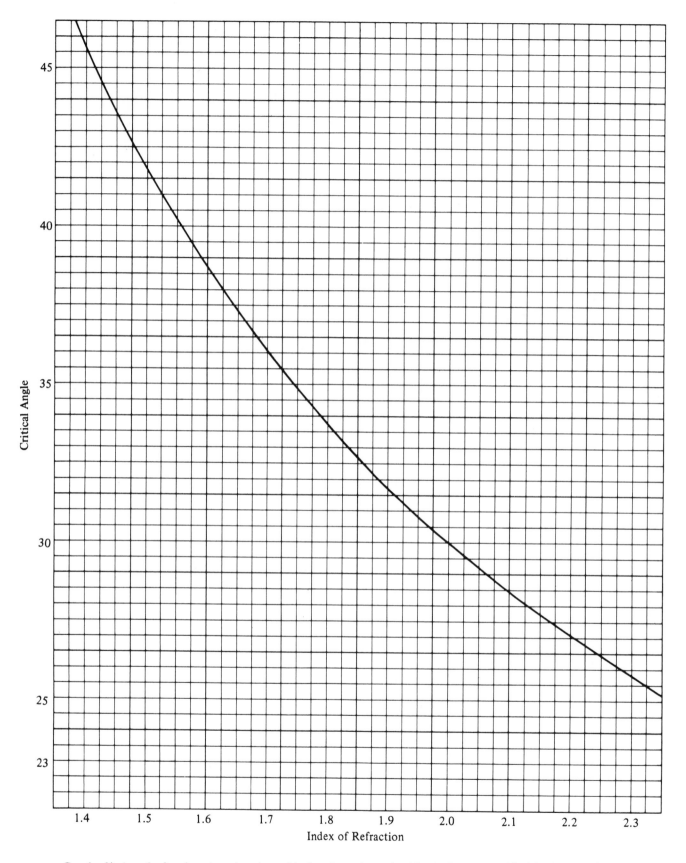

Graph of index of refraction plotted against critical angle, as determined by the formula: Critical Angle = arcsin (1/n) where n is the refractive index. This graph is most useful to the gem cutter for determining main pavilion angles. Maximum brilliance is achieved when the pavilion main angle is slightly greater than the critical angle. This can be determined for any given gem material with a quick refractive index measurement on a polished surface prior to cutting the pavilion.

PERIODIC CLASSIFICATION OF THE ELEMENTS

IA	IIA	IIIB	IVB	VB	VIB	VIIB	VIIIB			IB	IIB	IIIA	IVA	VA	VIA	VIIA	0
1 H Hydrogen 1.0079																	**2 He** Helium 4.00260
3 Li Lithium 6.941	**4 Be** Beryllium 9.01218											**5 B** Boron 10.81	**6 C** Carbon 12.011	**7 N** Nitrogen 14.0067	**8 O** Oxygen 15.9994	**9 F** Fluorine 18.99840	**10 Ne** Neon 20.179
11 Na Sodium 22.98977	**12 Mg** Magnesium 24.305											**13 Al** Aluminum 26.98154	**14 Si** Silicon 28.086	**15 P** Phosphorus 30.97376	**16 S** Sulfur 32.06	**17 Cl** Chlorine 35.453	**18 Ar** Argon 39.948
19 K Potassium 39.098	**20 Ca** Calcium 40.08	**21 Sc** Scandium 44.9559	**22 Ti** Titanium 47.90	**23 V** Vanadium 50.9414	**24 Cr** Chromium 51.996	**25 Mn** Manganese 54.9380	**26 Fe** Iron 55.847	**27 Co** Cobalt 58.9332	**28 Ni** Nickel 58.71	**29 Cu** Copper 63.546	**30 Zn** Zinc 65.38	**31 Ga** Gallium 69.72	**32 Ge** Germanium 72.59	**33 As** Arsenic 74.9216	**34 Se** Selenium 78.96	**35 Br** Bromine 79.904	**36 Kr** Krypton 83.80
37 Rb Rubidium 85.4678	**38 Sr** Strontium 87.62	**39 Y** Yttrium 88.9059	**40 Zr** Zirconium 91.22	**41 Nb** Niobium 92.9064	**42 Mo** Molybdenum 95.94	**43 Tc** Technetium 98.9062b	**44 Ru** Ruthenium 101.07	**45 Rh** Rhodium 102.9055	**46 Pd** Palladium 106.4	**47 Ag** Silver 107.868	**48 Cd** Cadmium 112.40	**49 In** Indium 114.82	**50 Sn** Tin 118.69	**51 Sb** Antimony 121.75	**52 Te** Tellurium 127.60	**53 I** Iodine 126.9045	**54 Xe** Xenon 131.30
55 Cs Cesium 132.9054	**56 Ba** Barium 137.34	**57* La** Lanthanum 138.9055	**72 Hf** Hafnium 178.49	**73 Ta** Tantalum 180.9479	**74 W** Tungsten 183.85	**75 Re** Rhenium 186.2	**76 Os** Osmium 190.2	**77 Ir** Iridium 192.22	**78 Pt** Platinum 195.09	**79 Au** Gold 196.9665	**80 Hg** Mercury 200.59	**81 Tl** Thallium 204.37	**82 Pb** Lead 207.2	**83 Bi** Bismuth 208.9804	**84 Po** Polonium (210)a	**85 At** Astatine (210)a	**86 Rn** Radon (222)a
87 Fr Francium (223)a	**88 Ra** Radium 226.0254b	**89** Ac** Actinium (227)a	**104** (260)a	**105** (260)a	**106** (263)*											metals →	← nonmetals

58 Ce Cerium 140.12	**59 Pr** Praseodymium 140.9077	**60 Nd** Neodymium 144.24	**61 Pm** Promethium (145)a	**62 Sm** Samarium 150.4	**63 Eu** Europium 151.96	**64 Gd** Gadolinium 157.25	**65 Tb** Terbium 158.9254	**66 Dy** Dysprosium 162.50	**67 Ho** Holmium 164.9304	**68 Er** Erbium 167.26	**69 Tm** Thulium 168.9342	**70 Yb** Ytterbium 173.04	**71 Lu** Lutetium 174.97
90 Th Thorium 232.0381b	**91 Pa** Protactinium 231.0359b	**92 U** Uranium 238.029	**93 Np** Neptunium 237.0482b	**94 Pu** Plutonium (242)a	**95 Am** Americium (243)a	**96 Cm** Curium (247)a	**97 Bk** Berkelium (249)a	**98 Cf** Californium (251)a	**99 Es** Einsteinium (254)a	**100 Fm** Fermium (253)a	**101 Md** Mendelevium (256)a	**102 No** Nobelium (254)a	**103 Lr** Lawrencium (257)a

a Mass number of most stable or best known isotope.

b Mass of most commonly available, long-lived isotope.

Index